IBDY 5625

OXFORD CLASSICAL MONOGRAPHS

Published under the supervision of a Committee of the Faculty of Literae Humaniores in the University of Oxford

The aim of the Oxford Classical Monographs series (which replaces the Oxford Classical and Philosophical Monographs) is to publish books based on the best theses on Greek and Latin literature, ancient history, and ancient philosophy examined by the Faculty Board of Literae Humaniores.

Lucan

Spectacle and Engagement

MATTHEW LEIGH

CLARENDON PRESS · OXFORD
1997

Oxford University Press, Great Clarendon Street, Oxford OX2 6DP

Oxford New York
Athens Auckland Bangkok Bogota Bombay
Buenos Aires Calcutta Cape Town Dar es Salaam
Delhi Florence Hong Kong Istanbul Karachi
Kuala Lumpur Madras Madrid Melbourne
Mexico City Nairobi Paris Singapore
Taipei Tokyo Toronto
and associated companies in
Berlin Ibadan

PA
6480
.L44
1997

Oxford is a trade mark of Oxford University Press

Published in the United States
by Oxford University Press Inc., New York

© *Matthew Leigh 1997*

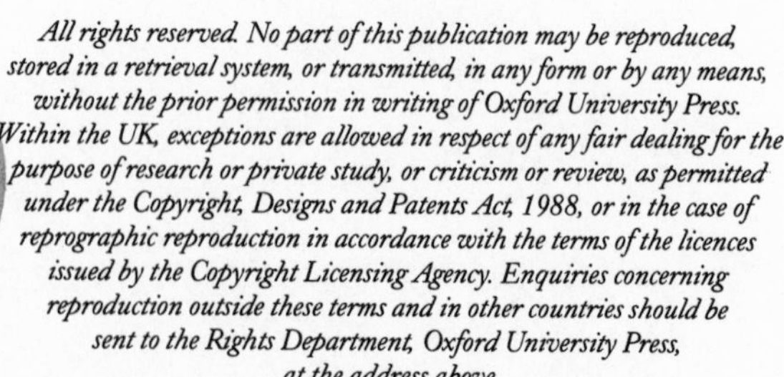

All rights reserved. No part of this publication may be reproduced, stored in a retrieval system, or transmitted, in any form or by any means, without the prior permission in writing of Oxford University Press. Within the UK, exceptions are allowed in respect of any fair dealing for the purpose of research or private study, or criticism or review, as permitted under the Copyright, Designs and Patents Act, 1988, or in the case of reprographic reproduction in accordance with the terms of the licences issued by the Copyright Licensing Agency. Enquiries concerning reproduction outside these terms and in other countries should be sent to the Rights Department, Oxford University Press, at the address above

British Library Cataloguing in Publication Data
Data available

Library of Congress Cataloging in Publication Data
Lucan : spectacle and engagement / Matthew Leigh.
(Oxford classical mmonographs)
Includes bibliographical references
1. Lucan, 39–65. Pharsalia. 2. Rome–History–Civil War, 49–48 B.C.–Literature and the war. 3. Pharsalus, Battle of, 48 B.C., in literature. 4. Epic poetry, Latin–History and criticism.
I. Title. II. Series
PA6480.L44 1996 873'.01–dc20 96-24547
ISBN 0-19-815067-9

1 3 5 7 9 10 8 6 4 2

Typeset by Joshua Associates Ltd., Oxford
Printed in Great Britain on acid-free paper by
Bookcraft (Bath) Ltd., Midsomer Norton

To my parents

Acknowledgements

I wish to acknowledge my debt to the following scholars for their help at different points in the composition of this study: to my undergraduate teacher, Oliver Lyne, for introducing me to Lucan; to my two doctoral supervisors, Robin Nisbet and Don Fowler, for their constant support; to my examiners Michael Winterbottom and Philip Hardie for invaluable criticism, and especially to the latter for suffering the lengthy metamorphosis from thesis into book; to my colleagues at the University of Exeter, John Wilkins and Peter Wiseman, for reading different chapters as they emerged; to my third-year Latin Epic class for their wisdom and their jokes. Hilary O'Shea, Enid Barker, Liz Alsop, and Jenny Wagstaffe at OUP have offered constant help and wise counsel during the final stages of composition, correction, and publication.

I must thank the British Academy for the doctoral grant which made this research possible. In addition, the award by the Oxford University Craven Committee of the Derby Scholarship permitted me to spend six months of my second year at the University of Pisa. The chance to study with Gian Biagio Conte and Antonio La Penna was an immense boon. A second visit to Pisa in early 1996 was made possible by a generous grant from the Wellcome Trust. I must also thank St Hugh's College for making me the Dorothea Gray Senior Scholar for the last two years of my research and Magdalen College for appointing me to the post of Junior Lecturer in Latin. Laetitia Edwards and Oliver Taplin have shown great kindness. Since October 1993, it has been my privilege to teach in the Department of Classics and Ancient History at Exeter University in what has been a golden period for classical studies in the south-west.

The Classics Departments of the Universities of London, Bristol, Exeter, Durham, Warwick, Pisa, Yale, Manchester, and Cambridge invited me to read papers and suggested new ways forward. Many others commented on parts of my work: Miriam and Jasper Griffin, Peter Brown, Bruno Currie, Ben Tipping, and Rolando Ferri. Finally, I must mention three friends without whom the happiness of this period would have been sadly diminished: Michael Clarke, Sam Hood, and Federica Bessone, each one the very best of companions.

Contents

Abbreviations

ACD	*Acta Classica Debrecensia*
AJAH	*American Journal of Ancient History*
AJPh	*American Journal of Philology*
AKG	*Archiv für Kulturgeschichte*
ANRW	*Aufstieg und Niedergang der Römischen Welt*
ASNP	*Annali della Scuola Normale Superiore di Pisa*
BAGB	*Bulletin de l'Association Guillaume Budé*
BCPE	*Bolletino del Centro Internazionale per lo Studio dei Papiri Ercolanesi*
BICS	*Bulletin of the Institute of Classical Studies, London*
CIL	*Corpus Inscriptionum Latinarum* (Berlin, 1863–)
ClAnt	*Classical Antiquity*
C&M	*Classica et Mediaevalia*
CPh	*Classical Philology*
CQ	*Classical Quarterly*
CR	*Classical Review*
FGH	*Die Fragmente der Griechischen Historiker*, ed. F. Jacoby (Berlin and Leiden, 1923–58)
Forcellini	E. Forcellini (ed.), *Totius Latinitatis Lexicon* (4th edn., Padua, 1926)
ICS	*Illinois Classical Studies*
ILLRP	*Inscriptiones Latinae Liberae Rei Publicae*, ed. A. Degrassi (Florence, 1957–63)
ILS	*Inscriptiones Latinae Selectae*, ed. H. Dessau (Berlin, 1892–1916)
JRS	*Journal of Roman Studies*
LCM	*Liverpool Classical Monthly*
LEC	*Les études classiques*
MD	*Materiali e discussioni per l'analisi dei testi classici*
MH	*Museum Helveticum*
OLD	*Oxford Latin Dictionary*, ed. P. G. W. Glare (Oxford, 1968–82)
PBSR	*Papers of the British School at Rome*
Peter	H. Peter (ed.), *Historicorum Romanorum Reliquiae*, 2nd edn. (Leipzig, 1914)

PhQ	*Philological Quarterly*
PCPhS	*Proceedings of the Cambridge Philological Society*
PLLS	*Papers of the Leeds Latin Seminar*
PVS	*Proceedings of the Virgil Society*
RE	A. Pauly, G. Wissowa, and W. Kroll (eds.), *Real-Encyclopädie der classischen Altertumswissenschaft* (Stuttgart, 1894–)
REA	*Revue des études anciennes*
REL	*Revue des études latines*
RhM	*Rheinisches Museum*
RIL	*Rendiconti dell'Istituto Lombardo*
SIFC	*Studi italiani di filologia classica*
SLG	*Supplementum Lyricis Graecis*, ed. D. Page (Oxford, 1974)
SO	*Symbolae Osloenses*
SVF	*Stoicorum Veterum Fragmenta*, ed. H. von Arnim (Leipzig, 1903–24)
TAPhA	*Transactions and Proceedings of the American Philological Association*
TLL	*Thesaurus Linguae Latinae* (Leipzig, 1900–)
TrGF	*Tragicorum Graecorum Fragmenta*, ed. B. Snell *et al.* (Göttingen, 1971–)
WS	*Wiener Studien*
ZPE	*Zeitschrift für Papyrologie und Epigraphik*

Texts of Lucan

The text of Lucan used throughout this study is the magisterial edition of A. E. Housman (Oxford, 1926). Where I disagree with Housman or print an alternative reading, this is noted in the text. Other editions referred to in the notes are:

C. E. Haskins (1887), *M. Annaei Lucani Pharsalia* (London)
G. Luck (1985), *Lukan: Der Bürgerkrieg* (Berlin)
D. R. Shackleton Bailey (1988), *Lucanus De Bello Civili* (Stuttgart)

Introduction

Lucan's *Pharsalia* is a document of fundamental importance for students of the history and literature of Rome in the early imperial period. By taking as his theme the civil war sparked by Caesar's invasion of Italy in 49 BC, Lucan engages with the coming of the autocratic political system under which Rome has lived for a century and of which his own family connections give him intimate experience. The decision to write in the epic genre, meanwhile, involves him in a dialogue with the tropes and formulations adopted by the Augustan poets, and particularly Vergil, in order to give expression to their approval of the values of the new regime. The historical theme encompassed by the *Pharsalia* engenders a no less significant relationship with Sallust, Pollio, Livy, and their successors. Whether one is a historian of the Republican opposition to Nero or a literary critic teasing out the ideological implications of intertextuality, it is impossible to ignore the *Pharsalia*.

Lucan was born in AD 39, only two years after the future emperor Nero. As the nephew of Nero's appointed tutor and counsellor, the philosopher and tragedian Seneca, Lucan could not hope to escape entanglement with the life of the court. His own prodigious abilities as a writer and rhetorician must have contributed further to his early involvement in public life, and the ancient lives record an early panegyrical oration in honour of Nero, a premature quaestorship, and appointment to the college of augurs.[1] They also record a rupture soon afterwards which led to a ban on the publication or recitation of Lucan's writings.[2] The ancient lives date this ban to after the publication of the first three books of the *Pharsalia* and, while they attribute it to Nero's artistic jealousy of Lucan's poetic achievement, it is very

[1] The principal sources for the career of Lucan are the lives composed by Suetonius and the late grammarian Vacca. For the text of Suetonius, see Rostagni (1964) 141–9; for Vacca, see Endt (1909) 1–3 and Rostagni (1964) 176–86. The poet is also referred to repeatedly in Books 15 and 16 of the *Annals* of Tacitus and celebrated in Statius, *Silvae* 2. 7, the *Genethliacon Lucani*.

[2] See Tac. *Ann.* 15. 49, Suet. *Luc.* 10–22, and Vacca, 32, 35—47.

likely that the disfavour shown towards Lucan arose as much from the overt political content of the poem as from the artist-emperor's distress at his surpassing poetic achievement. Modern interpretations of Books 1–3 as politically neutral or even overtly Neronian lean heavily on the surface evidence of the dedication to the emperor at 1. 33–66 and obfuscate the implications of a number of other passages.[3] While there is little doubt that Books 4–10 exhibit a spirit profoundly hostile to the imperial system and that this finds most concentrated expression in the Pharsalus narrative of Book 7, the text as a whole gives little support to the idea that Lucan's writing underwent any radical change in character after the ban.

Lucan's poem is unfinished and breaks off abruptly with Caesar cut off and in desperate straits. This incompletion must be attributed to the early death of Lucan, implicated in the Pisonian conspiracy against Nero and driven to suicide in AD 65.[4] The same fate awaited Seneca.[5] The extensive account of this conspiracy given by Tacitus in Book 15 of the *Annals* represents it not as an attempt to restore the full Republican system but rather as a bid to replace Nero with their favoured candidate, C. Calpurnius Piso.[6] The Tacitean pen-portrait of Piso does nothing to suggest a die-hard Republican and the historian even records that an excessive devotion to that cause could count as sufficient grounds for exclusion from the plot.[7] The alleged behaviour of Lucan when accused of participation is not the stuff of Stoic-Republican martyrology.[8] The most recent modern accounts depend substantially on Tacitus.[9]

It is not my intention here to offer a thoroughgoing reinterpretation of the Pisonian conspiracy. Suffice it to say that the evidence suggests a

[3] This position is argued most determinedly in Lebek (1976).

[4] For the death of Lucan, see Tac. *Ann.* 15. 70.

[5] For the death of Seneca, see the extended narrative at Tac. *Ann.* 15. 60–4. For the deliberate stylization of this event, see M. T. Griffin (1976) 367–88.

[6] Tac. *Ann.* 15. 48–74 is given over entirely to the account of the conspiracy. Tac. *Ann.* 15. 48 summarizes the motivation of the participants as 'cum odio Neronis tum favore in C. Pisonem'.

[7] Tac. *Ann.* 15. 48 depicts Piso as charismatic but frivolous; Tac. *Ann.* 15. 52 records the common belief that Piso excluded the consul Vestinus from the conspiracy 'ne ad libertatem oreretur vel delecto imperatore alio sui muneris rem publicam faceret'.

[8] Tac. *Ann.* 15. 56 and Suet. *Luc.* 27–31 both allege that Lucan responded to accusations of complicity by attempting to shop his mother.

[9] M. T. Griffin (1984) 166–70 is brief but preferable in many ways to Rudich (1993) 87–131 where Tacitean accounts of character and motivation are treated as objective data for psycho-history and the evidence for ideological commitment is consistently underplayed.

wide range of different grounds for participation and that the account of Suetonius indicates that Lucan's role was more ideological than Tacitus or Vacca imply.[10] More significantly, it is surely the case that the fundamental virtues of the Republican system provide a paradigm for the criticism of autocracy even when proposals for reform involve only a moderation of the imperial system and not its abolition. The assertion at Tacitus, *Annals* 1. 3 that there was almost nobody at the time of the accession of Tiberius who had known the Republic is true in only the most limited sense: the memory of the Republic survived long after the death of those who had been alive to see it, and the early imperial period, particularly the Neronian period, testified to the intense interest in the late Republic in works of history and tragedy as well as epic. Romans of the imperial period thought constantly about the Republic and did so with a view to the commentary it could offer on their own age.

The emphasis here placed on the ideological role of early imperial literature is crucial to Lucan. While the ancient biographical evidence provides some indication of Lucan's milieu and of the basic co-ordinates of his career, it is worse than useless as a guide to his thought as a politician and historian. For the only possible interest in the story of the artistic jealousy of Nero and the personal feud between the two can be as a curiosity for scholars and philologists delighted to see in the ancient world the mirror of their own disputes. Whatever personal reasons are alleged for Lucan's composition of the *Pharsalia*, none can detract from the final ideological seriousness of the work itself.

The aim of this study is not to provide a general guide to Lucan. Frederick Ahl's *Lucan: An Introduction* still offers an excellent initial survey of the poem as a whole, combining commentary on the narrative with an attempt to locate Lucan's work within the political culture of his time.[11] The scope of this work is more limited. Although comment is offered on episodes from throughout the poem as a whole and the aim, as with Ahl, is to investigate the ideological complexities of the poem, the seven studies which follow concentrate their aim on one particular concept: the tendency of the *Pharsalia* to highlight the idea of spectacle and the role of the viewer.

[10] While Rudich (1993) 95 uses the evidence of Suet. *Luc.* 23–6 merely to justify his contention that the poet's behaviour 'more closely resembled that of a capricious adolescent than of a conscientious politician', it is reasonable to note that Lucan's public speeches in celebration of tyrannicides must have given an ideological cast, however basic, to his critique of Nero.

[11] Ahl (1976).

All through the *Pharsalia*, Lucan shows an unusual concern for the manner in which his epic will be received. In particular, he is alert to the possibility that his narrative will be treated not so much as something to be read, but as something to be watched. This is a striking formulation and one which requires serious investigation.

The mediation of narrative through the point of view or focalization of a character involved encodes responses to the action often very different from those expressed by the primary narrator. The importance of this concept to modern evaluations of the ideology of the *Aeneid* from Heinze to Conte and on is well known.[12] What is striking about Lucan is that, while his narrative responds to the same fundamental analysis as that of Vergil, it does so in a manner almost diametrically opposed to that found in the *Aeneid*. For, if the point of view of a Dido, a Lausus, or a Turnus encodes dissident responses within a narrative dominated by the necessity of Rome's mission, Lucan's internal audience repeatedly transforms into spectacle and seeks an admiring audience for a civil war which the primary narrator affects to abhor.[13]

What is truly striking about the *Pharsalia*, however, is the ready acknowledgement by the primary narrator that his readers may share some of the attitudes of his internal audience. The comparison which this imposes between one set of spectators and another becomes the focus for ideological contention within the poem. The invitation to measure one's response against the burning enthusiasm for the spectacle of civil war displayed by Caesar and his men is a fundamental challenge to acknowledge any complicity with the system they represent.

Lucan's representation of his narrative as spectacle likens his reader to a member of the audience at a theatrical or amphitheatrical display. Whichever of these two models is operative, modes of response are proposed which aestheticize civil war and treat it as a source of pleasure. When the latter takes hold, when a sea battle is like a *naumachia* or a soldier like a gladiator, the reader as spectator is transported to one of the institutions on which the power and hegemony of the emperor rests. Yet there is a choice. If complicity with the coming of Caesarism is associated with the dispassionate gaze of the spectator, the mentality which Lucan represents as most appropriate to the

[12] Heinze (1915) cf. Conte (1986). For further bibliography on this problem and its relationship to the subjective interventions of the primary narrator, see Ch. 1 n. 21. The most recent contribution to the debate on the ideological implications of focalization is Fowler (1990).

[13] For an important early contribution on this subject, see Conte (1968).

Republican is that of constant emotional intervention against history. While he suggests that it is possible to respond like a spectator, the reaction which he wishes to engender and which he enacts is absolutely different. When Lucan breaks into his own narrative to address characters and call for a reversal of history, his attacks on various passive observers mean that the issue is not so much 'spectacle and engagement' as 'spectacle or engagement'.[14]

This choice is not easy to make and it has a habit of finding people out. If the *Pharsalia* as a whole is an ongoing challenge to the reader's Republican conscience, specific events present characters with a similar dilemma. What is to be made, for instance, of a Republican general who is unable either to watch Pharsalus through to the end or to take his part in the fight? How ambivalent is the poet's celebration of his role? It is an indication of Lucan's genius that what may first seem like a hopeless inconcinnity finally testifies to the sophistication of his thought.

When Lucan describes Pompey as a spectator, this figuration reveals more than just passivity. Rather, the opportunity to view the battle from Pompey's point of view gives access to the distorted mentality of the general. Similarly, later analysis of the devotion of the Caesarians to spectacle and display reveals them to be a disturbing community with a mental world all their own. As Lucan's extraordinary imagination veers from one form of spectacle to another, each one is further distorted by the antics of Caesar, his centurions, and their men.

The *Pharsalia* is a profoundly political poem. Chapter 1 expands on and exemplifies the patterns pointed to here. At the same time, it should serve to illustrate Lucan's uncanny tendency to take anecdotes, paradigms of philosophical behaviour, or doctrines in literary criticism and to politicize them all. At the centre of all of this, moreover, is the conflict between spectacle and engagement.

[14] A crucial element of the procedures examined in Chs. 1–3 is Lucan's unique manipulation of the tenses of narrative in order to move between different temporalities and perspectives. I have therefore included three appendices on apostrophe, the present historic, and the future tense, which outline the basic linguistic premises underlying my interpretation.

1

Gaius Cornelius and the Caesarian *Vates*

LUCAN, *PHARSALIA* 7. 185–213—LUCAN, CORNELIUS, AND *ENARGEIA* IN NARRATIVE

How does the *Pharsalia* activate the opposition between spectacle and engagement? The following movement, which closes Lucan's catalogue of omens before the battle of Pharsalus, offers an excellent starting-point for investigation. The account begins with the vague fears felt by Romans as far away even as Cadiz in the West and Armenia in the East. As it advances, it settles on two figures, each characterized by an uncanny clarity of vision:

> Quid mirum populos quos lux extrema manebat
> lymphato trepidasse metu, praesaga malorum
> si data mens homini est? Tyriis qui Gadibus hospes
> adiacet Armeniumque bibit Romanus Araxen,
> sub quocumque die, quocumque est sidere mundi,
> maeret et ignorat causas animumque dolentem
> corripit, Emathiis quid perdat nescius arvis.
> Euganeo, si vera fides memorantibus, augur
> colle sedens, Aponus terris ubi fumifer exit
> atque Antenorei dispergitur unda Timavi,
> 'Venit summa dies, geritur res maxima,' dixit
> 'inpia concurrunt Pompei et Caesaris arma',
> seu tonitrus ac tela Iovis praesaga notavit,
> aethera seu totum discordi obsistere caelo
> perspexitque polos, seu numen in aethere maestum
> solis in obscuro pugnam pallore notavit.
> Dissimilem certe cunctis quos explicat egit
> Thessalicum natura diem: si cuncta perito
> augure mens hominum caeli nova signa notasset,
> spectari toto potuit Pharsalia mundo.
> O summos hominum, quorum fortuna per orbem
> signa dedit, quorum fatis caelum omne vacavit!
> Haec et apud seras gentes populosque nepotum,
> sive sua tantum venient in saecula fama

sive aliquid magnis nostri quoque cura laboris
nominibus prodesse potest, cum bella legentur,
spesque metusque simul perituraque vota movebunt,
attonitique omnes veluti venientia fata,
non transmissa, legent et adhuc tibi, Magne, favebunt.

What wonder that peoples whose final day awaited them trembled with panic-stricken fear, if man has been given an intellect which presages ills? Whether the Roman guest is by Tyrian Gades or drinks the Armenian Araxes, under whatever sky, whatever star of the universe, he sorrows and does not know the cause and chides his grieving mind, unaware of what he is losing in the fields of Emathia. If those who tell the story are truly to be believed, an augur sitting on the Euganean hill, where smoky Aponus leaves the earth and the water of Antenor's Timavus divides its course, said, 'The final day has come, the crucial issue is at hand, the impious arms of Pompey and Caesar come to battle.' Either he noted the thunder and the prophetic weapons of Jupiter or he saw that all the sky and the poles were at war with hostile heaven or a sad deity in the sky indicated the battle by the gloomy paleness of the sun. Undoubtedly nature made the day of Thessaly unlike all the others which she unfolds: if through some skilled augur the mind of men had noted all the new signs in heaven, Pharsalia could have been watched all over the world. O highest of men, whose fortune indicated itself all over the globe, to whose fates all heaven paid heed! These events, even among late nations and the peoples of our descendants, whether they survive by their fame alone or whether the care of my labour can do any service to great names, when the wars are read, they will generate together hopes and fears and prayers doomed to perish and all will be shocked as they read what seem like fates that are coming and not yet past, and all, Magnus, will still side with you.

We begin with two story-tellers, two prophets, an augur and a *vates*. The one, Gaius Cornelius, sits on the Euganean hill, outside ancient Patavium, reads with eerie precision the message of his augury, exactly foretells and vividly describes the events of the battle of Pharsalus; the other, the poet Lucan, writing under Nero, born too late to fight, writes of his determination to perpetuate the illusion—but, yes, the illusion—that history can be reversed. The two figures offer an uncomfortable commentary on each other.

The story of Gaius Cornelius was made famous by his compatriot, the historian Livy. That Gaius featured in Book 111 of the *Ab Urbe Condita* is guaranteed by Plutarch, *Caes.* 47:

Ἐν δὲ Παταβίωι Γάϊος Κορνήλιος, ἀνὴρ εὐδόκιμος ἐπὶ μαντικῆι, Λιβίου τοῦ συγγραφέως πολίτης καὶ γνώριμος, ἐτύγχανεν ἐπ' οἰωνοῖς καθήμενος ἐκείνην τὴν ἡμέραν. καὶ πρῶτον μέν, ὡς Λίβιός φησι, τὸν καιρὸν ἔγνω τῆς μάχης καὶ πρὸς τοὺς παρόντας εἶπεν ὅτι καὶ δὴ περαίνεται τὸ χρῆμα καὶ συνίασιν εἰς ἔργον οἱ ἄνδρες. αὖθις δὲ πρὸς τῆι θέαι γενόμενος καὶ τὰ σημεῖα κατιδὼν ἀνήλατο μετ' ἐνθουσιασμοῦ βοῶν "Νικᾶις, ὦ Καῖσαρ". ἐκπλαγέντων δὲ τῶν παρατυχόντων περιελὼν τὸν στέφανον ἀπὸ τῆς κεφαλῆς ἐνωμότως ἔφη μὴ πρὶν ἐπιθήσεσθαι πάλιν ἢ τῆι τέχνηι μαρτυρῆσαι τὸ ἔργον. ταῦτα μὲν οὖν ὁ Λίβιος οὕτως γενέσθαι καταβεβαιοῦται.

Moreover, at Patavium, Gaius Cornelius, a man in repute as a seer, a fellow citizen and acquaintance of Livy the historian, chanced that day to be sitting in the place of augury. And to begin with, according to Livy, he discerned the time of the battle, and said to those present that even then the event was in progress and the men were going into action. And when he looked again and observed the signs, he sprang up in a rapture crying: 'You are victorious, O Caesar!' The bystanders being amazed, he took the chaplet from his head and declared with an oath that he would not put it on again until the event had borne witness to his art. At any rate, Livy insists that these things happened in this way.

The accuracy of Cornelius' prediction is borne out by history. More interesting still is the assertion of his skill as a narrator by two other ancient writers, Aulus Gellius and Dio. Thus, Aulus reports at *NA* 15. 18. 1–3 that:

Quo C. Caesar et Cn. Pompeius die per civile bellum signis conlatis in Thessalia conflixerunt, res accidit Patavi in transpadana Italia memorari digna. Cornelius quidam sacerdos et nobilis et sacerdotii religionibus venerandus et castitate vitae sanctus repente *mota mente conspicere se procul* dixit pugnam acerrimam pugnari ac deinde alios cedere, alios urgere, caedem, fugam, tela volantia, instaurationem pugnae, inpressionem, gemitus, vulnera, *proinde ut si ipse in proelio versaretur, coram videre sese vociferatus est* ac postea subito exclamavit Caesarem vicisse. Ea Cornelii sacerdotis hariolatio levis tum quidem visa est et vecors. Magnae mox admirationi fuit, quoniam non modo pugnae dies, quae in Thessalia pugnata est, neque proelii exitus qui erat praedictus, idem fuit, sed omnes quoque pugnandi reciprocae vices et ipsa exercituum duorum conflictatio vaticinantis motu atque verbis *repraesentata est.*

On the day when C. Caesar and Cn. Pompeius pitted their standards against each other in civil war and came to blows in Thessaly, a memorable event took place at Patavium in Transpadane Italy. A certain priest Cornelius, of high repute, much respected for the piety with which he fulfilled his priestly responsibilities, revered for the chastity of his life, his mind suddenly in a turmoil, said that far off he had caught sight of a most bitter battle being fought, and then proclaimed that he could see before him, just as if he himself were caught up in the battle, one side retreating, the other pressing, slaughter, flight, spears flying, the battle being renewed, a shove, groans, wounds, and afterwards suddenly cried out that Caesar had won. At first this prophecy of the priest Cornelius seemed unreliable and mad. Soon it was a source of amazement, for not only did he get right the day on which the battle was fought in Thessaly and the outcome of the battle which he predicted, but even every twist and turn of the battle and clash of the two armies was represented in the gestures and words of the prophet.

This should be compared with the account at Dio Cass., 41. 61. 4–5:

καὶ ἐν Παταουίωι τῆς νῦν Ἰταλίας τότε δὲ ἔτι Γαλατίας ὄρνιθάς τινας οὐχ ὅτι διαγγεῖλαι αὐτὴν ἀλλὰ καὶ δεῖξαι τρόπον τινά· Γάιος γάρ τις Κορνήλιος πάντα τὰ γενόμενα ἀκριβῶς τε ἐξ αὐτῶν ἐτεκμήρατο καὶ τοῖς παροῦσιν ἐξηγήσατο. ταῦτα μὲν ἐν αὐτῆι ἐκείνηι τῆι ἡμέραι ὡς ἕκαστα συνηνέχθη, καὶ παραχρῆμα μὲν ἠπιστεῖτο, ὥσπερ εἰκὸς ἦν, ἀγγελθέντων δὲ τῶν πραχθέντων ἐθαυμάζετο.

And in Patavium, which is now a part of Italy but was then still part of Gaul, some birds not only announced the battle but in some sense performed it. For a certain Caius Cornelius accurately adduced all that had happened from them and recounted it to those present. Each of these things happened on that very day and, though people were naturally sceptical at first, when the events were announced, they were amazed.

And with the important note at Lucan, 7. 192 in the *Commenta Bernensia*:

Euganeum nomen est collis Illiriae. [et] Gaium Cornelium augurem ante urbem ex more sedentem augurari dicunt, qui et haec praedixit quae poeta refert. Nam ** et Caesarem victorem ea die nuntiavit.

'Euganean' is the name of a hill in Illyria. [and] they say that Gaius Cornelius, an augur, who was seated before the city according to custom, interpreted the signs and foretold these events which the poet reports. For ** and he announced that Caesar was the winner on this day.[1]

[1] Cf. Julius Obsequens, 65, 'C. Cornelius augur Patavii eo die, cum aves admitterent, proclamavit rem geri et vincere Caesarem', and Sid. Apoll., *Carm.* 9. 194–6: 'Nec quos Euganeum bibens Timavum | colle Antenoreo videbat augur | divos Thessalicam movere pugnam'. Some may wonder what an augur is doing at Patavium. Suet. *Tib.* 14. 3 records the existence of an oracle of Geryon at Patavium and the practice of casting golden dice into the fount of the Aponus, but both these instances have little to do with augury. However, Servius at Verg. *Aen.* 1. 242 provides evidence for the central position of augury in the foundation myth and local cult of Patavium: Antenor fled Troy and then 'cum uxore Theano et filiis Helicaone et Polydamante ceterisque sociis in Illyricum pervenit, et bello exceptus ab Euganeis et rege Veleso victor urbem Patavium condidit; *id enim responsi acceperat eo loco condere civitatem quo sagittis avem petisset; ideo ex avis petitae auspicio Patavium nominatum*'. If Scherling, *RE* xxi. 2 (1952) 1601 is right to regard the reference to Polydamas the son of Antenor as indicating the same Trojan normally denoted as the son of Panthus, it is worth noting that Polydamas at Hom. *Il.* 12. 217–29 and 237–43 is notable for his unsuccessful attempt to make Hector pay attention to the warnings of bird-signs. For more on this, see Leigh (forthcoming).

While it is by no means certain that each of these authors depends directly on Livy, there can still be no doubt that, as Plutarch records, the first version in any chain at least is Livian.[2] It is equally difficult to state with any confidence which elements in the different versions are derived directly from Livy, but the assertion of an early date for one aspect of the ancient accounts of Cornelius would give particular point to Lucan's placing of the central statement of his poetics at this particular juncture in the narrative.[3] For the note in the *Commenta* that Cornelius 'foretold these events which the poet reports' (*haec praedixit quae poeta refert*) gains particular point when it is recalled that Lucan is matching himself with a figure who is noted in antiquity as a master not just of prophecy but also of the arts of narration.

The skill of Cornelius as a narrator is apparent in the assertion of Gellius that he had actually caught sight of the action (*conspicere*); that 'he proclaimed that he could see [the action] before him, just as if he himself were caught up in the battle' (*proinde ut si ipse in proelio versaretur, coram videre sese vociferatus est*), and that the battle 'was represented in the gestures and words of the prophet' (*vaticinantis motu atque verbis repraesentata est*). True, the attestation of a vision in one's mind's eye apparent in both these claims is typical of prophecy in ancient literature, but its application is not restricted to this field.[4] Rather, the language used is characteristic in narrative and in rhetorical theory of that form of vivid presentation or description which goes under the various titles of ἐνάργεια, διατύπωσις, ὑποτύπωσις, φαντασία, *subiectio sub oculos*, *ponere ante oculos*, *demonstratio*, and so on.[5] This point merits further investigation.

The ecstatic visions of prophecy and the narrative procedure which aims at ἐνάργεια are closely related categories in ancient thought. While Quintilian and Plutarch urge the speaker to generate φαντασία

[2] Apart from the evidence in Plutarch, one must also underline the significance of Gaius' origins in Patavium. Livy's enthusiasm for stories concerning his Transpadane *patria* is evident at 1. 1, the foundation by Antenor, and 10. 2, where he tells of the victory in 302 BC of the Patavians over the Greek fleet of Cleonymus. Sid. Apoll. *Carm.* 2. 189 talks of Livy's writing as 'Euganeae chartae'. The considerable influence of Livy's account of the civil war on Lucan is established in Pichon (1912).

[3] Leigh (forthcoming) engages with the complex problems involved in reconstructing Livy. This piece also investigates the local religious traditions and foundation myth of Patavium.

[4] For *cerno* in prophecies, see Verg. *Aen.* 6. 86–7, Sen. *Ag.* 730, and Val. Flacc. *Arg.* 1. 226.

[5] The ensuing remarks owe much to Lausberg (1960), Russell (1964), N. J. Richardson (1980), Walker (1993), and esp. Zanker (1981).

or ἐνάργεια by exploiting one's natural tendency to day-dream, Longinus associates them with a form of speaking in which the vision of the speaker seems to be owed to divine possession and to passion:

ἤδη δ' ἐπὶ τούτων κεκράτηκε τοὔνομα ὅταν ἃ λέγεις ὑπ' ἐνθουσιασμοῦ καὶ πάθους βλέπειν δοκῇς καὶ ὑπ' ὄψιν τιθῇς τοῖς ἀκούουσιν.

But currently the word is generally used in those cases where you seem, subject to divine possession and passion, to see what you describe and to place it before the eyes of your listeners.[6]

This is only one instance of the exploitation by Gellius in his description of the prophecy of Cornelius of the language applied by literary critics to the field of ἐνάργεια. The statement that the vision of the augur was 'just as if he himself were caught up in the battle' (*proinde ut si ipse in proelio versaretur*) is strikingly similar to the assertion of Dionysius concerning the ἐνάργεια of the orations of Lysias, that the reader cannot help but feel that:

γινόμενα τὰ δηλούμενα ὁρᾶν καὶ ὥσπερ παροῦσιν οἷς ἂν ὁ ῥήτωρ εἰσάγῃ προσώποις ὁμιλεῖν.

He sees the events shown as they happen and mingles with whichever characters the orator introduces as if they were present.[7]

In the Gellian instance, the prophet seems to achieve for himself that state which Dionysius attributes to the audience of Lysias, namely that of actual presence as spectators at the action described. Yet there is nothing solipsistic about the vision of Cornelius—the great point about 'was represented in the gestures and words of the prophet' (*vaticinantis motu atque verbis repraesentata est*) is that he contrives to communicate that experience to his listeners. And, again, the language of 'representation' is exactly that employed by Quintilian, *Inst.* 6. 2. 29 to describe the rhetorical figure of φαντασία or *visio*:

Quas φαντασίας Graeci vocant (nos sane visiones appellemus), per quas imagines rerum absentium ita *repraesentantur* animo ut eas cernere oculis ac *praesentes* habere videamur, has quisquis bene ceperit is erit in adfectibus potentissimus.

[6] Long. *Subl.* 15. 1 cf. Quint. *Inst.* 6. 2. 29–30. For the analogy between φαντασία or ἐνάργεια and dreaming, cf. Lucan's Pompey at 7. 9–10, 'Nam Pompeiani *visus sibi* sede theatri | innumeram effigiem *cernere* plebis'. For more on this passage and on the problem of Pompey as spectator in general, see Ch. 4 *passim*. At ps.-Sen. *Oct.* 727, 'cerno' expresses the vision of Poppaea in her dream.

[7] Dion. Hal. *Lys.* 7; I. 14, 17 Us.–Rad.

Whoever masters those experiences which the Greeks call φαντασίαι (and we, of course, may call visions), through which images of things absent are so presented to the mind that we seem to see them with our eyes and to have them present, he will have immense power over the emotions.

The great quality of the family of concepts clustered around the term ἐνάργεια is their capacity to offer the listeners to or readers of a literary text a representation so vivid as to be visual, at best even to transport them as spectators to the scene of the events described.[8] It is not possible to affirm with any absolute certainty that the qualities as a narrator attributed to Cornelius by Gellius were already present in Livy, but similar terms are employed by the Greek writers and it is surely to just such a tradition that Lucan refers when at 7. 202–4 he remarks with some sarcasm that:

Si cuncta perito
augure mens hominum caeli nova signa notasset,
spectari toto potuit Pharsalia mundo.

If through some skilled augur the mind of men had noted all the new signs in heaven, Pharsalia could have been watched all over the world.

The famous and resonant lines which follow are discussed in almost every study of the *Pharsalia*. It is perhaps both a tribute to and the fault of that special resonance that they are invariably condemned to consideration in isolation from the surrounding verses from which they gain so much of their sense. Lucan breaks into a two-line exclamation on the greatness of the men whose fates were noted the whole world over, then offers one single seven-line sentence outlining the historical role, the aims, and intended impact of his own narrative technique:

O summos hominum, quorum fortuna per orbem
signa dedit, quorum fatis caelum omne vacavit!
Haec et apud seras gentes populosque nepotum,
sive sua tantum venient in saecula fama
sive aliquid magnis nostri quoque cura laboris
nominibus prodesse potest, cum bella legentur,
spesque metusque simul perituraque vota movebunt,
attonitique omnes veluti venientia fata,
non transmissa, legent et adhuc tibi, Magne, favebunt.

[8] Note here the description of the figure of hypotoposis at Nicolaus, *Prog.* 7 at Spengel (1885–6), iii. 476. 12 as a κεφάλαιον εἰς ὄψιν ἄγον τὸ γεγενημένον καὶ δι' ἐκφράσεως θεατὰς τῶν ἀτόπων ἐργαζόμενον ἡμᾶς.

O highest of men, whose fortune indicated itself all over the globe, to whose fates all heaven paid heed! These events, even among late nations and the peoples of our descendants, whether they survive by their fame alone or whether the care of my labour can do any service to great names, when the wars are read, they will generate together hopes and fears and prayers doomed to perish and all will be shocked as they read what seem like fates that are coming and not yet past, and all, Magnus, will still side with you.

Lucan's subject-matter is of such moment that it will live on by its own repute alone (7. 208). Yet the poet has a special contribution: to transform the experience of reading the wars (*cum bella legentur* . . . *legent*). The essence of this transformation is that, just as Cornelius contrived by ἐνάργεια to turn the audience of his Pharsalus narrative into spectators present at the scene, so Lucan will generate in his readers the very emotional response at which it is characteristic of such vivid narration to aim. That Lucan's readers will be rendered present at the battle is expressed temporally rather than locally in the assertion that they will treat what they read as 'like fates that are coming and not yet past' (*veluti venientia fata, non transmissa*); that they will be emotionally engaged emerges from the claim to stir 'hopes and fears and prayers doomed to perish' (*spesque metusque perituraque vota*) and to render them 'shocked' (*attoniti*).

As in the case of Cornelius, comparison with a number of ancient texts makes clear the close relationship between the ambitions expressed here by the poet and the rhetorical theory of ἐνάργεια and its cognates. For Lucan's assertion that his readers will have the feeling of being present at the time of the narrative, a perfect parallel is offered in the praises of Xenophon's account of the Battle of Cunaxa at Plut. *Art.* 8. 1:

τὴν δὲ μάχην ἐκείνην πολλῶν μὲν ἀπηγγελκότων, Ξενοφῶντος δὲ μονονουχὶ δεικνύοντος ὄψει καὶ τοῖς πράγμασιν ὡς οὐ γεγενημένοις, ἀλλὰ γινομένοις, ἐφιστάντος ἀεὶ τὸν ἀκροατὴν ἐμπαθῆ καὶ συγκινδυνεύοντα διὰ τὴν ἐνάργειαν, οὐκ ἔστι νοῦν ἔχοντος ἐπεξηγεῖσθαι, πλὴν ὅσα τῶν ἀξίων λόγου παρῆλθεν εἰπεῖν ἐκεῖνον.

But since many have recorded that battle and Xenophon all but presents it to our sight and by the vividness of his description engages the listener in the emotions and dangers of events as if they were not past but still happening, it would be foolish to recount it again, save in those details worthy of consideration which he passed over.[9]

[9] The parallel between Plutarch's description of Xenophon and Lucan is first attested at Walker (1993) 359–60 and is related to Lucan's pursuit of tragic ἀπατή. Plut. *Art.* 8. 1 is

For his claim that the result will be different sorts of emotional perturbation, might be cited the definition of *inlustris oratio* at Cic. *Part. Or.* 6. 20:

Est enim haec pars orationis, quae rem constituat paene ante oculos; is enim maxime sensus attingitur, sed et ceteri tamen et maxime mens ipsa moveri potest.

For it is this department of oratory which almost sets the matter before the eyes [of the listener]; for this sense is particularly touched, though the others also and the mind itself in particular can be moved.

Even more striking is the abortive attempt to distinguish the forms of φαντασία characteristic of rhetoric and poetry at Longinus, *Subl.* 15. 2:

ὡς δ' ἕτερόν τι ἡ ῥητορικὴ φαντασία βούλεται καὶ ἕτερον ἡ παρὰ ποιηταῖς οὐκ ἂν λάθοι σε, οὐδ' ὅτι τῆς μὲν ἐν ποιήσει τέλος ἐστὶν ἔκπληξις, τῆς δ' ἐν λόγοις ἐνάργεια, ἀμφότεραι δ' ὅμως τό τε {παθητικὸν} ἐπιζητοῦσι καὶ τὸ συγκεκινημένον.

And you will not fail to notice that φαντασία aims at one thing in rhetoric and another in poetry, and that the aim of poetic φαντασία is shock and of rhetorical φαντασία vividness, but that both nevertheless seek to arouse the passions and to move.

Longinus almost immediately abandons the terms of his distinction, discussing what he appears very strongly to consider Euripidean ἐνάργεια and asserting the usefulness of 'the type of shock generated by φαντασία' (τὸ κατὰ φαντασίαν ἐκπληκτικὸν) in rhetoric.[10] At times ancient writers discuss ἐνάργεια as a rhetorical figure in its own right, at others as the desired effect consequent on the employment of a figure, in this case φαντασία, and it is to this that the confusion must be attributed. It is therefore significant for this argument to note that the ἐνάργεια generated by rhetorical φαντασία is still only a way-station to the final end of 'arousing the passions and moving [the listener]' (τό τε παθητικὸν . . . καὶ τὸ συγκεκινημένον), an end which

also discussed at Nicolai (1992) 148–9 and compared to Long. *Subl.* 25 where it is asserted that ὅταν γε μὴν τὰ παρεληλυθότα τοῖς χρόνοις εἰσάγῃς ὡς γινόμενα καὶ παρόντα, οὐ διήγησιν ἔτι τὸν λόγον ἀλλ' ἐναγώνιον πρᾶγμα ποιήσεις. For the dramatic resonance of εἰσάγειν, see below, 'Beyond Tragic History' and cf. Long. *Subl.* 9. 13, where the *Iliad* is described as ὅλον . . . δραματικὸν . . . καὶ ἐναγώνιον. It should be noted here, however, that what Longinus is discussing at *Subl.* 25 is the related but different problem of narrating in the present tense. For a discussion of the implications of narration in the present historic in Latin, see App. 2.

[10] On this point, see Russell (1964) at Long. *Subl.* 15. 2 and Zanker (1981) 304 n. 28.

poetic φαντασία reaches immediately when it produces 'shock' (ἔκπληξις).[11] When one applies this observation to Lucan, it is striking that the term *spesque metusque* is regularly used in Latin from Cicero onwards to stand for the two Stoic prospective passions and that *attonitus* is marked by the glossaries as the Latin equivalent of the Greek ἔκπληκτος.[12]

Lucan has found in Cornelius a counterpart who is no less his antitype. All the evidence so far has pointed to a considerable convergence in the achievements of the two. The rest of the story, however, is one of divergence, of the two modes of narration and of response to the civil war, which compete with each other throughout the *Pharsalia.* Both of these modes have been attributed to the same generic theory, both burst the bounds of that theory. For Lucan is not just an epicist, not just a narrative artist; rather he is possessed of a political and historical imagination able to transcend the categories he inherits, to render them the bearers of the most dynamic ideological conceptions. The closing section of this chapter, 'Beyond Tragic History', returns to Lucan's appeal to the theory of ἐνάργεια and to his position within the alleged genre of tragic history. It is the purpose of the intervening sections, meanwhile, to inform that discussion with a preliminary investigation of the ideological disputes which give particular point to his claims. The first task, therefore, is to examine more closely the terms of Lucan's relationship with Cornelius and to locate certain crucial elements within the basic conceptual framework of Augustan and post-Augustan epic.

[11] For ἐνάργεια and the generation of passion, see also Plut. *Mor.* 347 A and the discussion at Walker (1993) 360–1.

[12] *Spesque metusque* is a very common collocation in Latin: Cic. *Verr.* 2. 2. 135 and 2. 4. 75, *Clu.* 176, *Red. Sen.* 7; Livy, 7. 10. 9, 8. 13. 17, 25. 27. 5, 26. 37. 1, 27. 26. 1, 27. 45. 5, 30. 32. 5, 36. 10. 9, 42. 59. 8; Tac. *Ann.* 2. 12. 3, 3. 69. 2, 4. 50. 3, 15. 51. 1, *Hist.* 1. 62. 2, 2. 2. 1, 4. 59. 1, 4. 70. 3, *Ger.* 46. 3; Verg. *Aen.* 1. 218; Ov. *Fast.* 1. 486, 3. 362, 6. 245, *Ars Am.* 3. 478; Sen. *Epp.* 13. 12 and 13. 13, 82. 18, 110. 4, *Ben.* 4. 11. 5, 7. 1. 7, *Vit. Beat.* 15. 5, *Q. Nat.* 2. 50. 1, *Ag.* 283, *Phoen.* 516–7 and 631. While Stoic ἐπιθυμία is normally translated as *libido*, Cic. *Tusc.* 4. 80 (see Dougan and Henry (1934) ad loc. for textual problems) uses *spes* as an alternative, a practice followed by Seneca at *Constant.* 9. 2 (see Minissale (1977) ad loc.), *Tro.* 399 (see Fantham (1982) ad loc.), *Phaed.* 492, *Thy.* 348–9. See also *Epp.* 13. 13, 47. 17, 82. 18, 110. 4, and the lengthy epigram attributed to Seneca in which *spes* is demonized. For this last, see Baehrens (1882–3) iv. 65. For *attonitus* as ἔκπληκτος, see *TLL* ii. 1154. 35 ff.

LUCAN, CORNELIUS, AND THE POETRY OF THE *VATES*

The essential point is that both Lucan and Cornelius underline the significant place of Pharsalus on a far longer temporal axis and, in different ways, reveal their own position on that axis. When at Lucan, 7. 196–7 Cornelius announces that 'The final day has come, the crucial issue is at hand, the impious arms of Pompey and Caesar come to battle' (*Venit summa dies, geritur res maxima . . . inpia concurrunt Pompei et Caesaris arma*), his reference to the impious weapons of Caesar and Pompey rather excludes him from any simplistic association with Caesar's partisans.[13] At the same time, however, there is a *sotto voce* Vergilianism to *venit summa dies* which connects to one aspect of his story on which Plutarch, Gellius, and Obsequens all concur and which is therefore surely Livian. It is this aspect which Lucan must most vehemently oppose: the confident assertion that Caesar has won. For *venit summa dies* echoes Vergil's Panthus at the sack of Troy in order obliquely to indicate not just the imminence of the crisis but also the defeat and destruction of one side (Verg. *Aen.* 2. 324–7):

> 'Venit summa dies et ineluctabile tempus
> Dardaniae. Fuimus Troes, fuit Ilium et ingens
> gloria Teucrorum; ferus omnia Iuppiter Argos
> transtulit; incensa Danai dominantur in urbe.'

'The final day and the inescapable time has come to Dardania. We Trojans are dead, Troy and the great glory of the Teucrians is dead; savage Jupiter has taken all away to Argos; the Danaans lord it in the fired city.'

It remains the task of Lucan, however, to deny Cornelius his Caesarian certainties, to make his own contribution to the continuation of the struggle.[14] At 2. 1–15 Lucan turns his back on omens and asks, 2. 4–6:

[13] For more on the attitude of Cornelius to Caesar, see the partial reconstruction of Livy in Leigh (forthcoming).

[14] It might reasonably be objected that Luc. 7. 196, 'venit summa dies' has a different sense in the mouth of Cornelius to that given it by Panthus: that it implies only the coming of the crisis, not one specific outcome. This is true for any surface reading of the text but not for one which recognizes any intertextual dimension. For what Vergil's Panthus and Livy's Cornelius have in common is the certainty with which the former acknowledges his side's defeat, and the latter asserts Caesar's victory. The determination of Lucan to have the last word over Vergil is emphasized in the excellent study of the theme of 'the final day' in Conte (1988) 32–9. Note esp. p. 34, which demonstrates the overturning of the optimistic tone of Verg. *Aen.* 7. 145 in Luc. 7. 129–33.

Cur hanc tibi, rector Olympi,
sollicitis visum mortalibus addere curam,
noscant venturas ut dira per omina clades?

Why, O ruler of Olympus, did you see fit to give worried mortals this extra care, so that they might know of disasters to come through dire omens?

Here he goes one step further and promises a narrative which, however like that of Cornelius in its vividness, will still rebel against it, steadfastly refusing the augur's submission to the truths of history. While Cornelius' listeners in Plutarch marvel to see him doff the cap of prophecy and refuse again to don it until the victory of Caesar be proved, Lucan's achievement will be not just to convince his readers of the imminence of past events but actually to induce them, if hopelessly, to cheer for Magnus, for the losing side. The catalogue of omens opens at 7. 151–2 with the assertion that 'Fortune, however, did not abstain from revealing by various signs the events that were to come' (*Non tamen abstinuit venturos prodere casus | per varias Fortuna notas*), and closes with Lucan's determination to make his readers believe in 'fates that are coming and not yet past' (*venientia fata, non transmissa*). Where the omens of 7. 151–2 reveal events which are 'about to come' because inevitable, the fates of 7. 212 are 'coming and not yet past' for the opposite reason, because they still retain an element of contingency.

The powerful implicit opposition between these two figures finds its inspiration in the self-definition of the Augustan and post-Augustan Roman poets. If Cornelius is an *augur*, Lucan is a *vates*.[15] This role is advertised in the initial dedication of the *Pharsalia* to Nero, 1. 63–6:

Sed mihi iam numen; nec, si te pectore *vates*
accipio, Cirrhaea velim secreta moventem
sollicitare deum Bacchumque avertere Nysa:
tu satis ad vires *Romana in carmina* dandas.

But you now are my divine power; nor, if I receive you in my breast as your *vates*, will I have any wish to disturb the god who rules mysterious Delphi or to summon Bacchus from Nysa: you are enough to provide inspiration for my Roman songs.

[15] Wiseman (1992) 284 and n. 105 gives a number of instances in Ovid where *augur* actually functions as a synonym for *vates* but here the title *augur* appears to derive more specifically from the actual sacral role which Cornelius performs.

It is again present—though, tellingly, as something refused—at 7. 551–6, where Lucan, faced with the worst horrors of battle, exclaims:

> Hic furor, hic rabies, hic sunt tua crimina, Caesar.
> Hanc fuge, mens, partem belli tenebrisque relinque,
> nullaque tantorum discat *me vate* malorum,
> quam multum bellis liceat civilibus, aetas.
> A potius pereant lacrimae pereantque querellae:
> quidquid in hac acie gessisti, Roma, tacebo.

Here is madness, here rage, here is your damnation, Caesar. O mind, flee this part of the war and leave it to the darkness, and let no age learn from my vatic recollection of such great evils how much is possible in civil wars. O rather let our tears be shed, our laments be uttered in vain: whatever you did in this battle, Rome, I shall not report.

It returns finally in a further apostrophe of the poet to Caesar, this time as the 'pious grandson' and loyal heir to Aeneas returns to Troy and the birthplace of the epic tradition his servants will so devotedly appropriate in his name, 9. 980–6:

> O sacer et magnus *vatum* labor! Omnia fato
> eripis et populis donas mortalibus aevum.
> Invidia sacrae, Caesar, ne tangere famae;
> nam, siquid Latiis fas est promittere Musis,
> quantum Zmyrnaei durabunt *vatis* honores,
> *venturi* me teque legent; Pharsalia nostra
> vivet, et a nullo tenebris damnabimur aevo.

O great and holy labour of the *vates*! You snatch everything from death and grant mortal peoples immortality. Caesar, be not touched by envy of holy fame; for, if it is right for the Latin muses to promise anything, as long as the honour of the *vates* of Smyrna shall endure, men to come will read me and you; our Pharsalia will live and we will be damned to darkness by no age.[16]

Lucan's point of reference is fundamentally Vergilian. At *Aeneid* 7. 41, in the second proem which introduces the Iliadic half of the poem, Vergil calls himself *vates*, and at 6. 660–5 the pious *vates* who uttered words worthy of Phoebus mingle with the chaste priests, the inventors, and the band of men wounded in the service of the homeland. The decision of the Augustan poets to style themselves *vates* and thus to

[16] There are excellent discussions of this scene in Zwierlein (1986), Schrijvers (1990), and Quint (1993). Quint offers an important analysis of Caesar's prayer at Luc. 9. 990–9, of his relationship to 'Aeneae ... mei' and of his status as the 'pius nepos', underlining Lucan's response to the appropriation of Homeric epic by different despots, first Alexander, then the Caesars.

assert their allegiance to the new national programme and their self-association with the temple of Apollo on the Palatine has been studied in depth by Newman.[17] The term *vates* is not just the sturdily Roman alternative to the Greek calque *poeta* but also gives the activity of the poet the particular ideological significance of association with the demiurgic role of the priest and the prophet.[18] When so much of the *Aeneid* is given over to the anticipation in speeches and artistic representations of events understood by the characters as the future, but known to the reader as the past, the overlap between the roles of the prophet and the poet-historian is clear and of some considerable importance.[19] Lucan is profoundly engaged with the implications of this conception of epic time.

TIME AND RECONCILIATION

The speech of Panthus at *Aeneid* 2. 324–7 finds an answering voice at the very close of the poem and from the most embittered enemy of his people, Juno (*Aen.* 12. 826–8):

> 'Sit Latium, sint Albani per saecula reges,
> sit Romana potens Itala virtute propago:
> occidit, occideritque sinas cum nomine Troia.'

'Let Latium be, let there be Alban kings through the centuries, let there be Roman offspring mighty with Italian manliness: Troy has fallen, let it have fallen together with its name.'[20]

In Vergil, the final day of Troy is balanced against the redeeming rise of Rome. And what is true for the fate of a city is also essential for understanding Vergil's attitude to the fate of individuals. This point can be illustrated through the example of the central apostrophes to the followers of Aeneas—Nisus, Euryalus, and Pallas—and to his opponent, Lausus. In each of these cases, the empathetic engagement of the narrative with the most pitiful reverses of the defeated is suddenly broken by a subjective intervention, the paradoxical effect of

[17] Newman (1967) 99–206 modifies and extends Dahlmann (1948) and Bickel (1950–1).

[18] This association is apparent in the discussion of the term *vates* at Varro, *Ling.* 7. 36, cf. 6. 52. Wiseman (1992) 279–80 offers a considerable collection of evidence for 'the long history of inter-relation between the poet and the prophet'.

[19] Wiseman (1992) 286 observes that 'the business is still with revelation'.

[20] Note also the observation of Conte (1988) 34 that the 'venit summa dies' of Panthus is answered by the recognition of the men at Verg. *Aen.* 7. 145 that 'advenisse diem quo debita moenia condant'.

which is to locate this suffering in a grander historical process and thus to evoke the reconciling power of time.[21] In the description of Nisus and Euryalus as a lucky pair, of the dead Pallas as bringing back both grief and glory to his father, of Lausus as a memorable youth who performs excellent deeds, Vergil defines his characters by qualities which will continue to be admired long after their local loyalties, their historically situated hatreds, have lost meaning.[22] Whatever Lausus might think of Aeneas and the Roman destiny he died to resist, it is that same Rome which will grant him his admired immortality. Vergil announces at *Aen.* 10. 791–3 that:

> Hic mortis durae casum tuaque optima facta,
> si qua fidem tanto est operi latura vetustas,
> non equidem nec te, iuvenis memorande, silebo.

Here I shall not pass over in silence the cruel fortune of your harsh death, your excellent deeds (if antiquity be trusted as it tells of so great a feat), nor indeed shall I pass over you, O memorable youth.

Here, *nec te* surely serves to align Vergil's promise to Lausus most closely with that to Nisus and Euryalus at *Aen.* 9. 446–9:

> Fortunati ambo! Si quid mea carmina possunt,
> nulla dies umquam memori vos eximet aevo,
> dum domus Aeneae Capitoli immobile saxum
> accolet imperiumque pater Romanus habebit.

O happy pair! If my songs have any force, no day will ever remove you from the memory of time, as long as the house of Aeneas shall inhabit the immovable rock of the Capitol and the Roman father shall hold sway.

If the promise of the approbation of a *Roman* audience renders the poet's favour to Lausus rather double-edged, indeed almost impertinent, while it remains unclear whether Rome will finally create a complete harmony out of the discordant polyphony sung by Dido, Turnus, Camilla, and Mezentius, Vergil's anticipation of the future from the

[21] The most eloquent contribution on this subject is the intervention of Conte (1986) in the debate on Vergil's subjective style begun in Heinze (1915) with the identification of the twin techniques of 'Empfindung' and 'Subjektivität' and continued in Otis (1963) 41–96 and La Penna (1967). See Conte (1986) 166–72, esp. 171, 'Only Vergil knows the whole of the story he is telling and knows how to interpret its future developments; even if he has made room within the text for all the potential irreconcilability (halted at a point "not yet") of its contradictions, he can still recognise within the hidden meaning of Fate a faint gleam of hope and, at the same time, suggest a final meeting point of sense for all the various voices he has gathered.'

[22] Verg. *Aen.* 9. 446–9 cf. 10. 507–9 and 791–3.

perspective of the past is a powerful rhetorical bid to impose meaning on history and to generate the reader's consent.

What is here at issue is the central Vergilian modification of the epic form. Homeric epic almost never relates the time of the action to that of the narrator, and when it does it is in such a manner as to assert how utterly different the one is from the other.[23] The first extant epic to represent the events of the narrative as any sort of κτίσις for the world of the narrator is the *Argonautica* of Apollonius, but the ideological significance of such a stance is only fully apparent in Roman epic, where fate is nationalized and history represented as an onward path leading to the goal of Roman domination. In the speech of Vergil's Jupiter, moreover, the great characteristic of this goal, this end, is its final endlessness (*imperium sine fine dedi*).[24] This anticipation of a task and a destiny which will long outlive Vergil gives the notion that 'the first of the Romans can learn | his Roman history in the future tense' a force which is as prescriptive as it is descriptive.[25] The foundation myth, the statement of the original character of Rome, is also a myth of authentication: that which always was is also that which ever shall be. Vergil the poet-*vates* is supported by a succession of prophetic speakers and artists, from Jupiter in Book 1 to Anchises in Book 6 and Vulcan in Book 8, each of whom transcends the location of the action in the time 'before Rome was' in order to tell us what 'Rome will be'. In the degree to which this selective interpretation of Roman history and identity coincides with the values embodied by the great originator Aeneas, it is possible to identify the Augustan ideology of the poem.

FOUNDATION AND AETIOLOGY

The contrast between the *venit summa dies* of Cornelius and the determination of Lucan to create a narrative where fate is always only about to happen and subject to counterfactual wishing is therefore the expression *in minimo* of a broader pattern in the *Pharsalia*. Here, the aetiological formula is redeployed in order to mark individual elements, the totality of which is Caesarism, and, since that totality must be reached at the close of the action, as the detested goal of the poem, the narrative is studded with the emotional refusal of an ending.

[23] Cf. De Jong (1987) 44–5.

[24] Verg. *Aen.* 1. 279. For aetiology and the linking of temporalities in Apollonius, see Fusillo (1985). For the application of this terminology to Vergil, see G. Williams (1983), ch. 1, 'The Concept of Fate', esp. 16.

[25] Auden, 'Secondary Epic'.

The Vergilian αἴτιον underpins the system endorsed by the foundation myth, by claiming that things still visible in the day of the narrator go back to the earliest identity of his people and are present because of the deeds of the hero or some other good man.[26] This is central to the poet's authentication of the Augustan political programme of rebirth and renewal after civil war. When Propertius, 4. 1A embraces the themes of the *Aitia* of Callimachus, the poet's description of himself as the Roman Callimachus is a matter not just of language or nationality, but of the particular political coloration to be given to his αἴτια.[27] This coloration—apparent from the opening of the poem, cast as a guided tour around Rome, all her modern grandeur contrasted with the humility of her origins—is Vergilian, closely imitating the walk of Aeneas and Evander around the future city of Rome in *Aeneid* 8.[28]

In the *Pharsalia*, in Lucan's *Romana carmina*, the treatment of the civil war has an analogous function to the struggles of Aeneas: it is the war that created the world in which Lucan lives, that set the foundations for the imperial system. The difference is that the *Pharsalia* is a poem of burning dissent, that the αἴτιον is deployed to display the coming of corruption. This is evident at 3. 84–168, particularly in the description of the robbing of the treasury, 3. 167–8:

Tristi spoliantur templa rapina,
pauperiorque fuit tum primum Caesare Roma.

The temples were robbed in dismal plunder and then for the first time was Rome poorer than Caesar.[29]

[26] For αἴτια and anticipations of later Roman culture in the *Aeneid*, see 3. 408–9, 5. 121–3, 5. 545–603, esp. 597–603 ('Lusus Troiae'), 5. 718 (Acesta), 6. 234–5 (Misenum), 6. 242 (Avernus), 7. 1–4 (Caieta), 7. 59–63 (Laurentines from laurel tree), 7. 162–5 (martial exercises), 7. 173–82 (temples, Senate, fasces, statues), 7. 183–6 (displaying 'rostra'), 7. 409–10, 7. 601–23 ('Belli Portae'), 7. 678–81 (Praeneste), 7. 706–9 (Claudii), 7. 765–80 (altar of Diana), 8. 98–101 (town of Evander as first Rome 'quae nunc Romana potentia caelo | aequavit'), 8. 306–69 (Aeneas and Evander at site of Rome, esp. 348–9 'nunc' cf. 'iam tum'), 8. 600–1, 10. 145, 12. 819–28 (Troy must disappear). A crucial concomitant of the disappearance of Troy is the depiction, for instance at 7. 173–91, of essential elements of Roman military and political culture as Italian in origin. This is also the proof of the promise of Aeneas that the Italians will be equal partners in the new country, and perfectly in tune with Augustan attempts to exorcize the conflicts of civil war with a policy of *tota Italia*.

[27] Prop. 4. 1A 64 talks of 'Umbria Romani patria Callimachi'.

[28] Of course, however, any reading of Prop. 4. 1A cannot be conducted without regard for the much more disturbing 4. 1B, and the model of Vergilian aetiology provided is only a partial statement of the full complexities of the *Aeneid*. The analysis of 7. 385–459 in Ch. 4 shows Lucan both creating a crudely Augustan Vergil and offering an exegesis of the 'further voices' involved.

[29] Hunink (1992) at 3. 168 is needlessly hesitant about detecting a 'political allusion'

The same idea then returns very prominently at 5. 374–402 and the description of Caesar's extortion of the consulship, 5. 385–6:

> Namque omnes voces, per quas iam tempore tanto
> mentimur dominis, haec primum repperit aetas.

For all the words, with which we have for so long now been lying to our masters, this age first discovered.[30]

THE DEDICATION TO NERO AND THE AUGUSTAN RHETORIC OF FOUNDATION

'We lie to our masters'? It is worth pausing on this striking phrase, for it echoes only too well one passage which illustrates Lucan's eristic relationship with Vergil and Augustanism from the start of his poem. Analysis of the sincerity or otherwise of Lucan's initial dedication to Nero—already quoted for its attestation at 1. 63–6 of Lucan's vatic role and for his composition of Roman songs—has concentrated on the anticipation in lines 1. 45–62 of the apotheosis of Nero and of the consequent coming of world peace and contentment. Emphasis is therefore put on the subsequent scorn shown by Lucan for the cult of the emperors and on the suggestion first raised in the *Adnotationes super Lucanum* and the *Commenta Bernensia* that the physical attributes anticipated for the god Nero at 55–7 are in some sense an allusion to

and drawing the parallel with Lucan 5. 386. His deference to the view of Lebek (1976) 205 that this refers only to Julius Caesar is unjustified. Lebek's citation of Verg. *Aen.* 8. 222–3 and Lucan 3. 440–5 as examples of *tum primum* where what matters is the change from the previous state, not the new state consequent on the change, proves nothing. Syndikus (1958) 42 and Bömer (1969–86) at Ov. *Met.* 1. 119 tell a different story: *tum primum* is regularly used for the description of *Kulturentstehung* in Latin poetry and that is what Lucan is doing here. It is essential to recall that what Lucan describes in Book 3 is the plundering of the temple of Saturn, home of the *aerarium*. Luc. 3. 167–8 presents this scene as an aetiology for the imperial tendency to transfer responsibility and resources from the State *aerarium* to the *fiscus*, originally the private property of the emperor. On this issue, see the reply of Brunt (1966) to Millar (1963).

[30] Luc. 3. 154–68 four times refers to what happened 'then' ('tunc . . . tum . . . tunc . . . tum'), while 5. 397–8 evokes the historical significance of the extortion of the consulship ('Inde perit primum quondam veneranda potestas | iuris inops'). See also 8. 673. Syndikus (1958) 42 quotes all these passages and has a definite feel for their importance to Lucan's perspective on his narrative. For 'mentimur dominis', a striking parallel is Mart. *Ep.* 10. 72 on the appropriate way to address the new ruler. Martial opens, *Ep.* 10. 72. 1–3, 'Frustra, Blanditiae, venitis ad me, | attritis miserabiles labellis: | dicturus dominum deumque non sum', and, after banishing this mode of address to Parthia, continues, 10. 72. 7–12, 'Non est hic dominus sed imperator, | sed iustissimus omnium senator, | per quem de Stygia domo reducta est | siccis rustica Veritas capillis. | Hoc sub principe, si sapis, caveto | verbis, Roma, prioribus loquaris.'

corporeal defects apparent in life: obesity, baldness, a squint, and the like.[31] Yet it is in the opening lines of the dedication, 1. 33–45, that perhaps the most disturbing of the poet's remarks are made. Lucan embraces Nero as his consolation for the civil wars:

> Quod si non aliam venturo fata Neroni
> invenere viam magnoque aeterna parantur
> regna deis caelumque suo servire Tonanti
> non nisi saevorum potuit post bella gigantum,
> iam nihil, o superi, querimur; scelera ipsa nefasque
> hac mercede placent. Diros Pharsalia campos
> inpleat et Poeni saturentur sanguine manes,
> ultima funesta concurrant proelia Munda,
> his, Caesar, Perusina fames Mutinaeque labores
> accedant fatis et quas premit aspera classes
> Leucas et ardenti servilia bella sub Aetna,
> multum Roma tamen debet civilibus armis
> quod tibi res acta est.

But if the fates could find no other way for the coming of Nero and if the gods win their eternal kingdom at a great price and heaven could not enslave itself to its Thunderer until after the wars of the savage giants, no longer, O gods, do we complain: the crimes themselves, the unspeakable deeds, please us with this reward. Let Pharsalia fill its dire fields and let the Carthaginian ghosts be sated with blood; let the final battle be fought at murderous Munda; on top of these deaths, O Caesar, let there come the famine of Perugia and the sufferings of Mutina and the fleets sunk off fierce Leucas and the servile wars beneath burning Etna: much yet does Rome owe to the arms of civil war if the deed was done for you.

The Vergilian patterning is not hard to see. The assertion at 33–4 that 'the fates found a way for Nero' (*fata Neroni | invenere viam*) echoes the confident assurance that 'the fates will find a way' (*fata viam invenient*) of Helenus the prophet at *Aeneid* 3. 395 and of Jupiter at the close of the council of the gods at 10. 113. In this way it imposes on Rome's history from the civil wars to Nero the same model employed by Vergil to describe the coming of the Trojans to Rome, the victory of

[31] For Lucan's attitude to the cult of the emperors, see Luc. 6. 807–9, 9. 601–4, and esp. 7. 445–59. The only way in which it is possible to deny the impact of these assaults on the sincerity of the proem is to follow the story in the ancient lives of Lucan that poetic jealousy led Nero to ban Lucan from performance after the publication of his first three books. Yet the attempts by Lebek (1976) to deny any subversive tone in Books 1–3 and to blame that tone in 4–10 on the poet's personal quarrel with Nero are deeply flawed. For discussions of Nero's alleged physical defects, see Grimal (1960), Ahl (1976) 47 n. 54, and Brena (1988) 134–5 with bibliography.

Aeneas, and the resolution of Augustan Rome. Lucan's coup, however, lies in his capacity to point up the inadequacies of the figure as he employs it. These emerge on two levels. On the first level, the inevitable concern for Nero's capacity to serve as the balance to all of the ills of history is heightened by Lucan's remorseless piling up of woes in lines 38–43. Lines 37–8, 'the crimes themselves, the unspeakable deeds, please us with this reward' (*scelera ipsa nefasque* | *hac mercede placent*), describe the putative reward of Nero in the terms used by Vergil's Juno as she unleashes Allecto at *Aeneid* 7. 317–22 and look forward to the savage price to be paid before Aeneas and Latinus are united; lines 43–4, 'much yet does Rome owe to the arms of civil war if the deed was done for you' (*multum Roma tamen debet civilibus armis* | *quod tibi res acta est*) again demand calculation of profit and loss. All this is troubling. True, a dedication should be flattering and there would be nothing more flattering than sincerely to imply that Nero was worth the price paid, but it remains the case that the rest of the poem is studded with allusions to the destruction of Italy and is markedly free from attestations of the nation's rebirth under Nero. While the loss is ever visible, the profit is not there to be found.

If the first level of inadequacy emerges from the inconcinnity between Vergil's figure and the capacity of Lucan's material to make sense of it, the second level delivers itself of a far more radical critique. For within the consolation is seen Lucan's own twist on another favourite Vergilian motif, gigantomachy as an analogy for the struggle for power on Earth, 33–7:

Quod si non aliam venturo fata Neroni
invenere viam magnoque aeterna parantur
regna deis *caelumque suo servire Tonanti*
non nisi saevorum potuit post bella gigantum,
iam nihil, o superi, querimur.

But if the fates could find no other way for the coming of Nero and if the gods win their eternal kingdom at a great price and heaven could not enslave itself to its Thunderer until after the wars of the savage giants, no longer, O gods, do we complain.

Absolute power generates analogies for itself. The discussion of *Caesaris clementia* in Chapter 2 examines a number of these. Two here stand out: the king as Jupiter ruling the universe, the king as master to his slaves. Lucan's implication at 1. 33–6 is clear—'enslave itself to its Thunderer' (*suo servire Tonanti*) presupposes that you, Nero, are our

Jupiter and that we are your slaves. This is the ending which Vergil dissimulates and Lucan reveals, the ending which Vergil accepts and Lucan determinedly resists. Chapter 2 considers three episodes from the Spanish campaign where an end to the civil war is possible. In each of these endings, the immediate prospect is not just of a cessation of hostilities but also of the collapse of Caesar's ambitions. Trapped in history and subject to repeated frustration, Lucan's narrator throws himself directly into the action in order to make ever more perverse, more reflexive pleas for the sort of ending which cannot be. Overshadowing every one of his pleas, however, must be the pained consciousness of another of Lucan's vatic counterparts, the astrologer Nigidius Figulus, who warns at 1. 669–72:

> 'Et superos quid prodest poscere *finem*?
> Cum *domino* pax ista venit. Duc, Roma, malorum
> continuam seriem clademque in tempora multa
> extrahe civili tantum iam libera bello.'

'And what use is it to ask the gods for an ending? That peace comes with a master. Rome, carry on the continuous chain of disasters and drag out the slaughter as long as you can, free now only as long as the civil war endures.'

Lucan's dedication gestures at welcoming a Vergilian ending the true meaning of which it is actually concerned to expose. You can call it the *pax Augusta*, you can call it the nation reborn, but it is nothing more than the power of a master over his slaves.[32]

SPECTACLE AND ENGAGEMENT

When Lucan pairs himself with Cornelius, he makes a crucial assertion of affinity: the *augur* of Patavium overcomes through narrative ἐνάργεια the geographical separation of his audience from the action, the Neronian *vates* requires the same virtues in order to bridge the gap imposed by time. Yet when Lucan expresses in temporal terms his

[32] Lucan here puts into the mouth of Nigidius a version of the famous prophecy he is said to have uttered at the birth of Augustus in 63 BC. Suet. *Aug.* 94. 5 records that he 'affirmasse dominum terrarum orbi natum', Dio Cass., 45. 1. 5 that he told Octavius, father of Augustus, that δεσπότην ἡμῖν ἐγέννησας. It is evident that Nigidius was also a consistent opponent of Caesarism: Cic. *Att.* 7. 24 shows him joining Domitius in the civil war in 49 BC; Cic. *Fam.* 4. 13 is a consolation of 46 BC to Nigidius, who is still in exile; Suet. fr. 85 (Reifferscheid) shows that he died without returning to Rome. 'Cum domino pax ista venit' is surely as deliberately unspecific as the reference to 'Caesar' at 3. 167–8: Nigidius anticipates, Lucan records the experience of a people saddled with a succession of Caesars, of masters.

technical aim as a narrator again to make the action present for his audience, he brings to the surface a further and now ideological conception of time in narrative and one which implies a profound divergence between the two figures—the acceptance by Cornelius of the historical ending of Pharsalus gives voice to the consent of the Augustan *vates*, to his complicity with the political foundation brought about by the events he records. Lucan and his ideal reader will never share that consent.

To tell the story of the civil wars is to recount the great transformation of Rome, the death of the Republic and the birth of the Empire. Throughout the *Pharsalia*, characters as well as readers are presented with powerfully focused images of that transformation and are invited to respond. The contrast of Cornelius' Vergilian acceptance of the change and his representation of the battle as something to be *watched* with Lucan's oppositionist wish to induce his readers to deny the truths of historical time, to generate passion and counterfactual wishing, is one replicated at various crucial junctures in the narrative. Closer examination of these junctures, moreover, will introduce themes of continuous importance throughout this study and illustrate the corrosively political cast of Lucan's imagination.

The first instance of the opposition between watching and wishing emerges in Cato's justification of his own engagement in the war at 2. 289–92. What is striking is the manner in which Cato develops a conventional topos of Stoic imperturbability:

> 'Sidera quis mundumque velit *spectare* cadentem
> expers ipse *metus*? Quis, cum ruat arduus aether,
> terra labet mixto coeuntis pondere mundi,
> conpressas tenuisse manus?'

'Who would want to watch the stars and the universe in collapse without feeling any fear himself? Who, when the heights of heaven fell down, when the earth tottered amidst the weight of the collapsing universe, would not wish to lift a finger?'[33]

The connection drawn here between spectatorship and apathy or disengagement is again apparent at 4. 400–1. This is the *sententia* with which Lucan closes his account of the failed fraternization of the

[33] Fantham (1992*a*) is surely right to follow Shackleton-Bailey and Luck in rejecting Housman's 'complossas' (MZ) in favour of 'conpressas' (Ω). Livy, 7. 13 is a significant parallel.

armies in the Spanish campaign, the subsequent slaughter and final display of Caesar's clemency:

> Sic proelia soli
> felices *nullo spectant* civilia *voto*.

Thus they alone are happy watching a civil war who do so without a prayer.

If these lines offer a most eloquent encapsulation of the issues addressed in Chapter 2, a similar complaint at 7. 447–8 does the same for Chapter 3. At the close of Lucan's most consistent intertextual attack on the lies of the various Augustan *vates* comes his rebuke to the father of the gods whose benevolent guidance they were so enthusiastic to assert, 7. 447–8:

> *Spectabit* ab alto
> aethere Thessalicas, teneat cum fulmina, caedes?

Will he watch the slaughter of Thessaly from the heights of heaven, though he holds the thunderbolt?

In all these cases, the association of the spectator with dispassionate observation is made by one for whom the consequences of such disengagement are politically unacceptable. The terms employed are those of Senecan Stoicism but the sentiment is more complex. This pattern holds true throughout the *Pharsalia*. Consider, for instance, the question just quoted from the speech of Cato at 2. 289–90. This line of argument recalls a standard objection to Stoic teaching. At *Epistle* 74. 22, for instance, Seneca's notional opponent attacks the Stoics in these terms:

'Nihil agitis' inquit 'quod negatis ullum esse aliud honesto bonum: non faciet vos haec munitio tutos a fortuna et inmunes. Dicitis enim inter bona esse liberos pios et bene moratam patriam et parentes bonos. *Horum pericula non potestis spectare securi*: perturbabit vos obsidio patriae, liberorum mors, parentum servitus'.

'You are wrong', he says, 'to deny that there is any good save in what is virtuous: this defence will not keep you safe and sound from the blows of fortune. For you say that among the category of "good things" are dutiful children and a well-ordered homeland and good parents. You cannot look on these in a state of danger without feeling concern: the siege of your homeland, the death of your children, the enslavement of your parents will disturb you.'

Seneca's opponent derives his caricature of Stoic disengagement from the Stoics' own boasts. A classic statement of unconcern is Seneca, *Quaestiones Naturales* 6. 32. 4:

Pusilla res est hominis anima, sed ingens res contemptus animae: hanc qui contempsit, *securus videbit* maria turbari, etiamsi illa omnes excitaverunt venti, etiamsi aestus aliqua perturbatione mundi totum in terras vertet oceanum; *securus aspiciet* fulminantis caeli trucem atque horridam faciem, frangatur licet caelum et ignes suos in exitium omnium, in primis suum, misceat; *securus aspiciet* ruptis compagibus dehiscens solum, illa licet inferorum regna retegantur. Stabit super illam voraginem intrepidus et fortasse quo debebit cadere, desiliet.

A man's life is a small thing but contempt for life a huge thing: he who has contempt for life will see stormy seas without concern, even though all the winds have stirred them up, even though the swell, subject to some disturbance of the cosmos, casts the whole ocean onto the land; he will look without concern at the fierce and horrid sight of the thundering sky, though the sky be broken and commingle all its fires first to the destruction of itself, then of all; he will look without concern at the gaping of the earth as its frame bursts open, though those kingdoms of the shades below be revealed. He will stand over that chasm without fear and perhaps will leap down where he must fall.[34]

These passages draw on the same arguments in Stoicism as the speech of Cato. Cato's reply to Brutus, it should be noted, has a double function. On one level, it urges an attitude of engaged concern for others. Like Lucan's readers at 7. 205–13, Cato is not free from fear, but his fear is fear for the world, not himself. At 2. 240–1, he is 'fearful for all and untroubled for himself' (*cunctisque timentem* | *securumque sui*).[35] At the same time, Cato's words, like the narrator's accusation against Jupiter, posit the possibility of a disengaged spectatorship which simply does not care, which is marked by unconcern for the fate of others. This attitude is stated most eloquently in Roman verse in the opening lines of Book 2 of the *De Rerum Natura* of Lucretius, a passage which bears an obvious resemblance to that cited earlier from the *Quaestiones Naturales*:

> Suave, mari magno turbantibus aequora ventis,
> e terra magnum alterius spectare laborem;
> non quia vexari quemquamst iucunda voluptas,
> sed quibus ipse malis careas quia cernere suave est.
> Suave etiam belli certamina magna tueri
> per campos instructa tua sine parte pericli.

Sweet is it when out on the broad sea the winds disturb the waves to watch from land the great struggles of another; this is not because it is happy and

[34] Cf. Sen. *Constant.* 6, *Ep.* 85. 25.

[35] See the comments of Fantham (1992*a*) ad loc. and cf. Sen. *Ep.* 56. 12–14.

pleasant that another be distressed but because it is sweet to see the troubles from which you yourself are free. Sweet too to look at the great conflicts of war drawn up in the fields but at no risk to you.[36]

Lucretius ponders the pleasures of the theatre of war. He denies that there is any pleasure (*voluptas*) in watching the suffering of others save as a reminder of one's own well-being, but motives are not always so pure. In particular, it is the same term (*voluptas*) which emerges most consistently in moralizing accounts of the vicious world of the amphitheatre. When Lucan describes Cato's desert march, he employs so many references to spectatorship and so dense a crop of amphitheatrical metaphors that it is unclear where Stoic imperturbability ends and cruel pleasure begins. I discuss this problem at the close of Chapter 7. Even more significantly, when the Senecan 'untroubled spectator' (*securus spectator*) returns in the *Pharsalia*, he is the Sulla of 2. 207–8, the tyrant *par excellence* gloating over the bodies of his victims. What started as the attitude of the Stoic sage has taken on an alarmingly political tone and become the criminal gaze of the despot. The implications of this and similar manifestations are confronted directly in the Epilogue.

BEYOND TRAGIC HISTORY

If Lucan politicizes the categories he has drawn from Hellenistic philosophy, this is no less true of his relationship to Hellenistic historiography. This point may be illustrated by comparison of his assertion of the capacity of his narrative to generate passion with the comments of Seneca at *De Ira* 2. 2. 3–6:

Hic subit etiam inter *ludicra scaenae spectacula* et *lectiones rerum vetustarum*. Saepe Clodio Ciceronem expellenti et Antonio occidenti *videmur irasci*. Quis non contra Mari arma, contra Sullae proscriptionem concitatur? Quis non Theodoto et Achillae et *ipsi puero non puerile auso facinus infestus est*? Cantus nos nonnumquam et citata modulatio instigat *Martiusque ille tubarum sonus*; movet mentes et atrox pictura et iustissimorum suppliciorum tristis aspectus; inde est quod adridemus ridentibus et contristat nos turba maerentium et effervescimus ad aliena certamina. Quae non sunt irae, non magis quam tristitia est quae ad conspectum mimici naufragii contrahit frontem, non magis quam *timor qui Hannibale post Cannas moenia circumsidente lectorum percurrit animos*, sed omnia ista motus sunt animorum moveri nolentium, nec adfectus sed principia proludentia adfectibus. Sic enim *militaris viri in media pace iam togati aures tuba suscitat*

[36] Lucr. 2. 1–6.

equosque castrenses erigit crepitus armorum. Alexandrum aiunt Xenophanto canente manum ad arma misisse.

This crops up even amongst the spectacles of the theatrical stage and readings recording the events of history. Often we seem to grow angry at Clodius as he expels Cicero and at Antony as he kills him. Who is not stirred up against the arms of Marius and the proscriptions of Sulla? Who is not hostile to Theodotus and Achillas and the boy himself who dared no boyish deed? Sometimes singing and an excited modulation and that martial ring of the trumpets arouse us; even a horrible picture and the sorry sight of the most just punishments move our minds; this is why we laugh with those who laugh, why a crowd of mourners saddens us, why we grow excited at the conflicts of others. These experiences are no more forms of anger than is it sadness which furrows our brow at the sight of a fake sea-battle, no more than is it fear which runs through the minds of readers as Hannibal besieges the city walls after Cannae; all these, rather, are the emotions of minds reluctant to be moved, nor are they passions but the very initial stages prior to passion. For thus does the trumpet still excite the ears of the soldier now immersed in civilian life and dressed in a toga, thus does the din of arms awake war-horses. They say that when Xenophantus played, Alexander reached for his weapons.[37]

This passage contains many points of intersection with the claims for narrative examined in the initial discussion of Lucan and Cornelius. On a basic level, the themes it suggests are very familiar to readers of Lucan (the murder of Pompey) and of Silius (Hannibal at the walls of Rome). More significantly, Seneca's reference to the fear felt as Hannibal besieges the walls of Rome reveals the power of art to revive in passion the experience of prospection. Moreover, the reference to 'readings recording the events of history' (*lectiones rerum vetustarum*) and to the fear which 'runs through the minds of readers' (*lectorum percurrit animos*) parallels Lucan at 7. 205–13 in its assertion that these emotions can be experienced through reading and not just in the theatre.[38]

[37] The comparison is made at Hutchinson (1993) 71 n. 66.

[38] For this, cf. Cic. *Fam.* 5. 12. 4–5 for the *spes* and *timor* experienced in reading. The experience of prospection revived is not purely literary. For it is stated as a characteristic of both hope and fear at Sen., *Ep.* 5. 7–9. Here, Seneca expounds to Lucilius the maxim of Hecato that 'Desines . . . timere, si sperare desieris'. The linking of the two emotions is then expressed in these terms: 'Quemadmodum eadem catena et custodiam et militem copulat, sic ista quae tam dissimilia sunt pariter incedunt: spem metus sequitur. Nec miror ista sic ire; *utrumque pendentis animi est, utrumque futuri expectatione solliciti.* Maxima autem utriusque causa est quod non ad praesentia aptamur sed cogitationes in longinqua praemittimus; itaque providentia, maximum bonum condicionis humanae, in malum versa est. Ferae pericula quae vident fugiunt, cum effugere, securae sunt: *nos et venturo*

It is evident that Seneca's description of the impact of reading on the emotions owes much to the broad ancient critical tradition regarding ἐνάργεια in narrative. More specifically, however, one aspect of this passage intersects with a form of presentation with which both the spectacle of Cornelius and the narratorial interventions, the immediacy, and the pathos of Lucan have been associated. Seneca refers twice to the blast of the trumpet. The notion that a written account of the opening of a battle can be so vivid that it is actually possible to hear the battle-trumpets sound is paralleled by Hutchinson at Silius, *Pun.* 5. 190–2,[39] but it is important to look back rather earlier than this to the praises of Asinius Pollio at Horace, *Carm.* 2. 1. 17–18:

> Iam nunc minaci murmure cornuum
> perstringis auris, iam litui strepunt.

Even now you strike the ears with the menacing murmur of the horns, even now the cornets resound.

In this assertion of the capacity of a narrative to reproduce direct sensory experience has been identified the authentic boast of the tragic historian, and it is with this 'school' that Lucan's name is repeatedly linked.[40]

The association between the emphasis on spectacle in Hellenistic and Roman historiography and the tragic history of Phylarchus and Duris was made in the classic study of Borszák.[41] The notion that Lucan's radical development of the narrative voice in epic is to be explained by analogy with tragedy goes back at least as far as Guillemin and Syndikus and has since found particular favour in Italian scholarship of the 1960s and 1970s and in two significant articles by Marti.[42] In the first of these articles, moreover, Marti

torquemur et praeterito. Multa bona nostra nobis nocent; timoris enim tormentum memoria reducit, providentia anticipat; nemo tantum praesentibus miser est.'

39 Hutchinson (1993) 71 and n. 66. See also Cic. *Marcell.* 9, 'Sed tamen eius modi res nescio quo modo *etiam cum leguntur*, obstrepi clamore militum videntur et tubarum sono'.

40 For Asinius Pollio as a tragic historian, see Ullman (1942) 50–1. The most suggestive part of Horace's tribute must be *Carm.* 2. 1. 9–12: 'Paulum severae Musa tragoediae | desit theatris: mox ubi publicas | res ordinaris, grande munus | Cecropio repetes coturno'. Is the Muse of tragedy simply to quit the theatre and remain silent or to transfer her energies to the new task of tragic history?

41 Borszák (1973).

42 Guillemin (1951) 220, 'Avant le récit du combat trouve place un mouvement imité de la lyrique chorale de la tragédie, qui est une innovation dans l'épopée. Lucain y commente en son propre nom, et non pas par la voix d'un choeur ni par l'exposé des *rumores* à la manière de Tacite, l'état des événements.' These opinions are cited with approval by Syndikus (1958) 41. For Italian versions of the argument, see Gagliardi (1970) and

specifically addresses the concept not just of tragedy but also of tragic history.

The idea of a subgenre of tragic history is subject to much dispute. In particular, there is little sympathy for the original formulation of Schwartz and Scheller, which compares the remains of Duris with the critique of Phylarchus in Polybius and uses this as the foundation for the theory that Hellenistic historians of Peripatetic training applied to their narratives the plot-movements marked by Aristotle in the *Poetics* as characteristic of tragedy.[43] While it is possible to demonstrate that Phylarchus represents the fall of Mantinea as a form of περιπέτεια and that the account of his practice in Polybius features a succession of recognizably Aristotelian terms,[44] belief in a dogmatically Aristotelian school of history is hard to sustain in the face of the considerable evidence for the presence of tragic motifs and modes of presentation in historiography as early as Herodotus, Thucydides, and Isocrates.[45] Strasburger pushes the origins of tragic history as far back even as Homer.[46]

The current orthodoxy, therefore, is that the phenomena marked as characteristic of tragic history are not the property of one school but have a long tradition throughout ancient historiography. An extension

(1975), esp. at 7. 24–7; cf. Viansino (1974) 97–101 and Narducci (1979) 115–17. Gagliardi (1975) in particular is obviously influenced by Conte (1968) and the description of the recollection of Sulla and Marius by the old of Rome as a chorus. Conte, however, is less concerned with the role of the narrator than with the explosion of Lucan's epic into a mass of conflicting subjectivities. The most committed statements of the case for the influence of tragedy and tragic history are Marti (1964) and (1975).

43 The idea of a school of Peripatetic 'tragic history' is expounded in Schwartz (1897) and (1903) and Scheller (1911). The vagueness of the model is emphasized in Walbank (1955) 4–5, (1960) 233–5, and (1972) 34–9 and admitted even by Brink (1960) 14, who attempts to rebut some of Walbank's criticisms. See also the detailed discussion of previous research in Meister (1975) 109–26 and the remarks of Wiseman (1994) 18–20.

44 Polyb. 2. 56. 6 records that Phylarchus φησὶ τοὺς Μαντινέας γενομένους ὑποχειρίους μεγάλοις περιπεσεῖν ἀτυχήμασι, καὶ τὴν ἀρχαιοτάτην καὶ μεγίστην πόλιν τῶν κατὰ τὴν Ἀρκαδίαν τηλικαύταις παλαῖσαι συμφοραῖς ὥστε πάντας εἰς ἐπίστασιν καὶ δάκρυα τοὺς Ἕλληνας ἀγαγεῖν. It is hard to think that Plutarch's use of περιπεσεῖν is not meant to recall Aristotle, while the emphasis on Mantinea as the biggest and oldest of the cities of Arcadia only underlines the gravity of the reversal. This point is made explicit at Polyb. 2. 56. 13, where the enthusiasm of Phylarchus for περιπετειῶν is attacked, for which see Walbank (1957–79) ad loc. and Ullman (1942) 41–2. For an extended list of Aristotelian-sounding terms in Polybius, see Walbank (1972) 34–5 and esp. n. 16.

45 Ullman (1942) points to the prominence of tragic motifs in Isocrates and his school; Walbank (1955), (1960), and (1972) looks back to Herodotus and Thucydides. The views of Kebric (1977) 11–18, 38–41, 77 and of Sacks (1981)—especially in their treatment of *mimesis* in Aristotle—are those of Walbank.

46 Strasburger (1966) 78, 80.

of this position is to play down the Peripatetic education of Duris of Samos and assert that his stated views on *mimesis* have little or nothing to do with the *Poetics*.[47] There is in this an extremism potentially as misleading as that which it contradicts: where once it was assumed that tragic history was all about Aristotle, now it is held that he has nothing to do with it at all. An alternative strategy, however, can find points of connection between Homer, the wider historiographical tradition, and Aristotle.

For the conception of *mimesis* propounded by Duris, the crucial testimony is *FGH* 76 F1, the record at Photius, *Bibl.* 176 p. 121 a 41 of his censure of Ephorus and Theopompus:

Δοῦρις μὲν οὖν ὁ Σάμιος ἐν τῆι πρώτηι τῶν αὐτοῦ Ἱστοριῶν οὕτω φησίν· Ἔφορος δὲ καὶ Θεόπομπος τῶν γενομένων πλεῖστον ἀπελείφθησαν· οὔτε γὰρ μιμήσεως μετέλαβον οὐδεμιᾶς οὔτε ἡδονῆς ἐν τῶι φράσαι, αὐτοῦ δὲ τοῦ γράφειν μόνον ἐπεμελήθησαν.

In the first book of his *Histories*, therefore, Duris the Samian says as follows: 'Ephorus and Theopompus fell far short of what happened; for they engaged in no mimesis or pleasure in description but were concerned only with writing itself'.[48]

For many, there is no way to bridge the gap in Aristotle's thought between history as that which did happen and tragedy as that which might; even if Aristotle had explicitly conceded to historiography some part of *mimesis*, nothing in the fragments of Duris or Phylarchus could be said to apply to historical material the universalizing effect of tragic *mimesis*.[49] To Ullman, Duris' censure of Ephorus and Theopom-

[47] For the studies of Duris and his brother Lynceus under Theophrastus at Athens *c.*304–302 BC, see *FGH* 76 T1–2.

[48] A second passage is often compared to *FGH* 76 F1, that found at Diod., 20. 43. 7 but conventionally attributed to the influence of Duris: *ταύτηι δ' ἄν τις καὶ τὴν ἱστορίαν καταμέμψαιτο. θεωρῶν ἐπὶ μὲν τοῦ βίου πολλὰς καὶ διαφόρους πράξεις συντελουμένας κατὰ τὸν αὐτὸν καιρόν, τοῖς δ' ἀναγράφουσιν ἀναγκαῖον ὑπάρχον τὸ μεσολαβεῖν τὴν διήγησιν καὶ τοῖς ἅμα συντελουμένοις μερίζειν τοὺς χρόνους παρὰ φύσιν, ὥστε τὴν μὲν ἀλήθειαν τῶν πεπραγμένων τὸ πάθος ἔχειν, τὴν δ' ἀναγραφὴν ἐστερημένην τῆς ὁμοίας ἐξουσίας μιμεῖσθαι μὲν τὰ γεγενημένα, πολὺ δὲ λείπεσθαι τῆς ἀληθοῦς διαθέσεως.* This passage is perhaps less significant than it might first appear. For it concerns itself with a very limited field of reference in historiography—the problem of how to narrate events which occur simultaneously and are moving because of their simultaneity. While Diodorus attributes the quality of *mimesis* to that sort of history-writing which treats in separation events which occur simultaneously, he does so in the course of an argument which still attributes scant pathetic impact to such an approach compared to the experience of lived reality. In this way, *mimesis* emerges as conceptually quite insignificant. For the attribution of this passage to Duris, see Kebric (1977) 39–41, 77.

[49] Walbank (1960) 220, Kebric (1977) 17–18, and Sacks (1981) base their rejection of

pus employs Aristotelian terminology in order to express the much more banal opinion that these writers simply do not include enough recognizably tragic material.[50] Yet the emphasis on universality produces a very one-sided view of Aristotelian *mimesis*, while the analysis of tragic history purely by content ignores other, stylistic criteria for interpretation.

An important recent study compares the views of Duris on *mimesis* to the stylistic theories of later writers influenced by Peripatetic thought, particularly Demetrius and Dionysius.[51] Taking as her starting-point Duris' use of *ἐκμιμεῖσθαι* at *FGH* 76 F89 for Homer's skill in representing the irrigation of a garden, Gray examines the notion that use of language in narrative is mimetic as long as it is proper or fitting to the nature of the person or phenomenon it seeks to evoke. By contrast, artificial or unnatural language is good only for epideictic purposes and is incapable of conveying emotional states or character. This is a significant approach and one which—in its exploration of the deleterious effect on narrative *mimesis* of show-speaking and artifice—perhaps suggests a way back into the tradition of the *Poetics* and thereby back to Homer.

The point here is to consider how Duris and Phylarchus attempted to perfect historiography as a narrative art. While Aristotle may regard tragedy as the most perfectly mimetic literary form, other genres, most notably epic, are at their best when coming closest to what may be styled dramatic presentation. A heterodox interpretation of the praises of Homer at *Poetics* 1460a5–11 attributes to him the virtues of the 'showing narrator' which the overly-intrusive and ostentatious 'telling' narrator is doomed to lose and understands his qualities as a mimete as extending beyond the prominence of character-speech also to take in the manner in which he presents action.[52] Those epicists

Aristotelian influence on the mimetic theories of Duris entirely on Ar. *Poet.* 1447a21 (*mimesis* as the peculiar characteristic of poetry) and on the distinction at 1451b2–7 between the *τὰ γενόμενα* and *καθ' ἕκαστον* of history and the *οἷα ἂν γένοιτο* and *τὰ καθόλου* of tragedy.

[50] Ullman (1942).

[51] See Gray (1987).

[52] Ar. *Poet.* 1460a5–11 states that: *Ὅμηρος δὲ ἄλλα τε πολλὰ ἄξιος ἐπαινεῖσθαι καὶ δὴ καὶ ὅτι μόνος τῶν ποιητῶν οὐκ ἀγνοεῖ ὃ δεῖ ποιεῖν αὐτόν. αὐτὸν γὰρ δεῖ τὸν ποιητὴν ἐλαχίστα λέγειν· οὐ γάρ ἐστι κατὰ ταῦτα μιμητής. οἱ μὲν οὖν ἄλλοι αὐτοὶ μὲν δι' ὅλου ἀγωνίζονται, μιμοῦνται δὲ ὀλίγα καὶ ὀλιγάκις· ὁ δὲ ὀλίγα φροιμιασάμενος εὐθὺς εἰσάγει ἄνδρα ἢ γυναῖκα ἢ ἄλλο τι (ἦθος) καὶ οὐδέν ἀήθη ἀλλ' ἔχοντα ἦθος.* Two modes of interpretation have been offered for these lines. The orthodox—or at least most common—mode sees Aristotle as reproducing the distinction at Pl. *Resp.* 392–4 between

who do not follow his lead are then subjected to criticisms very similar to those applied by Demetrius and Porphyry to Ephorus and Theopompus.[53] To readers familiar with the narratological debates of modern but often avowedly neo-Aristotelian critics, this approach to *mimesis* will scarcely seem strange.[54] It may thus be said the narrative of the tragic historian—in so far as it presents the events as they happened and allows them to speak for themselves—is consonant with the criteria of dramatic presentation and therefore thoroughly Aristotelian in character. When Polybius 2. 56. 7–8 describes the technique of Phylarchus in narrating the sack of a city, it is evident that the tragic historian pursues vivid mimesis through graphic presentation of detail.

art that operates through diegesis, alias narration, or through *mimesis*, i.e. drama, or δι' ἀμφοτέρων. This tripartite division is reproduced repeatedly in antiquity, for instance Proclus in Scholia to Dionysius Thrax p. 450 Hilgard; Anon. Prolegomena to Hesiod, p. 5, 8 Gaisford; Probus on Vergil, *Eclogues* and *Georgics* 3. 2, p. 329 Thilo-Hagen. While this division is in conflict with the application of the term *mimesis* to narrative at *Poet.* 1448ᵃ19–24, Janko (1989) and Woodruff (1992) 79 imagine that *Poet.* 1460ᵃ5–11 makes a knowing allusion to the conventional Platonic model, one which may be underpinned by his fundamental belief that tragedy is the supreme art form, and thus perhaps most fully mimetic. For this, see Else (1957) *passim*. Halliwell (1986) ch. 4 thinks that Aristotle is conflating two conflicting conceptions of *mimesis*. The heterodox mode attempts to keep faith with the idea at *Poet.* 1448ᵃ19–24 that ἀπαγγέλλειν is a form of *mimesis* and therefore asserts a distinction in function between ἀπαγγέλλειν at 1448ᵃ19–24 and λέγειν and ἀγωνίζεσθαι at 1460ᵃ5–11. For this, see Ridgeway (1912), Kitto (1966) 25, 150, and de Jong (1987) 1–8. Crucial to this approach is its challenge to the presumption that the characters introduced (1460ᵃ5–11) are characterized solely by their speech and not also by their actions. Ridgeway (1912) 238 is particularly strong on this point, and is an important challenge to the assumptions of, for instance, Vahlen (1867) 292–3, Else (1957) 619–21, and Halliwell (1986) 126. De Jong argues to the same end when she stresses the brevity of Homer's 'non-mimetic' proem as opposed to the show speeches δι' ὅλου of his rivals. The Aristotle who emerges from this alternative tradition believes in the notion of 'dramatic presentation' in narrative and is a Jamesian *avant la lettre*. While this may seem somewhat anachronistic, I find it the most convincing interpretation of his text.

[53] Gray (1987) 480–1 cites Dem. *On Style* 27 for the inappropriateness of the artificial style of these writers for the expression of anger, the portrayal of emotion or character. She then likens this to *FGH* 115 F21 for Porphyry's attack on the artificiality of Theopompus' adaptation of the conversation between Agesilaus and Pharnabazus in Xen. *Hell.* and his zeal to ἐπιδείκνυσθαι. This compares very interestingly with Aristotle's censure of those who fail in *mimesis* because they δι' ὅλου ἀγωνίζονται.

[54] In Anglo-American criticism, the criteria of dramatic presentation are those extrapolated from the great late novels of James and prescribed in Lubbock (1921). They are vigorously challenged in the restatement of the 18th-c. 'telling' aesthetic in Booth (1961). The influence of the *Poetics* is particularly evident in German approaches to narrative such as Hamburger (1957). In French criticism, Genette (1980) 255–9 attempts to escape judgements of value, basing his structuralist typology of the five functions of the narrator on the linguistic model introduced in Jakobson (1960) of the six functions of a speech-event. Only Strasburger (1966) 80 draws the connection between *mimesis* in ancient historiography and the theory of the modern novel.

It is therefore striking that Polybius should describe this bringing onto the stage of scenes and details in the same technical theatrical terms as Aristotle uses in his praises of the master of dramatic narrative, Homer:

σπουδάζων δ' εἰς ἔλεον ἐκκαλεῖσθαι τοὺς ἀναγινώσκοντας καὶ συμπαθεῖς ποιεῖν τοῖς λεγομένοις, εἰσάγει περιπλοκὰς γυναικῶν καὶ κόμας διερριμμένας καὶ μαστῶν ἐκβολάς, πρὸς δὲ τούτοις δάκρυα καὶ θρήνους ἀνδρῶν καὶ γυναικῶν ἀναμὶξ τέκνοις καὶ γονεῦσι γηραιοῖς ἀπαγομένων· ποιεῖ δὲ τοῦτο παρ' ὅλην τὴν ἱστορίαν, πειρώμενος ἐν ἑκάστοις ἀεὶ πρὸ ὀφθαλμῶν τιθέναι τὰ δεινά.

And being keen to rouse the readers to pity and to involve them emotionally in the narrative, he brings on stage women clinging to one another, their hair torn and breasts bared, and, on top of these things, the tears and laments of men and women being led away to captivity with their children and their aged parents. And he does this throughout the history, trying in every instance always to place the terrible events before the eyes [of his readers].[55]

It is obvious that various set-piece moments in a narrative invite the full tragic-historical treatment. The sacking of a city has a privileged position amongst these.[56] The deliberate exclusion at Livy 1. 29. 1–3 of such 'Phylarchan' detail in his account of the sack of Alba must at least in part be in deference to Ennius, whose version of the same event formed the basis for Vergil's *Excidium Troiae*.[57] When later Livy comes to recount the Gallic sack of Rome, his account is full of references to the spectacle of woe. Quintilian, *Inst.* 8. 3. 66–9, even uses the sacking of a city as his example of how to achieve ἐνάργεια through detail:

Sine dubio ... qui dicit expugnatam esse civitatem complectitur omnia quaecumque talis fortuna recipit, sed in adfectus minus penetrat brevis hic velut nuntius.

Undoubtedly, the man who says that a city was sacked embraces each and every thing which such a fortune involves, but this has all the curtness of a dispatch, and fails to penetrate the emotions of the hearer.[58]

Lucan's *Pharsalia* compares oddly to the Phylarchan model. The problem here is not thematic: the close association between civil war

55 Both Walbank (1957–79) ad loc. and Ullman (1942) 41 note the technical theatrical register here of εἰσάγει. It is possible that Polybius alludes to the use of the same verb in order to describe Homer's dramatic presentation at Ar. *Poet.* 1460ᵃ10. For this, see Else (1957) 620 n. 94. For εἰσάγειν at Long. *Subl.* 25, see n. 9 above.

56 On this theme see Paul (1982).

57 See Serv. at Verg. *Aen.* 2. 486.

58 On this point, cf. Strasburger (1966) 84–5 and Meister (1975) 114 and n. 25.

and tragedy is guaranteed by Aristotle,[59] and as early as his proem Lucan introduces verses very similar to others from Seneca's tragedy of civil war, the *Phoenissae*.[60] The appeal of civil war as a theme to a self-consciously Aristotelian tragic historian may be assumed. Nor is there any great difficulty in Lucan's professed desire to generate emotion. While the equation made by Marti and Narducci between Lucan's 'hopes and fears and prayers doomed to perish' (*spesque metusque peri-turaque vota*) and Aristotle's 'pity and fear' (ἔλεος καὶ φόβος) is inevitably inexact, there can be no doubt tht the tragic historian appealed to the reader on the level of the passions.[61] The problems enter on the level of actual narrative practice.

Lucan 7. 205–13 is a programmatic statement of the poet's narrative intent. Its emphasis on escape from the constraints of historical time, on the transportation of the reader to the time of the battle, appears, moreover, to guarantee that the poet will reveal events to his witness as they happen.[62] Yet it is a noted characteristic of Lucan's indignant presentation of events—and a recurrent consequence of his own endeavours to intervene against history—that the Phylarchan generation of emotion through the depiction of details is lost along the way. It is simply impossible to reconcile Lucan's interventions with the prescriptions laid down in the *Poetics*. If the sacking of the city is to be taken as the standard for the generation of pathos through detailed

[59] Ar. *Poet.* 1453^{b}20, cf. Conte (1968) 251.

[60] On this point, see Conte (1966) 49–50 and cf. Gagliardi (1975) at 7. 24–7. Conte's observations on the proem are acute but it might be added that the use of doubling to describe a civil war is already seen in tragedy as early as Aesch. *Sept.* 674–5: ἄρχοντι τ' ἄρχων καὶ κασιγνήτωι κάσις, | ἐχρθὸς σὺν ἐχθρῶι στήσομαι. In Latin the theme is prominent at Livy, 8. 6. 15–16: 'Curam acuebat quod adversus Latinos bellandum erat, lingua, moribus, armorum genere, *institutis ante omnia militaribus* congruentes; *milites militibus, centurionibus centuriones, tribuni tribunis compares collegaeque iisdem in praesidiis, saepe iisdem manipulis permixti* fuerant'. Cf. 8. 7. 6 'conlata signa' and 8. 8. 2: 'Fuit autem *civili maxime bello pugna similis*; adeo nihil apud Latinos dissonum ab Romana re praeter animos erat'. The emphasis on the doubling of civil war is also apparent at 8. 8. 14–15, 'Alterum *tantum ex Latino dilectu adiciebatur, qui ea tempestate hostes erant Romanis* eodemque ordine instruxerant aciem; nec *vexilla cum vexillis* tantum, universi *hastati cum hastatis, principes cum principibus*, sed *centurio quoque cum centurione*, si ordines turbati non essent, concurrendum sibi esse sciebat'.

[61] Marti (1964) 182 and (1975) 89 cf. Narducci (1979) 116. While ἔλεος may find some reflection in the sympathy which future readers will feel for Pompey, it is not clear what relation it bears to Lucan's *spes*. Similarly, Aristotelian fear, generally regarded as the product of seeing something dreadful happen to someone 'like us', is considerably different from the altruistic, anticipatory emotion which Lucan suggests. On this point, see Halliwell (1986) ch. 6.

[62] This is certainly the interpretation of Marti (1964) 181, Narducci (1979) 116, and Viansino (1974) 97–101.

mimetic representation, it is worth noting that both Seitz and Bramble highlight Lucan's description of the flight from Rome in Book 1 in order to underline his abandonment of the pathetic motifs beloved of other writers in favour of ellipsis, of a recurrent negation antithesis, apostrophe, rhetorical question, and other figures designed to express the personal indignation of the narrator.[63] Throughout the next three chapters of this study, episodes will be examined where what may be called the dramatic interventions of Lucan's narrator as a character at the scene of the conflict are marked by a calculated non-naturalism, one which places the weight of the pathos on the historical and political experience of the generation born too late.

Lucan moves beyond tragic history, beyond ἐνάργεια. The poet's promise to render the action of his narrative present to his readers involves a claim very like that made for previous tragic historians; the description of his narrative as spectacle invokes a category with an important place in that school. His achievement, whether manipulating temporal perspectives in order to dramatize his resistance to the foreclosure of history, or confronting the reader with the narcotic effect of imperial spectator society, is to move these concepts out of the inert categories of literary codification and to grant them a significance which is richly contemporary and political. Battle narratives conducted from a standpoint of horror at the slaughter and hatred for the winners implicitly protest at others where death is only the amazing and amusing sport of a lazy afternoon. Battle narratives described by a narrator *qua* Caesarian ringmaster jab at the reader with an insistent and troubling question: how deep is your involvement, your Republicanism, your patriotic horror? Does not the emperor amuse you, put on a good show? How rigorous is your dissent?

It is vital that students of Lucan should endeavour a restatement of his politics. In the years after the Second World War, the *serae gentes populique nepotum* infused Lucan with the liberal, antitotalitarian spirit of the period, cheered for Pompey, and attempted to reverse the *venientia fata, non transmissa*. More recently, these readings have been exposed to more iconoclastic interpretations, to critical techniques better adapted to revealing the fault-lines in his account.[64] If it is the aim of this study to continue our engagement with the complex and reflexive character of Lucan's creation, it is nevertheless my wish to do so in a manner which underlines the force of his ideas and his dissent.

[63] Seitz (1965) cf. Bramble (1982).

[64] Apart from Masters (1992), see also Johnson (1987).

To say that a writer can present two contrary ideological positions in the same work is not to condemn him to the bland suspension of indeterminacy. Lucan's combination of elements produces an energizing friction, produces combustion, the end result of which is consciousness. There are few writers of Rome's past so acutely conscious of the world in which they live.

2

Passionate Viewing in the Spanish Campaign

At 4. 382–401, Lucan's ecstatic exclamation evokes the relief of the surrendering Pompeian soldiers now released by Caesar from any further participation in the civil war. This exclamation culminates in the following lines, 4. 398–401:

> Hoc quoque securis oneris fortuna remisit,
> sollicitus menti quod abest favor: ille salutis
> est auctor, dux ille fuit. *Sic proelia soli*
> *felices nullo spectant civilia voto.*

This favour too did fortune grant to the men now free of their burden: their mind was free from partisan care—one man was responsible for sparing them, the other had been their leader. Thus they alone are happy watching a civil war who do so without a prayer.

Although the final sentence refers in the immediate context to the new mentality of the troops, it is also recognizable as one of the generalizing *sententiae* with which Lucan is accustomed to place a coda on a piece of narrative or moralistic analysis.[1] It is in this spirit that Lucan's words will be taken in this discussion, for they serve as an encapsulation of the tensions apparent in three connected episodes from the Spanish campaign. In each of these episodes, it is the voice of the narrator which exemplifies the mentality of the second group posited in the *sententia*, those unable contentedly to watch, those still subject to the prayers of engagement and partisanship. And it is this tortured, convoluted and deeply reflexive voice which reveals the full unhappiness of one cherishing not just prayers but prayers doomed to perish, those which rage hopelessly against a historical process the inevitability of which is always close at hand.

The central section of this chapter is devoted to an analysis of the movement at 4. 157–401, which encompasses first the prospect of

[1] See Bonner (1966).

universal concord, then its bloody reversal, finally the clemency of Caesar to his defeated opponents. It is to this scene that I regard the first episode, that of the flood, as forming an introduction and the third, that of the mutiny, a rather sour coda. Linking motifs between all three scenes are noted throughout. At the same time, however, it is to the central section that particularly close attention is paid. This is not just because it is the most sophisticated in its construction and the most effective in its drama, but also because it raises ideological problems which require more sophisticated investigation. If concord coheres with the flood and the mutiny in providing a paradoxical means to defeat Caesar simply by ending the war, clemency reveals both the temptations and the perils of compliant acceptance of his rule. From the interaction of voices and perspectives which serve to make up the narrative of this episode emerges an understanding of why this narrator at least is unable to watch his civil war without a partisan prayer.

PHARSALIA 4. 110–20: PRAYING FOR RAIN

Pharsalia 4. 48, 'Thus far, the issue was decided by fighting' (*Hactenus armorum discrimina*), marks a new segment in the narrative. From here to 4. 143, the course of the civil war depends less on the outcome of armed battle than on the freak meteorological conditions of a disordered universe. At 4. 110–20, Lucan breaks into ecstatic prayer to the gods, urging them to maintain this weather so that the civil war may be rendered impossible:

> Sic, o summe parens mundi, sic, sorte secunda
> aequorei rector, facias, Neptune tridentis,
> et tu perpetuis inpendas aera nimbis,
> tu remeare vetes quoscumque emiseris aestus.
> Non habeant amnes declivem ad litora cursum
> sed pelagi referantur aquis, concussaque tellus
> laxet iter fluviis: hos campos Rhenus inundet,
> hos Rhodanus; vastos obliquent flumina fontes.
> Riphaeas huc solve nives, huc stagna lacusque
> et pigras, ubicumque iacent, effunde paludes
> et miseras bellis civilibus eripe terras.

Act thus, O greatest father of the universe, act thus, Neptune, who by the second lot hold the trident of the sea: may you cast constant storms over the air, may you forbid to return all those tides which you have sent forth. Let not the rivers glide smoothly down to the shores, but let them be borne back by the waters of the deep, and let the shaken earth loosen the way for the rivers: let the Rhine flood these fields, let the Rhône; let the rivers turn aside their mighty sources. Melt hither the Riphaean snows, pour forth hither pools and lakes and lazy marshes, wherever they lie, and save the wretched lands from civil wars.

This is recognized as one of the classic instances of the narrator's intervention as an agent in his own drama, seeking to reverse the course of history, uttering the futile prayers of a character in a Senecan tragedy.[2] The approach to be taken here builds on this position. However, closer examination of the manner in which the dramatic immediacy of the episode is constructed reveals other rather different qualities, most of all a paradoxicality and reflexivity born out of despair at the impossibility of wishing. In this continuity between dramatic illusion and historical disillusion are seen for the first time the features most characteristic of the narrator of the Spanish campaign.

It is important to study the dramatic outburst of 4. 110–20 in the context of the surrounding lines from which it emerges and into which it disappears. In particular, it is these lines that reveal first Lucan's creation, then his abolition of the prime prerequisite of dramatic intervention, the merging of the temporalities of narrator and narrative, and with this both the naturalistic immediacy and the reflexivity of the episode as a whole. In this episode, therefore, tension is created by the repeated use of *iam* to describe fresh stages in the build-up to the crisis, the term recurring at *Pharsalia* 4. 76, 4. 83, 4. 87, 4. 93 and, anaphorically, at 4. 98. The penultimate stage, the coming of famine, is expressed as *iamque* . . . | . . . *aderat*; the last as, 4. 98–9:

> *Iam* tumuli collesque latent, *iam* flumina cuncta
> condidit una palus vastaque voragine mersit.

Now the mounds and hills were hidden, now one marsh buried all the rivers and submerged them in a gigantic swell.

While none of these developing narrative stages can be said finally to merge the temporalities, while *iam* does not exactly equate to *nunc*, it is significant that Lucan observes the different stages in the

[2] See Syndikus (1958) 42–3: 'Er bedauert nicht nur das Ergebnis des Kampfes, er steigert sich einmal so sehr in die Illusion des Miterlebens, dass er 4. 110–20 in ein persönliches Gebet an die Götter ausbricht, den Bürgerkrieg doch zu ersticken, genau so, wie wenn er ein Zeitgenosse wäre, der das Verhängnis noch abwenden konnte.' Cf. Marti (1975) 86, who cites it as an example of 'the interruption of the narrative by an anonymous *persona* whose voice expresses sentiments identical with those of the author but who, unlike him, is totally ignorant of the future', and Hutchinson (1993) 250–3, who notes some of the paradoxicality of the speech.

escalation as they happened, now one and now another. This apparently naïve procedure, recording the succession of events without pause to reorder them or to analyse, facilitates absorption in the process *per se*.[3] As such, it provides the perfect springboard for the prayer of a narrator now entirely taken up with the lived presence of the action, repeatedly addressing Jupiter and Neptune and firing off a series of eleven imperatives.[4] This is the situation reached at *Pharsalia* 4. 110–20.

Reversal, however, is not far off. For a characteristic of Lucan's narrative interventions which will appear recurrently is his use of the same linguistic tools to open up and then to shut off the temporal space within which the narrator can function as a character. The result is an impressive unity of design and a frightening reminder of foreclosure. Here, this typical reflexive movement is created by the employment of the same *iam* that helped create the illusion of presence now to conspire to destroy it. 4. 121–3 briskly announces the inevitable reversal, and the move down the scale begins with a further *iam*, now combined with the pluperfect 'had broken up' (*sparserat*) and the imperfect 'were red' (*rubebant*) of 4. 123–5. The dramatic crisis has passed, a new narrative movement is announced, and the two temporalities have again moved apart.

Dramatic illusion, dramatic disillusion are conjured up by reference not just to time but also to space. It is in the spatial dimension, moreover, that the most striking aspect of this prayer is contained and, here again, further levels of paradox emerge.

Lucan acts to create a sense of actual presence by the employment of terms which equate the space occupied by the speaker with that in which the action takes place. In particular, the sense of the narrator present at the place of the action is communicated by his anaphoric use of deictics at 4. 116–17 (*hos campos Rhenus inundet,* | *hos Rhodanus*) and at 4. 118 (*Riphaeas huc solve nives, huc stagna lacusque*). There is little dramatic naturalism, however, in a character who can stand in Spain and pray for rivers as distant as the Rhine and the Rhône to come 'here'.[5] This geographical inconcinnity has an inevitable distancing effect. Yet it goes further than this. Hutchinson observes of the prayer for rain that Lucan 'enjoys the paradox of

[3] Cf. Casparis (1975) and the discussion in App. 2.

[4] 'facias . . . inpendas . . . vetes . . . non habeant . . . referantur . . . laxet . . . inundet . . . obliquent . . . solve . . . effunde . . . eripe'.

[5] For a similarly calculated violation of dramatic naturalism in geographical reference, see the analysis of the mountains of Thessaly and Ionia at Luc. 7. 445–59 in Ch. 3.

desiring what sounds like disaster for the earth in order to benefit it'. This is a significant observation, but it can be taken further. Consider, for instance, *Pharsalia* 1. 75–7:

> Ignea pontum
> astra petent, tellus extendere litora nolet
> excutietque fretum.

The fiery stars will seek the sea, the earth will refuse to stretch flat her shores and will shake off the deep.[6]

These lines might be compared with 7. 134–7:

> Quis litora ponto
> obruta, quis summis cernens in montibus aequor
> aetheraque in terras deiecto sole cadentem,
> tot rerum finem, timeat sibi?

Who, on seeing the shores submerged by the sea and the deep amidst the highest mountains, the heavens falling to earth with the sun cast down, the end of so many things, who could fear for himself?

The point is simple. In the metaphorical repertoire of the narrator as story-teller, the cataclysm at the end of the world serves as an analogy for the disasters wrought by civil war.[7] If the narrator as agent now prays for the Rhine and Rhône to flood the fields of Spain, for the waters of the rivers to merge with those of the seas, he must be seen to be begging for the very disaster to end civil war which he elsewhere treats as the equivalent of civil war. In this way, Lucan's eloquent and reflexive narrative destroys the illusion of dramatic intervention; the bid for reversal forces home the final awareness that truly there is no way out.

FOOTBALL IN THE TRENCHES: *PHARSALIA* 4. 157–401

The flood episode gives voice to the yearning to escape civil war. 4. 120, 'And save the wretched lands from civil wars' (*et miseras bellis civilibus eripe terras*), makes a non-partisan prayer, asking only that the war be stopped. This is the tone of the episode almost throughout but

[6] Luc. 1. 77, 'excutietque' is emended to 'excipietque' in Hudson-Williams (1952) but defended in Mackay (1953). While 'excipietque' more immediately communicates the experience of the cataclysm, it is perhaps excessively passive for the cosmic broils described by Lucan.

[7] The best discussion of Lucan's employment of Stoic cosmology remains Lapidge (1979).

one instance remains where a slightly different perspective is apparent. While 4. 16–18 tells us that Caesar and the Pompeians make camp on hills of equal height (*nec*. . . *colle minore* tells us that Caesar's camp is at least as high up as that of his opponents), at 4. 87–9, the narrator seems keen to emphasize that it is Caesar's camp that is swept away:

> Iam naufraga campo
> Caesaris arma natant, inpulsaque gurgite multo
> castra labant; alto restagnant flumina vallo.

Now Caesar's shipwrecked arms swam over the plain and the camps tottered, struck by the great current; the rivers formed a pool at the top of the rampart.

The point is never given any emphasis in this episode but it still creeps through—to end the civil war now is also to defeat Caesar. This awareness comes to far greater prominence in the next two scenes to be discussed.

It is at the close of *Pharsalia* 4. 157–401 that Lucan delivers the *sententia* with which this chapter began. The celebration of the joys of disengagement is expressed in terms of those who can look on civil war without a partisan prayer. If the *sententia* is taken as a coda to the episode as a whole, therefore, one of its effects is to set up a powerful contrast with the manner of the narrator in the dramatic crisis with which the action begins. In short, the episode opens with the narrator praying for a concord which will frustrate the kingly ambitions of Caesar, closes with his evocation of the relief felt at accepting a disengagement unattainable except by selling the pass to his kingship. In the space created between these two apparently conflicting voices Lucan permits the reader to investigate the consequences of the different ideological choices to be made.

Concord and Reversal—Rise and Fall of Lucan's Dramatic Crisis

Pharsalia 4. 157–205 describes a moment of repeated crisis in Lucan's narrative, that is the point where the opposing camps or lines of battle are sufficiently close together for father to see son or brother to see brother, 4. 169–79:

> Postquam spatio languentia nullo
> mutua conspicuos habuerunt lumina voltus,
> [hic fratres natosque suos videre patresque]
> deprensum est civile nefas. Tenuere parumper
> ora metu, tantum nutu motoque salutant
> ense suos. Mox, ut stimulis maioribus ardens

rupit amor leges, audet transcendere vallum
miles, in amplexus effusas tendere palmas.
Hospitis ille ciet nomen, vocat ille propinquum,
admonet hunc studiis consors puerilibus aetas;
nec Romanus erat, qui non agnoverat hostem.

After each side's sight, vision obscured by no distance of separation, held clearly the other's face, [here they saw their brothers, sons and fathers], the sin of civil war was grasped. For a moment they held from speech in fear, only greeted their relatives with a nod or a shake of the sword. Soon, when love, burning with more powerful impulse, overcame discipline, the soldiers dared to cross the rampart, to hold forth their outstretched hands and embrace. One recalled the name of a host, another hailed a relative, another was reminded of the years spent together in youthful study; and there was not a Roman who did not recognize a foe.

This is not the last occasion in the *Pharsalia* where the rush to slaughter will be halted by a moment of recognition, but the mentality here displayed gives far more hope of reversal than the hardened cynicism of 7. 460–9:

Ut rapido cursu fati suprema morantem
consumpsere locum, parva tellure dirempti,
quo sua pila cadant aut quam sibi fata minentur
inde manum, spectant. Vultus, quo noscere possent
facturi quae monstra forent, videre parentum
frontibus adversis fraternaque comminus arma,
nec libuit mutare locum. Tamen omnia torpor
pectora constrinxit, gelidusque in viscera sanguis
percussa pietate coit, totaeque cohortes
pila parata diu tensis tenuere lacertis.

When with rapid dash they crossed the ground that delayed the final ends of fate, separated by a small stretch of land, they looked to see where their spears would fall and with which hand the fates threatened them from the other side. That they might recognize the terrible deeds they were about to do, they saw the faces of their parents opposite them and at close quarters their brothers' arms, but they did not wish to change position. Yet dullness caught every breast and chill blood congealed in their guts, their moral sense struck, and every regiment long held the weapons aimed in straining arms.[8]

At Pharsalus, the men are stopped momentarily, but, 7. 466, *nec libuit mutare locum*, they show no wish to turn back. Here, something very

[8] The theme is also apparent at Luc. 3. 326–9, 4. 24–8, 5. 468–75.

different arises. 4. 180–2 makes it clear that the soldiers break ranks and restore the unity that civil war has shattered:

> Arma rigant lacrimis, singultibus oscula rumpunt,
> et quamvis nullo maculatus sanguine miles
> quae potuit fecisse timet.

Their arms were wet with tears, gulps punctuated their kisses, and the troops, though stained with no blood, feared for what they might have done.

This is the moment of crisis. It is at the emotional joining of the two armies that the narrator emerges as an agent in his own narrative, that the mixture of apostrophe and rhetorical question gives his exclamation the dramatic immediacy already seen in the prayer for cataclysm, 4. 182–5:

> Quid pectora pulsas?
> Quid, vaesane, gemis? Fletus quid fundis inanis
> nec te sponte tua sceleri parere fateris?
> Usque adeone times quem tu facis ipse timendum?

Why do you beat your breast? Why do you groan, madman? Why do you pour forth futile weeping and confess that you obey your criminal orders against your will? Do you so utterly fear the man whom you yourself make a cause of fear?

This is a striking example of the ability of the narrator to suspend consciousness and treat the action of the civil war as something coming and not yet passed. At 4. 181–2, *miles* could be read synecdochically, the one standing for the whole. Suddenly, with the mid-line shift at 182–5, that *miles* becomes an individual moral agent, called 'mad' (*vaesane*), challenged to justify his prevarications, urged no longer just to obey his criminal orders. Caesar is only terrifying because these soldiers, because you—'soldier!'—make him so.[9] What follows only heightens the sense of a situation still open, of the possibility of reversal, 4. 186–8:

[9] Cf. Marti (1975) 86–7, 'What is significant is the fact that, to this unidentified speaker, the future is not yet determined. He makes a promise which we and Lucan know cannot be fulfilled. He is not one of the combatants any more than he can be either the author or the omniscient narrator.' The view taken here is dependent on Marti's belief in an anonymous character intervening as a chorus who remains distinct from the narrator. More interesting are the remarks by Heyke (1970) 63, who emphasizes the 'Absicht der Desillusionierung' already present in the narrator's voice as he condemns the 'fletus . . . inanis' and the pathetic excuse that one acts 'non sponte'.

> Classica det bello, saevos tu neclege cantus;
> signa ferat, cessa: iam iam civilis Erinys
> concidet et Caesar generum privatus amabit.

If he sounds the trumpets for war, neglect the savage blast; if he advances the standards, stall; now, now the Fury of civil strife will fall and Caesar, a private citizen, will love his son-in-law.

The narrator fires off a series of imperatives to his character (*det*... *neclege* ... *cessa*). This creates an immediacy of involvement unparalleled in previous epic. The 'now' of the 'narrator' is the 'now' of the narrative, hence the power of the deictic *iam iam* at 187. Moreover, there is a second sense to *iam* as 'now', that is as a 'now' coming very soon in the future: the Fury of civil strife will fall (*concidet*) and Caesar, a private citizen, will love Pompey (*amabit*). Here, the future tense is clearly not a simple future historic. That the future historic appears only once in the *Aeneid* marks it as already a transgressive tense in narrative, but far more unusual is the use of this *contingent* future.[10]

The continuation of the exclamation at *Pharsalia* 4. 189–94 reveals why this scene is special for the narrator—it offers the chance to reverse history and in the process promises to reconcile his two irreconcilable desires: it will defeat Caesar, and it will do so without shedding blood. It is 'now or never':

> Nunc ades, aeterno conplectens omnia nexu,
> o rerum mixtique salus Concordia mundi
> et sacer orbis amor: magnum nunc saecula nostra
> venturi discrimen habent. Periere latebrae
> tot scelerum, populo venia est erepta nocenti:
> agnovere suos.

Now come, Concord, embracing all in your eternal bond, you who bring salvation to nature and the scattered cosmos, you holy love joining the world: our ages now can make the great decision of the time to come. So many criminal deeds no more can hide, the guilty people have lost their excuse: they have recognized their friends.

The use of the deictic *iam iam* to create immediacy at 4. 187 is now picked up by the anaphoric *nunc* of 189 and 191. Lucan moves from the apostrophe to the individual soldier to a much more daring locution, addressing the goddess Concordia and the abstract 'holy love of the world' (*sacer orbis amor*). The tone of 'Now come!' (*Nunc ades*) is that

[10] For this distinction, see App. 3.

of an invocation, the prayer perhaps of a *vates.*[11] The goddess must come because this is a crisis: 'our ages now can make the great decision of the world to come' (*magnum nunc saecula nostra* | *venturi discrimen habent*) emphasizes the degree to which these are 'fates coming and not yet past', begs the question which are 'our ages', who is speaking and from where. The crisis is then frozen with a series of perfects, *periere . . . est erepta . . . agnovere*, expressing what 'has happened'.

Sobriety soon sets in. At *Pharsalia* 4. 194–7 the narrator exclaims, but a shift in tense, combined with the actual information communicated, drains the immediacy and prepares for the reversal at 4. 205–10:

Pro numine fata sinistro
exigua requie tantas augentia clades!
Pax erat, et castris miles permixtus utrisque
errabat.

O the evil force of fates that exacerbate such great calamities with a tiny respite! Peace there was and the mingled soldiers wandered through both camps.

Instead of an apostrophe, Lucan now offers an accusative of exclamation. Further, the point of the exclamation is that the coming disasters are all the worse for the brief experience of peace, of harmony: now one can see what could have been.[12] From this, it is apparent that something is going to go wrong.[13] And this may also be inferred from 'Peace there was . . . the soldiers wandered' (*Pax erat . . . miles . . . errabat*): the desired situation is depicted as continuing, the individual soldier of 4. 181–8 is obeying the narrator's orders, but only in the *imperfect.* The exhilaration of immediacy has been drained away, and conventional narrative restored. The ground has been laid for the disaster to come.

Lucan and Caesar—Reformation of the Commentarii

It is essential to examine carefully the narrative premises on which Lucan builds the coming and the reversal of his dramatic crisis and to

[11] For the use of *Ades vel sim.* in Roman prayer language, see Livy, 2. 6. 7, 3. 25. 8, 6. 29. 2, 7. 26. 4, 24. 38. 8; Verg. *Aen.* 1. 734, 4. 578, 8. 78, 10. 255, 10. 460–1, 10. 774; Catull. 62. 5. These examples are culled from Hickson (1993) 67–9.

[12] This is also the point of Luc. 4. 204–5: 'Est miseris renovata fides, atque omne futurum | crevit amore nefas'.

[13] Cf. Heyke (1970) 65, who observes acutely that 'Die "numine fata sinistro" sind es, welche das Unheil nicht äusser Acht lassen, auch während die concordia der Soldaten den Frieden verheisst'. The effect of the narrator's intervention is thus double: it serves the function of temporary 'Dramatisierung', but also acts 'Die happy end—Illusion vorzeitig zu rauben und ihm die Brüchigkeit des Friedens, auf den die Soldaten noch naiv vertrauen, bewusst zu machen'.

investigate the relationship between the account offered in Lucan and that given at Caesar, *B. Civ.* 1. 74–5. Previous analyses of this episode have all emphasized the need to study Lucan's account as a response to Caesar's but have perhaps ignored the significance of certain crucial details.

The principal question is what Lucan is actually describing as the soldiers embrace. For it is the contention of Caesar that the Pompeians betrayed their own camp, and deliberately went over to *his* side. Yet the narrative from 4. 169 onwards is quite different: the recognition is mutual, both sides rush to embrace, to restore the concord they have abandoned. Lucan's exclamation at 4. 186–8 makes no sense unless it is understood that Caesar will be defeated because his men refuse any longer to slaughter their kinsmen in order to make him king.

This clear distinction between the accounts offered in Caesar and in Lucan is confused by the development of the scene in the *Pharsalia* and the coming of disaster. For the Caesarian account enters Lucan only from the perspective of the general Petreius, who infers from what he *hears and sees* that he has been betrayed, but whose perceptions are entirely in conflict with those of the narrator, 4. 205–10:

> Nam postquam foedera pacis
> *cognita* Petreio, seque et sua tradita venum
> castra *videt*, famulas scelerata ad proelia dextras
> excitat atque hostis turba stipatus inermis
> praecipitat castris iunctosque amplexibus ense
> separat et multo disturbat sanguine pacem.

For after Petreius learned of the peace treaty and saw that he and his camp had been sold, he roused the hands of his slaves to criminal battles and accompanied by this band drove the unarmed enemy from the camp and separated with his sword men joined in embraces and violated the peace with much blood.

At this point, Ahl observes that 'the reader unfamiliar with the Caesarian account must surely find these lines inexplicable. Lucan has given no inkling of any treachery behind the fraternisation'. This is an important observation but it is hard to accept Ahl's explanation for the discrepancy, one which presupposes that Lucan is engaged in a peculiarly incompetent process of deformation, suppressing the nasty Caesarian 'truth' up to this point, then foolishly allowing it to slip out.[14] Another line of interpretation surely merits consideration.

[14] Ahl (1976) 194. Masters (1992) 80 and n. 84 argues this point well.

What we are told of Petreius is in terms of what he is told and what he sees. Ahl assumes that he is right. To make this assumption is to attribute authoritative status to Caesar, to presume that the exclamation of the 'narrator as character' is either mendacious or the hopelessly flawed perspective of one seeing only what he yearns to see. The latter solution would certainly underline the trauma of Lucan's impassioned narrator, but there are good grounds for taking the opposite position, for asserting that it is Petreius who is mistaken. Petreius may have no reason on first sighting to realize that the camp has not been sold out and that the joining of the armies is the result of mutual love. And yet he will drive out the *hostis . . . inermis*, the enemy unarmed for the simple reason that in truth they are still subject to the mentality described before.

Echoes of Immediacy—Closing the Dramatic Crisis

Whatever the error which underpins it, it is hard to ignore the power of the rhetoric of Petreius.[15] That it can take effect is testimony partly to the authority of the politics underpinning it, partly to the warped mentality of those long exposed to civil war (4. 237–42). By what is surely a mistake, by breaking the truce before Caesar could, Petreius takes the guilt of civil war onto his side, and condemns the Pompeians to be the worse cause.[16] This is the significance of the apostrophe to Caesar at 4. 254–9 with which Lucan closes this movement, bitterly echoing the terms earlier employed to give it its openness and hope:

> Tu, Caesar, quamvis spoliatus milite multo,
> agnoscis superos; neque enim tibi maior in arvis
> Emathiis fortuna fuit nec Phocidos undis
> Massiliae, Phario nec tantum est aequore gestum,
> hoc siquidem solo civilis crimine belli
> dux causae melioris eris.

You, Caesar, though despoiled of many soldiers, recognize the favour of the gods; for your fortune was no greater either in the fields of Emathia or the

[15] Masters (1992) 82 rightly observes that the speech of Petreius is 'a faultless classic of Republican rhetoric', but that the consequence of his noble words is that Luc. 4. 235–6: '. . . omnis | concussit mentes scelerumque reduxit amorem'.

[16] I find this interpretation more satisfactory than that of Heyke (1970) 67, who talks of Petreius as the 'Vertreter einer anderen Denkweise' who 'betrachtet die Vorgänge im Lager nicht isoliert unter dem Aspekt der Menschen- und Friedensliebe, sondern beurteilt sie nach ihrer realen politischen Bedeutung und muss sich daher verraten und verkauft fühlen'.

waters of Phocaean Massilia, nor did you achieve so much in the sea of Egypt, since by this crime of civil war alone you shall be the leader of the better cause.

The apostrophe seems initially to create a sense of immediacy, the narrator perhaps standing with Caesar as he interprets the scene (*agnoscis*). Yet the form of 254–5 is swiftly undermined by both the form and content of 255–6, where the past tense 'was' (*fuit*) is used both of events of the previous book at Massilia, and of still-coming events at Pharsalus (Book 7) and in Egypt (Book 8). What this points to is the difficulty faced by the narrator in explaining history, in narrating the error of Petreius and the vicious behaviour of the Pompeian troops brutalized by the effect of civil war.[17] Thus, the future tense of 'you shall be the leader of the better cause' (*dux causae melioris eris*) at 4. 259, which on one level obviously forms an echo of the contingent futures of 4. 188, on another level is very different. It surely should be understood as a *future of literary immortality*: this is how people will read of Caesar and interpret him.[18] Later, at 9. 980–6, Lucan will talk to Caesar of their mutual literary immortality in a manner which sounds more like a threat than a promise. Here, however, he has been lucky: the arch-immoralist may be robbed of his troops, but, by cruel chance, he has emerged a figure of paradoxical, wronged virtue. The movement between the open, contingent futures of 4. 182–92 and the closed futures of literary immortality of 4. 254–9 gives the episode its own architectonic unity.

Caesaris Clementia *and the Caesarian Lucan?*

That the villainous Caesar remains the artistic hero of the *Pharsalia* is a position which has attracted a number of supporters in the twentieth century. At the same time, few have been willing to suggest that the artistic affinity between poet and character takes on a political dimension as well.[19] Were Lucan to end his account with the 254–9 apostrophe to Caesar, there would be little temptation to view this episode

[17] It is striking that here the Pompeian troops perform their criminality before their general in a manner which Ch. 6 marks as typical of Caesar's insane cohorts (Luc. 4. 250–2: '. . . Fervent iam castra tumultu, | ac, velut occultum pereat scelus, omnia monstra | in facie posuere ducum: iuvat esse nocentis'). Heyke (1970) 69 is good on the beast simile and the effect of civil war on the men, while 71 discusses the aspect of display, 'sie geniessen es, sich mit Schuld zu beflecken'.

[18] For this distinction, see App. 3.

[19] For artistic sympathy, see Thierfelder (1934–5), Malcovati (1940) 65–7, Haffter (1957), and Tandoi (1963) 87 n. 2. The last contrasts this with the political position of the poet in Books 4–10, arguing that 'naturalmente altro discorso è rilevare una costante "simpatia artistica" per Cesare, genio del male, creazione satanica e fascinosa'.

as challenging this version of the poet's politics; it would be apparent that Lucan was merely exploiting the paradox that the consistently worse figure should suddenly emerge the better. Yet the action carries on and in a manner which is far more troubling. When the troops of Afranius and Petreius surrender, the escape from civil war is provided by Caesar himself. The show of *clementia*, the decision to excuse the soldiers further military service, all of this is celebrated so effusively by the narrator at 4. 363–401 that the reader is left wondering whether Caesar is truly such a villain, whether Caesarism is so high a price to pay for peace.

To Ahl, the episode is evidence of the insuperability of the problems posed by the historical record for Lucan's bid to write an unflinchingly anti-Caesarian history.[20] For Masters, on the other hand, it serves as evidence of the actively Caesarian politics of Lucan's narrator.[21] Just as the landscape, the extispicy, and the forms of killing in the *Pharsalia* are permeated with the civil-war principle of fracture and division, so, Masters argues, the political positions adopted by the narrator are characterized by a half-Republican, half-Caesarian schizophrenia. Far from struggling in vain to write a deformation of an event favourable to his villain, Lucan goes out of his way to blacken the character of Petreius and to celebrate the *clementia* of Caesar.

On one level, this second position seems satisfyingly and properly iconoclastic. Too much post-war writing on Lucan has contented itself with combing his verse for apt quotations to be put to service in the ongoing opposition to Caesar, Nero, Hitler, Mussolini, and Stalin.[22] What is more, Masters seems to be operating on favourable ground, since all he need do is quote and regret Ahl's tortured reasoning as he struggles to reconcile his belief in the Republican Lucan with the thoroughly unpromising material which this passage offers.[23] Yet the situation is not so simple; the narrative contains dynamics which invite the deconstruction of the superficial Caesarism it purveys and which reveal the perils of resignation.

The Real Problem of Caesar's Clementia

The fundamental point is that Caesar gains the chance to exercise his clemency only after the failure of Concordia and the defeat of Petreius. At the height of the crisis, when the men seem set to leave Caesar's

20 Ahl (1976) 192–7.

21 Masters (1992) 78–90.

22 See Narducci (1979) 14 and n. 12 for some trenchant observations.

23 Ahl (1976) 192–7.

arms, the narrator perceives the consequence that 'Now, now the Fury of civil strife will fall and Caesar, a private citizen, will love his son-in-law' (*iam iam civilis Erinys | concidet, et Caesar generum privatus amabit*). The term *privatus* is used regularly in the *Pharsalia* to contrast with the kingly manner and mentality of Caesar.[24] When Petreius mistakes the concord of the troops for a Republican surrender, he assaults their presumed acceptance of Caesar's pardon as the admission of his right to be master, to be king.[25] It is impossible to say anything pertinent about the politics of this episode if it is isolated from other instances of *clementia* in the *Pharsalia*, from the attempts to theorize *clementia* as a doctrine in the Neronian period, or from the ideological struggles of which it was a part.[26] Beyond the investigation by Menz of Caesar's odious clemency to Domitius and of its relationship to Seneca's *De Clementia*, this is a task which modern critics have singularly failed to undertake.[27]

Ahl heads his discussion of 4. 157–401 'The Problem of Caesar's *Clementia*'. The genuine problem of *clementia*, however, does not lie in explaining away the friendly face which at times it adopts, but in examining the difficulty for Romans in accepting its ugly heart. Historians such as Jal,[28] Earl,[29] Wirszubski,[30] or Griffin,[31] all contextualize

[24] At 5. 538–9, Lucan describes Caesar as 'quamquam plebeio tectus amictu, | indocilis privata loqui'. Compare 3. 108–9, which describes the absolute power of the unelected conqueror in these terms, 'Omnia Caesar erat: privatae curia vocis | testis adest'. When Caesar describes himself at 7. 266–7 as 'privatae cupidus me reddere vitae | plebeiaque toga modicum componere civem', he cannot expect too many of his listeners to believe him.

[25] See below, pp. 65–7.

[26] The first odiously clement 'monarch' to appear in Lucan is Marius at 2. 113–8, who grants men their lives who kiss his hand. For Pompey's fear of Caesar's clemency, see 8. 133–7 and 314–16, and for Cato's see 9. 213–4 (cf. Plut. *Cat. Min.* 66). For Caesar's regret at his inability to spare Pompey, see 9. 1066–8 and 9. 1100–1 (cf. 9. 1058–62 for the narrator's relief at his being denied this right).

[27] Menz (1952) 49–65, 168–70 = Rutz (1970*b*) 360–76. There is very little on the significance of clemency for Domitius in Lounsbury (1975), (1976), and (1986) and Mayer (1978). Ahl (1976) 50–4 and 192–7 is not much more enlightening. The limitations to Ahl's approach are visible in comments such as (196): 'Lucan cannot deny Caesar's clemency in dealing with the surrendering army, but he can and does minimize it'. Masters (1992) 84 n. 88 hints at complications which he later ignores.

[28] Jal (1963) 464–72 is the most detailed discussion of the odious clemency of the civil wars.

[29] Earl (1967) 60: 'Mercy is a blessed virtue: not so the Latin concept . . . *Clementia* in fact denoted the arbitrary mercy, bound by no law, shown by a superior to an inferior who is entirely in his power. It is the quality proper to the *rex*. In the free Republic there was no place for *rex* or *regnum*. The only body which could properly show *clementia* was the Roman People itself in its historic role of pardoning the humbled'.

[30] Wirszubski (1950) 133–5 and 152–3.

[31] M. T. Griffin (1976), esp. 148–71. The obnoxious aspect of *clementia* is only left implicit in Cizek (1972) 96–105.

the act of forgiveness by reference to the kingship doctrine underpinning it and make clear the potential unacceptability of *Caesaris clementia* for a member of the Republican opposition living under Nero. Failure to acknowledge these further implications must, of course, vitiate any assessment of the meaning of Caesar's 'insidious clemency' for a Roman in the immediate aftermath of Corfinium, but it is a still greater weakness in the discussion of the meaning of *clementia* for a Neronian Roman living after the ideological watershed of Seneca's *De Clementia*.[32]

If *clementia* is contextualized within the theory of absolutism, it is possible to discern the traces of the anxiety which it provokes. Even when apparently most sympathetic to Caesar, Lucan's narrative leaves these traces only too visible. Masters, for instance, cites 4. 363–4:

> At Caesar facilis voltuque serenus
> flectitur atque usus belli poenamque remittit.

Yet Caesar, compliant and smiling serene, accedes and remits military service and punishment.

These lines are then taken as simple evidence of the 'gratuitous pro-Caesarian tone' of the narration.[33] This view seems obvious: Caesar listens to pleading, smiles, excuses the Pompeians from service in his army, and remits all punishment. In particular, the decision to free the men from further military service answers to the narrator's detestation of civil war, and it is to this emotion that the narrator gives vent soon afterwards at 4. 382–401.

On another level, however, it is necessary to read the reference to *remissio poenae* in the light of the crawling rhetoric of Afranius, most importantly at 4. 346–7:

> 'At nunc causa mihi est orandae sola salutis
> dignum donanda, Caesar, te credere vita.'

'Yet now my only reason to beg you to spare me, Caesar, is that I consider you worthy to grant life.'

Here, perhaps, we can see one reason for Caesar to smile: his Republican opponent concedes his right to punish or to spare. Such rhetoric surely cannot help but remind one that under the *ius gentium* anyone

[32] The phrase *insidiosa clementia* is used in Cic. *Att.* 8. 16. 2, written on 4th March 49 BC. For other instances in Cicero of seeing beyond the surface of Caesar's clemency, see Curio at *Att.* 10. 4. 8 and Cicero himself at *Phil.* 2. 116.

[33] Masters (1992) 85.

captured in war came under the absolute power over life and death of the captor. Anyone one chose to spare (*servare*) was one's slave (*servus*).[34]

This is very odd language for the behaviour of one Roman citizen to another. On the other hand, Lucan's Caesar sees himself, and is seen by his supporters, not as a citizen, but as a king.[35] He thus arrogates to himself the status of kingship which Seneca confesses in the *De Clementia* as the reality of Nero's rule. This work does, it is true, make some reference to the laws but its basic method of describing the constitutional position of the emperor is to analogize his role *vis-à-vis* the people with various relationships in which the one party holds absolute power of life and death over the other.[36] Thus, at 1. 1. 2–4, Nero has been chosen 'to play the part of the gods on earth' (*qui in terris deorum vice fungerer*), an analogy to which Seneca returns at 1. 5. 7, and 1. 8. 5, where Nero is likened to Jupiter omnipotent (*qui omnia potest*).

A second and more insidious analogy is invoked at 1. 14–15. Nero is the 'father of the fatherland' (*pater patriae*), holds *patria potestas*[37] over

34 Thus, Just. *Inst.* 1. 3. 2–3: 'Servitus autem est constitutio iuris gentium, qua quis dominio alieno contra naturam subicitur. Servi autem ex eo appellati sunt, quod imperatores captivos vendere iubent ac per hoc servare nec occidere solent'.

35 Note Luc. 2. 446, 'concessa pudet ire via civemque videri' and cf. 2. 508–9 for Domitius before Caesar, 'civisque superbi | constitit ante pedes'.

36 Note that this contrasts with the consistent tendency in the *Pharsalia* to figure the Republican cause as a defence of the laws. This position is announced by Brutus at 2. 281–4, 'Quod si pro legibus arma | ferre iuvat patriis libertatemque tueri | nunc neque Pompei Brutum neque Catonis hostem, | post bellum victoris habes' and is picked up at 2. 316 where Cato describes himself as 'me frustra leges et inania iura tenentem'. For further instances, see 3. 113 (though cf. 3. 119–21), 3. 137–40, 3. 151–2, 4. 26–8, 5. 7–9, 5. 12–14, 5. 31, 5. 44–7.

37 *Patria Potestas* is the term used to describe the power of a *paterfamilias* both over his kin and over his slaves. It is a lifelong condition and confers on the father or master the absolute right of life and death over his subjects. Thus, Gai. *Inst.* 1. 52: 'In potestate itaque sunt servi dominorum. Quae quidem potestas iuris gentium est: nam apud omnes peraeque gentes animadvertere possumus dominis in servos vitae necisque potestatem esse, et quodcumque per servum adquiritur, id domino adquiritur'. For a discussion of this doctrine, see Crook (1967) 107–13. It is to this Roman principle that Adam (1970) 28 points. Adam quotes the antique formula for adult adoption given at Gell. *NA* 5. 19. 9: 'Velitis, iubeatis, uti L. Valerius L. Titio tam iure legeque filius siet, quam si ex eo patre matreque familias eius esset, utique ei vitae necisque in eum potestas siet, uti patri endo filio est'. Adam's arguments are noted in Fears (1975) 492, but not considered with sufficient sympathy. Fears points to the notion of absolute rights over life and death in Hellenistic kingship treatises and in works clearly deriving from Hellenistic models (ps.-Aristeas *Letter to Philocrates* 253 cf. Gundel (1936) 75. 4 and 84. 29 and Critodemus at *Catalogus Codicum Astrologorum Graecorum*, VIII. i p. 260. 9), but this does not detract from the importance of different relations of absolute power recognized by Roman law, by analogy with and with reference to which the new powers of the emperor could be described and explained. When Manil. 4. 549 describes Augustus as 'iudex . . . vitaeque

his people, and could as easily be the bad Tricho (1. 15. 1) as the good Tarius (1. 15. 2–16.1).[38] On the same principle, at 1. 18 he is compared to a slave-master, again free to emulate the vicious Vedius Pollio. Finally, at 1. 26. 5, this last point is related gruesomely to the gift to the emperor of the *corona civica*. This award, traditionally reserved for a Roman soldier who saved a fellow citizen in the line of battle, was later awarded to Cicero and Caesar for saving the entire State by their victories. Now, *servare* is given the secondary sense of 'to spare', invoking the theory of the *ius gentium* described above, and Nero is rewarded for his wise decision not to execute his subjects, his slaves, *en masse*:

Felicitas illa multis salutem dare et ad vitam ab ipsa morte revocare et mereri clementia civicam. Nullum ornamentum principis fastigio dignius pulchriusque est quam illa corona ob cives servatos, non hostilia arma detracta victis, non currus barbarorum sanguine cruenti, non parta bello spolia. *Haec divina potentia est gregatim ac publice servare; multos quidem occidere et indiscretos incendii ac ruinae potentia est.*

That is good fortune: to grant many salvation, to call them back to life from death itself and to merit the civic crown by one's clemency. No ornament is more worthy of the rank of an emperor, nothing more fair than that crown awarded for the saving/sparing of citizens, not enemy arms stripped from the vanquished, not chariots stained with the blood of the barbarians, not the spoils won in war. This is a divine power—to spare *en masse* and by peoples; to kill many and indiscriminately is indeed the power of a fire or an earthquake.[39]

necisque', one need not presume that his understanding of the powers of the *princeps* derives exclusively from Greek theory.

[38] The punishment from which Tarius so admirably refrained, that of sewing the parricide up in a sack to be eaten by various beasts, is just that which (1. 23) 'pater tuus' Claudius indulged to appalling excess during his brief reign. The fact that Seneca highlights the potential abuse of the role of *pater patriae* should also be connected to the historical tradition of repugnance at the brutal Caesar's arrogation of the title. For this see Jal (1963) 468–71.

[39] Maxfield (1981) 70–4 is enlightening. The man saved by the winner of the *corona civica* was expected to treat his saviour as his father for the rest of his life (Plin. *HN* 16. 14, cf. Cic. *Planc.* 72 and Polyb. 6. 39. 6–7). Nor was this position difficult only in circumstances such as the saving of the elder Scipio by the younger. Cicero stresses the general reluctance to be put under such an obligation. We are thus in a position in which the original significance of the *corona civica* carried with it unpleasant traces of *patria potestas*, and in which Seneca's interpretation of *servare* appears as the unmasking of the scarcely hidden implications of the award of the crown to Caesar (Dio Cass. 44. 4. 5 ὡς τοὺς πολίτας σεσωκότος cf. App. *B.Civ.* 2. 106. 441 ὡς σωτῆρι τῆς πατρίδος) and to Augustus (*Res Gestae* 34 cf. Dio Cass. 53. 16. 4 τούς τε πολεμίους νικῶντι καὶ τοὺς πολίτας σώζοντι). That the confusing aspect of *servare* as both spare and save is a point of anxiety in Seneca's reading of *clementia* can also be seen from *Ben.* 2. 20. 3, where Seneca discusses the sparing of Brutus by Caesar, and where the principles behind the *corona*

Further, the passage of Lucan can surely be seen to activate one of these models for absolute power, that of the sway of Jupiter over the universe. This is the import of the adjective *serenus*. Domitius hated that a *civis* should be forgiven for following the cause of his country and the legitimate source of authority, the Senate,[40] but Caesar saw himself then, and sees himself now, in a very different light. For *serenitas* is a familiar quality of Jupiter,[41] and the serene role of the god is clear at Ennius, *Annals* frr. 446–7 (Skutsch):

> Iuppiter hic risit tempestatesque serenae
> riserunt omnes risu Iovis omnipotentis.

Now laughed Jupiter and all the storms grew serene and laughed at the laughter of omnipotent Jupiter.

It is also apparent at Vergil, *Aen.* 1. 254–5:

> Olli subridens hominum sator atque deorum
> vultu, quo caelum tempestatesque serenat . . .

The father of men and gods, smiling at her with the face with which he makes serene the sky and the storms . . .

Finally, we should note that the reign of Domitian will offer even clearer evidence of the equation of the emperor with Jupiter, vital corroboration coming from Martial, *Ep.* 5. 6. 9–11:

civica are again visible: 'Sed vitam accipere debuit, ob hoc tamen *non habere illum parentis loco*, quia in ius dandi beneficii iniuria venerat; non enim servavit is, qui non interfecit, nec beneficium dedit, sed missionem.' Jal (1963) 471–2 notes Plin. *HN* 16. 7, '. . . postquam civilium bellorum profano, meritum coepit videri civem non occidere', and Dio Cass. 47. 13. 3 for ancient awareness of the irony of granting the *corona* as a reward for not killing one's subjects. For the award of the *corona* to Cicero and Caesar, see Weinstock (1971) ch. 8, 'The Saviour', 163–7. The possible instance of an early award of the *corona* for saving the State *en masse* offered by Weinstock is dubious. One presumes that the minting of a coin *c.*110 BC with the image of a galley within an oak wreath should be attributed less to the victory of Q. Lutatius Cerco's ancestor C. Lutatius Catulus at the Aegates Islands in 241 BC than to a presumed etymology for the name Cerco, namely 'quercus'.

[40] Luc. 2. 519–21: 'Poenarum extremum civi, quod castra secutus | sit patriae Magnumque ducem totumque senatum, | ignosci'.

[41] Apul. *Mun.* 37 cf. *CIL* 6. 431 and 433. For more, see *OLD* 'Serenator' and 'serenus' 1, cf. Forcellini, v. 463 for 'Serenator' and 464 for 'serenus' 6. Livy 2. 62. 1–2 is an excellent example of the attribution of divine significance to *serenitas*. Cook (1914–40) i. 1 begins with discussion of 'Zeus of the Bright Sky'. Heyke (1970) 76 n. 1 describes Lucan's use of *serenus* as 'ironisch' and points to Pöschl (1950) 17, which discusses the serenity of Jupiter. Pöschl was Heyke's supervisor. No one else seems to have discussed *serenus* in this context.

Nosti tempora tu Iovis sereni,
cum fulget placido suoque vultu,
quo nil supplicibus solet negare.

You know the times when Jupiter is serene, when he shines with his own calm face, with which he is accustomed to deny nothing to suppliants.

Martial then returns to this theme at 9. 24. 1–6:

Quis Palatinos imitatus imagine vultus
  Phidiacum Latio marmore vicit ebur?
Haec mundi facies, haec sunt Iovis ora sereni:
  sic tonat ille deus cum sine nube tonat.
Non solam tribuit Pallas tibi, Care, coronam;
  effigiem domini, quam colis, illa dedit.

Who, representing the face of the emperor in a statue, has outdone the ivory of Phidias with Latin marble? This is the visage of the universe, this is the face of Jupiter serene: like this does the god thunder when he thunders from a cloudless sky. Carus, Pallas did not just give you a wreath; she gave you the lord's effigy which you worship.

Thus, Domitian is compared to *Jupiter serenus*, the poet clearly alluding to the self-representation of the emperor in the equestrian statue described in Statius, *Silvae* 1. 1. 32–3:

Ipse autem puro celsum caput aere saeptus
templa superfulgens et prospectare videris.

Yet you yourself, your lofty head wreathed in a clear air, glitter over the temples and seem to gaze forth.

Yet, as the second Martial epigram makes clear, *Jupiter serenus* can thunder even in a cloudless sky, and there is a considerable hinterland of ancient writing on the ominous significance of both thunder and lightning from a cloudless sky.[42] Bright, clear days give way to

[42] There are long notes on the significance attached by divination to thunder and lightning from a cloudless sky at Nisbet and Hubbard (1970) 376–7, Pease (1973) at Cic. *Div.* 1. 18, and in Skutsch (1985) at Enn. *Annals* fr. 541. Skutsch makes the point that, while thunder in a cloudless sky is generally taken for a good omen, lightning has the opposite import: Cic. *Div.* 1. 18, Verg. *G.* 1. 487–8, Suet. *Aug.* 95, and, most importantly for us, Luc. 1. 530–4: 'Fulgura fallaci micuerunt crebra *sereno,* | et varias ignis denso dedit aere formas, | nunc iaculum longo, nunc sparso lumine lampas. | Emicuit caelo tacitum sine nubibus ullis | fulmen . . .' etc. Thunder from a cloudless sky can also be a bad omen, e.g. Sen. *Thy.* 263, 'tonat dies serenus' and Tarrant (1985) ad loc. In Enn. *Ann.* fr. 541 (Sk.) and Verg. *Aen.* 9. 630–1, it is not clear whether the omen of thunder from a cloudless sky would be favourable were it not also on the left-hand side (cf. Cic. *Div.* 2. 82). The point I wish to stress is that Jupiter can do *either* of these things, and both are unexpected. You cannot hold the omnipotent one to laws.

bad as the weather flatters to deceive.[43] The god is marked by his complete unpredictability. I make this point in order to relate it to Caesar 'smiling serene' (*voltu serenus*); for, in the desperate insecurity of the Julio-Claudian period, the expression of the emperor becomes a point of immense anxiety. For Cremutius Cordus, it is fatal that Tiberius should listen to his defence 'with a fierce expression' (*truci vultu*),[44] and it is Tiberius who is described at *Annals* 4. 60. 2 as 'either grim or with an expression that shone with hypocrisy' (*torvus aut falsum renidens vultu*). The emperor as arch-dissimulator[45] requires an ever-vigilant audience, able not only to follow his expression, but to second-guess it.[46] Such are the toils of absolutism.

When one is aware of this way of talking about the power of Jupiter in earlier writers, and of its application to a specific emperor in a later author such as Martial, it is hard not to be struck by the manner in which Seneca compares Nero to Jupiter at *De Clementia* 1. 7. 1–3. The passage begins 'Since I have mentioned the gods' (*Quoniam deorum feci mentionem*) and then moves into a description of the desirable behaviour of Jupiter/Nero, in which, characteristically, the undesirable alternative figures prominently as an anxiety:

Quod si di placabiles et aequi delicta potentium non statim fulminibus persequuntur, quanto aequius est hominem hominibus praepositum miti animo exercere imperium et cogitare, uter mundi status gratior oculis pulchriorque sit, *sereno et puro die*, an cum fragoribus crebris omnia quatiuntur et ignes hinc atque illinc micant! *Atqui non alia facies est quieti moratique imperii quam sereni caeli et nitentis.*

But if the gods, placable and fair, do not immediately punish the crimes of the powerful with thunderbolts, how much fairer is it for a man placed in authority

[43] At Calp. *Ecl.* 4. 82–6, the poet seems to employ the concept of Jupiter of the smiling heaven: 'Ab Iove principium, si quis canit aethera, sumat, | si quis Atlantiaci pondus molitur Olympi: | at mihi, qui nostras praesenti numine terras | perpetuamque regit iuvenili robore pacem, | *laetus et augusto felix arrideat ore*.' Yet it is hard here to forget the return of *arridere* in the description of the spring at Calp. *Ecl.* 5. 46–8: 'modo *fronte serena* | blandius *arrisit*, modo cum caligine nimbos | intulit et miseras torrentibus abstulit agnas'. For the political allegorization of weather in Calpurnius, see Leach (1973), esp. 56–7. The imperative to meteorological piety mixed with pessimism finds its *locus classicus* at Verg. *G.* 1. 311–34, where the behaviour of 'Ipse Pater'(*G.* 1. 328) cannot help but worry us.

[44] Tac. *Ann.* 4. 34. 2. For more on the *vultus* of Tiberius, see Woodman and Martin (1989) ad loc.

[45] For Tiberius the dissimulator, see ibid. at Tac. *Ann.* 4. 1. 2.

[46] It should be added that *serenus* is repeatedly used for a dissimulating expression of happiness or benevolence. The *locus classicus* is Verg. *Aen.* 4. 477, 'Consilium vultu tegit ac spem fronte serenat', but Pease (1935) ad loc. also suggests Sil. *Pun.* 11. 367, Nemes. 4. 17, and Hor. *Carm.* 1. 37. 26.

over men to exercise power with a gentle mind and to consider whether the state of the universe is more pleasing to the eyes and more fair on a serene and clear day or when all is shaken with repeated crashing and fires gleam now from here, now from there! Yet the appearance of a peaceful and well-ordered kingdom is no different from that of a serene and gleaming sky.

The worldly kingship of Nero is described by analogy with the absolute power of Jupiter over the universe.[47] This comparison is not isolated, but can be paralleled with evidence from coinage, official decrees, and poetry.[48] Most importantly here, one of the choices offered to Nero in Lucan's panegyric is that of deification as Jupiter. Further, the other option, that of becoming Phoebus-Apollo, is even better attested as one of Nero's preferred self-images, and carries with it the same sense of the bright, clear light of the serene monarch.[49] Proper weight must therefore be given to the terms in which Lucan expresses his wish at *Pharsalia* 1. 57–9:

Librati pondera caeli
orbe tene medio; pars aetheris illa *sereni*
tota vacet nullaeque obstent a Caesare nubes.

Hold the weights of a balanced heaven in the middle of the sphere; let all that part of the sky be serene and clear to view and let no clouds block our vision of Caesar.

However, it must also be stressed that this is only a wish. One may yearn for the gods to stay serene, but must remain powerless to stop them from doing the opposite. Moreover, one cannot even count on them to change their face before they act: a god can thunder even from a cloudless sky. In other words, to see unalloyed endorsement of the

[47] The significance of this analogy is recognized in Fears (1975) 491. A significant parallel is that offered at Plin. *Pan.* 80, where a tribute to the *clementia* of Trajan involves first comparison of Trajan's work with the benevolent guidance of Jupiter, then the assertion that Jupiter and Trajan work in tandem. The comparison in Roman politics of the absolute ruler with Jupiter goes as far back as Cic. *Rosc. Am.* 131 and the description of Sulla.

[48] The evidence is collected and discussed in Nock (1926) 17–18, Schumann (1930) 23–6, and in Fears (1981), esp. 66–74. Fears, however (p. 70), makes the important qualification that the appearance of Jupiter on coins is a feature of life after the Pisonian conspiracy: 'However, in the Neronian period, the association of "princeps" and Jupiter served as more than a literary and philosophical topos. At a critical moment in the reign, its appearance on the coinage marks its re-entry into the mainstream official imperial ideology.'

[49] For the evidence, see Schumann (1930) 23–6, L'Orange (1947) 61–3, and Grimal (1971).

description of the clement Caesar as *serenus* is entirely to overlook the fundamental insecurity of the adjective and of the act. Where once Roman citizens could depend on the defence of the law, now as slaves they must look in trembling at the expression of their master.

Serenity and the Stoic Sage—Another Perspective

I have used the significance of the word *serenus* to conduct a critique of *clementia* from a position outside the ideology of the Empire, from the stance of an unreconciled Republican malcontent. However, a scholar more inclined to make peace with the Empire might simply reply that Caesar was described as *serenus* because blessed with the calm ἀπάθεια required by Seneca in the second book of the *De Clementia*. The rigorous analysis of Griffin shows how Seneca carefully casts *clementia* as the work of reason.[50] That which 'turns off to a point below what rightly could be decided' (*se flectit citra id quod merito constitui posset*) is in line with the rational *severitas* of the Stoic sage and cannot be characterized as 'moderation which remits something from the proper and deserved punishment' (*moderationem aliquid ex merita ac debita poena remittentem*).[51] There is a scale of merited punishments and it is the work of *clementia* to choose one which, while to the lower end of that scale, still gives the guilty man what he deserves. Thus, Caesar *serenus* is in just the right state of mind rationally to punish, for he shows the very quality which marks the wise man at Seneca, *Ep.* 59. 16:

Hoc ergo cogita, hunc esse sapientiae effectum, gaudii aequalitatem. Talis est sapientis animus qualis mundus super lunam: *semper illic serenum est.*

Therefore consider this, that this is the result of wisdom: an unbroken continuity of joy. The mind of the wise man is like that part of the universe beyond the moon: there the air is ever serene.[52]

So, this is a case of clemency, and, if you accept the imperial ideology, you will also be gratified to see that it is being done just right. Seneca would have smiled. Or would he? Unfortunately, he would not. For it is an essential characteristic of all Lucan's three *clementia* scenes that they consistently describe the act with the terms which the second book of the *De Clementia* is concerned to reject. This point needs to be made in some detail.

At *Pharsalia* 2. 511, 2. 515, 4. 231, 4. 343, 4. 510 (if with built-in

[50] M. T. Griffin (1976) 155–61.

[51] Sen. *Clem.* 2. 3. 2.

[52] For the calm of the superlunary firmament, cf. Sen. *Ira* 3. 6. 1.

irony), 7. 604, 8. 136, 8. 784, 9. 276, 9. 1089 *clementia* is defined as a 'pardon' (*venia*). As Menz[53] observes, this term is deliberately rejected by Seneca at *De Clementia* 2. 7. 1.[54] As he outlines his rejection, Seneca defines the *venia* as the 'remission of the proper punishment' (*poenae meritae remissio*), thus as off the scale of rational punishments to the lower end of which clemency 'turns' (*se flectit*). It will therefore be noticed that, at 4. 363–4, which appears so egregiously pro-Caesarian, Caesar 'is turned / accedes' (*flectitur*) and consequently 'remits the punishment' (*poenam . . . remittit*). The reference to Seneca and the obvious contradiction of his terms is clear. Further, the *venia* is a form of forgiveness (*ignoscere*), again a concept alien to Seneca's system.[55] We will therefore be struck that *ignoscere* is the concept which Lucan and Domitius find so obnoxious about Caesar's *clementia* at 2. 519–21, while it is the feeble Afranius who begs of Caesar at 4. 355–6:

> 'Hoc hostibus unum,
> quod vincas, ignosce tuis.'

'Forgive your enemies this alone: that you conquer.'

Further, it is Afranius who wheedles at 4. 346–7:

> 'At nunc causa mihi est orandae sola salutis
> dignum *donanda*, Caesar, te credere vita.'

'Yet now my only reason to beg you to spare me, Caesar, is that I consider you worthy to grant life.'

Seneca, however, rejecting the concept of forgiveness, remarks of the wise man that, Sen. *Clem.* 2. 7. 1:

> Itaque poenam, quam exigere debet, non *donat.*

Therefore he does not excuse anyone the punishment which he ought to exact.

[53] Menz (1952) = Rutz (1970*b*) 373–4.

[54] Two passages from the *De Clementia* are here essential: (i) 2. 7. 1: '"At quare non ignoscet?" Agedum constituamus nunc quoque, quid sit venia, et sciemus dari illam a sapiente non debere. Venia est poenae meritae remissio. Hanc sapiens quare non debeat dare, reddunt rationem diutius, quibus hoc propositum est; ego ut breviter tamquam in alieno iudicio dicam: "Ei ignoscitur, qui puniri debuit; sapiens autem nihil facit, quod non debet, nihil praetermittit, quod debet; itaque poenam, quam exigere debet, non donat. Sed illud, quod ex venia consequi vis, honestiore tibi via tribuet; parcet enim sapiens, consulet et corriget; idem faciet, quod, si ignosceret, nec ignoscet, quoniam, qui ignoscit, fatetur aliquid se, quod fieri debuit, omisisse."' (ii) 2. 7. 3: 'Ignoscere autem est, quem iudices puniendum, non punire; venia debitae poenae remissio est. Clementia hoc primum praestat, ut, quos dimittit, nihil aliud illos pati debuisse pronuntiet; plenior est quam venia, honestior est.'

[55] See *Clem.* 2. 7. 1 and 2. 7. 3 cited at n. 54.

Giving is not part of the intended scheme, a point underlined at 2. 7. 1, where Seneca defines the *venia* with the comment:

Et sciemus *dari* illam a sapiente non debere.

And we will know that that should not be granted by the wise man.

By contrast, at 2. 512, in a passage stressing the *venia*, Caesar describes his *clementia* to Domitius as a 'gift' (*munus*) and, at 2. 524–5, Domitius resolves:

'Rue certus et omnis
lucis rumpe moras et Caesaris effuge *munus*.'

'Hasten on, sure of your purpose, and break off all dawdling in the light and flee the gift of Caesar.'[56]

At *De Clementia* 2. 7. 4, Seneca enters an apology for his terminological exactitude:

De verbo, ut mea fert opinio, controversia est, de re quidem convenit. Sapiens multa remittet, multos parum sani, sed sanabilis ingenii servabit.

The argument, to my mind, is about a term, concerning the essential issue there is agreement. The wise man will remit many punishments, will spare many men of insufficiently sound but still curable character.

The sudden disavowal of terms is a *captatio benevolentiae*, the daring inexactitude of 'will remit' (*remittet*) serving the rhetoric of that mode. We should not be taken in. Lucan's Domitius scenes are explicit. For him, it is the essential issue which is in dispute and the doctrine of *clementia* is rejected from without. It cannot in any sense be good, because it is the stuff of absolute monarchy. This too is the implication of my first interpretation of *serenus*, and it is the explicit intent of the speech of Petreius at 4. 212–35. He appeals to the factors which legitimated Domitius and made the concept of his being forgiven so appalling.[57] As Petreius goes on, he sees his troops as a 'liberator' (*adsertor*) against Caesar, thus echoing and rebutting the claims of Augustus in the *Res Gestae*;[58] he represents Caesar as a 'master' (*dominus*) and the

56 Domitius fulfils his resolution when he rushes to his death at Luc. 7. 603–4 and '*venia* gaudet caruisse secunda'.

57 Cf. n. 40 for Luc. 2. 519–21. This finds an answering voice at Luc. 4. 212–14: 'Immemor o *patriae*, *signorum* oblite tuorum, | non potes hoc causae, miles, praestare, *senatus* | *adsertor* victo redeas ut Caesare?'

58 Augustus, *Res Gestae* 1. 1, claims that 'rem publicam dominatione factionis oppressam in libertatem vindicavi'. Both speakers thus use the language of the archaic manumission ritual of *vindicta*, for which the slave required an *adsertor libertatis*. See

surrendering Pompeians as his 'slaves' (*famuli*).[59] Peace is a betrayal and is bought at the price of freedom.[60] The enemy will stay loyal (*sacramenta*, 4. 229), while it is the very justice of the cause which offers his men the chance of a *venia*. Here again, the use of *venia* for pardon, that is remission of deserved punishment, is highly uncomfortable. For one of the circumstances in which *clementia*, as opposed to *venia*, may be exercised is just this one, *De Clementia* 2. 7. 2–3:

Hostes dimittet salvos, aliquando etiam laudatos, si honestis causis pro fide, pro foedere, pro libertate in bellum acciti sunt.

He will dismiss enemies unharmed, sometimes even commended, if they were driven to war for good reasons: out of loyalty, to defend a treaty, in the name of freedom.

A *venia* requires actual fault; Seneca's ideal of *clementia* allows for the victor to admit the justice of his opponents' resistance. The paradox built into Petreius' words is that now Caesar can regard the Pompeians as having done something wrong in defending their homeland, or, worse, that they must go to him and admit as much themselves.

The speech of Petreius reveals dispute both over the fundamental issue of clemency and over the terms used to describe it. For anyone insisting that *serenus* only implies the proper rationality of the clement *sapiens*, for anyone who will not step outside the imperial ideology, there remains the ugly problem that the terms used by Lucan to describe *clementia* simply do not add up. The speech of Afranius and the description of Caesar's response, as the two Domitius scenes, systematically employ all the terms which Seneca had tried to define out of his model of *clementia*. The result of this intertextual and terminological onslaught is simple. Petreius ends his speech with the paradoxical lament, 4. 231–5:

'Pro dira pudoris
funera! Nunc toto fatorum ignarus in orbe,
Magne, paras acies mundique extrema tenentis
sollicitas reges, cum forsan *foedere nostro*
iam tibi sit promissa *salus*'.

J. A. C. Thomas (1975) 19. The difference is that Augustus saw his actions as restoring freedom to Rome, while, as Nigidius Figulus perceives, Luc. 1. 670, 'cum domino pax ista venit'.

[59] Luc. 4. 218–19. For Caesar the *dominus*, cf. Cic. *Fam.* 15. 19. 4, where Cassius describes him as 'veterem et clementem dominum'. For more on this theme, see Jal (1963) 467.

[60] Luc. 4. 222 cf. 227.

'O the dire death of shame! Now, Magnus, ignorant of your fate, you muster armies all over the globe and rouse the kings who rule the very edges of the world, when perhaps by our treaty you have already been promised your life.'[61]

Now, for Afranius and his men 'the terms of a just treaty were agreed' (*iustae placuerunt foedera pacis*), but it is possible to smell the injustice, the rottenness of it all.

Conclusion

At *Pharsalia* 6. 244, Scaeva scorns his Republican assailants, 'Or do you think me like you and reluctant to die?' (*An similem vestri segnemque ad fata putatis?*) The note in the *Commenta Bernensia* is surprising and intriguing: 'He touches on Afranius and Petreius' (*Afranium et Petreium tangit*). To the commentator there seems to be something wrong with the Republicans' pursuit of forgiveness in this episode. Similarly, the reader accustomed to a narrator yearning to defeat Caesar cannot expect him unambiguously to endorse Caesar's most contentious doctrine. Indeed, the same lines, 4. 363–4, which give grounds for gratitude also contain traces of something very different: *clementia* is a kingship doctrine, the ideology of absolutism, and, as a consequence, highly insecure. I am sufficiently intentionalist to take the unpleasant implications of *serenus* as evidence not of Lucan being unable to compose a successful panegyric, but of the Republican poet leading us by the nose through his own ironies.

This episode is marked by the bitter ironies of *fortuna* (4. 256). Caesar when winning the civil war was never so lucky as when he won the judgement of posterity. At 4. 169–205, the two sides come together and Lucan's aim seems to have been achieved. He who is split between his wish to end the civil war and his yearning to defeat the Caesars suddenly sees a way to achieve both his aims. Then, with the error of Petreius, things fall apart again, and with it the mind of the narrator. One side of him can go with Afranius and the men, can yearn for escape and celebrate it in the *Georgic* voice.[62] This second side is clearly antiphrastic to the speech and values of Petreius. Yet the rhetoric of the latter is authoritative, strong, and good. Moreover, in its scorn for the *clementia* of Caesar, it is echoed both by the manner in which Lucan represents the odious self-abasement of Afranius, and by

[61] Cf. Luc. 4. 510, where Vulteius cries '. . . promittant *veniam*, iubeant sperare *salutem*': his men will prefer death to disgrace.

[62] The concept of the *Georgic* voice goes back to Paratore (1943).

the assault on the grounds for and nature of Caesar's *venia*. In this way, Petreius too must be seen to rebut Afranius.

In his depiction of the serene Caesar, of the joy of the troops of Afranius, Lucan gives air both to the terrible temptation to resign autonomy and abandon opposition, and to the perilous consequences of resignation. The temptations explored are not isolated. The discussion of Pompey in Chapter 4 investigates the lines of tension around the Republican 'hero', the political compromise of treating him as the embodiment of his cause; the examination in Chapter 7 of references to the amphitheatre considers the cultural confusion of reading a Republican epic as an imperial *munus*. The *Pharsalia* is a historical epic which derives its vigour from its radical engagement with its own period, and it must be read with an eye to the disputes of that period.

Ahl responds to this scene by trying to show how Lucan minimizes the kudos accruing to Caesar from his offer of *clementia*. On one level, this approach is sound: not even Lucan, pushing his taste for paradox to the limit, could find more to lament in Caesar's *clementia* than he could in a massacre. On another, however, he is not radical enough: the point which emerges so strongly from Seneca's *De Clementia* is that the acts of forgiveness and the acts of brutality are two sides of the same absolutist coin. All depends on the emperor's whim and mood. *Pharsalia* 4. 157–401 begins with a crisis in which the narrator intervenes with the specific wish that civil war be ended and Caesar deprived of the right to be king. In the action which follows it is the misapplied rhetoric of Petreius that does the immediate damage, but it is the odious wheedling of Afranius which truly creates the conditions for the disasters to come.

Pharsalia *5. 237–373: The Caesarians Mutiny*

This episode is clearly closely related to the 'football in the trenches' of Book 4. It depicts a mutiny among the Caesarian troops occurring *en route* from Spain to the East (5. 237–8), thus appearing most similar to that at Placentia in 49 BC, but also includes elements from the Campanian mutiny of 47 BC.[63] It is dominated by the speeches of the mutineers at 5. 261–95 and of Caesar at 319–63 and features two interventions on the part of the narrator: the first immediately after the

[63] Suet. *Jul.* 69–70 handles both mutinies, App. *B. Civ.* 2. 47. 191–5 that at Placentia, and 2. 92–4. 386–96 that in Campania. Dio Cass. 41. 27–35 records the lengthy address of Caesar to his men at Placentia, while 42. 52–5 gives a brief account of affairs in Campania. The relationship of Lucan's account to the historical sources is discussed in Fantham (1985). This excellent piece seems to be the only full discussion of the scene.

speech of the mutineers, the second immediately before that of Caesar. As before, the hope offered by the dramatic immediacy of an unresolved crisis is countered by the bitterness of swift reversal and co-exists with the reflexivity and painful self-awareness of even Lucan's most impassioned interventions.

Pharsalia *5. 297–9: The First Appeal*

The importance of the dominance of the speeches of the soldiers and of Caesar is that they embed the immediacy of the characters caught up in the crisis. Lucan's two outbursts both come between these two speeches, and depend on the openness of the situation.[64] The first emerges as a direct response to the speech of the mutineers, 5. 295–9:

> Haec fatus totis discurrere castris
> coeperat infestoque ducem deposcere voltu.
> Sic eat, o superi: quando pietasque fidesque
> destituunt moresque malos sperare relictum est,
> finem civili faciat discordia bello.

This said they began to run about all over the camp and call for the general with hostile expression. So be it, gods: when loyalty and trust fail and there is nothing left to hope for save bad morals, let discord make an end to civil war.

Here, one cannot miss the tone of weary cynicism in the narrator's outburst, almost an abnegation of involvement: 'If that's the way the gods want it, well, fine, but I give up . . .'. The obvious source of this is the expression given to their dissatisfaction by the troops at 5. 270–3:

> 'Cepimus expulso patriae cum tecta senatu,
> quos hominum vel quos licuit spoliare deorum?
> Imus in omne nefas manibus ferroque nocentes,
> paupertate pii.'

'When we expelled the Senate and captured the houses of our fatherland, which men, which gods were we permitted to plunder? We enter into every crime, guilty with our hands and our steel, innocent in our poverty.'

Further, the necessity of such plunder is recognized at 5. 305–9, while at 7. 736–60 the Battle of Pharsalus ends with Caesar encouraging his men to ransack the Pompeian camp. To plunder the temples of the

[64] Cf. Heyke (1970) 91 on Luc. 5. 297–9: 'Der Wunsch fällt zeitlich zwischen die Rede der Meuterer und die Reaktion Caesars; zu diesem Zeitpunkt wäre es noch möglich, dass die discordia der Soldaten Caesar in Bedrängnis versetzte.'

gods is the worst sin,[65] but its long-frustrated desire revives the possibility of Caesar's defeat. In this episode of mutiny, therefore, Lucan will play on the same paradoxes of power and fear which so preoccupied him in Book 4.[66] For instance, there Lucan moves from his usual tactic of describing the troops *pars pro toto* as *miles* to the direct address to one individual soldier (4. 181–8). However, at 4. 185 onwards, the paradox is that the *miles* in the sense of 'the soldiers' is/are quite capable of seeing off Caesar: 'Do you so utterly fear the man whom you yourself make a cause of fear?' (*Usque adeo times quem tu facis ipse timendum?*) Similarly, in Book 5, the soldiers have to overcome the period of mutual suspicion but then, once in rebellion, reveal the isolation of the general.[67] This is brought out most clearly at 5. 252–4, where it is said of Caesar's position that:

> Tot raptis truncus manibus gladioque relictus
> paene suo, qui tot gentis in bella trahebat,
> scit non esse ducis strictos sed militis enses.

Shorn of all the hands he had lost and left almost with his own sword alone, the man who was dragging so many peoples into war knew that the swords drawn belonged not to the general but to the soldiers.

As the episode advances, great emphasis is placed on the fears of Caesar;[68] this is most strikingly the case at 5. 316–18, where Lucan introduces Caesar's lone challenge to his troops:

> Stetit aggere fulti
> caespitis intrepidus voltu meruitque timeri
> non metuens, atque haec ira dictante profatur.

He stood with untroubled expression on a mound of heaped-up turf and deserved to be feared for his want of fear and, prompted by anger, made the following declaration.

Finally, at the close of the speech, we see the effect of Caesar's fearlessness in the new fear, new irresolution of the men, 5. 364–7:

[65] Barratt (1979) at 5. 305–7 cites Menz (1952) 135, who comments that 'Das 'spoliare templa' gilt als charakteristisch für den Tyrannen und wurde als Deklamationsthema behandelt'. Barratt also cites Luc. 3. 167, Sen. *Controv.* 5. 8 and 9. 4, and Pl. *Resp.* 574D.

[66] In this passage, the characters are constantly afflicted by the anticipatory emotions which Lucan attributes to his readers at 7. 205–13. In my discussion, I concentrate on the prominence of fear, but Lucan also points to the wishes of Caesar at 5. 307–8 ('vult . . . | . . . vult') and to his hopes at 5. 370 ('spem ducis'). We should perhaps not be surprised that it is in such a passage that the narrator emerges as character.

[67] For the mutual suspicion of the troops, see esp. 5. 257: 'dum quisque pavet, quibus ipse timori est'.

[68] Luc. 5. 300: 'Quem non ille ducem potuit terrere tumultus?' cf. 5. 309: 'militis indomiti tantum mens sana timetur'.

Tremuit saeva sub voce minantis
volgus iners, unumque caput tam magna iuventus
privatum factura timet, velut ensibus ipsis
imperet invito moturus milite ferrum.

The idle mass trembled at the savage sound of his threats and the group of youths so numerous feared the one head it was about to consign to private life, as if he gave orders to the swords themselves and would direct the steel even against the will of the soldiers.

In this passage is seen the same *pars pro toto* use of *miles* as has been seen in the previous passage, and again it serves to express the moral challenge which each one of the soldiers faces. Yet there is more. In particular, the description of the men as 'about to consign [him] to private life' (*privatum factura*) should remind us of the hopes so passionately expressed at 4. 187–8:

Iam iam civilis Erinys
concidet et Caesar generum privatus amabit.

Now, now the Fury of civil strife will fall and Caesar, a private citizen, will love his son-in-law.

As in the previous episode, the return of Caesar to the status of private citizen is synonymous with his defeat. Equally, the coming of peace will mean the frustration of his hopes. Thus, at 4. 196, the narrator's ecstatic exclamation at the reunification of the two sides breaks off with the simple statement 'Peace there was' (*Pax erat*) and, at 5. 293–5, the mutineers close their address to Caesar with the selfsame threat:

'Licet omne deorum
obsequium speres, irato milite, Caesar,
pax erit.'

'Though you hope for the utter indulgence of the gods, Caesar, if the soldiers are angry, there will be peace.'

The parallels between Books 4 and 5 are numerous, and are both ideologically and thematically significant. They also, I would argue, make it possible to explain the particular jaundiced tone adopted by the narrator at 5. 297–9. As has been seen, Book 4 sees the chance to defeat Caesar and end the civil war by the intervention of mutual love. As the men gather and tell stories, 4. 204, 'the mutual trust of the wretches was renewed' (*est miseris renovata fides*). Now, 'loyalty and trust fail' (*pietasque fidesque | destituunt*) but the potential result is the same.

Thus, while the naïve, optimistic narrator of 4. 190–1 can pray to 'Concord, you who bring salvation to nature and the scattered cosmos you holy love joining the world' (*o rerum mixtique salus Concordia mundi et sacer orbis amor*), now he simply urges the gods: 'let discord make an end to civil war' (*finem civili faciat discordia bello*).[69] I return to this point below.[70]

Pharsalia *5. 310–16: The Second Appeal*

Lines 4. 182–95 were followed by a second outburst from the narrator at 4. 254–9, the latter addressed to Caesar. In Book 5, the second outburst is again addressed to Caesar, 5. 310–16:

> Non pudet, heu, Caesar, soli tibi bella placere
> iam manibus damnata tuis? Hos ante pigebit
> sanguinis? His ferri grave ius erit, ipse per omne
> fasque nefasque rues? Lassare et disce sine armis
> posse pati; liceat scelerum tibi ponere finem.
> Saeve, quid insequeris? Quid iam nolentibus instas?
> Bellum te civile fugit.

Caesar, alas, are you not ashamed that you alone favour wars now condemned by your men? Will these men grow weary of blood ahead of you? Will these men resent the rule of the sword, while you hasten through every moral, every immoral act? Grow tired and learn that one can comply with a life without warfare; let it be possible for you to put an end to your crimes. Why do you press them, savage one? Why do you compel men who are no longer willing? The civil war is running away from you.

The address to the gods at 5. 295–9 combined apostrophe with the

[69] Concordia is an important leitmotiv in Book 4. Thus, at 4. 5–6, Lucan says of Afranius and Petreius that 'concordia duxit in aequas | imperium commune vices', and, at 4. 197–8, one of the consequences of the peace is that 'duro concordes caespite mensas | instituunt et permixto libamina Baccho'. The move from Concordia in 4 to Discordia in 5 is noted by Heyke (1970) 88 and by Masters (1992) 73 n. 73. Heyke (1970) 91 is succinct and clear: 'Da fides und pietas fehlen, muss Lucan, sonst ein Gegner der "mali mores", "discordia" Erfolg wünschen'. Also useful is Moretti (1984) 46–7. Moretti points out that the idea of 'Concordia discors', which first appears in Lucan at 1. 98–100, but which has also been used in Hor. *Epist.* 1. 12. 19 and Ov. *Met.* 1. 433, derives from the Hymn of Cleanthes, *SVF*. I: 537 14–15: *ἀλλὰ σὺ καὶ τὰ περισσὰ ἐπίστασαι ἄρτια θεῖναι, καὶ κοσμεῖν τ' ἄκοσμα καὶ οὐ φίλα σοὶ φίλα ἐστίν*. For the cosmic aspect to Concordia in Lucan, see Lapidge (1979) 365–7, although Lapidge stresses the terminology of Chrysippus and not of Cleanthes. Jal (1982) 85 also stresses the Stoic aspect of the Concordia–Discordia opposition. For this, cf. Jal (1961) 225 and 229, where the Stoic interpretation of Concordia is related more closely to its political and ideological significance in the first centuries BC and AD.

[70] See below, 'Ending the "Bellum Civile"'.

ussive subjunctives *eat* and *faciat.* The tone of disenchantment only somewhat lessened the vividness of direct involvement. Here, however, the questioning and exhortation of Caesar at the moment of crisis is far more dramatic. The combination of apostrophe and imperative directed at a character follows the same pattern seen in the address to the soldiers and to Concordia at 4. 182–94 and which will appear again in that to the guards at 7. 24–7; the men are referred to by the anaphoric use of the deictic *hos* ... *his* (5. 311–12); and the simultaneity of the appeal with the time of the action is emphasized by the pattern *iam*... *ante*... *iam*. As the first outburst concluded 'let discord make an end to civil war' (*finem civili faciat discordia bello*), so this turns directly to the author of the conflict and urges 'let it be possible for you to put an end to your crimes' (*liceat scelerum tibi ponere finem*).

This passage is also striking for the apparent absence of factors reversing the impression of immediacy and recalling the Neronian temporality of the narrator.[71] Rather, the narrative moves straight back to the position and attitude of Caesar before his speech, then to the record of the speech itself. At 5. 368–9, Caesar is still fearful for the success of his speech ('Ipse pavet ne tela sibi dextraeque negentur | ad scelus hoc'), but he who was urged to 'comply with' (*pati*) a life without arms is pleasantly surprised by the 'compliance' (*patientia*) of his troops, and the hardened criminality of the men leads them to join in the betrayal of their peers, 5. 369–72:

> Vicit patientia saevi
> spem ducis, et iugulos, non tantum praestitit enses.
> Nil magis adsuetas sceleri quam perdere mentis
> atque perire tenet.

Their compliance outdid the hopes of their savage general and provided him with victims as well as executioners. Nothing has a greater hold on minds accustomed to crime than the instinct to kill and to die.

And thus the men return to the ranks and the progress of crime continues unabated.

Ending the 'Bellum Civile': 'Narrator as Character' and 'Narrator as Narrator'

Analysis of the contrasting futurities of 4. 182–8 and 4. 254–9 highlighted Lucan's tendency to focus the pathos of his work on the

[71] However, Heyke (1970) 93 sees 'bellum te civile fugit' as ironic because it represents the narrator, 'der Allwissende des Epos' as nothing more than a 'Parteigänger der Meuterer' who 'Unwissenheit vortäuschen muss'.

distress of the Neronian composer. This factor is also visible in a metaliterary leitmotiv connecting the flood and mutiny episodes.

On three occasions in these episodes, the 'narrator as character' expresses the wish that the world should be saved from civil war. Thus, at 4. 118–20, he urges:

> Riphaeas huc solve nives, huc stagna lacusque
> et pigras, ubicumque iacent, effunde paludes
> *et miseras bellis civilibus eripe terras.*

Melt hither the Riphaean snows, pour forth hither pools and lakes and lazy marshes, wherever they lie, and save the wretched lands from civil wars.

This appeal is then paralleled at 5. 297–9:

> Sic eat, o superi: quando pietasque fidesque
> destituunt moresque malos sperare relictum est,
> *finem civili faciat discordia bello.*

So be it, gods: when loyalty and trust fail and there is nothing left to hope for save bad morals, let discord bring an end to civil war.

It appears for a third time at 5. 315–16:

> Saeve, quid insequeris? Quid iam nolentibus instas?
> *Bellum te civile fugit.*

Why do you press them, savage one? Why do you compel men who are no longer willing? The civil war is running away from you.

Civil war is both what the 'narrator as character' sees and what the Neronian narrator composes. The latter is even more radically the case if one accepts that the title of Lucan's poem was *Bellum Civile* or *De Bello Civili*, but supporters of the alternative title *Pharsalia* can still point out that Lucan summarizes the content of his poem at 1. 1 as 'Wars *worse than civil* through the fields of Emathia' (*Bella per Emathios plus quam civilia campos*).[72] The idea, therefore, that an end to the civil war is also an escape for Lucan from writing The Civil War should not

[72] This last point is significant. The theme of the poem is wars in Emathia. This locates Pharsalus as the moral centre of the poem and urges that the theme of the *Pharsalia* is something worse than conventional civil wars. Ahl (1976) 326–32 is good on the title of the poem. Stat. *Silv.* 2. 7. 68, 'Pharsalica bella' is important corroborative evidence for the obviously metapoetic Luc. 9. 980–6, esp. 985–6, 'Pharsalia nostra | vivet'. Housman (1926) ad loc., 'Pharsalia nostra: proelium a te [sc. Caesare] gestum, a me scriptum' sets up a bogus opposition, since the *Pharsalia* is now the poem in which the condemned Caesar will achieve an unwelcome immortality. If the title *De Bello Civili* appears on many manuscripts, it is surely because that is just the sort of title to which an uninspired editor would resort.

on the face of things seem implausible. Further, this hypothesis is considerably strengthened if one considers more closely the wish at 5. 299 that discord should end the civil war.

It has already been noted that the appeal for discord to bring an ending is a sign of the dramatic development and growing cynicism of the 'narrator as character', who, in Book 4, has already seen the disastrous failure of concord. It also, however, has clear metaliterary overtones, which play on the relationship of opening and closure in the *Pharsalia* to that seen in previous Roman epic. For it is the personified Discordia who opens the Gates of War (*Belli Portae*) at Ennius, *Annales* frr. 225–6 (Skutsch), and Juno, making common cause with Discordia's analogue Allecto, who does the same at *Aeneid* 7. 622.[73] As at Petronius, 124. 253, 271–2 and especially 295, 'Whatever Discordia ordered was done on earth' (*Factum est in terris, quicquid Discordia iussit*),[74] the passages of Ennius and Vergil mark *the end of the beginning*, that is the start of the bloodshed. Similarly, *Aeneid* 1. 294, 'The Gates of War will be closed' (*Claudentur Belli Portae*), equates the final end of the *Aeneid* with the undoing of the work, historically first done by Juno in *Aeneid* 7, but in literature by Discordia in Ennius.[75] When we know that, for the Romans of this period, Concordia was taken as the stable alternative to the insecure and potentially vicious cessation of Pax, that is as a genuine ending, we can see quite how perverse it is for Lucan to seek a conclusion to the civil war, to his Civil War, in its absolute antithesis, the figure of violent beginnings, *Discordia*.[76] In this sense, Lucan's appeal to discord in Book 5 is doubly reflexive, operating on the level both of political theory and of literary composition. Once again, the 'narrator as character' and the Neronian narrator coexist as twin centres of Lucan's pathos.

[73] Skutsch (1985) ad loc. points to Verg. *Aen.* 7. 335 ff. and esp. 545 ('En, perfecta tibi bello discordia tristi') as acknowledgements of the analogous relationship between the Discordia of Ennius and the Allecto of Vergil. Both furies appear at the start of the seventh book of their respective works, both follow a second proem and introduce the second onslaught of conflict.

[74] Most editors regard line 295 as spurious.

[75] Cf. Cairns (1989) 85–108, 'Concord and Discord'. I agree with Cairns that the rhetoric of Aeneas at 12. 189–94 is indicative of a wish for final Concordia in its Roman political sense, though I see no reason to anticipate such an ending in the marriage with Lavinia, or perhaps at any time before Augustus. I remain uneasy about Cairns's critical method in this chapter.

[76] For the suspicion of Pax and the ideology of Concordia in the period of the civil wars and their aftermath, see Jal (1961).

CONCLUSION

Books 4 and 5 provide three connected instances not just of the bridging but of the merger of epic temporalities. The dramatic appearance of the narrator as a character in his own drama is motivated by the twin emotions of detestation of civil war and yearning to defeat Caesar. The flood, the fraternization, and the mutiny each provide the opportunity to reconcile these two emotions, but, in each case, disaster intervenes. In the case of the fraternization, it is essential to trace this narrative dynamic and to relate it to the underlying critique of the doctrine of *clementia*. If Lucan measures the temptations of resignation, he also gives air to the perils it entails.

In all these scenes, there are more or less prominent elements which highlight the pain of composition of the Neronian narrator. In the case of the flood and mutiny scenes, this is achieved through the motif of civil war as Lucan's Civil War; in the fraternization scene, the dramatic open future of 4. 182–94 is balanced by the closed, literary future of 4. 254–9. This creates an architectonic unity, a phenomenon visible again at 7. 385–459 and 7. 545–96. It is to these episodes that the following chapter is devoted.

3

Pharsalus—Wishing and Watching

If the narrator of the *Pharsalia* is repeatedly subject to intense emotional involvement in the various crises of the Spanish campaign, there is nevertheless a discernible heightening of engagement as the epic reaches its decisive conflict, Pharsalus. One passage from the Pharsalus narrative, 7. 185–213, has already been discussed as a programme for Lucan's anguished and involved narrative voice; two others, 7. 1–44 and 7. 647–711, provide the focus for investigation in the following chapter. The purpose of this chapter is to consider three further points in Book 7 where the narrator invades the world of the action, or the action that of the narrator. These are all analysed with a view to their complexity and reflexivity. Once again, the impassioned manner of the narrator is contrasted with an alternative perspective, that of the indolent spectator Jupiter.

PHARSALIA 7. 630–46: 'WE ARE ALL LAID LOW'

Mors nulla querella
digna sua est, nullosque hominum lugere vacamus.
Non istas habuit pugnae Pharsalia partes
quas aliae clades: *illic* per fata virorum,
per populos *hic* Roma perit; quod militis *illic*,
mors *hic* gentis erat: sanguis ibi fluxit Achaeus,
Ponticus, Assyrius; cunctos haerere cruores
Romanus campisque vetat consistere torrens.
Maius ab hac acie quam quod sua saecula ferrent
volnus habent populi; plus est quam vita salusque
quod perit: in totum mundi prosternimur aevum.
Vincitur his gladiis omnis quae serviet aetas.
Proxima quid suboles aut quid meruere nepotes
in regnum nasci? Pavide num gessimus arma
teximus aut iugulos? Alieni poena timoris
in nostra cervice sedet. Post proelia natis
si dominum, Fortuna, et bella dedisses.

No death is worthy of its own lament and we have no room to mourn individuals. Pharsalia did not have those features of battle which other massacres have: there Rome died through the destinies of men, here through whole peoples; what there was the death of soldiers, here was the death of a race—there flowed Achaean, Pontic, Assyrian blood; the Roman torrent prevents all that gore from sticking or from settling on the fields. The peoples suffered a greater wound from this battle than their generations could endure; it is more than life and salvation that is lost—we are laid low for all the time of the world to come. Every age which shall be enslaved is conquered by these swords. Why did the next generation, why did the grandsons deserve to be born into a monarchy? Did we bear arms like cowards or cover our throats? The penalty of another's fear sits on our necks. Fortune, if you gave those born after the battle a master, you should also have given them wars.

I begin my discussion of Lucan's Pharsalus narrative with this brief passage because it features, in condensed form, almost all the elements of his literary style and political outlook to be highlighted in this chapter.[1] In its anger and search for someone to blame, it also raises issues which will form the central preoccupation of the ensuing discussion of the heroism and *devotio* of Pompey.[2]

Lines 7. 597–616 describe the heroic death of Domitius. Yet this is not to be a poem of individual *aristeiai*. This is the message of 7. 617–30, where Lucan's expression of shame at discussing individual deaths goes hand in hand with a grotesque account of the violence done by Roman to Roman, kinsman to kinsman.

Lines 7. 630–46 return to the futility of mourning individuals: Pharsalus is a universal disaster. Moreover, it is this expression of universality, conceived both spatially and temporally, which underpins the striking intensification of involvement visible in this scene.

The universal impact of Pharsalus is expressed spatially at lines 7. 632–40. These lines represent all other battles as more distant (*illic* . . . *illic*) while presenting Pharsalus as 'here' (*hic* . . . *hic* . . . *hac*). Lucan moves beyond the standard adversative relationship of *hic* and *ille*, emphasizing the nearness of 'this' battle. Just as all the kings and races of the world are drawn into the confined space of Pharsalus, so the narrator undergoes a transformation, taking on an engaged presence at the scene of the conflict. At times, his presence is that of a character intervening in the action, at others the *hic* of Pharsalus represents the

[1] A similar approach to that taken here is apparent in Quint (1993) 147–51, which analyses this scene in the context of the ongoing opposition of the defeated, of the literary and political refusal of an ending. For Quint, Luc. 7. 630–46 is the most pessimistic moment in the poem.

[2] See Ch. 4.

horribly vivid reality of a battle which the Neronian narrator must recount. This second aspect of Lucan's use of deixis emerges very strongly at 7. 545–59, where the immediacy of *hic* gives body to the place considered in memory.[3]

The temporal universality of the battle emerges most powerfully at 7. 638–41:

> Maius ab hac acie quam quod sua saecula ferrent
> volnus habent populi; plus est quam vita salusque
> quod perit: in totum mundi prosternimur aevum.
> Vincitur his gladiis omnis quae serviet aetas.

The peoples suffered a greater wound from this battle than their generations could endure; it is more than life and salvation that is lost—we are laid low for all the time of the world to come. Every age which shall be enslaved is conquered by these swords.

These lines outline the historical significance of Pharsalus. They treat the battle as the great transformatory episode, and exploit the Vergilian conception of epic as aetiology or foundation myth. The depiction of Pharsalus as the evil cause of present woes coheres with a radical engagement with Vergilian prophecy and Augustan intimations of immortality at 7. 385–459.[4]

Yet the battle is not just an αἴτιον. The temporalities are not so much bridged as merged. The narrator engages with the battle as something continuous and present—we are all still being laid low. This merger of times and perspectives is achieved through the introduction of those normal tenses and voices already familiar from the previous chapter.

Variation of tense emerges in the lines just quoted. The imperfect subjunctive 'could endure' (*ferrent*) suggests that 'suffered' (*habent*) is present historic; 'is lost' (*perit*) can be either present or progressive present historic; but 'we are laid low' (*prosternimur*) marks a clear shift. While its tone is of soldiers laid low in battle, the use of the first-person plural and the expansion of the temporal focus (*in totum mundi . . . aevum*) makes it clear that the people being laid low are not just the soldiers, but all Romans to come; both those, one might say, between the battle and the time of Lucan, and those who will live after him. This is peculiarly resonant for a civil war. In conventional narratives of war, it is possible to use notions of 'us' to imply the Romans against the

[3] See below, pp. 99–103.
[4] See below, pp. 82–99.

foreign enemy (*milites nostri*).[5] Here, 'we are laid low' has an entirely different implication.[6]

Prosternimur thus allows Lucan both to associate himself with the immediacy of death in battle and to point to Pharsalus as the αἴτιον for Rome's destruction. Line 7. 641 has the same double effect:

> Vincitur his gladiis omnis quae serviet aetas.
>
> Every age which shall be enslaved is conquered by these swords.

The combination of 'these swords' (*his gladiis*) with 'shall be enslaved' (*serviet*) may be taken as an instance in miniature of the phenomenon which was first noted with reference to 4. 254–9: the illusion of immediate presence undermined by the self-conscious reference to historical information available only to one living after the battle.[7] The future historic again features as a distancing, analytical device. Alternatively, the sense of merged temporalities, of *his gladiis* still drawn and ready for use, allows 'omnis quae serviet aetas' a further sense: that is, of the future faced by the Neronian narrator and his readers, the very future to which he refers at 7. 205–13 and 9. 980–6. In either case, the main point of reference, the focus of pathos, is the Neronian world of the unfree survivors. The interaction of different conceptions of futurity is prominent at 7. 385–459.

With lines 7. 638–41, Lucan achieves a smooth but complex transition to 7. 642–7, where the concluding focus is explicitly that of the subsequent generations, hence the first-person plural perfect tense of 'did we bear?' (*gessimus*) and 'did we cover?' (*teximus*). Lucan wishes 'you should also have given them wars' (*et bella dedisses*) and laments that his time did not have the chance to fight against monarchy. 'He' was beaten at Pharsalus.

On one level, these closing lines are entirely consonant with the engaged, Republican Lucan prominent in Books 4 and 5: they reverse the terms of Vergilian epic, the αἴτια, the sense of foundation and futurity, in order to write a dissenter's anti-*Aeneid*. However, the hatred of Caesarism is now combined with a second and equally violent resentment, that of those who 'let us down':

[5] For *milites nostri* in Caesar, see *B. Gall.* 1. 52. 5, 2. 11. 5, 2. 33. 6, etc. For *nostri* as 'the Roman soldiers', see Caes. *B. Gall.* 1. 26. 4 and 5, 1. 52. 3, 1. 53. 3.

[6] The effect of *prosternimur* is enhanced by its double sense: 'We prostrate ourselves before a tyrant' (*OLD* 'prosterno' 3) and 'We are defeated/slain' (*OLD* 'prosterno' 5).

[7] See Ch. 2 above, pp. 52–3.

Proxima quid suboles aut quid meruere nepotes
in regnum nasci? Pavide num gessimus arma
teximus aut iugulos? Alieni poena timoris
in nostra cervice sedet. Post proelia natis
si dominum, Fortuna, et bella dedisses.

Why did the next generation, why did the grandsons deserve to be born into a monarchy? Did we bear arms like cowards or cover our throats? The penalty of another's fear sits on our necks. Fortune, if you gave those born after the battle a master, you should also have given them wars.

These are the words of a generation not just defeated but sure that it has been betrayed. 'The penalty of another's fear' (*Alieni poena timoris*) is a markedly unspecific expression, and one which begs some obvious questions: 'Who let us down? Whose cowardice?' On the surface, the answer to these questions may seem clear. Lucan, after all, gives the reader a positive answer. Rambaud,[8] Lounsbury,[9] and Heyke[10] all point to 7. 525–7 and the collapse of the barbarian cavalry:

Inmemores pugnae *nulloque pudore timendi*
praecipites fecere palam civilia bella
non bene barbaricis umquam commissa catervis.

Forgetful of battle and unashamed of their fear, by their headlong flight they made it evident that civil wars are never well entrusted to barbarian troops.

To this they add the summary of the collapse at 7. 543–4:

Semel ortus in omnis
it timor, et fatis datus est pro Caesare cursus.

Once it rose, the fear spread to all and the fates allowed things to run in favour of Caesar.

Yet it is a measure of the complexity of the question that Lucan also feels bound to give a second, negative answer, and one which replies to his complaint in its own terms. Pompey, the reader is assured, was not afraid, 7. 669–70:

Nec derat robur in enses
ire duci iuguloque pati vel pectore letum.

Nor did the general lack the courage to enter the fight and meet death with a blow to the throat or the breast.

[8] Rambaud (1955) 271–2.
[9] Lounsbury (1976) 214–17.
[10] Heyke (1970) 86, esp. n. 2.

Blame attributed and blame denied are an intriguing combination. Blame attributed bespeaks the need to blame someone, the sense that the defeat of the Republic was not just due to the positive superiority of the opposition. Blame denied reveals the suspicion which the denial controverts, gives air to the notion that Pompey's generalship was perhaps cowardly or his conduct reprehensible.[11] It is the purpose of my chapter on Pompey closely to investigate the suspicion that Lucan's ostentatious refusal to blame Pompey is not as simple as it may appear. In this chapter, my analysis of 7. 545–96 examines the actions of the senators, and shows how the address to Brutus may be taken as the sarcastic and frustrated complaint of the die-hard oppositionist revealed in these lines. As in the mutiny and the appeal to Discordia, it is thus possible to measure the true degree of Lucan's disillusion, of his rage against history.

PHARSALIA 7. 385–459: HEADING FOR THE BATTLEFIELD

This is a complete and complex narrative movement, which should be printed in full:

Ergo utrimque pari procurrunt agmina motu
irarum; metus hos regni, spes excitat illos.
Hae *facient* dextrae, quidquid non expleat aetas
ulla nec humanum genus reparet omnibus annis,
ut vacet a ferro.[12] Gentes Mars iste futuras
obruet et populos aevi venientis in orbem
erepto natale *feret*. Tunc omne Latinum
fabula nomen *erit*; Gabios Veiosque Coramque
pulvere vix tectae *poterunt* monstrare ruinae
Albanosque lares Laurentinosque penates,
rus vacuum, quod non habitet nisi nocte coacta
invitus questusque Numam iussisse senator.

[11] Or, as Serv. at Verg. *Aen.* 1. 242 would have it when discussing the tradition that Aeneas and Antenor betrayed Troy, Horace's reference to 'ardentem sine fraude Troiam' does not work because 'nemo . . . excusat nisi rem plenam suspicionis'.

[12] The text printed at 387–9 is that transmitted and restored by Shackleton-Bailey in his Teubner edition. The Latin is difficult, and the text cannot be free from suspicion, but it is possible to translate adequately if 'ut vacet a ferro' is taken as concessive. Housman's 'Hae facient dextrae quidquid nona explicat aetas | ut vacet a ferro' objects to 388 as pleonastic, and presumes that it is an interpolation designed to explain 387 and 9. However, his 'nona aetas' is suspect, and does not express the absolute desolation wrought by the battle.

Non aetas haec carpsit edax monimentaque rerum
putria destituit: crimen civile videmus
tot vacuas urbes. Generis quo turba redacta est
humani! Toto populi qui nascimur orbe
nec muros inplere viris nec possumus agros:
urbs nos una capit. Vincto fossore coluntur
Hesperiae segetes, stat tectis putris avitis
in nullos ruitura domus, nulloque frequentem
cive suo Romam sed mundi faece repletam
cladis eo dedimus, ne tanto in corpore bellum
iam possit civile geri. Pharsalia tanti
causa mali. Cedant feralia nomina Cannae
et damnata diu Romanis Allia fastis.
Tempora signavit leviorum Roma malorum,
hunc voluit nescire diem. Pro tristia fata!
Aera pestiferum tractu morbosque fluentis
insanamque famem permissasque ignibus urbes
moeniaque in praeceps laturos plena tremores
hi *possunt*[13] explere viri, quos undique traxit
in miseram Fortuna necem, dum munera longi
explicat eripiens aevi populosque ducesque
constituit campis, per quos tibi, Roma, ruenti
ostendat quam magna cadas. Quae latius orbem
possedit, citius per prospera fata cucurrit?
Omne tibi bellum gentis dedit, omnibus annis
te geminum Titan procedere vidit in axem;
haud multum terrae spatium restabat Eoae,
ut tibi nox, tibi tota dies, tibi curreret aether,
omniaque errantes stellae Romana viderent.
Sed retro tua fata tulit par omnibus annis
Emathiae funesta dies. Hac luce cruenta
effectum, ut Latios non horreat India fasces,
nec vetitos errare Dahas in moenia ducat
Sarmaticumque premat succinctus consul aratrum,
quod semper saevas debet tibi Parthia poenas,
quod fugiens civile nefas redituraque numquam
libertas ultra Tigrim Rhenumque recessit
ac, totiens nobis iugulo quaesita, vagatur
Germanum Scythicumque bonum, nec respicit ultra
Ausoniam, vellem populis incognita nostris.

[13] 'possunt' = PGV, Housman, 'possint' = (M), Shackleton Bailey, 'possent' = ZUC, Haskins and Luck. Housman's 'fingit se proelio adesse' can be applied to any of the conditions created by the variant readings.

Volturis ut primum laevo fundata volatu
Romulus infami conplevit moenia luco,
usque ad Thessalicas servisses, Roma, ruinas.
De Brutis, Fortuna, queror. Quid tempora legum
egimus aut annos a consule nomen habentis?
Felices Arabes Medique Eoaque tellus,
quam sub perpetuis tenuerunt fata tyrannis.
Ex populis qui regna ferunt sors ultima nostra est,
quos servire pudet. Sunt nobis nulla profecto
numina: cum caeco rapiantur saecula casu,
mentimur regnare Iovem. *Spectabit* ab alto
aethere Thessalicas, teneat cum fulmina, caedes?
Scilicet ipse *petet* Pholoen, *petet* ignibus Oeten
inmeritaeque nemus Rhodopes pinusque Mimantis,
Cassius hoc potius *feriet* caput? Astra Thyestae
intulit et subitis damnavit noctibus Argos:
tot similis fratrum gladios patrumque gerenti
Thessaliae *dabit* ille diem? Mortalia nulli
sunt curata deo. Cladis tamen huius habemus
vindictam, quantam terris dare numina fas est:
bella pares superis *facient* civilia divos,
fulminibus manes radiisque *ornabit* et astris
inque deum templis *iurabit* Roma per umbras.

Therefore from both sides the armies ran forwards each with as great an angry impulse; fear of monarchy aroused one side, hope the other. These right hands will do a deed which no age can make right nor can the human race in all the years repair, even if it desists from warfare. This fight will destroy the nations of the future and will take away the peoples of the time still to come to the world, stealing their birth from them. Then all the Latin name will be a tale; the ruins covered in dust will scarce be able to indicate Gabii and Veii and Cora and the houses of Alba and the settlements of Laurentum, an empty stretch of country which nobody inhabits save the senator who is compelled against his will to spend the night there and who complains of Numa's orders. The tooth of time did not eat away at these things and bring down the crumbling monuments of the past: we see in so many empty cities the sin of civil war. To what has the mob of the human race been reduced! We peoples who are born all over the world can neither fill the walls nor the fields with men: one city holds us. The corn of Hesperia is cultivated by a chained ditcher; the house stands crumbling with its ancient roof, doomed to fall but on no occupants; and Rome, populated by no citizens of her own but full of the dregs of the world, we have brought to such a point of destruction that in so great a body it is no longer possible to fight a civil war. Pharsalia is responsible for so great an ill. Let the fatal names give way,

Cannae and the Allia long damned on the Roman calendar. Rome marked the date of lesser ills, this day she preferred not to know. O sorry fates! These men can satiate air poisonous to inhale and the spread of plagues and mad hunger and cities set on fire and earthquakes that will bring full cities to the ground—these men whom Fortune has drawn from every side to wretched slaughter, the gifts of long ages which she steals away as she displays them to you, the peoples and the generals whom she has set on the field, by whom she may show you, Rome, in collapse how great you are as you fall. Which city possessed a greater expanse of the globe, which ran faster from one success to another? Every war gave you nations, every year the Sun saw you move further towards the North and South; very little of the Eastern land remained before all of night and day, all the heavens, should run for you and the wandering stars should see nothing that was not Roman. Yet the fatal day of Emathia, a match for all the years, turned back your destiny. By this bloody day it was ensured that India should not tremble at the Latin rods; that the consul should not forbid the Dahae to roam and lead them into city walls or gird himself up and lean on a Sarmatian plough; that still Parthia should owe you savage retribution; that Freedom, fleeing the crimes of civil strife and never to return, has retreated beyond the Tigris and the Rhine and, so often sought by us at the expense of our lives, wanders, the property of the Germans and the Scythians, and never more looks back on Ausonia—if only she had never been known to our peoples! Would that, ever since Romulus filled the city walls he had founded on the auspices of a vulture's flight on the left with the people of the notorious grove, you had been a slave, Rome, right down to the disaster of Thessaly! Fortune, I complain of the Bruti. Why did we enjoy times of legal administration and years which took their names from the consuls? Lucky are the Arabs, the Medes and the Eastern land, which destiny has held under a succession of tyrants. Of the peoples who endure monarchies our lot is the worst, for we are ashamed to be slaves. Truly we have no divine powers: when the generations are carried along by blind chance, we lie to say that Jupiter rules. Will he watch the slaughter of Thessaly from the heights of heaven, though he holds the thunderbolts? Will he, of course, attack Pholoe, will he attack with his fires Oeta and the grove of innocent Rhodope and the pines of Mimas, will Cassius strike this head instead? He brought night to Thyestes and damned Argos to sudden darkness: will he grant day to Thessaly as she bears so many like swords of brothers and of fathers? No god has cared for mortal affairs. Yet we have as great a revenge for this slaughter as it is right for the divine powers to give to mortals: civil wars will make gods equal to those above; Rome will decorate shades with thunderbolts and haloes and stars and in the temples of the gods will swear by ghosts.

This is a classic example of Lucan's technique of narrative delay. Lines 7. 382–4 round off the *paraceleusis* of Pompey, and are then followed by two lines of consequent action:

> Ergo utrimque pari procurrunt agmina motu
> irarum; metus hos regni, spes excitat illos.

Therefore from both sides the armies ran forwards with equal angry emotion; fear of monarchy aroused one side, hope the other.

The reader is then treated to seventy-two lines of magniloquent analysis and exclamation from the narrator, itself rounded off by the surely ironic 7. 460–1:

> Ut *rapido cursu* fati suprema *morantem*
> *consumpsere locum*...

When with rapid dash they crossed the ground that delayed the final ends of fate ...[14]

Needless to say, Lucan shares none of the haste of his characters.

These brief segments of narrative advance encircle a remarkable instance of the indignant reflection and final intervention of Lucan's narrator. It is my contention that the movement of the passage demands its reading as a unified whole, that the temptation should be resisted to mark off certain sections as coming from the primary narrator, others from an anonymous chorus.[15] The case for a resulting architectonic unity may be made by a series of observations.

It is essential from the outset to emphasize the significance of 7. 386, 'fear of monarchy aroused one side, hope the other' (*metus hos regni, spes excitat illos*). Lucan fills his characters with the very emotions which he expects to generate in his readers at 7. 211. Of course, the distinction applies to the emotions of the Pompeians on the one hand, and of the Caesarians on the other, and thus summarizes the reactions to the speeches of the two generals; but it is also programmatic for the dramatic involvement of the narrator in this segment.[16]

[14] For *mora*, see Masters (1992) 3–10, 43, 54–5, 60, 95–6, 119–22, 183 and Ch. 5, pp. 186–7. For *locus* as textual space or rhetorical theme, see *OLD* 'locus' 23 and 24.

[15] For the approach here resisted, see Marti (1975).

[16] The density of reference to the anticipatory emotions grows ever greater the closer Pharsalus approaches. O'Higgins (1988) and Masters (1992) argue for the metapoetic quality of the Erictho scene at the close of Book 6. It is striking therefore that Sextus Pompeius should travel to visit her at a time when his comrades, 6. 419, '*spemque metumque* ferunt' and when his emotional state can be described as, 6. 423–4, 'stimulante *metu* fati praenoscere cursus, | inpatiensque *morae venturisque* omnibus aeger'. For further references to anticipation at the start of Book 7, see 7. 20 for Pompey's rest 'anxia venturis' (contra Housman 'anxia mens curis'), 7. 105 'venturi timor', cf. 106 'metuenda', 7. 133–8, esp. 'maiore metu', 'timeat sibi', 'pro se ferre metus', 'urbi Magnoque timetur', 7. 248 for Caesar advancing 'formidine mersa', 7. 252 'nil opus est votis', 7. 297 'spe

The text printed at 7. 387–9 is not free from suspicion but the possible corruption is not such as to obscure the sweeping movement and complex literary effects at which Lucan aims through 387–407. These lines divide into two answering sections. The first, 387–96, takes its inspiration from the anticipatory emotions of the troops at 386. The primary narrator, by employing a succession of future indicatives, evokes the immediacy of expectation: 'will do . . . will destroy . . . will take away . . . will be . . . will scarce be able' (*facient . . . obruet . . . feret . . . erit . . . poterunt*). Though it soon becomes apparent that the future is not open, that these verbs use a prospective mode of expression to convey a strictly historical proposition, it is essential to the functioning of the passage as a whole that the sense of some potential vivid presence should be injected from the start.

The future historic again serves to underline the extreme significance of the event.[17] That these are future historics and not the vivid futures of a separate character or chorus is made explicit by the answering movement of perfects and presents at 7. 397–407, outlining the state of the world 'in which we live'. Essential here are the expressions in the first person plural: 'we see the sin of civil war . . . we are born . . . we can . . . one city holds us . . . we have brought to such a point of destruction' (*crimen civile videmus . . . nascimur . . . possumus . . . urbs nos una capit . . . cladis eo dedimus*).

The two answering movements at 387–407 combine to produce a two-pronged attack on Augustan poetry: at once assaulting directly its optimistic prophecies and, more subtly, providing an exegesis of the points of anxiety already present within them. It is the second tendency, in particular, that is apparent at lines 391–6, which enter into a complex dialectic with the prophecy of Anchises at *Aeneid* 6. 773–6:

> 'Hi tibi Nomentum et Gabios urbemque Fidenam,
> hi Collatinas imponent montibus arces,
> Pometios Castrumque Inui Bolamque Coramque;
> haec tum nomina erunt, nunc sunt sine nomine terrae.'

'These men will put Nomentum and Gabii and the city of Fidenae and the Collatine citadel atop the mountains for you, and Pometii and Castrum Inui and

trepido', 7. 298–9 'camporum limite parvo | absumus a votis', etc. One of the aims of this chapter is to demonstrate that while this community of emotion between characters, readers, and narrator is in part a literary device to create suspense, it is also something much more than this.

[17] This function of the future historic is underlined in App. 3.

Bola and Cora; these then will be famous names, now they are lands without name.'[18]

Anchises understands the power of naming as one imposes one's civilization, one's buildings, on the countryside. Yet the names evoked have a particular and troubling resonance. Anchises tells of the future glory of cities, but it is not an unconditional future. It is the destiny of Rome as she expands to render other civilizations mere ghost-towns, and it cannot escape the Augustan reader that, by his time, Gabii and Fidenae are mere names because destroyed by Rome.[19]

The speech of Anchises is a complex phenomenon. It is impossible to escape the sense that, in its totality, this is an 'eternal' statement of Roman destiny and identity. At the same time, a detailed reading of the speech reveals an indisputable partiality and selectivity. The downplaying or exclusion of the creative arts at 6. 847–53, which has long been recognized as highly incongruous in the context of Vergil's poetry, is also marked by Ovid as true only for an early period of Roman history.[20] And the celebration of Gabii and Fidenae is a classic instance of the 'optimistic prophecy'[21] in the *Aeneid*: a prophecy delivered by one character to another, often with the effect of consoling the listener, but which reveals its own omissions and obfuscations to the 'Augustan' reader. It is this inconcinnity which Lucan exploits at 7. 391–6:

> Tunc omne Latinum
> fabula nomen erit; Gabios Veiosque Coramque
> pulvere vix tectae poterunt monstrare ruinae
> Albanosque lares Laurentinosque penates,
> rus vacuum, quod non habitat nisi nocte coacta
> invitus questusque Numam iussisse senator.

Then all the Latin name will be a tale; the ruins covered in dust will scarce be able to indicate Gabii and Veii and Cora and the houses of Alba and the settlements of Laurentum, an empty stretch of country which nobody inhabits save

[18] For previous treatments of this intertext, see Guillemin (1951) 221–2, Thompson and Bruère (1968), Feeney (1986*b*) 7–8, and Labate (1991) 179.

[19] Already in the Augustan period, Hor. *Epist.* 1. 11. 7–8 describes a 'Gabiis desertior atque | Fidenis vicus', while of Veii, Prop. 4. 10. 29–30 states: 'Nunc intra muros pastoris bucina lenti | cantat, et in vestris ossibus arva metunt'. For Cora, Gagliardi (1975) gives Livy 2. 16, Serv. at Verg. *Aen.* 7. 672, and ps.-Aur. Vict. *Orig.* 17. See Feeney (1986*b*) for the fate of all the cities cited.

[20] For Vergil's own discomfort, see Lyne (1987) 214–16, but most importantly Broch (1983) 268–9. Hine (1987) collects a mass of material on this issue but does not entirely dispel anxiety. For Ovid's attitude, see *Fast.* 3. 79–104, esp. 101–2, and Hinds (1992) 124–7.

[21] See O'Hara (1990).

the senator who is compelled against his will to spend the night there and who complains of Numa's orders.

Lucan blames on the civil wars the destruction of cities ruined years earlier and by the expansion of Rome. The function of this anachronism is surely to point up the literary relationship to Vergil and to offer an exegesis of his predecessor's text.[22] Lucan does not so much write an anti-*Aeneid* as draw out the troubling 'further voice' audible in the prophecy of Anchises.[23]

Lucan's prospective, prophetic voice at 387–96 interacts strikingly with its retrospective counterpart at 397–407. If the former offers an exegesis of the problems which Vergil discreetly invites the reader to perceive in Anchises' prophecy, the latter noisily rebuts the illusions of Horace's Augustan verse. *Pharsalia* 7. 397–8 opens:

> Non aetas haec carpsit edax monimentaque rerum
> putria destituit.

The tooth of time did not eat away at these things and bring down the crumbling monuments of the past.

Lucan thus savages the conceits of Horace at *Carm.* 3. 30. 1–5:

> Exegi monumentum aere perennius
> regalique situ pyramidum altius,
> quod non imber edax, non Aquilo impotens
> possit diruere aut innumerabilis
> annorum series et fuga temporum.

I have built a monument more lasting than bronze and higher than the regal pomp of the pyramids, which neither biting rain nor mighty Aquilo nor the numberless succession of the years and the flight of times can bring down.

Another target is perhaps the boast of Ovid at *Met.* 15. 871–2:

> Iamque opus exegi, quod nec Iovis ira nec ignis
> nec poterit ferrum nec edax abolere vetustas.

And now I have built a work, which neither the anger of Jupiter nor fire nor steel nor the tooth of time can destroy.[24]

22 Dilke (1960) ad loc. finds it 'somewhat strange' to blame the destruction of Veii on Pharsalus but does not perceive the Vergilian intertext.

23 At the same time, 7. 391–2, 'omne nomen Latinum | fabula erit', recalls first the description at 3. 211–13 of Caesar's claim to descent from Iulus and Troy as a *fabula*, that is as Vergil's literary fiction; second 6. 48–9 (Troy), 6. 355–9, and 8. 406–7 (both Thebes) where the greatness of cities is attested only by a *fabula*.

24 For *edax* and the tooth of time, cf. Ov. *Am.* 1. 15. 41–2, 'Ergo etiam cum me supremus adederit ignis, | vivam, parsque mei multa superstes erit' and *Anth. Lat.* 415. 8 (SB), 'edetque'.

What is significant about both these Augustan claims to immortality is that the survival they claim is conditional on the continuation of the political culture which can make sense of them. Though *Carm.* 3. 30 begins with the claim of longer life for the poet's verse than for mere physical monuments, it closes with the assertion of the vital interrelation of Roman verse and the public buildings of the Roman state, *Carm.* 3. 30. 7–9:

Usque ego postera
crescam laude recens, dum Capitolium
scandet cum tacita Virgine pontifex.

I shall ever rise, fresh with the praises of posterity, as long as the priest climbs the Capitol with the silent Virgin.[25]

This association of the immortality of Augustan verse with the survival of the political buildings of the Augustan State also underpins the apostrophe of Vergil to Nisus and Euryalus at *Aeneid* 9. 446–9,[26] is parodied in Apollo's words to Daphne the laurel tree at Ovid, *Met.* 1. 557–67, and explored much more seriously at the very close of the poem, especially 15. 877–9:

Quaque patet domitis Romana potentia terris,
ore legar populi, perque omnia saecula fama,
siquid habent veri vatum praesagia, vivam.

And where Roman power opens out over the conquered lands, I shall be read in the mouths of the people, and through all the generations, if the prophecies of the poets have any truth, I shall live in fame.[27]

The Augustan poets premise their claim of immortality on the survival of Augustan Rome.[28] Lucan, however, protests that Rome has

[25] The contrast between the immortality of poetry and the mortality of buildings is traced back to Ennius, *Ann.* frr. 12–13 and 404–5 (Skutsch) in Zwierlein (1982). It is still apparent in *Anth. Lat.* 415 and 416 (SB) and is appropriated for philosophy in Sen. *Brev.* 15. 4, 17. 1, 19. 1. By contrast, the association between immortal verse and State building seems typically Augustan.

[26] Verg. *Aen.* 9. 446–9: 'Fortunati ambo! Si quid mea carmina possunt, | nulla dies umquam memori vos eximet aevo, | dum domus Aeneae Capitoli immobile saxum | accolet imperiumque pater Romanus tenebit'.

[27] Anderson (1963) 26–7 notes that Ov. *Met.* 15. 876–9 first acnowledges dependence on Roman power, then defiantly transcends it. This connects to the song of Pythagoras at the beginning of the book with its uncomfortable implications for *Roma aeterna* in its account of the rise and fall of cities.

[28] This is not true, however, of Ov. *Am.* 1. 15. Galinsky (1969) 95–6 contrasts the unconditional immortality claimed by Ovid for his own verse at *Am.* 1. 15. 33–4 with the conditional survival of Vergil at 1. 15. 25–6, 'Tityrus et fruges [segetes (Mckeown)] Aeneiaque arma legentur, | Roma triumphati dum caput orbis erit'. Galinsky treats this as evidence of the dissident mentality of the *Amores*.

been destroyed, and, what's more, that it was destroyed by the very war, the *crimen civile*, which brought their Augustus to power. The poets who praise the new regime are not the celebrants of the great Rome but the lackeys of its destroyer. This is powerfully expressed at 7. 402–3, where 'The corn of Hesperia is cultivated by a chained ditcher' (*Vincto fossore coluntur* | *Hesperiae segetes*), an allusion to the replacement of the native Italian farmer with the chain-gang labour of the *ergastulum*, also bears the stamp of Ovid's exile poetry, of the latter's final experience of tyranny. For Ovid, in *Tristia* 4. 1. 5–6, apologizing for the inadequacy of his verse, claims that he writes only for *requies* and compares his motivation to that of the chained ditcher:

> Hoc est cur cantet vinctus quoque compede fossor,
> indocili numero cum grave mollit opus.

This is why even the ditcher bound in fetters sings as he eases his hard labour with an untaught tune.

The same poet, at *Epistulae ex Ponto* 1. 6. 31–2, protests that he has not yet lost hope, and adds that:

> Haec [i.e. spes] facit ut vivat fossor quoque compede vinctus
> liberaque a ferro crura futura putet.

This [hope] makes even the ditcher bound in fetters live and hope that his legs will be free from the irons.[29]

Lines 387–407 introduce the notion of the narrator operating on two different stages at once. The Neronian narrator is able also to speak as if he is a character watching the drama develop. This perspective will now come to prominence. At the same time, the presence and prospection of the narrator at 387–96 is not that of a dramatically involved and naïve character, but a highly self-conscious production constantly entangled intertextually with the Augustan visions of Rome it unmasks or deplores. The intertextual dimension will again become prominent at the close of the speech.

All the emphasis of 397–407 is on what has happened, does happen, no longer can happen. The explanation is simple and brief, 7. 407–8:

[29] 'Hesperiae segetes' at Luc. 7. 403 raises two further issues. First, *Hesperia* is used regularly by Lucan as a term for *Italia* in deliberate allusion to Ennius and Vergil and thus as an extension of his anti-*Aeneid*. Second, *segetes* has a Vergilian resonance of its own, used at Prop. 2. 34. 78, as an encapsulation of the *Georgics*, alluding to Verg. *G.* 1. 1, 'Quid faciat laetas segetes . . .'. It is for this reason that McKeown at Ov. *Am.* 1. 15. 26 emends 'fruges' to 'segetes'.

. . . Pharsalia tanti
causa mali.

Pharsalia is responsible for so great an ill.[30]

From here, the emotion of the narrator grows. The reference to Cannae and Allia at 7. 408–11 is in the form of what one might call an imperative of literary immortality, and one which derives its force from the response of the Roman calendar: 'only Pharsalus have we refused to recall'. The perspective here is still firmly that of the Neronian poet looking back on and analysing the battle and its consequences, but a slightly different movement seems to emerge in the following lines, 7. 411–19. The initial exclamation 'O sorry fates!' (*Pro tristia fata!*) seems still to maintain the position of retrospection. On the other hand, *fata* can be viewed as coming as well as past, and this interpretation is consonant with the easiest translation of the following sentence: that is, that it is addressed by the 'narrator as character' to Rome, the best part of which are the men who die, as he stands on or by the field of battle. As they fall, so does Rome (*quam magna cadas*). Thus, *possunt* is read 'can glut', *traxit* and *constituit* as 'has drawn' and 'has arrayed'. The apostrophe to 'you, Rome, in collapse' (*tibi, Roma, ruenti*) and the purpose clause 'by whom she may show you' (*per quos . . . ostendat*) would seem to support this interpretation.[31]

The intervention of the narrator is only fleeting. It acts as much as anything to demonstrate the emotional pressure generated by awareness that Pharsalus is the one great and destructive day. The address to Rome at 7. 418–19 is an address to the men of Rome on the battlefield, who, by destroying themselves, destroy the city as well, but it is also an address to the idealizing conception of Rome. This ideal of Rome remains Lucan's addressee throughout the section introduced with the rhetorical question at 419–20:

Quae latius orbem
possedit, citius per prospera fata cucurrit?

Which city possessed a greater expanse of the globe, which ran faster from one success to another?

The rise and fall of the city is traced in the second person.[32] It is as if

[30] Lucan employs a version of the ἀρχὴ κακῶν motif. For this, see Pease (1935) at Verg. *Aen*. 4. 169.

[31] See n. 13 for the alternative readings 'possint' and 'possent', neither of which invalidates the suggestion of immediate presence.

[32] Luc. 7. 421–31, 'tibi . . . te . . . tibi . . . tibi . . . tibi . . . tua . . . tibi'.

the ideal of Rome is to be separated from the men, the generation which is to be blamed. For the point of this passage is again that Pharsalus destroyed everything, 7. 426–7:

> Sed retro tua fata tulit par omnibus annis
> Emathiae funesta dies.

Yet the fatal day of Emathia, a match for all the years, turned back your destiny.

The true nadir is the world of Nero and of Lucan.

At 7. 427–36, the narrator gives four lines of external, imperial decline (7. 428–31) and five of internal (7. 432–6), and all the product of Pharsalus. Again, we are in the territory of the *αἴτιον*. The civil wars were the period of transformation which created the Rome in which Lucan lives. The theme of lost liberty now prompts the narrator to a retrospective and paradoxical mode of expression, offering a wish (7. 437–9, esp. *servisses*), a complaint (7. 440, *queror*), a rhetorical question (7. 440–1), and a tortured *sententia* (7. 442–5). Finally, as his emotion and indignation builds, the narrator draws what ought to be his climactic conclusion: that is, that the fact of the civil wars proves that there are no gods, or at least no caring gods. However, lines 7. 445–7, self-consciously literary in their final swipe at Horace,[33] do not so much complete the process of retrospection as act as the pivot to introduce the emergence of the narrator as *dramatis persona*:

> Sunt nobis nulla profecto
> numina: cum caeco rapiantur saecula casu,
> mentimur regnare Iovem.

Truly we have no divine powers: when the generations are carried along by blind chance, we lie to say that Jupiter rules.

At this point, it is important to recapitulate. *Pharsalia* 7. 387–459 is a consistent sweeping movement, deploying a variety of perspectives to evoke the significance for Lucan's Rome of the coming battle. While Pharsalus and its consequences are past, historical events for the narrator and his audience, it is a past which remains alive in the world it created. The inclusion of so long a piece of intense analysis at this point in the action is in violation of any traditional conception of epic

[33] Hor. *Carm.* 3. 5. 1–2, 'Caelo tonantem credidimus Iovem | regnare' associates the power of Augustus over the world with that of Jupiter over the heavens. Now, Lucan cites the coming of the emperors as proof of the non-existence or unconcern of Jove. See Zetzel (1980) and Feeney (1991) 281–2. Assaults on Hor. *Carm.* 3. 5 open and close this section of Lucan, for Luc. 7. 390, 'aevi venientis in orbem' must be an echo of 'veniens in aevum' at Hor. *Carm.* 3. 5. 16.

narration. What is seen, in fact, is a radical transformation of customary epic practice, though one which, by its assault on the imperial aetiology, the bridging of temporalities of the *Aeneid*, can be seen as an explosion of forces inherent in previous *Romana carmina*.

The variation of perspective, the appeal to futurity—all this will now return as the movement, architectonic in its structure, reaches its climax. 7. 387–96 begins with a series of future historics, which act to underline the significance of the battle, also to disconcert the reader by their likeness to those futures which express a contingent situation or which promise immortality in a literary work.[34] Similarly, 7. 411–19 hints at the actual intervention of the narrator as character, this being treated as the paradoxical extension of his retrospective rage. At 7. 447–54, where previously this was only a possible interpretation, now it is evident. The contingent future of the narrator emerges directly from the conclusion to his retrospection:

> *Spectabit* ab alto
> aethere Thessalicas, teneat cum fulmina, caedes?
> Scilicet ipse *petet* Pholoen, *petet* ignibus Oeten
> inmeritaeque nemus Rhodopes pinusque Mimantis,
> Cassius hoc potius *feriet* caput? Astra Thyestae
> intulit et subitis damnavit noctibus Argos:
> tot similis fratrum gladios patrumque gerenti
> Thessaliae *dabit* ille diem?

Will he watch the slaughter of Thessaly from the heights of heaven, though he holds the thunderbolts? Will he, of course, attack Pholoe, will he attack with his fires Oeta and the grove of innocent Rhodope and the pines of Mimas, will Cassius strike this head instead? He brought night to Thyestes and damned Argos to sudden darkness: will he grant day to Thessaly as she bears so many like swords of brothers and of fathers?

The sentiment expressed accuses Jupiter of watching, of reading the *Pharsalia* with a culpable absence of passion.[35] The contrast between the anguished engagement of the poet and the apathy attributed to the god recalls the terms of Cato's question at 2. 289–92 and Lucan's own comment at 4. 400–1. The wishes implicit in Lucan's question are those which he anticipates in his readers at 7. 211. Moreover, it is surely possible to envisage the manner of the complaint. Just as

[34] For these distinctions, see App. 3.

[35] Stat. *Theb.* 1. 79–80 picks up on the terms of Lucan's complaint when Oedipus, lamenting his mistreatment by his sons, exclaims, 'Et videt ista deorum | ignavus genitor?'

Lucan's readers will feel as if they are present at the battle, so too here the 'narrator as character' seems to stand on the field of battle, to hold up his hands to heaven, to point to the high mountains all around him, and thus to deliver his despairing complaint: history must be reversed.

Further, all the above observations take on a particular point when one considers two passages of Seneca of obvious intertextual importance for the narrator's complaint. The first of these is *De Otio* 4. 2, where one of the catalogue of philosophical questions listed by Seneca is:

Qui sit deus; *deses* opus suum *spectet* an tractet.

Who is god; whether he indolently watches his creation or takes it in hand.[36]

The implication of Jupiter's spectatorship in Lucan is the same as that posited here by Seneca, that it stands for his inaction, his want of care.[37] The second passage is more complex. My discussion of spectatorship and spectacle in Lucan stresses his allusion to the experience of the audience in the amphitheatre.[38] Yet consideration is also given to Rosenmeyer's discussion of Seneca, where the world is a stage on which man acts out the good life for the gods to observe.[39] The two conceptions of spectacle are scarcely separate from each other; for the amphitheatre, in Seneca as much as in Cicero, is a constant source of exemplary deeds of various sorts.[40] This blending is apparent in the second passage to be examined, Seneca, *De Providentia* 2. 7–9:

Miraris tu, si deus ille bonorum amantissimus, qui illos quam optimos esse atque excellentissimos vult, fortunam illis cum qua exerceantur adsignat? Ego vero non miror, si aliquando impetum capiunt spectandi magnos viros conluctantis cum aliqua calamitate. *Nobis interdum voluptati est, si adulescens constantis animi inruentem feram venabulo excepit, si leonis incursum interritus pertulit, tantoque*

[36] The Latin text printed is the emendation of Gertz, which I prefer to the version offered by Reynolds in the OCT, '. . . quae sit dei sedes, opus suum spectet an tractet'.

[37] *Comm. Bern.* at Luc. 7. 447–8 explains that Lucan 'astruit deos non curare terrena'. It is interesting to note that while Seneca cites this as one of many questions to be considered in *otium*, Cato's refusal to hold his hands together and watch the end of the universe is expressed in the context of a debate with Brutus over whether the correct response to civil war is to engage or to pursue the philosophical *otium* of retreat. Thus, Brutus at Luc. 2. 266–7 urges that 'melius tranquilla sine armis | *otia solus ages*', while Cato responds at 2. 292–5, 'Gentesne furorem | Hesperium ignotae Romanaque bella sequentur | diductique fretis alio sub sidere reges, | *otia solus agam*?'

[38] See Ch. 7, 'A View to a Kill'.

[39] Rosenmeyer (1989). For my response to Rosenmeyer, see esp. the discussions of Cato and Vulteius.

[40] For Lucan's contamination of the exemplary with the amphitheatrical, see Ch. 7, esp. pp. 236–40.

hoc spectaculum est gratius quanto id honestior fecit. Non sunt ista quae possint deorum in se vultum convertere, puerilia et humanae oblectamenta levitatis: *ecce spectaculum dignum ad quod respiciat intentus operi suo deus*, ecce par deo dignum, vir fortis cum fortuna mala compositus, utique si et provocavit. *Non video, inquam, quid habeat in terris Iuppiter pulchrius, si {eo} convertere animum velit, quam ut spectet Catonem iam partibus non semel fractis stantem nihilo minus inter ruinas publicas rectum.*

Are you surprised if that god, who is most devoted to good men, who wishes them to be as good and as excellent as possible, assigns them a fortune with which they may be exercised. I indeed am not surprised, if sometimes they get the urge to watch great men wrestling with some calamity. Occasionally it is a source of pleasure for us if a young man of unflinching mind has caught an onrushing beast with his spear, if unshaken he has borne the attack of a lion, and this spectacle is the more pleasing the more virtuous is the man who has provided it. Those things are not the sort which can attract the attention of the gods, the puerile entertainments of human folly: lo! a spectacle worthy of the observation of a god intent on his work, lo! a pair worthy of a god—a hero pitted against ill fortune just as if he had issued the challenge. I tell you, I cannot see what Jupiter can have on earth more fair, if thither he should wish to turn his mind, than to watch Cato, his party already broken more than once, still standing no less straight amidst the disaster of the State.

The argument is complex, in that the exemplarity of the young hunter goes hand in hand with the entertainment of the watching audience. On the other hand, Seneca the philosopher denies the element of simple pleasure for Jupiter in watching the struggles of a Cato and emphasizes that our actions amidst disaster are not futile, for they are there to be observed and judged by the gods.[41] The voice of the narrator in Lucan is very different: it takes Seneca's hypothetical situation, gives it a dramatic reality, and condemns Jupiter the spectator for his disengagement. This has two obvious effects. On the one hand, it accuses Jupiter of an attitude too close to the 'pleasure' (*voluptas*) and 'folly' (*levitas*) of the human audience at the amphitheatre; on the other, it makes Seneca sound uncannily like his second self, the Seneca of the tragedies: the narrator of the *Pharsalia* now sounds far more like the chorus at *Phaedra* 959–88 than he does like Seneca in *De Providentia* 2. 7.

This is one way of looking at this passage. As in the flood episode, however, there are further elements, local and temporal, which undermine the surface naturalism of the intervention. On the local level, for

[41] Note that at *Prov.* 1. 1 Seneca promises that 'deorum causam agam'. This is hardly Lucan's perspective.

instance, it is somewhat disingenuous to describe the narrator as holding his hands up to the mountains of Thessaly all around. While Mount Oeta is genuinely Thessalian, Pholoe is Arcadian, Rhodope Thracian and Mount Mimas Ionian. Though Keil presumes that there existed a second, Thracian Mount Mimas, it is evident that Lucan's juxtaposition of Rhodope with Mimas is owed rather to his quotation of Ov. *Met.* 2. 222–3:

> Et tandem nivibus Rhodope caritura Mimasque
> Dindymaque et Mycale natusque ad sacra Cithaeron.

And Rhodope at last set to lose its snow and Mimas and Dindyma and Mycale and Cithaeron born for holy rites.

While some may take this as evidence of Lucan's geographical incompetence, it is surely more rewarding to follow Kroll and regard this and the subsequent imitation at Sil. *Pun.* 3. 494, *Rhodopeque adiuncta Mimanti*, as the self-conscious acknowledgement of the poetic inheritance.[42] There is an inevitable distancing effect in the recognition that the character we see so directly engaged with the crisis of civil war is also a poet rather knowingly quoting his predecessor, Ovid.

Temporal naturalism lasts little longer. Where the futures of 7. 387–96 were all historics, 'will he watch . . . will he attack . . . will he attack . . . will he strike . . . will he grant' (*spectabit*, *petet*, *petet*, *feriet*, and *dabit*) might all be taken as contingent. This is especially obvious for *spectabit* and *dabit*. The problem emerges with the second question, and particularly with *feriet*. This question plays on the Neronian narrator's knowledge of history subsequent to Pharsalus and of the assassination of Caesar. 'This head' (*hoc . . . caput*) imagines the character pointing to Caesar in person, but the information offered, the reference to Cassius, contradicts the implications of the deictic. In other words, even in those moments where Lucan feigns to seek the reversal of history, he displays great self-consciousness, reverses his own illusion, and puts the weight of the pathos on the Neronian narrator. It is in these terms that the close of this passage achieves its special point.

[42] For the presumed Thracian Mt. Mimas, see Keil at Pauly, *RE* xv. 2. 1714. Kroll (1924) 153 is far more plausible. Bömer (1969–86) at Ov. *Met.* 2. 222 is also sceptical. *Adiuncta* in Silius points to his awareness of the chain of imitation he is joining—the sense is as much rhetorical as geographical. *Adiunctus* has the geographical sense of 'next to' at Curt. 8. 11. 25 and 10. 10. 2, while *adiungere*, *adiunctus*, and *adiunctio* have a range of different rhetorical senses, of which Cic. *De Or.* 3. 206 and *Part. Or.* 16 would seem to conform to the sense of putting two or more words together.

The passage concludes with a return to the perspective of the opening lines and demonstrates the capacity of the future tense as a formal device, 7. 454–9:

> Mortalia nulli
> sunt curata deo. Cladis tamen huius habemus
> vindictam, quantam terris dare numina fas est:
> bella pares superis facient civilia divos,
> fulminibus manes radiisque ornabit et astris
> inque deum templis iurabit Roma per umbras.

No god has cared for mortal affairs. Yet we have as great a revenge for this slaughter as it is right for the divine powers to give to mortals: civil wars will make gods equal to those above; Rome will decorate shades with thunderbolts and haloes and stars and in the temples of the gods will swear by ghosts.

The theology of the passage has been commented on by many.[43] The Epicurean statement with which it begins can also be read as atheism if we treat *nulli* as indicating simply that there are no gods out there to care.[44] The atheism of the last lines, asserting that the old gods are equal to the new in the sense of being only shades and ghosts, may also indicate another revenge: the crazily antagonistic spirit of the Caesars will bring civil war, the amphitheatre even, to heaven (*pares*).[45] This is just what the spectator Jupiter of 7. 447 deserves.[46] At the same time, however, little has been said about the return to the future historic as a coda to the movement begun at 7. 387–96. Where that section began with a 'will do/make' (*facient*), so does this one, closely followed by 'will decorate' (*ornabit*) and 'will swear' (*iurabit*). The notion of futurity serves as the leitmotiv of the passage, but only a futurity cruelly conditioned and closed. At 7. 447–54, indignant recollection turns into an impotent plea for reversal; the narrator enacts the emotions anticipated at 7. 211; but he also, with *feriet*, includes at the height of his intervention a necessary intellectualizing distance. As his rhetoric sweeps on, and the future form avoids any change in the mode of

[43] Due (1962) 101–2 and (1970) 213–14 argues that Lucan denies the existence of the gods absolutely and then revels in the absurdity of any idea of mortal revenge. Feeney (1991) 281–2 sees Lucan protesting against divine unconcern. Gagliardi (1985) 2054 and Johnson (1987) 89–90 are surely correct to see Lucan flirting with both positions.

[44] *Comm. Bern.* at Luc. 7. 449 notes the movement between the two poles of atheism and Epicureanism, 'Duas opiniones posuit: prima non esse deos, secunda non curare mortales'.

[45] Cf. Feeney (1991) 297–8. A similar form of civil war seems to be going on in the Underworld at 6. 797–9, 'Aeternis chalybis nodis et carcere Ditis | constrictae plausere manus, camposque piorum | poscit turba nocens'.

[46] One thinks of Plin. *Pan.* 33. 1: 'e spectatore spectaculum factus'.

locution, gradually we become aware of the change in the propositional content of his words. The promise of 7. 205–13 is now completely fulfilled: fate is still fate; it may be coming and not past but is still immutable. The prayers perish on their speaker's lips.

PHARSALIA 7. 545–96: CAESAR ATTACKS THE SENATORS

Ventum erat ad robur Magni mediasque catervas.
Quod totos errore vago perfuderat agros
constitit *hic* bellum, fortunaque Caesaris haesit.
Non *illic* regum auxiliis collecta iuventus
bella gerit ferrumque manus movere rogatae:
ille locus fratres habuit, locus *ille* parentis.
Hic furor, *hic* rabies, *hic* sunt tua crimina, *Caesar*.
Hanc fuge, *mens*, partem belli tenebrisque relinque,
nullaque tantorum discat *me vate* malorum,
quam multum bellis liceat civilibus, aetas.
A potius pereant lacrimae pereantque querellae:
quidquid in *hac* acie gessisti, *Roma*, tacebo.
Hic Caesar, rabies populis stimulusque furorum,
nequa parte sui pereat scelus, agmina circum
it vagus atque ignes animis flagrantibus addit.
Inspicit et gladios, qui toti sanguine manent,
qui niteant primo tantum mucrone cruenti,
quae presso tremat ense manus, quis languida tela,
quis contenta ferat, quis praestet bella iubenti,
quem pugnare iuvet, quis voltum cive perempto
mutet; obit latis proiecta cadavera campis;
volnera multorum totum fusura cruorem
opposita premit ipse manu. Quacumque vagatur,
sanguineum veluti quatiens Bellona flagellum
Bistonas aut Mavors agitans si verbere saevo
Palladia stimulet turbatos aegide currus,
nox ingens scelerum est; caedes oriuntur et instar
inmensae vocis gemitus, et pondere lapsi
pectoris arma sonant confractique ensibus enses.
Ipse manu subicit gladios ac tela ministrat
adversosque iubet ferro confundere voltus,
promovet ipse acies, inpellit terga suorum,
verbere conversae cessantis excitat hastae,
in plebem vetat ire manus monstratque senatum:

scit cruor imperii qui sit, quae viscera rerum,
unde petat Romam, libertas ultima mundi
quo steterit ferienda loco. Permixta secundo
ordine nobilitas venerandaque corpora ferro
urguentur; *caedunt Lepidos caeduntque Metellos*
Corvinosque simul Torquataque nomina, rerum
saepe duces summosque hominum te, Magne, remoto.
Illic plebeia contectus casside voltus
ignotusque hosti quod ferrum, Brute, tenebas!
O decus imperii, spes o suprema senatus,
extremum tanti generis per saecula nomen,
ne rue per medios nimium temerarius hostis,
nec tibi fatales admoveris ante Philippos,
Thessalia periture tua. Nil proficis istic
Caesaris intentus iugulo: nondum attigit arcem,
iuris et humani columen, quo cuncta premuntur,
egressus meruit fatis tam nobile letum.
Vivat et, ut Bruti procumbat victima, regnet.

The fight had come to the strong-point of Magnus and to the middle of his troops. The war which had spread in random wandering all over the fields stopped here and Caesar's fortune was checked. Not there did young men wage war who had been collected from the auxiliaries of kings, but hands unbidden plied the steel: that place held brothers, that place fathers. Here is madness, here rage, here is your damnation, Caesar. O mind, flee this part of the war and leave it to the darkness, and let no age learn from my vatic recollection of such great evils how much is possible in civil wars. O rather let our tears be shed, our laments be uttered in vain: whatever you did in this battle, Rome, I shall not report. Here Caesar, rage and goad to madness of the peoples, lest criminality be lost in any part of his force, goes wandering around the ranks and adds fires to burning minds. And he inspects the swords, to see which drip all over with blood, which shine and are bespattered only at the very end of the blade, which hand trembles as it grips the sword, who bears his weapons weakly, who with exertion, who goes into action when ordered, who is delighted to fight, who changes his expression when he has slain a citizen; he goes around the corpses scattered on the broad fields; he himself uses his hand to staunch the wounds which would otherwise shed all the blood of many men. Wherever he wanders, like Bellona brandishing her bloody whip or Mars as he urges on the Bistones, when with savage blows he lashes on his horses that have been thrown into confusion by the aegis of Pallas, there is a huge night of crimes; slaughter rises and a groaning the size of a huge voice, and the breastplates resound with their own weight as a man falls, so too swords broken on swords. He himself with his own hand supplies swords and hands out spears and orders the men to disfigure with the steel the faces of their enemies. He himself pushes forward the line, drives onward the backs of his men, rouses the dawdlers with a blow from the butt of his spear, orders his men not to attack the ordinary soldiers and points the way to the Senate; he knows which is the lifeblood of the empire, which are the guts of the State, from where to attack Rome, in which place what remains of freedom in the world has taken her stand, ready to be struck. Senators commingled with knights and venerable bodies are pressed by the steel; they chop the Lepidi and they chop the Metelli and at the same time the Corvini and the famous Torquati, often leaders of the State and, you apart, Magnus, the loftiest of men. There, masking your face in a plebeian helmet and unnoticed by the enemy, what a sword did you hold, Brutus! O glory of the empire, O final hope of the Senate, the last name of a family so great across the centuries, do not rush too rashly through the midst of the enemy and do not bring on yourself ahead of time the doom of Philippi, you who are destined to die in your own Thessaly. [T]here you achieve nothing by aiming at Caesar's throat: he has not yet reached the citadel, and, by passing the summit of human law to which all things are subject, has not yet by his destiny earned so famous/noble a death. Let him live and, that he may fall a victim to Brutus, let him reign.

This is the worst moment of the war. The point at which Caesar's attack turns away from the foreign cavalry to assault the leaders of Rome is when the war becomes most truly civil. The narrator twice breaks into the narrative, and it is on these interventions that I wish to concentrate. While the first derives all its pathos from the evil of Caesar, the second may be interpreted as expressing equal frustration with the pious inertia of the Pompeians.

Pharsalia *7. 545–57: Refusal to Narrate*

Lucan's introduction is very striking, *Pharsalia* 7. 545–57:

> Ventum erat ad robur Magni mediasque catervas.
> Quod totos errore vago perfuderat agros
> constitit *hic* bellum, fortunaque Caesaris haesit.
> Non *illic* regum auxiliis collecta iuventus
> bella gerit ferrumque manus movere rogatae:
> *ille* locus fratres habuit, locus *ille* parentis.
> *Hic* furor, *hic* rabies, *hic* sunt tua crimina, *Caesar.*
> *Hanc* fuge, *mens*, partem belli tenebrisque relinque,
> nullaque tantorum discat *me vate* malorum,
> quam multum bellis liceat civilibus, aetas.
> A potius pereant lacrimae pereantque querellae:
> quidquid in *hac* acie gessisti, *Roma, tacebo.*
> *Hic* Caesar . . .

The fight had come to the strong-point of Magnus and to the middle of his troops. The war which had spread in random wandering all over the fields stopped here and Caesar's fortune was checked. Not there did young men wage war who had been collected from the auxiliaries of kings, but hands unbidden plied the steel: that place held brothers, that place fathers. Here is madness, here rage, here is your damnation, Caesar. O mind, flee this part of the war and leave it to the darkness, and let no age learn from my vatic recollection of such great evils how much is possible in civil wars. O rather let our tears be shed, our laments be uttered in vain: whatever you did in this battle, Rome, I shall not report. Here Caesar . . .

The situation described is just that which brought the soldiers to full consciousness of the horrors of civil war at 4. 169–79 and at 7. 463–9.[47] The peculiar problems posed by this for the narrator are underlined by Lucan's self-description at 7. 553 as a *vates*, that is, the Augustan national priest-prophet-poet. Chapter 1 has already discussed the connection of the term *vates* with patriotic verse (and implicitly its contingent problems for Lucan). The poet's attitude to his inheritance is illustrated not only by this passage but also by the final lines of the proem to the *Pharsalia*, 1. 63–6 and by the reaction to Caesar's visit to Troy at 9. 980–6. In each instance, the usage of the term is founded on the irony of gesturing at a tradition to which Lucan knows that he cannot belong. It is surprising how little Newman makes of this tension;[48] far more is to be gained from the analysis both of Lucan as *vates* and of the various surrogate *vates* appearing in the *Pharsalia* given by Masters and O'Higgins.[49] The latter in particular far outdoes her predecessors in showing how Lucan plays on the mixture of prospection and retrospection in the prophet-poet.[50] It is surely this

[47] For more on this, see Ch. 2, pp. 46–8. For the particular problem of facing one's relatives as *adversi*, see my discussion of Lucan's development of the traditional paradigm of the front and the back in Ch. 6, pp. 206–20.

[48] Newman (1967) 99–206 cf. (1986) 204–6 and esp. 219.

[49] O'Higgins (1988) cf. Masters (1992), esp. 138–9 and 205–6 and the surrounding discussions of Phemonoe and Erictho. Discussing this passage, in particular, both emphasize Lucan's simultaneous reluctance and urge to narrate. Thus, O'Higgins (1988) 215 compares Lucan at 7. 552–5 to Apollo and Phemonoe in Book 5, and observes that 'A similar abhorrence of the "nefas" of civil war is detectable in Lucan. If Apollo hesitates to create a world so alien to the gods, Lucan—to an extent—shrinks from recreating it. Although the impulse to write is stronger, there is evident a counter-impulse to maintain a decent silence'. O'Higgins then (p. 216) talks of him proceeding 'in spite of his scruples', despite knowing that as *vates* he will win an 'invidious distinction'. Masters (1992) 148 talks of the split in Lucan's poetic persona, the will to silence represented by Phemonoe, the 'grisly relish and Silver Latin exuberance' by her fellow *vates*, Erictho. 'Infandum, regina, iubes renovare dolorem' is, of course, a chat-up line.

[50] Moore (1921), esp. 142–51, and Dick (1963) 46–9 offer little more than brief catalogues of instances.

concept of telling a story from the past in order to set a prescription for the future which fuels Lucan's constant dialectic with the Augustan poets as *vates*. At this of all moments in Lucan's epic, the collapse of their national, patriotic role is most keenly felt.[51]

Lucan's use of apostrophe is intense and complex.[52] He addresses *Caesar*, *mens*, and *Roma*, all as characters or composers of literature, always with a retrospective stance, never himself intervening as a character in the action. As at 7. 418, the address to *Roma* is effectively an address to the soldiers on the battlefield, refusing to recall what she/they did at Pharsalus. More complicated is the sentence in which Lucan addresses first Caesar and then his own mind. This sentence is dense with *hic*-form deictics. These contrast with the *illic . . ./ ille . . . ille* of the previous sentence, and serve to show how the objective, distanced 'there' suddenly becomes an immediately present 'here' for the poet. The first impression given by the combination of *hic* deixis with address to Caesar is that the narrator has intervened as a character on the field of battle, but it is soon revealed that *hanc . . . partem belli* is, so to speak, a 'part of the narrative of war'. The address to Caesar as a character is similar to Vergil's address to Nisus and Euryalus at *Aeneid* 9. 446–9 or to Lausus at 10. 791–3, but while the promise of fame seems a favour happily granted by Vergil to his characters, Caesar forces his way into Lucan's Roman songs, and later, when Lucan promises his villain poetic immortality, the offer can be taken as a menace as well as a boon (*Pharsalia*, 9. 980–6).

Dear Brutus: Pharsalia *7. 586–96*

The poet's reluctance to narrate is, of course, a feint. Lines 7. 557–85 take us through a long description of the actions of Caesar, conducted as a grotesque parody of the conduct of the archetypal 'good general'.

[51] O'Higgins (1988) 211 n. 11 notes that 'Newman . . . has shown how "vates" was, in part, a political concept for the Augustan poets. There is a political element in Lucan's understanding of his role also', but then abandons the point in favour of some more general reflections on Lucan's politics. Johnson (1987) 98–9 has something to say on the point, but does not stray into specifics. Gagliardi (1970) ch. 5, 'Aspetti della Nuova Tecnica Epica e Letteraria', 104–39 is perhaps the best discussion of the political aspect of the *vates*.

[52] A significant factor is that noted by Gagliardi (1975) ad loc., namely that apostrophe to abstracts such as *mens* is an innovation which Lucan has drawn from tragedy, e.g. Eur. *Heracl.* 433 (with Wilkins (1993) ad loc.) and *Bacch.* 1287. This is thus 'un altro elemento significativo . . . della trasformazione dell'epica tradizionale in Lucano dietro la spinta della nuova vocazione drammatica a cui è portato dalla storia'. The comparison of Lucan's narrative voice to a tragic chorus is an important element in the tradition of likening him to a tragic historian discussed in Ch. 1.

At 7. 578–85, much stress is placed on the cutting-down of the representatives of the great aristocratic families, and this then introduces the address to Brutus at 7. 586–96, which closes the scene. This extended apostrophe places the whole scene in a most interesting light and it is on this section that analysis will be concentrated:

> Illic plebeia contectus casside voltus
> ignotusque hosti quod ferrum, Brute, tenebas!
> O decus imperii, spes o suprema senatus,
> extremum tanti generis per saecula nomen,
> ne rue per medios nimium temerarius hostis,
> nec tibi fatales admoveris ante Philippos,
> Thessalia periture tua. Nil proficis istic
> Caesaris intentus iugulo: nondum attigit arcem,
> iuris et humani columen, quo cuncta premuntur,
> egressus meruit fatis tam nobile letum.
> Vivat et, ut Bruti procumbat victima, regnet.

There, masking your face in a plebeian helmet and unnoticed by the enemy, what a sword did you hold, Brutus! O glory of the empire, O final hope of the Senate, the last name of a family so great across the centuries, do not rush too rashly through the midst of the enemy and do not bring on yourself ahead of time the doom of Philippi, you who are destined to die in your own Thessaly. [T]here you achieve nothing by aiming at Caesar's throat: he has not yet reached the citadel, and, by passing the summit of human law to which all things are subject, has not yet by his destiny earned so famous/noble a death. Let him live and, that he may fall a victim to Brutus, let him reign.

Caesar is depicted at 7. 557–81 as the great immoralist, the one who 'ordered them to mangle the faces of the enemy with their steel' (*adversosque iubet ferro confundere voltus*). He is also a figure of immense activity, always on the move, always driving men forward. As Aeneas becomes like Aegaeon at *Aeneid* 10. 565–70, so here Caesar is like Bellona and Mars (*Pharsalia* 7. 567–71). At 7. 578, Caesar urges his men to turn their destructive energy on the senators. The massacre of the great names of Rome must call forth particular lament, for with them dies freedom, *Pharsalia* 7. 579–85:

> Scit, cruor imperii qui sit, quae viscera rerum,
> unde petat Romam, libertas ultima mundi
> quo steterit ferię̨nda loco. Permixta secundo
> ordine nobilitas venerandaque corpora ferro
> urguentur; caedunt Lepidos caeduntque Metellos
> Corvinosque simul Torquataque nomina, rerum
> saepe duces summosque hominum te, Magne, remoto.

He knows which is the lifeblood of the empire, which are the guts of the State, from where to attack Rome, in which place what remains of freedom on the earth has taken her stand, ready to be struck. Senators commingled with knights and venerable bodies are pressed by the steel; they chop the Lepidi and they chop the Metelli and at the same time the Corvini and the famous Torquati, often leaders of the State and, you apart, Magnus, the loftiest of men.

This scene effectively excludes the senators from the accusation of *timor* at 7. 644. This need not have been the case. It has been noted above that 7. 575 records Caesar's order to his men to 'mangle the faces of the enemy with their steel' (*adversos . . . confundere voltus*). This is Lucan's version of Caesar's famous stratagem to combat the aristocratic *jeunesse dorée* who had followed Pompey, by exploiting their reluctance to receive the scars of which men would be proud.[53] This sounds very like the anti-aristocratic, Marian rhetoric that later will be identified as typical of Caesar in my discussion of the Caesarian centurion.[54] Yet Lucan does not reproduce the slur, insists that the aristocrats did not run.

If this scene excludes the senators from accusations of cowardice, it does not spare them the frustration often shown at the Pompeians' propensity for moral victories. The senators do not run, but they do not fight either. Rather, the frenzied mobility of Caesar is contrasted with the saintly inaction of the Pompeians, a vice which they share with or derive from their general. The contrast between the constant movement of Caesar and the inertia of Pompey is first brought out at *Pharsalia* 1. 135–57 in the comparison of the former to lightning, the latter to an ancient oak tree,[55] and there is surely an allusion to this fatal weakness of the Pompeian side when, at the start of this passage, Lucan announces that 'The fight had come to the strong-point of Magnus' (*Ventum erat ad robur Magni*). Caesar's Commentaries blame Pompey for ordering his men to stand and await the attack of the Caesarians at Pharsalus,[56] and the fatal passivity of the Pompeians has already been evoked at *Pharsalia* 7. 501–3:

Civilia bella
una acies patitur, gerit altera; frigidus inde
stat gladius, calet omne nocens a Caesare ferrum.

[53] Plut. *Caes.* 45. 1–3, *Pomp.* 71. 4–5; Appian *B. Civ.* 2. 76. 318; Flor. *Epit.* 2. 13. 50; Frontin. *Str.* 4. 7. 32; Polyaenus, 8. 23. 25; Oros., 6. 15. 26.

[54] See Ch. 6, pp. 194–206 and 228–31.

[55] See Rosner-Siegel (1983).

[56] See Caes. *B. Civ.* 3. 92 and cf. Plut. *Caes.* 44. 4, Plut. *Pomp.* 69. 4–5, and App. *B. Civ.* 2. 79. 33, who states that Caesar also voiced this criticism in his letters.

One side suffers civil war, the other wages it; on one side the sword stands cold on Caesar's side every guilty weapon is hot.[57]

The combination of the arboreal and the culpably passive is well evoked at 7. 580–5 with *steterit*,[58] *ferienda*,[59] and *caedunt*,[60] and the theme is rounded off at 7. 597–8, when:

> Iacet *aggere* magno
> patricium campis non mixta plebe cadaver.

The patrician corpses lie in a huge mound on the fields, unadulterated with the common soldiers.[61]

Lucan may loathe civil war, but he also yearns for someone, even a Sulla, with the spirit to resist Caesar.[62] It is in this context that the apostrophe to Brutus gains its special bite.

[57] Cf. Luc. 7. 485–7 and 533.

[58] At Luc. 1. 135, the simile of Pompey as oak tree begins famously 'Stat magni nominis umbra'. At 7. 502–3, Lucan says of the Pompeians 'frigidus inde | stat gladius'.

[59] Used relatively rarely of chopping a tree, but cf. Columella, *Arb.* 10. 3, Claud. *De Rapt. Proserp.* 3. 378, and particularly Luc. 3. 430, where the soldiers are fearful for the consequences 'si robora sacra ferirent'.

[60] Constantly used of chopping. See *TLL* iii. 56 A. For *caedere* in Lucan *re* trees, see 2. 670, 3. 413, 3. 450, 9. 332. Further, at 2. 172 and 6. 584, *caedere* vel. sim. is used of humans now described as *truncus*. Masters (1992) 27 n. 40 notes the argument that Caesar's cutting-down of the sacred grove in Book 3 of the *Pharsalia* is symbolic of his defeat of Pompey, while 29 n. 44 notes of 3. 450 that 'caesi nemoris' 'plays on the name "Caesar"'. One might add that Ovid uses the term *incaeduus* to describe sacred groves at *Fast.* 1. 243 and 2. 435–6 and at *Am.* 3. 1. 1, while *Met.* 2. 418 talks of 'nemus, quod nulla ceciderat aetas', *Met.* 8. 329 of the 'silva' 'quam nulla ceciderat aetas', cf. *Met.* 8. 769, 'repetitaque robora caedit'. The destruction of the sacred grove in Lucan is discussed in Phillips (1968) and in Dyson (1970). Of the two parallels attested, Dyson's contemporary historical parallel has been less well received than Phillips's comparison with Erysichthon in Ov. *Met.* 8. However, the manner in which Caesar dares 'primus' to wield the axe and fell an oak suggests a blasphemous perversion of the famed leadership-skills of Alexander. I would therefore like to suggest a third source in the story of Alexander at Aornus. Curt. 8. 11. 8 reads: 'ipse primus truncam arborem iecit, clamorque exercitus, index alacritatis, secutus est, nullo detrectante munus quod rex occupavit'. In support of this parallel, one might note that Curt. 8. 9. 34 underlines the sacred status of trees among the Indians ('Deos putant quidquid colere coeperunt, arbores maxime, quas violare capital est'). Finally, if it is protested that Curtius is probably subsequent to Lucan and therefore imitating the Caesar of the *Pharsalia*, one might respond that Alexander is also depicted as leading the way at Arr. *Anab.* 4. 29. 7 (esp. καὶ αὐτὸς ἐχώννυεν), allowing us to speculate that the claim is made earlier still in the Alexander tradition. For another instance of this 'topos' in Curt., see 5. 6. 14 for Alexander leading his men across the ice. Very similar is Sil. *Pun.* 1. 242–4 on Hannibal: 'primus sumpsisse laborem, | primus iter carpsisse pedes partemque subire, | si valli festinet opus'. Spaltenstein (1986–90) ad loc. discusses the topos. Examples include Luc. 9. 394–5 and 618; Sil. *Pun.* 3. 516, 4. 216–19, 4. 512–15, 8. 551–5; Livy 10. 41. 4 and 21. 4. 8; Tac. *Hist.* 2. 5. 1; Suet. *Jul.* 57. 2; Dio Cass. 69. 9. 3; and, for the topos reversed, Just. *Epit.* 2. 10. 23.

[61] For the importance of the Caesarian *agger* in Lucan, see Masters (1992) 29–34.

[62] For the wish that Pompey should act as Sulla, see Luc. 6. 299–313.

The notion suggested by 7. 545–56 of Lucan wrestling with the composition of the *Pharsalia* and the narration of the battle, thus addressing his characters as literary figures, is enhanced by the address to Brutus. It is true that the 'narrator as character' appears to intervene on the battlefield and urge a course of action on Brutus, but any sense of immediacy is disrupted by a glaring anachronism the impact of which is heightened by Lucan's cruel intertextual allusion.

The narrative of 7. 557–85 does not endeavour to create immediacy. It is conducted throughout in the present historic but only one apostrophe (7. 585, *Magne*) appears and no attempt is made to set up a vivid present or to depict a possible turning-point. When Lucan first addresses Brutus, he assiduously maintains temporal separation by simply asking him what he was doing then:

> Illic plebeia contectus casside voltus
> ignotusque hosti quod ferrum, Brute, tenebas!

There, masking your face in a plebeian helmet and unnoticed by the enemy, what a sword did you hold, Brutus!

If the sentence is punctuated with an exclamation mark at the end, the effect approximates to the sarcastic 'What a brave man you were!' If it is punctuated with a question mark, there emerges the probing 'What exactly were you doing?'[63] For there is an obvious question as to why Brutus, amidst the nobles and himself 'the last name of a family so great across the centuries' (*extremum tanti generis per saecula nomen*), should be skulking in a plebeian helmet.[64] Evidently, Brutus here stands as a representative of the inadequacies of the aristocrats at Pharsalus. This is then brought out in the imperative of the 'narrator as character'. After two lines of laudatory epithets, Lucan then urges his 'hero':

> Ne rue per medios nimium temerarius hostis,
> nec tibi fatales admoveris ante Philippos,
> Thessalia periture tua.

Do not rush too rashly through the midst of the enemy and do not bring on

[63] It is striking that Duff (1928) prints the Latin text with an exclamation mark and the English translation with a question mark.

[64] Another similarity between the arboreal senators and Pompey is that they are now merely *nomina*. Apart from Brutus, Caesar also cuts down the 'Torquata . . . nomina'. Pompey, we recall, 1. 135, 'Stat magni nominis umbra'. For Brutus in plebeian armour, cf. Masters (1994) n. 65.

yourself ahead of time the doom of Philippi, you who are destined to die in your own Thessaly.

The first aspect of this sentence which one notes is that it functions in the same way as the reference to Cassius discussed above: in the very sentence in which the narrator appears as a character on the field of battle, the reference to information available only to one living after the battle, that is to Philippi, reverses the illusion. This architectonic linking of temporalities and perspectives should now be familiar. The second aspect is that the imperative from 'narrator as character' to 'character' alludes to the repeated Vergilian formula in which the noble warrior rushes into the middle of the enemy *moriturus* or *periturus*, that is, essentially, 'intending to die'.[65] This action, which takes on a stylized religious function in the *devotio* of the Decii in Livy, is fundamentally a response to the political pressure on the aristocratic general to show personal *virtus* in the line of battle when his troops are in retreat or facing defeat.[66] It is thus peculiarly appropriate that Brutus should be the focus of one of its central appearances in the *Pharsalia*. On the other hand, the formula is here used with a sarcastic edge to it. For, *periture* here means 'destined to die' or 'later to die', not 'intending to die'.[67] Lucan plays cruelly on the question: 'Brutus, what did you do in the war?' This is easy to see when we consider the particular intertextual referent invoked by Lucan. This is the address of Aeneas to Lausus at *Aeneid* 10. 811–12:

> 'Quo moriture ruis maioraque viribus audes?
> Fallit te incautum pietas tua.'

'Why do you rush to your death, why do you dare deeds too great for your strength? Your sense of responsibility betrays you in your heedlessness.'

The reading of *Pharsalia* 7. 385–459 offered above showed how

[65] This formula is investigated in Ch. 4 and in Leigh (1993). The anthropological and political assertions which I now make are all based on the evidence collected in these two pieces.

[66] See Leigh (1993) 98–103 and Ch. 4, pp. 128–34.

[67] Gagliardi (1975) ad loc. is clearly confused by the ambiguity, first translating 'periture' as 'esponendoti a morte certa', then suggesting that the future participle actually has a 'funzione predicativa'. *Periturus* and *moriturus* mean doomed to die at Luc. 2. 74, 3. 211, 3. 665, 4. 748, 4. 776, 6. 788, 7. 329, 7. 730, 8. 692, 9. 318, 9. 611 but the distinction between fate and intention is blurred in the soliloquy of Domitius at 2. 523–5 'in medios belli non ire furores | iam dudum *moriture* paras? *Rue* certus et omnes | lucis rumpe moras et Caesaris effuge munus', while the sense of 'intending to die' is clear at 4. 277, for which cf. 4. 271–2, 'ut effuso Caesar decurrere passu | vidit et ad certam *devoto*s tendere mortem'.

Lucan extracted effects from the narrator speaking lines which in Vergil are left to a character, Anchises. Here, the effect is no less radical. Where Aeneas upbraided Lausus for his death-rush (*moriture ruis*)—the future participle indicating perhaps a mixture of intent and inevitable consequences—and called the loyal youth 'heedless' (*incautus*), now Lucan urges Brutus not to rush through the enemy and calls him 'too rash' (*nimium temerarius*). Yet the use of the future participle *periture* and the reference to Philippi emphasize that there was never any question of Brutus acting with foolish bravery at Pharsalus, and the great aristocrat hiding in a plebeian helmet hardly seems a figure of headstrong heroism and loyalty.[68] When the narrator observes that Caesar has not yet earned 'so famous / noble a death' (*tam nobile letum*), one is reminded also of Brutus' failure to die like the aristocrat that he is.[69] *Pharsalia* 7. 596, 'Let him live and, that he may fall a victim to Brutus, let him reign' (*Vivat et, ut Bruti procumbat victima, regnet*), it is true, draws from the episode a form of long-term consolation in the assassination of Caesar which emerges throughout the poem, but this instance is charged with further, more troubling implications.[70] The aim of the next chapter is to investigate how Lucan approaches these implications, the suggestion of want of spirit and desertion, in the leader of the Republican cause, Pompey.

[68] For another example of the 'narrator as character' quoting Vergil while urging a course of action on his characters, see Conte (1974) at Luc. 6. 196–201. The effect of the intertextuality is again to give the 'involved' imperative a sarcastic distance.

[69] When we consider the failure of Brutus' aristocratic valour, it is useful to bear in mind the intervening imitation of Vergil in the address of the narrator to the Fabii at Ov. *Fast.* 2. 225–6: 'Quo ruitis, generosa domus? Male creditis hosti! | Simplex nobilitas, perfida tela cave!' The episode of the Fabii seems to have exercised some hold over Lucan's imagination, for the description of the swollen Cremera and the comparison of the Fabii to Libyan lions at *Fast.* 2. 205–13 is highly reminiscent of Luc. 1. 185 and 213–19 on the swollen Rubicon and of 1. 205–12 for Caesar as a suicidal Libyan lion.

[70] It is in these terms that Ahl (1976) 45–6 and Feeney (1991) 282 interpret the apostrophe. For Ahl, it is the first instance of the 'secretive confidence' increasingly often displayed by Lucan in 8–10; Feeney emphasizes 'fatales' and sees Lucan recovering faith in destiny. For other anticipations of Brutus' role in the assassination of Caesar, see Luc. 5. 206–8, 6. 791–2, 10. 338–44. None of these has anything to equate to the ironies of 'periture'.

4
Pompey—The View from the Hill

The dissenting voice with which Lucan narrates the *Pharsalia* emphasizes the degree of its engagement by contrasting itself with others and deploring their inaction. Frequently the contrasting figure of disengagement is represented as simply watching the action, as a spectator. When that spectator is clearly the Jupiter of the Augustan poets, the refusal to intervene is testimony not just to a generalized apathy but actually to a culpable complicity with the politics of the regime Lucan detests. These are the principal conclusions to be drawn from the previous two chapters. As the three chapters that follow examine the enthusiasm of Caesar's army to transform the civil wars into a show to be performed for the sake of their general, the ideological significance of spectacle will become ever more apparent. Meanwhile the mentality to be examined in this chapter stands at a revealing point between the poles that have been established: a Republican general who can bear neither to watch a civil war nor to engage, and whose perspective on the civil war betrays his underlying bad faith; a Republican narrator whose instinct to praise that general can never be carried through with complete conviction.

POMPEY AND THE SPECTACLE OF CIVIL WAR

The passage which provides the focus for this chapter is *Pharsalia* 7. 647–711. Here Lucan introduces a narrative element apparently unique in the extant accounts of Pharsalus. By placing Pompey on a raised point on the battlefield, he is able to reproduce the dire *imago* of battle through the eyes of the general, to recount his motives and actions as he departs from Pharsalus. Having established this perspective, he concludes with an extended apostrophe delivered from the position almost of one by Pompey's side:

> Iam Magnus transisse deos Romanaque fata
> senserat infelix, tota vix clade coactus

fortunam damnare suam. Stetit aggere campi,
eminus unde omnis sparsas per Thessala rura
aspiceret clades, quae bello obstante latebant.
Tot telis sua fata peti, tot corpora fusa
ac se tam multo pereuntem sanguine vidit.
Nec, sicut mos est miseris, trahere omnia secum
mersa iuvat gentesque suae miscere ruinae:
ut Latiae post se vivat pars maxima turbae,
sustinuit dignos etiamnunc credere votis
caelicolas, vovitque, sui solacia casus.
'Parcite,' ait 'superi, cunctas prosternere gentes.
Stante potest mundo Romaque superstite Magnus
esse miser. Si plura iuvant mea volnera, coniunx
est mihi, sunt nati: dedimus tot pignora fatis.
Civiline parum est bello, si meque meosque
obruit? Exiguae clades sumus orbe remoto?
Omnia quid laceras? Quid perdere cuncta laboras?
Iam nihil est, Fortuna, meum.' Sic fatur et arma
signaque et adflictas omni iam parte catervas
circumit et revocat matura in fata ruentis
seque negat tanti. Nec derat robur in enses
ire duci iuguloque pati vel pectore letum.
Sed timuit, strato miles ne corpore Magni
non fugeret, supraque ducem procumberet orbis;
Caesaris aut oculis voluit subducere mortem.
Nequiquam, infelix: socero spectare volenti
praestandum est ubicumque caput. Sed tu quoque, coniunx,
causa fugae voltusque tui fatisque negatum
parte absente mori. Tum Magnum concitus aufert
a bello sonipes non tergo tela paventem
ingentisque animos extrema in fata ferentem.
Non gemitus, non fletus erat, salvaque verendus
maiestate dolor, qualem te, Magne, decebat
Romanis praestare malis. Non inpare voltu
aspicis Emathiam: nec te videre superbum
prospera bellorum nec fractum adversa videbunt;
quamque fuit laeto per tres infida triumphos
tam misero Fortuna minor. Iam pondere fati
deposito securus abis; nunc tempora laeta
respexisse vacat, spes numquam inplenda recessit;
quid fueris nunc scire licet. Fuge proelia dira
ac testare deos nullum, qui perstet in armis,
iam tibi, Magne, mori. Ceu flebilis Africa damnis

et ceu Munda nocens Pharioque a gurgite clades,
sic et Thessalicae post te pars maxima pugnae
non iam Pompei nomen populare per orbem
nec studium belli, sed par quod semper habemus,
libertas et Caesar, erit; teque inde fugato
ostendit moriens sibi se pugnasse senatus.
Nonne iuvat pulsum bellis cessisse nec istud
perspectasse nefas? Spumantes caede catervas
respice, turbatos incursu sanguinis amnes,
et soceri miserere tui. Quo pectore Romam
intrabit factus campis felicior istis?
Quidquid in ignotis solus regionibus exul,
quidquid sub Phario positus patiere tyranno,
crede deis, longo fatorum crede favori,
vincere peius erat. Prohibe lamenta sonare,
flere veta populos, lacrimas luctusque remitte.
Tam mala Pompei quam prospera mundus adoret.
Aspice securus voltu non supplice reges,
aspice possessas urbes donataque regna,
Aegypton Libyamque, et terras elige morti.

By now the unhappy Magnus had sensed that the gods and the destiny of Rome had crossed over to the enemy, though even the totality of the slaughter scarce could force him to despair of his fortune. He stood on a mound on the field from where far off he could see the slaughter scattered over the countryside of Thessaly, which lay invisible with war to block the view. He saw his life sought by so many weapons, so many bodies laid out and himself dying in so much blood. Yet he did not, as is the habit of the wretched, wish to drag everything down to destruction with him and to involve nations in his own ruin: he bore even now to consider the gods worthy of his worship and prayed, as solace for his fortune, that the greatest part of the Latin band might live after him. 'Hold back, O gods', he said, 'from laying every nation low. Though the world endure and Rome stay alive, Magnus can be wretched. If you wish to wound me further, I have a wife, I have sons; I have given so many hostages to the fates. Is it not enough for the civil war if it crushes me and my family? If the world is not included are we a tiny disaster? Why do you tear everything? Why do you endeavour to destroy everything? Fortune, I have nothing left of my own.' Thus he spoke and he went round the army and the standards and the troops beaten on every side and called them back as they rushed to a ready death and denied that he was worth so much. Nor did the general lack the courage to enter the fight and meet death with a blow to the throat or the breast; but he feared lest, when the body of Magnus had been laid low, the soldiers should not flee and the whole world fall over the general; or rather he wanted to remove his death from Caesar's eyes. In vain, unhappy man: your head must be presented to your father-in-law who desires to look wherever it may be. Yet you too, wife, are a cause of his flight, you and your face and the dictate of fate that he should not die with a part of him missing. Then a spurred steed carried Magnus away from battle unafraid of a spear in his back and bearing his great spirit to its final destiny. There was no groaning, no weeping, and a noble grief which preserved dignity, the sort which it was fitting for you, Magnus, to offer to the ills of Rome. You look on Emathia with an unchanged expression: success in war did not see you arrogant, nor will defeat see you broken; and just as faithless Fortune was less than you through your happy days of the three triumphs, so she is when you are wretched. Now, laying aside the burden of destiny, you go away unconcerned; now there is room to look back on the happy times; ambition fated never to be satisfied has retreated; now it is possible to know what you were. Flee the dire battle, Magnus, and take the gods as your witness that no man who stays to fight any longer dies for you. Like Africa lamentable for its losses and like guilty Munda and the slaughter by the stream of the Nile, so too the greatest part of the fight in Thessaly is no longer about the popularity and fame of Pompey throughout the world or about zeal for war, but rather the pair will be that which ever we have: Freedom and Caesar. With you put to flight, the senate by dying shows that it fought for itself.

Is it not pleasing to have been defeated and quit the battle and not watched that horror through to the end? Look back at the regiments foaming with gore, the rivers disturbed with the flow of blood, and feel sorry for your father-in-law. With what sentiments will he enter Rome when made the more fortunate by those fields? Whatever you endure as a lonely exile in unknown lands, whatever you endure at the mercy of the tyrant of Egypt, have faith in the gods, have faith in the enduring favour of destiny: it was worse to conquer. Let not the lamentation sound, forbid the peoples to weep, call off the tears and the mourning. Let the world revere the ill fortune of Pompey no less than the good. Look on kings without concern, with an expression which asks no favour, look on the cities you captured and the kingdoms you granted, on Egypt and on Libya, and choose a land for your death.

This representation of the feelings of Pompey as he looks on the battle of Pharsalus is as calculated and as well prepared as it is innovative. As early as *Pharsalia* 5. 747–9, the general himself, aware like Homer's Hector of the doom which he faces, seeks to remove his wife Cornelia from Thessaly to the greater safety of Lesbos and urges:

> 'Satis est audisse pericula Magni;
> meque tuus decepit amor, civilia bella
> si *spectare* potes.'

'It is enough to have heard of the perils which Magnus faces; and your love has deceived me if you can look on civil wars.'

When Pharsalus finally comes, Cornelia is spared the pain of watching a civil war, her husband is not. Rather, Pompey's words to Cornelia come back to him as his experience of the battle and the drastic reversal of his fortune is evoked through the description of two framing visions, each one accompanied by a telling apostrophe from the narrator. The first of these visions has some bearing on the problem of ἐνάργεια with which this study began, 7. 7–12:

> At nox felicis Magno pars ultima vitae
> sollicitos vana decepit imagine somnos.
> Nam Pompeiani *visus sibi* sede theatri
> innumeram effigiem Romanae *cernere* plebis
> attollique suum laetis ad sidera nomen
> vocibus et plausu cuneos certare sonantes.

Yet the night, the last part of happy life for Magnus, beguiled his troubled sleep with an empty vision. For he seemed to himself, from his seat in the Theatre of Pompey, to see the innumerable mass of the Roman plebs, his name being raised to the stars in jubilant cries and the resounding rows vying with each other in applause.[1]

Lucan's Pompey is a showman, never happier than when amidst the adoring audience of his own theatre at Rome.[2] On the eve of the battle he conjures up a show for himself, finding solace amidst present ills by escaping to the happy memory of his past. Yet he himself has acknowledged to Cornelia that the civil wars are preparing a quite different show for them and one which they will not have the stomach to watch. It is this show, the vision which the day to come will inflict, which is anticipated in the narrator's apostrophe to the guards at 7. 24–7:

> Ne rumpite somnos,
> castrorum vigiles, nullas tuba verberet aures.
> Crastina dira quies et *imagine maesta diurna*
> undique funestas acies feret, undique bellum.

Break not his sleep, guards of the camp, let not the trumpet strike any man's ears. The next day's sleep, dire and woeful with the image of the day's events, from all sides will bring murderous battle-lines, from all sides war.

[1] Cf. Ch. 1 for Quint. *Inst.* 6. 2. 29 and the advice to the orator to generate ἐνάργεια by exploiting his natural tendency to day-dream. Lucan confirms the relationship between the concepts when he expresses the vividness of Pompey's dream through the now familiar terms of 'seeming to see'.

[2] Luc. 1. 131–3, 'famaeque petitor | multa dare in volgus, totus popularibus auris | inpelli plausuque sui gaudere theatri'. For the famous theatre built by Pompey in Rome and dedicated in 55 BC, see Greenhalgh (1981) 54–61 and 278.

In the end, Lucan does not ascribe a second dream to Pompey. Instead, it is part of the elaborate vengeance of the defeated that that dream should be the one which punishes the victorious Caesarians at 7. 760–86. As for Pompey, the reader is left to infer the quality of his dreams from the waking nightmare shared with him in the passage above. The crucial sentiment is surely that expressed in the address to the general at 7. 698–9, when the Pompey fleeing is figured as a disgusted, horrified spectator:

> Nonne iuvat pulsum bellis cessisse nec istud
> perspectasse nefas?

Is it not pleasing to have been defeated and quit the battle and not watched that horror through to the end?

At 7. 213, Lucan has asserted his ambition to make the readers of the future cheer for Pompey. The combination of sympathetic and empathetic engagement apparent throughout 7. 647–711 and particularly in the two lines quoted above ought to contribute to this. It is not certain, however, that it does: sympathetic apostrophe in Lucan is rarely less than double-edged, empathy can give just too much access to someone's mind, can raise more problems than it puts to rest. The argument which follows is designed to expose just this sort of ambivalence in Lucan's account. At all stages, that which is deemed inadequate in Pompey can be connected directly to his role as a spectator.

POMPEY, CAMILLUS, AND THE VIEW FROM THE HILL

Although Lucan's interventions in the Pharsalus narrative of Book 7 identify him with the losing side, he repeatedly gives vent to his frustration with a number of those individuals and groups he might be expected to endorse. If the flight of Pompey's barbarian cohorts is most explicitly marked as responsible for the defeat, a degree of frustration with the virtuous passivity of the senators can also be detected in Lucan's double-edged address to Brutus. It is therefore almost inevitable that, however much one part of Lucan can celebrate the philosophical dignity of Pompey's retreat from ambition, that other part which can never give up the fight should be troubled by a commander who turns his back on the battle and rides away.

The situation faced by Lucan's Pompey and the quality of his response merit comparison with a Livian paradigm. This choice is not arbitrary, for Livy was almost certainly Lucan's main historical referent and the basic narrative formula apparent here recurs often in the course of Livy's work: an experienced general who wisely delays engagement with the enemy but who is driven to precipitate and often disastrous action by the impatience of his subordinates or of the common soldiers. In particular, the complaint of the foreign kings at Lucan 7. 57 that the wars are being dragged out (*bella trahi*) is one familiar to any reader of Livy.[3]

If the experiences of Pompey recall in outline those of a number of different Livian generals, in detail they are closest to those of the aging Camillus at Satricum in Book 6. At 6. 23. 1, Livy emphasizes that Camillus alone resisted an immediate battle (*nec praesentis dimicationis fortunam ulla res praeterquam unius viri consilium atque imperium morabatur*) and that he sought the chance to compensate for want of strength by the strategy of prolonging the war (*trahendo bello*). Just as Lucan's Pompey is challenged by the Eastern kings and by Cicero, so here the strategy of Camillus is attacked by the young military tribune, L. Furius Medullinus. Where the parallel becomes truly striking, however, is in the conduct of Camillus when he realizes that he cannot thwart his colleague, 6. 23. 10–12:

Dis bene iuvantibus ageret quod e re publica duceret: aetati suae se veniam eam petere, ne in prima acie esset. Quae senis munia in bello sint, iis se non defuturum: id a dis immortalibus precari ne qui casus suum consilium laudabile efficiat. Nec ab hominibus salutaris sententia nec a dis tam piae preces auditae sunt. Primam aciem auctor pugnae instruit, subsidia Camillus firmat validamque stationem pro castris opponit; *ipse edito loco spectator intentus in eventum alieni consilii constitit.*

[He said] Let him do with the aid of the gods what he considered to be in the interests of the State: he asked them to excuse him, old as he was, from fighting in the front line; those military tasks appropriate to an old man he would not shun. This he prayed the immortal gods, that no event should render his plan praiseworthy. But his salutary counsel was ignored by the men and his so pious prayers by the gods. The man responsible for the fight drew up the front lines,

[3] Cf. Livy, 7. 12. 10–14, where the general who 'bellum trahebat' is mocked as 'eximium imperatorem, unicum ducem'. At Livy, 4. 18. 1–2, Lars Tolumnius cannot 'bellum trahere' because of the impatience at being held away from home; at Livy, 5. 10. 7 and 5. 11. 8 popular politicians accuse the patricians of *bellum trahere* in order to prevent unwelcome agitation and legislation at home. Luc. 7. 296–7, where the frantically energetic Caesar pleads 'veniam date bella trahenti: | spe trepido', gains all its impact from the contrast with the Livian typology.

Camillus strengthened the supports and set out a strong garrison before the camp; *he himself took his place on a raised ground whence he could watch intently for the results of the other man's plan.*

The point is that at a crucial moment in the battle, both Pompey and Camillus find themselves presented with the unwelcome spectacle of their own vindication. A recurring concern in this chapter will be the disturbing impact on the reader of the access granted to Pompey's reflections at this point, the unwelcome implications of his perspective. In this way, the view from the hill is a crucial innovation. For now, another factor is of the essence: the parallel Camillus story presents the reader with an alternative to the subsequent conduct of Pompey and one which that part of Lucan that yearns to fight on would find it much easier to endorse, Livy 6. 24. 4–7:

Iam non recipiebat se Romanus miles sed immemor recentis ferociae veterisque decoris terga passim dabat atque effuso cursu castra repetebat, cum Camillus subiectus ab circumstantibus in equum et raptim subsidiis oppositis 'Haec est' inquit, 'milites, pugna, quam poposcitis? Quis homo, quis deus est, quem accusare possitis? Vestra illa temeritas, vestra ignavia haec est. Secuti alium ducem sequimini nunc Camillum et quod ductu meo soletis vincite. *Quid vallum et castra spectatis*? Neminem vestrum illa nisi victorem receptura sunt.' Pudor primo tenuit effusos; inde, ut circumagi signa obvertique aciem viderunt in hostem, et *dux, praeterquam quod tot insignis triumphis, etiam aetate venerabilis inter prima signa ubi plurimus labor periculumque erat se offerebat,* increpare singuli se quisque et alios, et adhortatio in vicem totam alacri clamore pervasit aciem.

No longer were the Roman soldiers retreating in order but, forgetful of their recent ferocity and of their valour of old, were fleeing in every direction and heading back for the camp in swift flight, when Camillus, mounted on his horse by his attendants and quickly throwing the supporting troops into the fight, said, 'Soldiers, is this the fight you asked for? Which man, which god can you accuse? Yours then was the rashness, yours now is the cowardice. You have followed another general, follow now Camillus and, as you are accustomed when I am your leader, win. Why do you look at the rampart and the camp? They will receive none of you save who has won.' Shame first checked their flight; then, when they saw the standards moving round and the battle-line turning to face the enemy, and, when the general, not just glorious for his so many triumphs but also venerable for his years, presented himself amidst the foremost standards and where the toil and the risk were the greatest, each man urged on himself and the rest, and the eager cry of mutual exhortation spread through the whole army.

Neither Camillus nor Pompey can endure the spectacle of defeat even of a defeat foreseen, the coming of which vindicates each man's military judgement. Yet their responses are diametrically opposed while each mounts his steed, Camillus does so in order to charge the line, Pompey in order to flee. Without a doubt, it is the latter decision which is the more troubling. For, if Lucan is associated with the demand that passive spectatorship be transformed into active engagement, he would surely find it much less difficult unconditionally to heroize Camillus than Pompey.

Camillus is only one instance of the paradigmatic response of a general to imminent or actual defeat. While his example demonstrates the value of measuring Lucan's Pompey against a model in Livy, the pages which follow consider a succession of figures all of whom relate broadly to a further Livian paradigm which has often been thought of as relevant to Lucan's Pompey: the *devotus*.[4] If this investigation takes us temporarily some way from the view from the hill, its purpose is to establish conceptually what is so peculiar not just in Pompey's decision to flee but also in the content of the vision which leads him to do so. In short, the act of *devotio* is premised on an understanding of the relationship between the body of the general and the body of the State which is entirely at odds with what Pompey is represented as seeing. By extension, the demonstration of what is dysfunctional about Pompey's *devotio* has far-reaching consequences for understanding of the *Pharsalia* as a Republican poem: propaganda pamphlet or sophisticated political meditation?

POMPEY'S DEATH POSTPONED: *MORS INOPPORTUNA* OR WORSE?

Camillus enters the line of battle, charges the line of the enemy, and wins. What is ethically significant about his action, however, is not the salutary outcome but rather his readiness to join his troops himself in risking something much worse (*ubi plurimus labor periculumque erat*

[4] The argument in this chapter engages in particular with Rambaud (1955), but see also Brisset (1964) 75–6 and 114–27 and Le Bonniec (1970) 159–60. Pompey's flight is taken as Stoic wisdom in Marti (1945). Conte (1968) 239–41, Lounsbury (1976), and Narducci (1979) 125 endorse Marti and Rambaud, though not explicitly the *devotio*. Lounsbury (1975) and (1976) also adheres closely to Rambaud's theory of counter-deformation. Gagliardi (1970) 174–8 sees the flight as heroic, but is sceptical of the idea of *devotio*. Hardie (1993) 54–6 injects a necessary note of scepticism. A number of the ideas expressed in this chapter are common to Leigh (1993).

se offerebat). In the case of Pompey, it is possible to imagine that his entry into the battle would have turned the tide, but, as Lucan makes clear, the real issue is his willingness or otherwise to meet a noble death.[5] The first task therefore is to locate this argument within the ancient tradition concerning Pompey's death.

The headless corpse of Pompey left unburied on the shore of Egypt is a source of horror not just for Lucan. Servius notes that the sudden transfer of the corpse of Priam from altar to shore at *Aen.* 2. 557–8 alludes to Pompey as Magnus. Vergil thus sets up an implicit synkrisis of the two as figures of reversal of fortune, *Aen.* 2. 554–8:

> Haec finis Priami fatorum, hic exitus illum
> sorte tulit Troiam incensam et prolapsa videntem
> Pergama, tot quondam populis terrisque superbum
> regnatorem Asiae. Iacet ingens litore truncus,
> avolsumque umeris caput et sine nomine corpus.

This was the final destiny of Priam, this allotted end took him as he saw Troy on fire and Pergamum in collapse, he who was once the ruler of Asia, proud of his so many peoples and his lands. He lies a huge trunk on the shore and the head is torn off from the shoulders and the body is without name.[6]

This, however, is only the most famous instance of the topos which treates the execution of Pompey as a paradigm for the mutability of fortune. The lacuna at line 44 cannot disguise that this is the sense of Ovid, *Pont.* 4. 3. 41–4, and the theme is taken up again at Manilius, *Astronomica* 4. 50–6:

> Quis te Niliaco periturum litore, Magne,
> post victas Mithridatis opes pelagusque receptum
> et tris emenso meritos ex orbe triumphos,
> cum te iam posses alium componere Magnum
> crederet, ut corpus sepeliret naufragus ignis
> eiectaeque rogum facerent fragmenta carinae?
> Quis tantum mutare potest sine numine fati?

Magnus, who, after you had conquered the might of Mithridates and won back the seas and thrice returned in triumph from the world you had travelled, when now you could represent yourself as another styled the Great, could have believed that you would die on the shore of the Nile, that fire kindled from

[5] Luc. 7. 669–72.

[6] For this synkrisis, and its reactivation in Lucan, see Narducci (1973) and (1979) 43–8 and n. 23, Feeney (1986*a*) and Bowie (1990). When Lucan reactivates the theme, he offers a disturbing exegesis of Vergil, in which the sack of Troy is a symbol for the sack of Rome. For Pompey and Fortuna, see Dick (1967).

driftwood would cremate your body and the remains of a wrecked ship would furnish a pyre? Who can undergo such change without the power of fate?[7]

Further, the sentiments of Manilius are paralleled in those of another Tiberian writer, Velleius Paterculus, who concludes his account of the death of Pompey at 2. 53. 3:

Hic post tres consulatus et totidem triumphos domitumque terrarum orbem sanctissimi ac praestantissimi viri in id evecti, super quod ascendi non potest, duodesexagesimum annum agentis pridie natalem ipsius vitae fuit exitus, *in tantum in illo viro a se discordante fortuna, ut cui modo ad victoriam terra defuerat, deesset ad sepulturam.*

This, after three consulates and as many triumphs and the conquering of the world, was the end of the life of a most revered and excellent man who rose to a point so high that it cannot be surpassed, the day before his fifty-eighth birthday, subject to a fortune so variable in his case that the same man who no longer had lands left to defeat no more could find land for burial.

Most importantly, this topos is a familiar refrain in Seneca, for instance at *Epistle* 4. 7, where he remarks that:

De Pompei capite pupillus et spado tulere sententiam . . . neminem eo fortuna provexit ut non tantum illi minaretur quantum permiserat.

A schoolboy and a eunuch passed judgement on the head of Pompey . . . fortune has advanced no man so far that she did not threaten him with as much as she had granted.

Note how similar are the sentiments of Sen. *Tranq.* 16. 1:

Sequitur pars quae solet non inmerito contristare et in sollicitudinem adducere. Ubi bonorum exitus mali sunt, ubi Socrates cogitur in carcere mori, Rutilius in exilio vivere, Pompeius et Cicero clientibus suis praebere cervicem, Cato ille, virtutium viva imago, incumbens gladio simul de se ac de re publica palam facere, necesse est torqueri tam iniqua praemia fortunam persolvere.

There follows the part which is not unjustifiably accustomed to cause sorrow and to leave people distressed. When the deaths of good men are bad, when Socrates is forced to die in prison, Rutilius to live in exile, Pompey and Cicero to allow themselves to be beheaded by their clients, that Cato, the living image of the virtues, to fall on his sword and admit the end of himself and of the State, it is inevitable that people are concerned that fortune should give such unjust rewards.[8]

[7] Cf. Manil. 1. 508–17 and 4. 63–6, esp. 64–5, 'Priamique in litore truncum, | cui nec Troia rogus'. For these as treating the same material as *Catalepton* 3, see Alfonsi (1947).

[8] Cf. Sen. *Brev.* 13. 7: 'Ille se supra rerum naturam esse tunc credidit, cum tot miserorum hominum catervas sub alio caelo natis beluis obiceret, cum bellum inter tam disparia animalia committeret, cum in conspectu populi Romani multum sanguinis

That the death of Pompey in Egypt demonstrated the terrible mutability of fortune was a truism. Equally commonplace was the notion that it would have been better for him to die somewhere else. Thus, at 8. 27–32, Lucan depicts Pompey fleeing Thessaly in a single craft as one who has lived too long:

Sic longius aevum
destruit ingentis animos et *vita superstes*
imperio. Nisi summa dies cum fine bonorum
adfuit et celeri praevertit tristia leto,
dedecori est fortuna prior. Quisquamne secundis
tradere se fatis audet nisi morte parata?

Thus the passage of time and a life which survives power destroy great spirits. Unless the final day has come together with the end of good fortune and has obviated sorrow by a swift death, [comparison with] one's previous fortune brings disgrace. Does any man dare to trust prosperity unless a way to death is already planned.

Pompey's 'life which survives power' (*vita superstes imperio*) is echoed at Florus 2. 13. 51, where he is described as 'surviving his own dignity' (*superstes dignitatis suae*).[9] Florus reproduces the traditional opinion that Pompey lived too long and thus ruined the glory of his early years. There is also general agreement as to when it would have been better for Pompey to die: that is, at the time of the serious illness which struck him at Naples in 50 BC. This sentiment is first expressed by Cicero at *Tusc.* 1. 86:

Pompeio, nostro familiari, cum graviter aegrotaret Neapoli, melius est factum ... Utrum igitur, si tum esset exstinctus, a bonis rebus an a malis discessisset? Certe a miseris. Non enim cum socero bellum gessisset, non inparatus arma sumpsisset, non domum reliquisset, non ex Italia fugisset, non exercitu amisso nudus in servorum ferrum et manus incidisset ... Qui, si mortem tum obisset, in amplissimis fortunis occidisset, is propagatione vitae quot, quantas, quam incredibilis hausit calamitates!

funderet, mox plus ipsum fundere coacturus. At idem postea Alexandrina perfidia deceptus ultimo mancipio transfodiendum se praebuit, tum demum intellecta inani iactatione cognominis sui.' The contrast repeatedly drawn in the epigrams of the *Anthologia Latina* between the grandeur of Pompey in life and the lowly indignity of his burial is discussed in Tandoi (1963).

[9] For 'vita superstes imperio', cf. Sen. *Ag.* 709 for Hecuba as 'superstes ... sibi' and Tarrant (1976) ad loc. Cf. Sen. *Tranq.* 11. 12 for Croesus 'non regno tantum, etiam morti suae superstes' and *Her. O.* 198 for 'sibi Tantalis ... facta superstes'. Mayer (1981) ad loc. offers Livy, 2. 7. 8, 'superstitem gloriae suae' (for which cf. Livy, 42. 50. 8, 'ubi privatus superstes regno suo ... consenescat'), and Plin. *Ep.* 2. 1. 2, 'gloriae suae supervixit'. See also Sen. *Suas.* 6. 6 where Cicero is 'rei publicae superstes' and 7. 8, where his agreement to the burning of his books will render him 'ingenii tui superstitem'.

My friend Pompey, when he was gravely ill in Naples, was cured ... Would he therefore, had he then passed away, have avoided happy or unhappy experiences? Unhappy, for sure. For he would not have waged war with his father-in-law, would not have taken up arms when unready, would not have left home, would not have fled from Italy, would not have lost his army and fallen naked into the weapons and the hands of slaves ... If he had died then, he would have fallen while at the height of his fortune; how many, how great, how incredible were the calamities he underwent by prolonging his life!

The idea is subsequently endorsed by a number of writers.[10]

It is also presumed that this is the meaning of Propertius, 3. 11. 33–8:

Noxia Alexandria, dolis aptissima tellus,
   et totiens nostro Memphi cruenta malo,
tris ubi Pompeio detraxit harena triumphos!
   Tollet nulla dies hanc tibi, Roma, notam.
Issent Phlegraeo melius tibi funera campo,
   vel tua si socero colla daturus eras.

Guilty Alexandria, land most fitted to deceit, and Memphis so often covered in the blood of our suffering, where the sand stripped Pompey of his three triumphs! Rome, no day will free you from this stain. It would have been better for you to die on the fields of Phlegra or if you had bowed your neck to your father-in-law.[11]

The reference to the field of Phlegra is ambiguous. While it is conventional to treat lines 37–8 as referring to Naples, it has been argued that, since one tradition (Serv. at *Aen*. 3. 578) located the field of Phlegra in Thessaly, they may actually refer to Pharsalus.[12] Fedeli discounts this possibility,[13] but it is not clear that Propertius' terms are not deliberately ambiguous. Evidently, the suggestion that Pompey would have done better to go down fighting at Pharsalus is considerably less anodyne than the reference to his illness at Naples, but then the

[10] Livy, 9. 17. 6 (though with no explicit reference to Naples); Vell. Pat. 2. 48. 2; Sen. *Marc*. 20. 4; Juv. 10. 283–6; Plut. *Pomp*. 46. 1–2 and 57. 1–3.

[11] The text printed is that of Barber's OCT. Butrica (1993) emends 'harena' at 35 to 'verna' and 'tua' at 38 to 'sua'. However, the arguments raised against 'harena' are insubstantial, while the desire with 'sua' to avoid a sudden shift of addressee within an apostrophe ignores parallels in Latin for this practice, such as Luc. 8. 512–17, where Pothinus fails initially to signal the fact that he is no longer speaking to Ptolemy but rather to Pompey. On this last point, see Shackleton Bailey (1956) 171.

[12] See Paratore (1936) 48–52.

[13] Fedeli (1985) ad loc., Rothstein (1924) ad loc., and L. Richardson (1977) ad loc. consider only Naples, while Butler and Barber (1933) discuss Pharsalus as a possibility, before endorsing the traditional view.

continuation of Propertius' thought at line 38 is no more conciliatory.[14] Further, this alternative version of the *mors opportuna* can be paralleled in Sen. *Marc.* 20. 4:

Cogita quantum boni opportuna mors habeat, quam multis diutius vixisse nocuerit. Si Gnaeum Pompeium, decus istud firmamentumque imperii, Neapoli valetudo abstulisset, indubitatus populi Romani princeps excesserat: at nunc exigui temporis adiectio fastigio illum suo depulit. Vidit legiones in conspectu suo caesas et ex illo proelio in quo prima acies senatus fuit—quae infelicis reliquiae sunt!—*ipsum imperatorem superfuisse*; vidit Aegyptium carnificem et sacrosanctum victoribus corpus satelliti praestitit, etiam si incolumis fuisset *paenitentiam salutis acturus*; quid enim erat turpius quam Pompeium vivere beneficio regis?

Consider the advantages of a timely death, how many men it has harmed to have lived too long. If illness had carried off Gnaeus Pompey, that glory and mainstay of the empire, at Naples, he would have died the unquestioned leader of the Roman people: yet now the addition of a tiny amount of time deposed him from his place of pride. He saw legions cut down before his eyes and from that battle in which the Senate formed the front line—what is left of the unhappy band!—the general himself survive; he saw the Egyptian executioner and he granted to a minion a body inviolable to the conquerors, bound to regret his salvation even if he had been unharmed; for what was more foul than for Pompey to live by the favour of a king?

Here, the principal instance of *mors opportuna* is still that of Naples, but one of the woes of surviving then was that Pompey should go to Pharsalus—and survive there as well. As with Propertius, the claim that Pompey would have done better to die in battle at Pharsalus bears dangerous implications. For a latter-day Republican, it is harsh to suggest that Pompey should have followed his troops in death at

[14] The exact sense of Prop. 3. 11. 38 is made obscure by the expression used. Camps (1966) ad loc. and Fedeli (1985) ad loc. equate 'si . . . daturus eras' with 'si dedisses', though the former does describe it as 'a remarkable periphrasis'. Butler and Barber (1933) offer a similar interpretation, though one which is variable according to the location of Phlegra. If this is taken to mean Pharsalus, they offer 'even though you were doomed to bow the neck before Caesar'. Goold's Loeb tries 'or had you been doomed to bow your neck to your father-in-law'. Two points arise. First, what does 'colla dare' imply? Unlike the options offered by Phlegra and by Egypt, it seems not to imply death or execution but rather the acceptance of servitude (Prop. 2. 10. 15, cf. Hor. *Sat.* 2. 7. 92, Sen. *Apocol.* 12. 3). Second, is 'si . . . daturus eras' the exact equivalent of 'si dedisses'? A rather verbose alternative translation might be 'or if [as some said you planned to do] you had bowed your head to your father-in-law'. The point about this alternative is that it allows Propertius to suggest both (i) that death in Egypt was the worst fate of all, and (ii) that death in Egypt precluded a course of action which, while better than what Pompey suffered, would still have been a disgrace. Cato at Luc. 9. 208–10 (see below) is an unkind commentary on the likelihood of Pompey making just such a compromise.

Pharsalus, because it implies that the general's valour was inadequate. For a supporter of the emperors, it is difficult to be told that Pompey should have fought Caesar to the death, and not risked survival, for it implies distaste for the imperial system. Neither of these problems is raised by locating the *mors opportuna* at Naples.

Lucan's Pompey is, of course, a sick man from the start. He is aging (1. 129–30, *vergentibus annis* | *in senium*), and the oak-tree simile demonstrates that the one thing which he does not have is a *viridis senectus* (1. 135–42). Pompey himself alludes to his brush with death at Naples at 7. 352–5:

> 'Si socero dare regna meo mundumque pararent,
> praecipitare meam fatis potuere senectam:
> non iratorum populis urbique deorum est,
> Pompeium servare ducem.'

'If they were preparing to give kingly power over the world to my father-in- law, they could have cut short my old age in death: it is not the act of gods angry at the peoples and at Rome to keep Pompey alive to command.'

The *Commenta Bernensia* at 7. 353 appreciate Pompey's sense, quoting Juvenal, 10. 283–4: 'Provident Campania had given Pompey the fevers he should have wished for' (*Provida Pompeio dederat Campania febres* | *optandas*). Pompey's profession of faith in divine good will comes in the context of a speech which impresses its listeners with its sad and fearful tone—the sense that death at Naples was to be desired is present, however obliquely, in his words. This, however, must be balanced against the repeated assertion of the second theme—the desirability of death at Pharsalus. This point of view is surely expressed in Cato's obituary for Pompey at 9. 208–10:

> 'O felix, cui summa dies fuit obvia victo
> et cui *quaerendos* Pharium scelus obtulit *enses*.
> Forsitan in soceri potuisses vivere regno.'

'O lucky man, whose last day followed soon on his defeat and to whom the Egyptians' crime brought the swords which he should have sought. Perhaps you could have lived under your father-in-law as king.'

Cato knows that Pompey should have sought to die, and fears that Pompey might have preferred enslavement to Caesar to death. Perhaps, like Cato, he should simply have sought the sword by his own suicide; more likely, surely, he should have done so in battle, when he had the chance. This certainly is the harsh judgement of Pothinus at 8. 505–11:

'Rapitur civilibus umbris.
Nec soceri tantum arma fugit: fugit ora senatus,
cuius Thessalicas saturat pars magna volucres,
et metuit gentes quas uno in sanguine mixtas
deseruit, regesque timet quorum omnia mersit,
Thessaliaeque reus nulla tellure receptus
sollicitat nostrum, quem nondum perdidit, orbem.'

'He is dragged down by the ghosts of those who died in civil war. Nor does he flee the arms of his father-in-law alone: he flees the faces of the senators, the great part of whom fatten the birds of Thessaly, and he fears the nations which, commingled in one pool of blood, he deserted, and he is frightened of the kings whose all he sank, and, guilty of his deeds in Thessaly and shunned by every land, he harasses our realm which he has yet to destroy.'

Books 8 and 9 introduce judgements of Pompey's actions in leaving Pharsalus which may not seem entirely consonant with the apparent heroization of 7. 647–711. It is therefore worth noting that Lucan too introduces his own homily on living too long only at the start of the eighth book, immediately after Pharsalus. His reference to 'life which survives power' (*vita superstes imperio*), Seneca's lament that 'the general himself survived' (*ipsum imperatorem superfuisse*), by extending reference to Thessaly, make problematic the rhetorical topos of reversal of fortune and *mors inopportuna* which, when centred only on Naples and Egypt, was truistic and banal. More important still, they both draw on the same nexus of expectations, the ideological underpinning of which is of signal importance for the appreciation of the *devotio* motif at 7. 647–711.

DEFEAT AND THE GOOD GENERAL

Seneca and Lucan are not the only Roman writers to express suspicion of the general who survives a defeat. An intriguing parallel is offered by the account of the battle fought between the returning Tarquinius and the consuls L. Junius Brutus and P. Valerius Publicola at Livy, 2. 6. 5–11. This battle is described at 2. 6. 10–11 as indecisive but it is not difficult to detect in Livy's account the traces of a possible hostile tradition which represented it as a defeat.[15] It is therefore striking to note the construction put on the contrasting fates of the two generals. Brutus spurs his horse against Arruns and enjoys a

[15] Cf. Plut. *Publ.* 9. 2, which again stresses the equal losses on each side but does not shy away from describing the battle as a calamity.

heroic death;[16] his colleague may count it a misfortune that he survives. Livy, 2. 7. 5–6 records the resentment felt against Publicola in terms now familiar from Neronian verdicts on the actions of Pompey:

Consuli deinde qui superfuerat, ut sunt mutabiles volgi animi, ex favore non invidia modo sed suspicio etiam cum atroci crimine orta.

The minds of the crowd being as fickle as they are, the favour originally felt for the consul who had survived changed to a mixture of resentment and suspicion combined with shocking accusations.

If the phrasing of this section parallels Seneca, that of Publicola's speech of self-defence at 2. 7. 8–9 may be equated with Lucan:

Ibi audire iussis consul laudare fortunam collegae, quod liberata patria, in summo honore, pro re publica dimicans, matura gloria *necdum se vertente in invidiam*, mortem occubuisset: *se superstitem gloriae suae ad crimen atque invidiam superesse*; ex liberatore patriae ad Aquilios se Vitelliosque recidisse.

Then the consul bade them listen and praised the fortune of his colleague in that he had met his death after liberating his country, while held in the highest honour, fighting for the State, with his glory ripe but not yet turning to resentment: he himself had outlived his glory and had survived only to meet accusations and resentment and had turned from the liberator of his country into an Aquilius or a Vitellius.

A general who survives defeat risks the hostility of the people when he returns home.[17] Some of the grounds for resentment of the general who survives may be inferred from the motivation ascribed to a further Livian commander, Hasdrubal, at 27. 49. 4:

Ne superstes tanto exercitui suum nomen secuto esset concitato equo se in cohortem Romanam immisit; ibi, ut patre Hamilcare et Hannibale fratre dignum erat, pugnans cecidit.

Lest he should survive the great army which had followed his name, he spurred on his horse and cast himself into the Roman army and there, as was worthy of his father Hamilcar and his brother Hannibal, he fell fighting.

[16] Livy, 2. 6. 8–9 says of Brutus that '[Arruns] Concitat calcaribus equum atque in ipsum infestus consulem derigit. Sensit in se iri Brutus; *decorum erat tum ipsis capessere pugnam ducibus; avide itaque se certamini offert*; adeoque infestis animis concurrerunt, neuter dum hostem volneraret, sui protegendi corporis memor, ut contrario ictu per parmam uterque transfixus duabus haerentes hastis moribundi ex equis lapsi sint'. The assertion that the behaviour of Arruns and Brutus is typical of the mores of archaic, not modern, Rome is striking but does not render the parallel inapplicable to Pompey. For the specific pressures on the general to take action in order to avert defeat remain true. For more on this, see below.

[17] The situation of Publicola in Livy is similar to that of Varro at Sil. *Pun.* 10. 605–39 in that both are resented for living on when a consular colleague is killed. Pompey's case is somewhat different at least in this respect.

Hasdrubal, like Camillus, spurs on his horse and sends himself into the ranks of the enemy. In this, he too shows the anxiety of the good general: 'followed his name' (*suum nomen secuto*) recalls the military oath of loyalty from soldier to general, an oath which itself placed certain implicit reciprocal obligations on the commander.[18] Livy's admiration for Hasdrubal is evident, so too that of Polybius, who underlines the exemplary character of his death.[19] The broad pattern too is widespread: the military manuals may emphasize the folly of excessive risk-taking on the part of the general,[20] but the literary ideal tends to be that embraced by Alexander the Great, according to which one should be 'both a good king/general and a mighty warrior'.[21] As a rule, admiration is felt for the general seen fulfilling the duty of kinship to his troops and fighting zealously in the front line.[22]

More particularly, fighting in the front line is the action which one *expects* of the leader of an army facing disastrous defeat. Thus, in the

[18] At Verg. *Aen.* 10. 672, Turnus frets over the men 'qui me meaque arma secuti', recalling the self-description of Aeneas' men at *Aen.* 3. 156 as 'nos te Dardania incensa tuaque arma secuti'. The exact mutual obligations of the *sacramentum* for soldier and general remain obscure, but Hor. *Carm.* 2. 17. 8–12 is suggestive: 'Ille dies utramque | ducet ruinam. Non ego perfidum | dixi sacramentum: ibimus, ibimus, | utcumque praecedes, supremum | carpere iter comites parati'. For more on the military oath, see Ch. 6, pp. 205–6. Vretska (1976) at Sall. *Cat.* 60. 6–7 connects the charge to death of Hasdrubal with those of Catiline and the Decii, and sees each as an instance of 'Feldherrnpflicht'.

[19] Polyb. 11. 2. 7 states that the attitude of Hasdrubal makes him worthy of imitation, while others αἰσχρὰς μὲν ἐποίησαν τὰς ἥττας . . . κατῄσχυναν δὲ τὰς πρὸ τούτου πράξεις, ἐπονείδιστον δὲ σφίσι τὸν καταλειπόμενον ἐποίησαν βίον. Cf. Polyb. 30. 6–9, on the reactions to defeat of the various anti-Roman statesmen of Greece, which condemns those who disgraced themselves in their attempt to cling on to life. Polyb. 30. 6. 3–4 emphasizes the exemplary character of his catalogue, stating that it will be useful if τίνες φανήσονται τὸ κατὰ λόγον πεποιηκότες καὶ τίνες παραπεπαικότες τοῦ καθήκοντος, ἵνα οἱ ἐπιγινόμενοι, ὡσανεὶ τύπων ἐκτιθεμένων, δύνωνται κατὰ τὰς ὁμοίας περιστάσεις τὰ μὲν αἱρετὰ διώκειν, τὰ δὲ φευκτὰ φεύγειν ἀληθινῶς. For the theme of the proper response of the general to defeat, see also Polyb. 18. 37. 7 and the words of T. Quinctius Flamininus to the Aetolians in 197 BC: πολεμοῦντας γὰρ δεῖ τοὺς ἀγαθοὺς ἄνδρας βαρεῖς εἶναι καὶ θυμικούς, ἡττωμένους δὲ γενναίους καὶ μεγαλόφρονας, νικῶντάς γε μὴν μετρίους καὶ πραεῖς καὶ φιλανθρώπους. For more on *exempla*, see Ch. 5.

[20] e.g. Onas. 33. 3: . . . εἰ γάρ ἐν ὧι τοῦ σύμπαντος ἡ σωτηρία στρατεύματός ἐστιν, οὗτος οὐδὲν εἰ τεθνήξεται πεφρόντικε, τὸ πᾶν αἱρεῖται συνδιαφθεῖραι, καὶ ὀρθῶς δ' ἄν τις αἰτιάσαιτο τοῦτον ὡς ἄπρακτον στρατηγὸν μᾶλλον ἢ ἀνδρεῖον. For a historical investigation of the actual actions of a Greek general, see Wheeler (1991).

[21] Plut. *Mor.* 331 c quoting Hom. *Il.* 3. 179, ἀμφότερον βασιλεύς τ' ἀγαθὸς κρατερός τ' αἰχμητής. McGushin (1977) at Sall. *Cat.* 60. 4 cites a number of parallels for the double role: Caes. *B. Gall.* 5. 33. 2 (see below), Livy, 9. 1. 2, Suet. *Aug.* 10. 4, Curt. 3. 11. 7, Plin. *HN* 7. 140. La Penna (1978) 214 cites and discusses Antonius Primus at Tac. *Hist.* 3. 17. 1.

[22] e.g. Livy, 2. 19. 6, 4. 41. 4, 30. 18. 4, 35. 5. 1, cf. App. *B. Civ.* 2. 104. 432 for Caesar at Munda.

same chapter in which he has warned against foolish adventurism on the part of the general, Onasander offers rather different counsel for when times are bad:

ὅθεν ἐπιφαίνειν μὲν δεῖ τῶι πλήθει τὸ φιλοκίνδυνον, ἵνα τὴν προθυμίαν ἐκκαλῆται τῶν στρατιωτῶν, ἀγωνίζεσθαι δὲ ἀσφαλέστερον, καὶ τοῦ θανάτου μὲν καταφρονεῖν, εἴ τι πάσχοι τὸ στράτευμα, μηδ' αὐτὸν αἱρούμενον ζῆν, σωζομένου δὲ καὶ τὴν ἰδίαν φυλάττειν ψυχήν.

Hence the general must show himself brave before the army, that he may call forth the zeal of his soldiers, but he must fight cautiously; he should despise death if his army is defeated, and not desire to live, but if his army is preserved he should guard his personal safety.[23]

There are many examples of Roman generals acting according to these instructions and in the spirit of Alexander: from Sallust's Catiline to Caesar's Cotta, the representation of the heroic general in defeat returns to the same formula.[24] In the case of Cotta, moreover, the qualities of this good general are brought into clearer focus by comparison with the failings of his inept colleague Titurius: Cotta is struck while urging on his men,[25] steadfastly refuses to join Titurius in negotiating for surrender,[26] and finally dies fighting; Titurius, whose foolish plan is responsible for the disaster, is surrounded and killed as he attempts to parley.[27]

DEVOTIO AND THE MYTH OF THE GOOD GENERAL

Riding to the Enemy

What was true of Camillus is as true of almost all the generals discussed: the decision to charge the line of the enemy has an ethical as

[23] Onas. 33. 5.

[24] Sall. *Cat.* 60. 4, 'strenui militis et boni imperatoris officia simul exequebatur', cf. Caes. *B. Gall.* 5. 33. 2, 'in appellandis cohortandisque militibus imperatoris et in pugna militis officia praestabat'.

[25] Caes. *B. Gall.* 5. 35. 8: 'Lucius Cotta legatus omnis cohortis ordinesque adhortans in adversum os funda vulneratur'.

[26] Ibid. 5. 36. 3: 'se ad armatum hostem iturum negat atque in eo perseverat'.

[27] Cf. Curio at Caes. *B. Civ.* 2. 42. 3: 'Hortatur Curionem Cn. Domitius, praefectus equitum, cum paucis equitibus circumsistens, ut fuga salutem petat atque in castra contendat, et se ab eo non discessurum pollicetur. At Curio numquam se amisso exercitu quem a Caesare fidei commissum acceperit in eius conspectum reversurum confirmat atque ita proelians interficitur'. Flor. *Epit.* 2. 8. 13–14 extends the compliment to the rebel gladiator Spartacus at the end of his revolt: 'Eruptione facta, dignam viris obiere mortem ... Spartacus ipse in primo agmine fortissime dimicans *quasi imperator* occisus est'.

well as a tactical dimension.[28] The exemplary death of Hasdrubal is treated as the response to binding social obligations—the shame of surviving the defeat of one's army, of caring more for self-protection than for the good of the troops—which it is hinted that Pompey's actions at Pharsalus may have violated. It is not accidental that the same terms—*superstes, superfuisse*—recur in the description of both their cases and can be paralleled in the closely related experiences of Valerius Publicola. The purpose of the section which follows is to examine a cluster of further motifs common to Camillus, Pompey, Hasdrubal, and others and to establish their relationship to a central Roman myth-historical conception of virtue in generalship: *devotio*.

The crucial lines to be discussed here are those which describe the retreat of Pompey from Pharsalus, Lucan 7. 677–9:

> Tum Magnum *concitus* aufert
> a bello *sonipes* non tergo tela paventem
> ingentisque animos extrema in fata ferentem.

Then a spurred steed carried Magnus away from battle unafraid of a spear in his back and bearing his great spirit to its final destiny.

When Livy, 2. 6. 8, recounts the charge against each other of Brutus and Arruns, he notes that they spur on their horses (*Concitat calcaribus equum*). Yet here there is no sacrificial motif. When, at 27. 49. 4, he describes the charge of Hasdrubal, the spurring of the horse (*concitato equo se in cohortem Romanam immisit*) has no attendant religious activity but is at least motivated by the desire to find a noble death. When the charger in Lucan leads Pompey away to his final destiny, a much stronger religious context has been set by the general's lengthy prayer to the gods at 7. 656–66 and the offer of himself or his family as substitute victims for the Rome he sees being destroyed. Pompey's assurance to the gods that he can be wretched 'though Rome survives' (*Roma . . . superstite*) demonstrates the same ambition as Cato, who, at 2. 306–13 prays:

[28] For the charge to the enemy as a successful tactic, cf. Caesar at Caes. *B. Gall.* 2. 25. 2–3 and the Fabii at Livy, 2. 46. 4–47. 1. For the social pressures faced by the Republican Roman commander, see Rosenstein (1990), esp. ch. 4, 'The Aristocratic Ethos and the Preservation of Status', 114–52. For the importance of demonstrating heroism in defeat, see esp. ibid. 117–18, 'A general was expected to display courage and self-control when things were falling apart all around him—a willingness to fight hard, take risks, and, if necessary, meet death fighting bravely . . . Generals died in battle frequently enough during the last two and a half centuries of the Republic to indicate that crisis often led commanders to put themselves in harm's way, and those who survived took pains to advertise the fact.'

'O utinam caelique deis Erebique liceret
hoc caput in cunctas damnatum exponere poenas!
Devotum hostiles Decium pressere catervae:
me geminae figant acies, me barbara telis
Rheni turba petat, cunctis ego pervius hastis
excipiam medius totius volnera belli.
Hic redimat sanguis populos, hac caede luatur
quidquid Romani meruerunt pendere mores.'

'O would that it were possible to offer this head in full repayment to the gods of heaven and hell to suffer the punishments of all! The enemy troops crushed Decius when he devoted himself: let the twin battle-lines fix me, let the barbarian band of the Rhine aim their arms at me, let me stand in the middle, pierced by every spear, and suffer the wounds of an entire war. Let this blood redeem the peoples, by this slaughter may payment be made in expiation for whatever penalty the sins of Rome deserve to pay.'[29]

The terms of Cato's prayer betray the myth-historical prototype which is replicated, if only in reverse, by Pompey: the self-devotion performed by two or three generations of the family of the Decii.[30] For, at Livy, 8. 9. 1–11, the Roman consul and commander, P. Decius Mus, faced with defeat against the Latins at Mons Vesuvius and acting on the instructions of haruspicy, delivers an elaborate prayer formula and then:

Ipse incinctus cinctu Gabino, *armatus in equum insiluit ac se in medios hostes immisit*, conspectus ab utraque acie, aliquanto augustior humano visu, sicut caelo missus piaculum omnis deorum irae qui pestem ab suis aversam in hostes ferret.

He himself girt himself up in the Gabine style, armed himself, jumped on a horse and cast himself into the midst of the enemy, visible to both armies and with an air rather more venerable than is customary in mortals, as if he had been sent from heaven as an expiation of all the anger of the gods to bear the pestilence away from his men and to the foe.[31]

[29] See Fantham (1992*a*) ad loc. for the interpretation of this speech as 'the Livian tradition of physical self-dedication by Roman battle commanders ... converted into moral dedication by the Stoic exemplar'.

[30] Cic. *Fin.* 2. 60–1 and *Tusc.* 1. 89 tell of the *devotio* of a third Decius, the son of the second and grandson of the first, but this story is generally treated with scepticism. For a full list of references to all three Decii, see Litchfield (1914).

[31] Cf. Val. Max. 5. 6. 5: 'P. Decius Mus, qui consulatum in familiam suam primus intulit, cum Latino bello Romanam aciem inclinatam et paene iam prostratam videret, *caput suum pro salute rei publicae devovit ac protinus concitato equo in medium hostium agmen patriae salutem, sibi mortem petens inrupit* factaque ingenti strage plurimis telis obrutus super corruit. Ex cuius vulneribus et sanguine insperata victoria emersit.' Further instances of the formula are to be found at Oros. 3. 9. 3, 'in confertissimos hostes sponte prolapsus occubuit' and at Sen. *Ep.* 67. 9 (*re* second Decius), 'in aciem confertissimam incucurrit, de hoc sollicitus tantum ut litaret'.

At Livy, 10. 28. 12–18, Decius' son, commanding the Roman forces at Sentinum and again on the brink of disaster, summons the *pontifex* M. Livius, repeats the prayer formula, and, 10. 28. 18:

Haec exsecratus in se hostesque, *qua confertissimam cernebat Gallorum aciem, concitat equum inferensque se ipse infestis telis est interfectus.*

Delivering this curse against himself and the enemy, he spurred his horse to where he saw the battle-line of the Gauls most thickly set and, bearing himself in, was slain by the enemy arms.

The question to ask now is what different levels of meaning the Decian *devotio ducis* can have for Pompey's flight.

Interpretation and Reception of the Devotio

Previous work on *devotio* in Livy has concentrated on the nature of the religious ritual involved in the prayer and sacrifice. In particular, there is some dispute over whether the prayer of P. Decius Mus constitutes a genuine promise of exchange of the sort seen in the *devotio hostium* recorded at Macrobius, *Saturnalia* 3. 9. 9–12, or a *consecratio*, the body of the general being transferred directly to the world below.[32] In some ways it is difficult to relate this type of argument to Lucan. For, from the first, those who perceived the stylized depiction of Pompey's flight as a form of inverted *devotio*, have argued for a loose and innovative understanding of the act.[33] The Decian *devotio ducis* does, however, throw up other categories which it is easier to apply to Lucan.

The very looseness of the religious dimension to the *devotio* in Lucan testifies to a further phenomenon: in many Roman writers, where technical distinctions between *devotio* and *consecratio* take a less than central position in the reception of the story and the Decii come to stand in a more general way for heroic self-sacrifice in battle, it is observable that the act is given more attention than the prayer, and the idea of *devotio* becomes increasingly closely identified with the recurrent formula for the charge to death. This is apparent at Livy, 9. 4. 10–11, where the charge is held to be the essential characteristic of the Decian *devotio ducis*. Thus L. Lentulus, trapped with the rest of the Roman army at the Caudine Forks, comments:

[32] Versnel (1976) and (1981), cf. Pascal (1982) 12–13, 15 and (1990).

[33] Rambaud (1955) 273, 'L'héroïsme de Magnus paraît contestable. La tradition romaine connaissait une façon de se dévouer: en avant, en se jetant au milieu des ennemis, et le sacrifice était sanglant. *En voici une seconde: en arrière, et l'on se jette dans la fuite, devenant le fuyard-type, absolu et quasi-métaphysique*, dont se satisfera le courroux des dieux; ce sacrifice est moral.' Cf. Brisset (1964) 75–6 and Le Bonniec (1970) 159–60.

'Equidem *mortem pro patria praeclaram esse fateor* et *me vel devovere pro populo Romano legionibusque vel in medios immittere hostes paratus sum*; sed hic patriam video, hic quidquid Romanarum legionum est; quae nisi pro se ipsis *ad mortem ruere* volunt, quid habent quod morte sua servent?'

'Indeed I confess that a death for the fatherland is glorious and I am ready to devote myself for the sake of the Roman people and the legions and to cast myself into the midst of the enemy, but it is here that I see the homeland, here whatever of the Roman legions is left, and, unless they wish to rush to death to please themselves, what do they have that they can save by their death?'[34]

The terms of this speech are easily paralleled. Moreover, the tendency to summarise the *devotio* by reference to the formula for the charge considerably antedates Livy. This is demonstrated by *Rhetorica ad Herennium* 4. 57, which, giving a specimen *tractatio* of the theme 'the wise man will avoid no danger in the name of the State' (*sapiens nullum pro re publica periculum vitabit*), cites Decius as an *exemplum*:

Quod mihi bene videtur Decius intellexisse, qui se devovisse dicitur et pro legionibus *in hostes immisisse medios.*

Which it seems to me that Decius understood well, who is said to have devoted himself and to have cast himself into the midst of the enemy for the sake of the legions.

Two points must therefore be asserted. First, the self-sacrifice of the Decii has a special resonance for Roman historians and one which it would be foolish to underestimate. Second, most descriptions of the *devotio* tend to combine two characteristics: the desire to save something else, normally the State or the legions, and the charge to the ranks of the enemy which ensues.[35] An important illustration of the

[34] One should not be confused by the suggestion of two alternative actions via 'vel . . . vel'. Weissenborn and Müller (1965) ad loc. comment that 'statt der beiden korrespondierenden "vel" erwartete man ein blosses "et" an der zweiten Stelle', observing that the second action is just the consequence of the first. For copulative *vel . . . vel* in Livy, see also 1. 42. 5. Livy, 9. 10. 2–4 emphasizes the expiatory aspect of the *devotio*, the Senate comparing Postumius to Decius and stating that 'ipsum se cruciatibus et hostium irae offerre piaculaque pro populo Romano dare'. At 9. 17. 13, however, Livy puts more emphasis on the rush, talking of the Decii as 'devotis corporibus in hostem ruentes'.

[35] Certain terms for the charge to the enemy recur. The spurring of the horse recurs, for instance, at Sen. *Ep.* 67. 9: 'Decius se pro re publica devovit et in medios hostes *concitato equo* mortem petens inruit'. Versnel (1981) 153 argues that the spurring of the horse creates 'the element of *furor*, ecstasy and rapture realised by means of the uncheckable impulse of the frantic animal'. This should be compared to Versnel's discussion of 'se immittere'. Here Versnel compares the *devotio* of Decius with the equally famous *devotio* of Curtius at Livy, 7. 6. 5, observes how Curtius 'equo . . . exornato insidentem, armatum se in specum immisisse', and notes other examples of sacrifice or execution involving the simultaneous death of the horse. These tend to follow the Curtius theme of direct

resonance of the Decian paradigm is the manner in which often rather surprising figures are attracted into its field. Such instances also underline the significance of the characteristic modes of description. A striking example is the description of the Athenian King Codrus at Cic. *Tusc.* 1. 116. It is known that Codrus sacrificed himself for the good of the Athenian State but there is nothing in the Greek tradition to equate to Cicero's very Decian 'who cast himself into the midst of the enemy' (*qui se in medios immisit hostes*).[36] Were it not for the observations already made about the quality of his generalship, one might be even more surprised by the identification by commentators of the presence of the formula in Sallust's description of the death of Catiline at Pistoia. Catiline may be a model of *ferocia*, not *pietas*, but he is somewhat redeemed by the manner of his going:

> [Catilina] postquam fusas copias seque cum paucis relicuom videt, memor generis atque pristinae suae dignitatis *in confertissumos hostis incurrit ibique pugnans confoditur.*
>
> Catiline, after he saw that his forces had been defeated and that he was left with a few men, remembering his family and his antique dignity, ran into that spot where the enemy were most thickly set and there was struck down fighting.[37]

The observations made by Skard and Vretska on the affinity of Catiline's charge to death with that of the Decii might as easily be applied to the death of Hasdrubal. One possible approach to the study of *devotio*, therefore, is to examine those phenomena to which it bears the closest resemblance and analyse the social pressures which underly events in each category. This is the approach which I adopt in a

dispatch to the gods below, for instance by the dropping of the traitor Philumenus and his horse down a well at Livy, 27. 16. 4. In land battle, in the absence of the chance to send oneself down, 'to cast oneself into the midst of the enemy' (*se inmittere in medios hostis*) replicates on the horizontal plane the direct self-consecration of the *devotus* to the gods below, while the falling or gliding resonance of *ruere* and *labi* can express the ease of movement of the warrior as he cuts his way through the foe. On this point, see above p. 130 n. 31 for Oros. *Hist.* 3. 9. 3.

[36] I owe this example to a note in Vessey's discussion of Menoeceus, a Greek *devotus* celebrated in most Livian terms by Statius. See Vessey (1971) 239 n. 13. Cicero's version of the deed of Codrus draws on Roman terms which find no equivalent in the Greek account at Lycurgus, *In Leocraten* 84–7.

[37] Sall. *Cat.* 60. 7. Here, cf. Sall. *Cat.* 61. 4: 'Catilina vero longe a suis inter hostium cadavera repertus est, paululum etiam spirans ferociamque animi quam habuerat vivos in voltu retinens'. Vretska (1976) at Sall. *Cat.* 61. 4 observes of this scene that 'Die Erzählung wiederholt sich in breiterem Ausmass bei Liv. 8.9.10 über P. Decius Mus bis in die Einzelzüge'. This point is first made by Skard (1956) 32–3.

separate study on the dispute over the *devotio* of Turnus in the *Aeneid*.[38] This piece identifies as one of the structuring repetitions of the *Aeneid* the persistent description of a warrior's charge to the enemy, the deliberate intention or readiness to meet death signalized by the use of the future participle *moriturus* or *periturus*.[39] While the stylistic tone of this repetition is Homeric, the mentality described has little to do with the world of the Iliadic warrior, who is not accustomed to charge the line of the enemy with the deliberate intention or expectation of getting killed. On the other hand, it is possible to identify within this cluster motivating factors and characteristic actions regularly found in Roman *devotio* narratives.[40] If the claim of Turnus to have devoted his soul to the Latins and final self-sacrifice is equated with the actions clustered around this formula, then there is space to think of *devotio* in relatively broad terms and to study it in the context of the social pressures described in previous sections.

In the case of Pompey, it is necessary to think on two different levels at once. On the one hand, what first marks his actions as akin to those of the Decii is his prayer to the gods and the offering of his own suffering in exchange for that of his men. There is therefore a significant religious dimension to be considered. On the other hand, as in the case of the *Aeneid*, Roman accounts of Pharsalus throw up a cluster of further self-sacrificial charges which, when taken together, offer a more socio-political commentary on Pompey's deeds. The section which follows attempts to engage with both these dimensions.

[38] Leigh (1993). A similarly sociological approach to self-sacrifice in the *Aeneid* is hinted at in Skard (1956) 32 n. 3 and McGushin (1977) at Sall. *Cat.* 60. 7, who both cite *Aen.* 9. 400 as a parallel for the heroic charge of Catiline, but do not note the extensive pattern of such charges in the *Aeneid*.

[39] The formula is apparent at Verg. *Aen.* 2. 353 cf. 2. 407–8, 2. 509–11, 9. 399–401 cf. 9. 438, 9. 554–5, 10. 811–12, 10. 867–70 cf. 878–82, 11. 741–4. Conington (1883) and Mackail (1930) make the point at 11. 741, Austin (1964) at 2. 408; while only Quinn (1968) 12 n. 1 cites the entire list. He does not take the question any further. Conington's note at 11. 741 reports discussion as to whether the 'et ipse moriturus' of Tarchon indicates an intention or willingness to die as well as those he slays (Servius), as well as his men, not just exhorting, but also setting the example, or as well as those who have fallen already. As will be seen from this argument, I, like Conington, have some sympathy with the second view, though I also regard 'et ipse moriturus' as characterizing Tarchon intratextually by reference to the other figures cited above, and intertextually, by reference to the Decii. The implication of intentionality in Vergil's use of the future participle is what distinguishes the charge to death from other scenes in which a hero storms the line of the enemy or rushes to battle, for instance at Verg. *Aen.* 9. 799–800, 10. 20–2, 10. 379, 10. 575–6, 10. 729, 12. 477–8, 12. 497–9.

[40] Leigh (1993) 93–6 discusses characteristic actions, 98–103 societal pressures.

DEFORMATION OR DIALECTIC—APPROACHES TO *DEVOTIO* IN BOOK 7 OF THE *PHARSALIA*

Deformation

The self-sacrificial charge of the warrior to the midst of the enemy, on foot or more commonly on horseback, becomes the basic identifying mark of the *devotio*. The actions of Lucan's Pompey therefore have an inevitably paradoxical aspect: while his prayer demands the chance to substitute his suffering for that of Rome, the manner in which he goes about this substitution is the exact opposite of that conventionally expected of a *devotus*. The question here is how Lucan's readers are to interpret this paradox.

The predominant current in interpretation of this scene is that which regards the introduction of the concept of *devotio* as excusing or even celebrating a potentially reprehensible action by representing it according to a trope which implies the highest merit. The most sophisticated example of this approach is that of Rambaud, who conceives Book 7 as Lucan's counter-deformation of the hostile propaganda of Caesar's Commentaries. Rambaud's study of Lucan is an extension of his earlier work on Caesar,[41] and his methodology, like that of Stevens and of Carcopino,[42] applies insights, often gathered first-hand through wartime employment, into the propagandist method of composition employed by certain Latin authors, not least Caesar. Together with the image of Lucan as propagandist comes a further metaphor, that of the poet as counsel for the defence, an analogy which is revived by Lounsbury, whose work is acknowledgedly in debt to, and a deepening of, that of Rambaud.[43] Lounsbury then takes the propagandist case one step further and asserts that Book 7 is a free-standing entity, to be recited to Lucan's cohorts as a covert manifesto for the Pisonian conspiracy.

Is Lucan's account a deliberate attempt to rewrite the highly prejudicial description of Pompey's flight visible in Caesar? Caesar's *Bellum Civile* 3. 94 and 96 offers the following version:

> Sed Pompeius, ut equitatum suum pulsum vidit atque eam partem cui maxime confidebat perterritam animum advertit, aliis diffisus acie excessit protinusque

[41] See Rambaud (1953) for his work on propagandist deformation in Caes. *B. Civ.* and (1955) for his application of this methodology to Lucan.

[42] Carcopino (1947) and Stevens (1952).

[43] Lounsbury (1975) and (1976).

se in castra equo contulit et eis centurionibus quos in statione ad praetoriam portam posuerat clare, ut milites exaudirent, 'Tuemini', inquit, 'castra et defendite diligenter, si quid durius acciderit. Ego reliquas portas circumeo et castrorum praesidia confirmo'. Haec cum dixisset, se in praetorium contulit summae rei diffidens et tamen eventum exspectans ... Pompeius, iam cum intra vallum nostri versarentur, equum nactus detractis insignibus imperatoris decumana porta se ex castris eiecit protinusque equo citato Larisam contendit.

Yet when Pompey noticed that his cavalry had been defeated and that that section in which he particularly put his trust had been sent into panic, he lost faith in the others and left the line of battle and immediately took himself off on horseback to the camp and, so that the soldiers might hear, said in a loud voice to those centurions whom he had placed in charge of the entrance to the general's quarters, 'Watch over the camp and defend it diligently should anything go wrong. I am going round the other entrances with a view to fortifying the defences of the camp.' When he had said these words, he took himself off into the general's quarters, despairing of the crucial issue but still waiting for the outcome ... Pompey, when our men were now inside the defences, obtained a horse, stripped off his general's insignia, fled from the camp by the back entrance and immediately spurred his horse and made for Larisa.

Plutarch, *Pomp.* 72–3, Appian, *B. Civ.* 2. 81. 339–44, and Dio Cass., 42. 1–2 give equally unflattering accounts. Plutarch describes Pompey in battle as so paralysed as to be 'like a man deranged and mad of mind' (ὅμοιος παράφρονι καὶ παραπλῆγηι τὴν διάνοιαν), and both he and Appian liken him to Homer's Ajax. These writers also emphasize the eerie silence of Pompey sitting in the camp, and, like Caesar, report that Pompey stripped off his general's insignia before retreating to Larisa. Is Lucan any more sympathetic?

One crucial difference between Lucan and the historians is the manner in which he gives the reader access to his character's mentality prior to the flight. Where Plutarch reports that 'it is hard to say what reasoning he employed' (ὧι μὲν ἐχρήσατο λογισμῶι χαλεπὸν εἰπεῖν), and Caesar reflects Pompey's state of mind only through his actions (and then unfavourably), Lucan at 7. 647–711 mediates the narrative through the perspective of Pompey and goes on to record the terms of his prayer to the gods.[44] Some of these reflections, however, do not do

[44] For Rambaud (1955) 272 this distinction is of the essence: 'Différence capitale: cette halte de Pompée ne doit pas seulement prouver qu'il n'était point trop pressé de quitter son armée, elle permet en outre au poète de faire connaître les réflexions qu'inspirent à ce chef de parti le spectacle du combat où succombent les défenseurs de la république. Le récit de César est comparable aux romans d'une école américaine qui, ne rapportant que des gestes et quelques paroles, laissent au lecteur le soin de comprendre les états psychologiques qu'ils traduisent; dans le cas de Pompée, lâche, effroi, dérobade

im much credit. In the conclusion to this chapter, I examine the olitically (and generically) disturbing aspects of what Pompey is ortrayed as seeing in the battle. The weaknesses displayed are very imilar to those present in the prayer to the gods to turn their wrath n him *or on his family*. While it may have been customary for a Roman nale constantly to identify his family with himself, this still seems carcely Decian. It is as if, at the moment where Pompey starts to face esponsibility, he suddenly makes to shift it onto someone else, onto extus, onto Cornelia.

As for the account of his motives before leaving battle, it is their very nultiplication which causes concern. The first motive is the most onourable—Pompey envisages himself perhaps as Homer's Patroclus, he whole world fighting for possession of his corpse. Yet the second nd third motives destroy any impression of selflessness. If the *aut* vhich follows the first motive offers an exclusive 'either . . . or', then ucan admits to knowing as little of Pompey's actual motives as he did f his dream,[45] of the tides[46] or of the nature of causation.[47] If *aut* mplies that various motives worked together, then the rather gocentric selflessness of the first motive coexists with the self-nslavement of the second and third.

The account of Pompey's actions is no less ambiguous. Lounsbury otes that Lucan's Pompey rides only one horse to Caesar's two, and bandons the battlefield directly without recourse to the camp. This is aken as superior to the account given by the historians, in which ompey retreats to the camp, and only abandons it when it is hreatened by the Caesarians, a rather undignified procedure.[48] Instead f rushing to find any horse from the camp, Pompey rides away on the ame steed which he took to the battlefield.[49] Nor does he dissemble is status in Lucan, the poet omitting any reference to *mutatio vestis*.[50] 'he general who rides away from the field without need of disguise is o longer tainted with the presumption of cowardice. All this con-ributes to the eulogy of the fearless Pompey 'unafraid of a spear in his ack' (*non tergo tela paventem*).

riminelle, désertion dans la bataille, petitesse de l'âme. Le poème de la Pharsale invite à articiper aux sentiments du héros. L'idée dominante est que trop désintéressé, trop bon atriote, il ne put se résoudre à voir massacrer à cause de lui des troupes venues de tout e monde romain, et surtout pas l'élite de la race latine.'

[45] Luc. 7. 19–24: 'Seu . . . sive . . . seu.'

[46] Luc. 1. 412–7: 'an . . . an'.

[47] Luc. 2. 7–15: 'Sive . . . sive'. For multiple causation, see Feeney (1991) 279–83.

[48] Lounsbury (1976) 230.

[49] Ibid.

[50] Ibid.

The argument is attractive but frail. For even those who asser Lucan's propagandistic purpose are compelled to confess that it is ver short-lived. Where Book 7 required a fearless Pompey, 8. 5–8 nov represents the historical reality quietly slipping past the poet' suddenly less vigilant eye:

> Pavet ille fragorem
> motorum ventis nemorum, comitumque suorum
> qui post terga redit trepidum laterique timentem
> exanimat.

He is frightened by the sound of the trees rustling in the wind and any of hi allies who comes up to him from behind terrifies him in his anxiety and fear c attack.[51]

Similarly, it is hard to reconcile Lounsbury's heroic Pompey, to brave to engage in *mutatio vestis*, with the picture of the general a 8. 18–21:

> Gravis est Magno quicumque malorum
> testis adest. Cunctis ignotus gentibus esse
> mallet et obscuro tutus transire per urbes
> nomine.

Magnus finds it hard to bear any witness to his ills. He would rather b unknown to all the nations and to pass secure in anonymity through cities.

The apparent collapse of the propagandistic purpose is striking One conclusion to draw is that Lucan is an incompetent. Another is that there is a flaw in the counter-deformatory model. Is it not possibl that the inconcinnity between the close of Book 7 and the opening o Book 8 is indicative of a more complex rhetorical relationship, that th latter might function as the explicit acknowledgement of the irony implicit in the former? What, after all, does it actually mean to cele-brate the courage of someone riding away from battle 'unafraid of a spear in his back' (*non tergo tela paventem*)? Certainly, the alliteration o *tergo* and *tela* has a magniloquent tone, but it is unclear how the con-tent can match the form. Later in this study, I examine the systemati

[51] Postgate (1913) ad loc. claims of 'non tergo tela paventem' that 'Lucan lets out th truth at 8. 5 ff.'; Gagliardi (1975) remarks of the same phrase 'parole di puro omaggio scaturente dalla concitazione del momento; si dice *infatti* [my italics] di Pompeo fugitiv a VIII. 5–8'; cf. Ahl (1974) 313, 'At 7. 677 ff., Pompey is fearless as he gallops away fror Pharsalus, but at 8. 7–14 he is frightened by the rustling of leaves in the woods, and by the noise created by his companions', and Rambaud (1955) 293. Narducci (1979) 128 an n. 69 is more sceptical.

deformation of the relationship of *pectus* and *tergum* in the mentality of Lucan's Caesarians, but here is a prime example from Pompey himself.[52] For all the surface praise, there is truly nothing heroic about the absence of fear for his back of one galloping ever further away from the battle-lines he should have entered. There is nothing in this which might be equated with Antigone's description of Hypseus at *Thebaid* 7. 311–12:

> Ter insuto servantur pectora ferro,
> pectora: nam tergo numquam metus.

His breast is protected by three layers of woven mail—his breast, for there is never any fear for his back.

Hypseus has no fear for his back because he will never turn it—would that one could say the same for Pompey.

The *devotio* of Pompey simply does not serve the cause of exculpation. If it is posited that Lucan sought to explain away or even heroize the undignified retreat of Pompey recorded in Caesar, it is unclear why he should introduce a prayer formula the effect of which is to encourage ever further the presumption that Pompey the good general will charge the line of the enemy. To follow this with the assurance that Pompey was not afraid to suffer the wounds consequent on such a charge, that is those to the throat or chest, only enhances the sense of disappointment consequent on his doing exactly the opposite. Endorsing the theories of Rambaud, Le Bonniec extolled their ingenuity.[53] On closer examination, they, and those of Rambaud's followers, especially Lounsbury, seem more ingenious than convincing. The theory of counter-deformation requires us to close off too many areas of the text as non-pertinent, to make too many uncomfortably counter-intuitive judgements, and to invent a Roman reader implausibly passive and bone-headed.

Dialectic

The effect of Lucan's construction of the retreat of Pompey as a form of *devotio* is to highlight the distortion of the trope. The reader holds present the ideal form of the self-sacrificial charge and uses it as a measure by which to assess the inadequacies of the actions of the general. Pompey's deeds are put into sharper focus when matched against the nexus of expectations implicit in the myth-historical ideal of the Decii. This is how they become meaningful.

52 See Ch. 6, pp. 208–20.

53 Le Bonniec (1970) 159–60.

It is not necessary, however, simply to judge Pompey's actions from the implicit cultural model which he fails to follow. Book 7 of the *Pharsalia* contains the traces of three other heroic charges to the enemy, each of which may be held up as a more or less flattering parallel to the general.

The first parallel is by now familiar. The apostrophe of the narrator to Brutus at 7. 586–96, especially 590–2, has already been shown in Chapter 3 to turn on its imitation of the address of Aeneas to Lausus at *Aen.* 10. 811–12, and to play on the distance between the intent or willingness of Lausus (*moriture*) and the ignoble skulking (*plebeia contectus casside voltus*) of Brutus, who we know will not die (*periture*) until Philippi. Lucan's sarcastic attitude to the conduct of Brutus at Pharsalus is justified by the evidence for his less than vigorous conduct on the day and decidedly late-flowering Republicanism.[54] The scorn which is showered on Brutus is telling; for that which he fails to do is what Pompey can manage only by inversion. The two 'heroes' sit well together.

The second charge to the enemy is that of Crastinus. Lounsbury highlights the reversal of Caesar's portrayal of his centurion Crastinus and of the Pompeian Domitius in Book 7 of the *Pharsalia*.[55] While Caesar celebrates the boast of Crastinus, that that day Caesar will thank him whether alive or dead, and the heroism he shows in leading the charge, Lucan curses him as a Pandarus (Hom. *Il.* 4. 85–126) or a Tolumnius (Verg. *Aen.* 12. 257–69). While Caesar claims (with Cic. *Phil.* 2. 71)[56] that Domitius was caught and killed when fleeing from the battle, Lucan represents him as charging the enemy and there dying in arms, to the end the resolute defender of the Republic and Pompey.

Lounsbury's point is that these are the only two individual deaths recorded by Caesar. In Lucan, the only individual death recorded is

[54] Plut. *Brut.* 4. 3–4 records that Brutus spent the campaign in close attendance on Pompey and reading Polybius. But Plut. *Brut.* 6. 1–2 also reports that after the battle Brutus took refuge in Larisa, wrote to Caesar to ask his pardon, and betrayed the route of Pompey's flight. In 46 BC Caesar left Brutus as governor of Cisalpine Gaul while he went off to pursue Cato and Metellus Scipio in Africa (Plut. *Brut.* 6. 6).

[55] Lounsbury (1975). For Crastinus, see Caes. *B. Civ.* 3. 91 and 99, both of which passages are printed in full in my discussion of the Caesarian centurion in Lucan in Ch. 6 pp. 192–3. Note that Carter (1993) ad loc. sees elements of the *devotus* even in Caesar's Crastinus. For Domitius, see Caes. *B. Civ.* 3. 99. 5.

[56] Cicero says that 'L. Domitium, clarissimum et nobilissimum virum, occideras multosque praeterea qui e proelio effugerant, quos Caesar, ut non nullos, fortasse servasset, crudelissime persecutus trucidaras'. From this it is presumed that Domitius too was killed while in retreat.

hat of Domitius, the Republican hero now inheriting the praises granted to Crastinus, who, in turn, is condemned by the narrator. A certain symmetry is identified, and with it proof positive of Lucanian counter-deformation.

Yet the Crastinus story is not told only by Caesar. Livy speaks of Crastinus, and in a manner which marks him as Lucan's primary referent.[57] This alone should encourage reconsideration of simple one-on-one counter-deformation of Caesar. Moreover, Crastinus appears again at Plut. *Pomp.* 71. 1–3, Plut. *Caes.* 44. 5–6 and App., *B. Civ.* 2. 82. 347–8, and, since Asinius Pollio is cited at App., *B. Civ.* 2. 82. 346 as an eyewitness authority for the day's casualties, it seems reasonable to presume that he is also the source of Appian's Crastinus story, and perhaps for those of Plutarch as well.[58]

What is striking about the versions of Crastinus in Plutarch and Appian is that they all appear to translate the formula for the charge to death. Plutarch, *Caes.* 44. 6 records that 'with these words, he led the charge against the enemy' (ταῦτ᾽ εἰπὼν πρῶτος ἐμβάλλει τοῖς πολεμίοις δρόμωι), while Plut. *Pomp.* 71. 2 offers: 'he assaulted the middle of the enemy' (προσέβαλε κατὰ μέσους τοὺς πολεμίους) and App., *B. Civ.* 2. 82. 347: 'the army testified that he ran into the enemy rank like one possessed and performed many distinguished deeds' (ἡ στρατιὰ δ᾽ ἐμαρτύρει, καθάπερ ἔνθουν ἐς ἑκάστην τάξιν μεταθέοντα πολλὰ καὶ λαμπρὰ δρᾶσαι). This last is most significant, for the description of the centurion as ἔνθους gives him just that state of ecstasy or possession which is characteristic of the *devotus*. It is therefore reasonable to infer that Lucan, who has long been presumed to have known the works of Pollio as well as those of Livy and Caesar, was faced with a matrix of possible representations

[57] *Comm. Bern.* at Luc. 7. 470 reads: 'Crastinus dictus est hic qui primus iaculatus in Pompei aciem pilum bella commisit, qui, ut historia refert, adacto in os gladio, sic inter cadavera repertus est, libidinem ac rabiem qua pugnaverat ipsa novitate vulneris praeferebat. De quo Titus Livius dicit 'tunc fuisse evocatum, proximo anno deduxisse primum pilum Gaium Crastinum qui a parte Caesaris primus lanceam misit.' Endt (1909), *Adnotationes super Lucanum* at Luc. 7. 471, 'Proprium nomen est "Crastine" eius militis, qui primus tela iaculatus est, ut ait Titus Livius "primus hostem percussit nuper pilo sumpto primo Gaius Crastinus".' For discussion of the account in the *Commenta Bernensia* of the madness and the wounds of Crastinus, see Ch. 6, pp. 215–16. There is an obvious similarity between Livy and Lucan's accounts of Crastinus casting the first spear, but it is quite unclear whether the further information supplied in the *Commenta* is taken from Livy, 111 or from a further source. Certainly, the reference to the 'libidinem ac rabiem' of his engagement is very similar to the ecstasy apparently described by Pollio.

[58] See Syndikus (1958) 1–11 for Pollio as the presumed source for Appian and Plutarch.

which included the depiction of Crastinus as a latter-day, Caesarian Decius.[59]

Lounsbury's argument may therefore be enriched: Lucan resolves to deny Crastinus the kudos of *devotio*, chooses instead to transfer this mode of heroization to the Republican Domitius. The death of Domitius in Book 7—Lucan's most striking reformation of the historical account—has been shown in Chapter 2 to conform to the function first given to him in Book 2, that is as a representative of the rejection of *clementia*. His 'outstanding' death is also now represented as a rush to the enemy conducted with the falling or gliding ecstasy of the *devotus*, 7. 599–604:

> Mors tamen eminuit clarorum in strage virorum
> pugnacis Domiti, quem clades fata per omnis
> ducebant: nusquam Magni fortuna sine illo
> succubuit. Victus totiens a Caesare salva
> libertate perit: tunc mille in volnera laetus
> labitur ac venia gaudet caruisse secunda.

Yet in the slaughter of famous men the death of doughty Domitius stood out. Destiny was leading him through every disaster, Magnus' luck never went under without him as a companion. Beaten so often by Caesar he died with his Freedom intact: now [then] he fell gladly to a thousand wounds and rejoiced to have escaped a second pardon.

We see four deaths or near-deaths, all possessing qualities which relate to one primary model. Each of them is a presence in Lucan's text, each has left its traces. The argument that Lucan's Domitius is dressed in the clothes of Crastinus opens up a fertile area of investigation; the instant attribution of this phenomenon to a partisan yearning to rebut Caesar rather closes it off. To a less mechanical reading, however, the text will yield other possibilities. Lucan says that the outstanding death was that of Domitius, but the one to which he devotes most attention and which raises most anxieties is obviously that of Pompey. The presumption of excellence in the death of Domitius, the endorsement of his refusal to live on, give it a dialectical relationship with the deaths refused of Brutus and Pompey. These two Republican heroes do not so easily coexist with Domitius in an even pattern of exculpation and glorification, but are constantly questioned by him.

[59] For Lucan and Pollio, see Syndikus (1958) 8–11, Grimal (1970) 62, 66 f., 73, Ahl (1976) 23, 82–4, and Nisbet and Hubbard (1978) 9. Pichon (1912) 55 dismisses Pollio as too Caesarian in his sympathies to be consulted by Lucan. Yet on p. 54 he sets up the insane premise that Lucan can have consulted only one authority.

Domitius dies to the last the loyal Pompeian, but his general does not have it in him to reciprocate the devotion he is shown.

POMPEY—THE VIEW FROM THE HILL AND THE BODY OF THE STATE

Concentration on the representation of Pompey's flight as a form of *devotio*, close analysis of the social pressures and ideals implicit in this action, are not motivated by the vindictive desire to brand him a coward, a runaway. Rather, it is essential to look and to look again at this scene for the manner in which Lucan employs meditation on the idea of *devotio*, on the twin concepts of the body of the general, the body of the State, to evolve a far more sophisticated understanding of Pompey's position in a Republican ideology than could ever emerge from a crude desire to celebrate the cause by exculpating its leader. It is to this ideological construction that the rest of this chapter is given over. While the concept of *devotio* should never be lost from view, it is now essential to integrate more fully into the argument those factors the introduction of which by Lucan has already been marked as a crucial modification of the account presented by the historians: narration from the point of view of the general and the narrator's apostrophe to his character. First, however, some remarks, historical and generic, on the political meaning of fighting for Pompey.

King Pompey

Pompey is the commander of the forces of the Republic. At the same time, there is a widespread suspicion of him as the man who would be king. Seneca repeatedly equates Pompey with Caesar, contrasting the two despots with the one true Republican, Cato. At *Ep.* 14. 12–13, for instance, he discusses the problem of Cato, who 'while some fell foul of Pompey and some of Caesar, attacked them both' (*aliis Pompeium offendentibus, aliis Caesarem, simul lacessit duos*), and invents a notional objector to urge Cato not to fight:

> 'Quaeritur utrum Caesar an Pompeius possideat rem publicam: quid tibi cum ista contentione?'

> 'What is at issue is whether Caesar or Pompey should possess the state: what interest is there for you in that dispute?'[60]

[60] For the repunctuation of this passage to include the imaginary speaker, see M. T. Griffin (1968).

In Book 2 of the *Pharsalia*, Lucan dramatizes this debate.[61] Brutus urges Cato not to join the State in enslaving itself to Pompey, 2. 277–81:

> 'Pars magna senatus
> et duce privato gesturus proelia consul
> sollicitant proceresque alii; quibus adde Catonem
> sub iuga Pompei, toto iam liber in orbe
> solus Caesar erit.'

'When the large part of the senate and the consul and the rest of the chiefs are set on waging war under an unelected general, it is tempting to join up; but if you add Cato to these subjects of Pompey, the only free man now left in all the world will be Caesar.'

The response which he receives, while arguing the necessity of following Magnus, has no illusions as to the aims of the leader, 2. 319–23:

> 'Quin publica signa ducemque
> Pompeium sequimur? Nec, si fortuna favebit,
> hunc quoque totius sibi ius promittere mundi
> non bene conpertum est: ideo me milite vincat
> ne sibi se vicisse putet.'

'Why should I not follow the standards of the State and the command of Pompey? Yet, if fortune favours him, I know full well that he too promises himself dominion over all the world: for this reason let him win with my support lest he think that he won for himself.'[62]

Cato is, of course, talking to the same Brutus who composed the *De Dictatura Pompei*.[63] The hostility which this expressed to Pompey's ambitions was widespread. The sort of suspicion which Pompey provoked in his lifetime can be perceived from a succession of anecdotes recorded by Valerius Maximus.[64] Cn. Lentulus Marcellinus at 6. 2. 6 attacks Pompey in public and then responds to the applause of the audience with the barbed:

'Adclamate . . . adclamate, Quirites, dum licet: iam enim vobis inpune facere non licebit'.

[61] George (1991) gives a good discussion of this scene.

[62] For other instances of this theme in Seneca, see *Ep.* 95. 70: '. . . simul contra Caesarem Pompeiumque se sustulit et aliis Caesareanas opes, aliis Pompeianas . . . foventibus utrumque provocavit ostenditque aliquas esse et rei publicae partes'; *Ep.* 104. 29: '. . . et hunc licet dicas non minus quam Socraten in servis se libertati addixisse, nisi forte Cn. Pompeium et Caesarem et Crassum putas libertatis socios fuisse'; *Prov.* 3. 14, cf. *Constant.* 1. 3.

[63] A speech of 51 BC mentioned at Quint. *Inst.* 9. 3. 95 and Suet. *Jul.* 49. 2 and evidently designed to oppose Pompey's dictatorship.

[64] Val. Max. 6. 2. 6–9.

'Applaud . . . applaud, Citizens, while you can: soon you will not be able to do so with impunity.'

Likewise Favonius at 6. 2. 7, on seeing a silver band round Pompey's leg, quips:

'Non refert . . . qua in parte sit corporis diadema.'

'It matters not . . . on what part of the body the diadem is worn.'[65]

A related phenomenon in the imperial period is the tendency to talk of Pompey as a notional first *princeps*. This can be seen, for instance, at Sen. *Marc.* 20. 4 and Manil. 1. 794. In the latter he is even described as 'first man before the god' (*ante deum princeps*).[66] This is particularly interesting when one bears in mind the parallel tendency of the Republican opposition to the emperors to describe themselves as *Pompeiani*. It is a sign of the times that a political movement which should stand for the principles of separation and limitation of powers has to talk of itself in terms of the one man who led the cause.[67] Lucan is alert to this difficulty.

The political meaning of fighting for Pompey remains problematic throughout the *Pharsalia*. This can be seen in the obituaries conferred on Pompey by Lucan[68] and by Cato:[69] the praises of the general are

[65] Cf. ibid. 6. 2. 9 for the famous jibe of the tragic actor Diphilus: 'miseria nostra magnus est'.

[66] See Grenade (1950) 58–9. Similar ideas are expressed at Ov. *Pont.* 4. 3. 43, and Vell. Pat. 2. 40. 2 and 2. 53. 3. Note that Goold emends 'ante deum princeps' to 'ante diem princeps'.

[67] For the association of the Republican cause with celebration of Pompey, see Cic. *Phil.* 1. 36 and the 'Pompei statuae plausus infiniti'. But note also ibid. 13. 26–9, 13. 32, 13. 38, 13. 45 where *Pompeianus* is used by Antony as a term of disparagement for the senatorial cause in the civil war. The equation of 'Pompeian' with 'Republican' is apparent in the description of Labienus at Sen. *Controv.* 10, pref. 5 as one who 'Pompeianos spiritus nondum in tanta pace posuisset'. Sen. *Ira* 3. 30. 5 reveals the sort of misgivings that were felt concerning the general, describing some of the assassins of Caesar as 'aliosque post Pompeium demum Pompeianos'. See below for Luc. 7. 61 and 9. 24. In general, see Grenade (1950).

[68] Luc. 8. 813–15: 'Dic semper ab armis | civilem repetisse togam, ter curribus actis | contentum multos patriae donasse triumphos'.

[69] Luc. 9. 190–210. Note here the tendency to suggest a possible vice and then remark on Pompey's avoidance of it. Thus, at 192–5, he is 'salva | libertate potens, et solus plebe parata | privatus servire sibi, rectorque senatus, | sed regnantis, erat'. With particular regard to Pompey's military zeal, Cato observes that he, 9. 198–200, 'Invasit ferrum, sed ponere norat. | Praetulit arma togae, sed pacem armatus amavit. | Iuvit sumpta ducem, iuvit dimissa potestas'. The political significance of this most reflexive eulogy is summarized at 9. 204–7, and in a manner which leaves us with the clear impression that, whatever his restraint, there was something still very wrong with Pompey: 'Olim vera fides Sulla Marioque receptis | libertatis obit: Pompeio rebus adempto | nunc et ficta perit. Non iam regnare pudebit, | nec color imperii nec frons erit ulla senatus'.

expressed in such a way as ever to highlight the uncertainty felt for him during his career. Another sign is that even when the status of Pompey is said to be constitutional, that of the general of the Republic, this tends to be expressed by the now-familiar rhetorical procedure of negative assertion, that which is denied figuring prominently as an anxiety. Thus, the meeting of the exiled Senate at the start of Book 5 confers on Pompey the legal authority which is marked as absent in Caesar's subsequent march on Rome and usurpation of the consulship,[70] but Lucan's summary of the resolution is revealing, 5. 13–14:

Docuit populos venerabilis ordo
non Magni partes sed Magnum in partibus esse.

The venerable order taught the world that they were not the party of Magnus but that Magnus was one of their party.

Here, Lucan's phrasing raises, if only in order to deny, the sort of misgivings apparent in the words of the notional objector at Sen. *Ep.* 71. 9:

Sed Cn. Pompeius amittet exercitum, *sed illud pulcherrimum rei publicae praetextum, optimates, et prima acies Pompeianarum partium, senatus ferens arma*, uno proelio profligabuntur et tam magni ruina imperii in totum dissiliet orbem.

But Cn. Pompeius will lose an army, [but] that most lovely ornament of the State, the optimates and the front line of the Pompeian party, the senate at war, will be overthrown in one battle and the ruins of that great power-group will be scattered throughout the world.

The senate at 5. 13–14 deny what is implied in Seneca: that they fight for Pompey and not he for them. Yet the anxiety does not go away. Discussing *Pharsalia* 7. 45–85, for instance, Lounsbury argues that Lucan exculpates the senators.[71] Plutarch and Appian record the feuding among the *optimates* in Pompey's camp and the jibes of Domitius, calling Pompey King of Kings and Agamemnon.[72] Lucan cannot exclude this dispute, but attributes the complaints to the (7. 47) 'largest part of the wretched mass' (*miseri pars maxima volgi*) and to the barbarian kings, 7. 51–7:

Dira subit rabies: sua quisque ac publica fata
praecipitare cupit; segnis pavidusque vocatur
ac nimium patiens soceri Pompeius, *et orbis*
indulgens regno, qui tot simul undique gentis

[70] See Luc. 5. 381–402, esp. 385–6: 'Namque omnis voces, per quas iam tempore tanto | mentimur dominis, haec primum repperit aetas . . .' etc.
[71] Lounsbury (1976) 212–13.
[72] Plut. *Pomp.* 67. 3, *Caes.* 41. 1–2; App. *B. Civ.* 2. 67. 278.

iuris habere sui vellet pacemque timeret.
Nec non et reges populique queruntur Eoi
bella trahi patriaque procul tellure teneri.

Dire madness entered: each man sought to hasten his own and the state's destiny; Pompey was accused of being slow and fearful and too indulgent of his father-in-law, and of pursuing universal rule, who wished to hold so many nations together from all over at one time under his rule and feared peace. And the kings and the peoples of the East complained at the prolongation of the war and at their being held away from their homelands.

When finally Cicero lends his voice to the complaint, Pompey is forced to bow, and Rambaud and Lounsbury can treat this as a mark of his Republican constitutionalism.[73] Yet none of this will wish away the terms of the narrator's lament at 7. 58–61. 'We' are *Pompeiani* and 'we' have asked for war:

Hoc placet, o superi, cum vobis vertere cuncta
propositum, nostris erroribus addere crimen?
Cladibus inruimus nocituraque poscimus arma;
in Pompeianis votum est Pharsalia castris.

Is it your pleasure, gods, when you have decided to destroy everything, to add guilt to our errors? We rush to the slaughter and we demand arms that will do us harm; in the Pompeian camp Pharsalia is the prayer.

With this one might compare the double nature of the soldiers' fear at 7. 137–8:

Non vacat ullos
pro se ferre metus: urbi Magnoque timetur.

There is no time to fear for themselves: they fear for Rome and for Magnus.

Most important of all, however, is the attitude of the Cilician auxiliaries at 9. 215–93. At 9. 227–30, their representative is quite frank in expressing his loyalties:

'Nos, Cato, da veniam, Pompei duxit in arma,
non belli civilis amor, partesque favore
fecimus. Ille iacet quem paci praetulit orbis,
causaque nostra perit.'

'Cato, forgive us, love of Pompey not of civil war induced us to fight and it was personal favour that decided which party we followed. He is dead whom the world loved better than peace and our cause is lost.'

[73] Rambaud (1955) 262–6 cf. Lounsbury (1976) 213–17.

Cato's reply at 9. 256–8 is crucial:

> 'Ergo pari voto gessisti bella, iuventus,
> tu quoque pro dominis, et *Pompeiana* fuistis
> *non Romana* manus?'

'So, young men, did you too wage war with the same aim of serving a master and were you a Pompeian, not a Roman band?'[74]

Throughout the *Pharsalia*, therefore, the Republican side is also, and more troublingly, Pompeian. Moreover, that which is disturbing in the attitude of the troops is more radically problematic in that of the general. It is to this question that I now wish to turn in the following section. In the process, I shall investigate the importance of the epic framework of the *Pharsalia* for the observations which hitherto have been made on a political and historical level.

Pompey: Epic Hero, General, King

Epic is not a democratic form. If this is just banally true for Homeric epic, if the verse of the *Iliad* mirrors the monarchical reality of the society in which it is composed, this is not the case for Vergil. It is not accidental that the *Aeneid*, written in a Rome emerging from the crisis of the dying Republic, should offer a national foundation myth which is also a foundation myth for monarchy. Aeneas is given an extra dimension, becomes the figure with whose identity and destiny the meaning of Vergil's epic is inextricably linked.

The epic hero is expected to transcend the historical hierarchy of State–general–army and in some way to represent all the elements of this triad: the lone warrior of the *aristeia* assuming the role of the anonymous masses, the 'kingly' Aeneas both commanding his troops and embodying the State for which they fight. It is this to which Hardie refers when he introduces the concept of the 'synecdochic hero.'[75] Thus, he observes of Aeneas that his isolation is not that of an Odysseus deprived of comrades, but rather: 'the loneliness of power and responsibility . . . of the representative and original ancestor of a race; in him we meet the first clearly defined example of the "synecdochic hero", the individual who stands for the totality of his people

[74] Cf. Scaeva at Luc. 6. 245–6: '*Pompei* vobis minor est *causaeque senatus* | quam mihi mortis amor'.

[75] Hardie (1993), esp. 4–5 and 29 *re* Verg. *Aen.* 12. 693–6: 'Here the language of the sacrificial victim and the language of the pre-eminent hero coincide: "unus pro omnibus" may refer either to the epic warrior in his "aristeia" fighting on behalf of his people, or the scapegoat singled out to bear the guilt of his community.'

present and future, part for whole'.[76] The synecdoche is not simply generic to epic as a whole, but carries with it the acceptance of a new political order. Aeneas as father of the race is an analogous figure for Augustus, the *pater patriae*.[77]

The problem for Pompey is that that which unites the heroic figure of Aeneas with the monarchical ideology he represents is radically incompatible with the Republican values of the Senate. It is therefore worth noting that a consistent feature of Lucan's narrative is to compromise the 'constitutional' Pompey by decking him out in the trappings of epic. This is the function of the simile for the withdrawal of Pompey to Brundisium at 2. 601–7:

> Pulsus ut armentis primo certamine taurus
> silvarum secreta petit vacuosque per agros
> exul in adversis explorat cornua truncis
> nec redit in pastus, nisi cum cervice recepta
> excussi placuere tori, mox reddita victor
> quoslibet in saltus comitantibus agmina tauris
> invito pastore trahit . . .

As a bull driven from the herd in the first fight makes for the inner parts of the woods and through the empty fields tests his horns on the facing tree-trunks and does not return to the pasture until he has back the strength of his neck and the vigour of his flexed muscles satisfies him, and soon victorious leads the herd into whichever woods he chooses, even against the will of the herdsman, with the other bulls in his train . . .

This is, of course, a rather ironic contrast simile, in that Pompey will never properly return to the pasture, and will follow the exile of Brundisium with that of Epirus and then of Thessaly.[78] Further, however, it is also a simile with clear epic precedents,[79] and thus one that figures Pompey and, implicitly, Caesar, as epic heroes: the cause of the Republic and the Senate is put in the shade by the *aemulatio* of the two bulls jousting over the passive and dependent herd.

Secondly, and rather obviously, 2. 728–30 casts Pompey as Aeneas, Priam, and Augustus as he quits Italy and enters exile:

[76] Ibid. 4.

[77] Ibid. 5, 'National salvation ensured by the extension over the whole state of the family head's "patria potestas" justifies the synecdochic hero in Virgil.'

[78] Don Fowler points out to me that 'cervice recepta' is particularly mordant in the context.

[79] Aymard (1951) 50, offers Ap. Rhod. 2. 88–9; Verg. *Aen.* 12. 103–6 and 715–24; Ov. *Met.* 9. 46–9; but particularly stresses the obvious model of Verg. *G.* 3. 220–41.

> Cum coniuge pulsus
> et natis totosque trahens in bella penates
> vadis adhuc ingens populis comitantibus exul.

Driven out together with your wife and children and taking all the household deities off to war, you go a still huge exile with peoples in your train.

For Priam, one is reminded of *Aen.* 2. 557–8 and the presumed allusion to Pompey as Magnus:

> Iacet ingens litore truncus,
> avulsumque umeris caput et sine nomine corpus.

He lies a huge trunk on the shore and the head is torn off from the shoulders and the body is without name.

For Aeneas, the crucial intertext is *Aen.* 3. 11–12:

> Feror exsul in altum
> cum sociis natoque penatibus et magnis dis.

I was borne into the sea, an exile, together with my companions, my son, the household deities and the great gods.

For Augustus, it is the shield's depiction of Actium at *Aen.* 8. 678–9:

> Hinc Augustus agens Italos in proelia Caesar
> cum patribus populoque, penatibus et magnis dis.

On one side is Augustus Caesar leading the Italians into battle together with the senators and the people, the household deities and the great gods.

It is tempting to pause on some of the ironies in Lucan's description of Pompey, on the contrast between his sorry pair of sons and the splendid Ascanius, on the people of Augustus and the peoples of Pompey (he has just summoned all the conquered races of the East); but the main point is that Lucan's Pompey, the constitutional general of the Roman Senate, when refigured as King Augustus and Hero Aeneas, stands less as the leader of the whole than as the whole itself.

Lucan compromises Pompey by encouraging the reader to regard him as the synecdochic hero. Pompey, meanwhile, talks of himself as if he were that hero. This tendency is sadly appropriate to one who is recorded by Quintilian for the eloquence of his self-praise and condemned by Seneca for his mad love of false grandeur.[80]

[80] Quint. *Inst.* 11. 1. 36, 'Pompeius abunde disertus rerum suarum narrator', cf. Sen. *Ep.* 94. 64, 'insanus amor magnitudinis falsae'. The passage in Quintilian is particularly interesting for the contrast between the rhetoric appropriate to a 'princeps' as opposed to his subjects, to 'imperatorum ac triumphalium' (Pompey) as opposed to the 'eloquens senator' (Cato).

Pompey's epic self-figuration emerges in his harangue at 2. 531–95. The start of this speech is pervaded with assertions of constitutionalism. Pompey gives great emphasis to the authority conferred by the Senate[81] and by Rome[82] and then, finishing with another reassertion of his submission to the constitution, gives a clear expression of the democratic limits placed on his heroic *aemulatio*, 2. 562–7:

'Quo potuit civem populus perducere liber
ascendi, supraque nihil nisi regna reliqui.
Non privata cupis, Romana quisquis in urbe
Pompeium transire paras. Hinc consul uterque,
hinc acies statura ducum est. Caesarne senatus
victor erit?'

'I have climbed as far as a free people could raise a citizen and have left nothing beyond save monarchy. If you seek in a Roman city to surpass Pompey, your ambitions are not those of a citizen. On this side will stand both the consuls, on this side an army of generals. Will Caesar be the conqueror of the Senate?'

Yet the rhetoric of Pompey takes a decided turn in the second half of the speech and adopts the perspective of the epic hero who represents the whole of his people, for whose *aemulatio* the war offers an ideal expression. This *aemulatio* emerges at 2. 575, where Pompey apostrophizes Caesar and explains the flight of the peoples:

'Heu demens, non te fugiunt, *me* cuncta secuntur.'
'Alas, madman, the world does not flee you, it follows me.'

The appointed servant of the Senate forgets his position and represents the war as 'my affair'. This way of thinking gradually takes control of Pompey's mind and dominates the close of the harangue, Luc. 2. 583–95:

'Pars mundi *mihi* nulla vacat, sed tota tenetur
terra *meis*, quocumque iacet sub sole, tropaeis:
hinc *me* victorem gelidas ad Phasidos undas
Arctos habet, calida medius *mihi* cognitus axis
Aegypto atque umbras nusquam flectente Syene,
occasus *mea* iura timent Tethynque fugacem
qui ferit Hesperius post omnia flumina Baetis,
me domitus cognovit Arabs, *me* Marte feroces

[81] Luc. 2. 531–3: 'O scelerum ultores melioraque signa secuti, | *o vere Romana manus, quibus arma senatus* | *non privata dedit*, votis deposcite pugnam'.

[82] Luc. 2. 537–9: 'Di melius, belli tulimus quod damna priores: | coeperit inde nefas, iam iam *me praeside Roma* | *supplicium poenamque petat*'.

Heniochi notique erepto vellere Colchi,
Cappadoces *mea* signa timent et dedita sacris
incerti Iudaea dei mollisque Sophene,
Armenios Cilicasque feros Taurumque subegi:
quod socero bellum praeter civile reliqui?'

'No part of the world is left to me, but all the earth, under whichever sun it lies, is occupied by my trophies: the North on one side has seen me the victor at the icy waters of the Phasis; the middle zone [the South] is known to me in hot Egypt and in Syene where the shadows fall straight down; the West and Spanish Baetis, most distant of all rivers which strikes the ebbing tides, fear my authority. The conquered Arab, the Heniochi ferocious in war and the Colchians famous for the stolen fleece know me; the Cappadocians and the Jews devoted to the worship of an unknown god and soft Sophene fear my standards; I have conquered the Armenians and the wild Cilicians and Taurus: which war save civil war have I left to my father-in-law?'

This is not just the rhetoric of a general seeking to inspire his troops.[83] It is also a revealing portrait of Pompey's mentality, of the straining tensions between the role granted him by the Senate and the epic, heroic delusions to which he clings. The constant repetition of the first-person pronoun is italicized with reason. Here, it may be interpreted as the bluster of a general representing his soldiers' war as a quarrel 'between me and him'. Yet, when the repetition returns, at the point of Pompey's *devotio*, that is at the crisis of Pompey's representative status, it reveals a delusion far more disastrous and destructive.

The View from the Hill—Pompey's Kingly Perspective

The crucial lines are those with which the *devotio* narrative begins at 7. 647–69:

Iam Magnus transisse deos Romanaque fata
senserat infelix, tota vix clade coactus
fortunam damnare *suam*. Stetit aggere campi,
eminus unde omnis sparsas per Thessala rura
aspiceret clades, quae bello obstante latebant.
Tot telis *sua* fata peti, tot corpora fusa
ac *se* tam multo pereuntem sanguine vidit.
Nec, sicut mos est miseris, trahere omnia *secum*
mersa iuvat gentesque *suae* miscere ruinae:
ut Latiae post *se* vivat pars maxima turbae,

[83] Which, of course, Luc. 2. 596–7 makes plain to be exactly what he fails to do.

sustinuit dignos etiamnunc credere votis
caelicolas, vovitque, *sui* solacia casus.
'Parcite', ait 'superi, cunctas prosternere gentes.
Stante potest mundo Romaque superstite Magnus
esse miser. Si plura iuvant *mea* volnera, coniunx
est *mihi*, sunt nati: dedimus tot pignora fatis.
Civiline parum est bello, si *meque meosque*
obruit? Exiguae clades sumus orbe remoto?
Omnia quid laceras? Quid perdere cuncta laboras?
Iam nihil est, Fortuna, meum'. Sic fatur et arma
signaque et adflictas omni iam parte catervas
circumit et revocat matura in fata ruentis
seque negat tanti.

By now the unhappy Magnus had sensed that the gods and the destiny of Rome had crossed over to the enemy, though even the totality of the slaughter scarce could force him to despair of his fortune. He stood on a mound on the field from where far off he could see the slaughter scattered over the countryside of Thessaly, which lay invisible with war to block the view. He saw his life sought by so many weapons, so many bodies laid out and himself dying in so much blood. Yet he did not, as is the habit of the wretched, wish to drag everything down to destruction with him and to involve nations in his own ruin: he bore even now to consider the gods worthy of his worship and prayed, as solace for his fortune, that the greatest part of the Latin band might live after him. 'Hold back, O gods', he said, 'from laying every nation low. Though the world endure and Rome stay alive, Magnus can be wretched. If you wish to wound me further, I have a wife, I have sons; I have given so many hostages to the fates. Is it not enough for the civil war if it crushes me and my family? If the world is not included are we a tiny disaster? Why do you tear everything? Why do you endeavour to destroy everything? Fortune, I have nothing left of my own.' Thus he spoke and he went round the army and the standards and the troops beaten on every side and called them back as they rushed to a ready death and denied that he was worth so much.

The synecdochic hero stands for his entire nation. In heroic epic, he fights alone in the *aristeia*, one man against whole armies. In Lucan, it is a mark of the reduced circumstances of his world that neither Caesar nor Cato nor Pompey contrives personally to kill anyone else in the course of the poem. Yet the idea of the synecdochic hero is present first in the imaginings of Pompey, second in the suggestive figurations of the narrator.

The synecdochic hero is troubling for Lucan, for the Republican reader, because he is the creation of a genre rewritten to speak for monarchy. Pompey, the Republican leader, is the man who threatens to be king, the man whom too many of his followers already regard as king. The more he is figured as the hero, the more he sees himself in such a light, the more urgent are the political misgivings aroused.

The *devotio* scene acts as a focus for these misgivings. The charge to death amidst the enemy is the action of a Republican hero. The good general temporarily commands absolute devotion from his men. They 'follow his name', obey his word, but, should disaster strike, he follows them into the line of battle, endeavours to substitute his death for theirs.

This is the model to which Pompey should conform. Yet the version of the *devotio* which he does perform is botched because the product of his own inversion of the heroic. While the true synecdochic hero fights as the embodiment of his people, Pompey looks on the battle and sees not just his people dying for him, but, worse, 'himself dying in so much blood' (*se tam multo pereuntem sanguine*). He sees 'his life sought by so many weapons' (*tot telis sua fata peti*) and, standing on the edge of the slaughter, he laments that whole nations should be mixed in 'his ruin' (*suae ruinae*). This is a terrible delusion, and, worse, one that is thoroughly Augustan, thoroughly Vergilian in character. The ancient commentators make the point better than anyone:

> Nam exercitus corpus est imperatoris, ut ait Vergilius: 'toto certatum est corpore regni'.

For the army is the body of the general/emperor, as Vergil says: 'they fought with all the body of the kingdom'.[84]

What the commentator identifies is the definitively monarchical perspective of Pompey. It is a commonplace in Roman political writing to represent the State as a body and to represent civil war as discord between the different members.[85] While the struggle for dominion in

[84] See Endt (1909) for *Adnotationes super Lucanum* at Luc. 7. 653.

[85] The best discussion of the Roman concept of the body of the State is Béranger (1953) 218–51. The representation of civil strife as a conflict between different parts of the same State is familiar from the fable of Menenius Agrippa at Livy 2. 32. 8–12, cf. Dion. Hal. *Ant. Rom.* 6. 86. Lucan repeatedly exploits Anchises' vain plea to Caesar and Pompey at Verg. *Aen.* 6. 832–3, 'Ne, pueri, ne tanta animis adsuescite bella | neu patriae validas in viscera vertite viris', starting at 1. 2–3 with the reference to the 'populumque potentem | in sua victrici conversum viscera dextra' and concretizing this notion through the deeds of Caesar, for instance at 7. 579–81 and 721–3. At Luc. 7. 406–7, I follow Housman in printing 'cladis eo dedimus, ne tanto in corpore bellum | iam possit civile geri', preferring 'corpore' ZMG over 'tempore' PUV (for Lucan's phrasing and the enormous body of the State, cf. Sen. *Clem.* 2. 2. 1, 'per omne immane imperii corpus').

civil war is represented as a multiplication of rival heads, Roman celebrations of the coming of Augustus (or of the latest of his successors) emphasize the restoration of a single benevolent head or intellect to the body of the State.[86] At Seneca, *De Clementia* 1. 5. 1, the essential corollary of this last position is drawn out and in terms strongly reminiscent of the judgement of the *Adnotationes*: 'you are the mind of your State, it is your body' (*animus rei publicae tuae es, illa corpus tuum*).

Pompey's perspective is the final product of the heroic *aemulatio* which could treat the civil war as his fight with Caesar. It is a delusion so shocking as to force the reader to awareness of the political tensions, the implicit Augustanism, which have underlain the concept of heroism throughout the poem. Pompey's inverted version of the synecdoche sees not the part standing for the whole, the hero for his people, but rather the whole standing for the part. For the general watching the slaughter of his men and seeing in it only his own death, the only solution is to run away. Lucan's apostrophe fully exploits the ironies implicit in this situation, 7. 680–97:

> Non gemitus, non fletus erat, salvaque verendus
> maiestate dolor, qualem te, Magne, decebat
> Romanis praestare malis. Non inpare voltu
> aspicis Emathiam: nec te videre superbum
> prospera bellorum nec fractum adversa videbunt;
> quamque fuit laeto per tres infida triumphos
> tam misero Fortuna minor. Iam pondere fati
> deposito securus abis; nunc tempora laeta
> respexisse vacat, spes numquam inplenda recessit;
> quid fueris nunc scire licet. Fuge proelia dira
> ac testare deos nullum, qui perstet in armis,
> iam tibi, Magne, mori. Ceu flebilis Africa damnis
> et ceu Munda nocens Pharioque a gurgite clades,
> sic et Thessalicae post te pars maxima pugnae
> non iam Pompei nomen populare per orbem
> nec studium belli, sed par quod semper habemus,
> libertas et Caesar erit; teque inde fugato
> ostendit moriens *sibi se pugnasse senatus*.

There was no groaning, no weeping, and a noble grief which preserved dignity, the sort which it was fitting for you, Magnus, to offer to the ills of Rome. You look on Emathia with an unchanged expression: success in war did not see you

[86] For the monarch's head restoring order to the discordant limbs of the State, see esp. Curt. 10. 9. 1–6. For the monarch as head or intellect, see Sen. *Clem.* 2. 2. 1; Tac. *Ann.* 1. 12–13; Flor. *Epit.* 2. 14. 5.

arrogant, nor will defeat see you broken; and just as faithless Fortune was less than you through your happy days of the three triumphs, so she is when you are wretched. Now, laying aside the burden of destiny, you go away unconcerned; now there is room to look back on the happy times; ambition fated never to be satisfied has retreated; now it is possible to know what you were. Flee the dire battle, Magnus, and take the gods as your witness that no man who stays to fight any longer dies for you. Just as Africa lamentable for its losses and just as guilty Munda and the slaughter by the stream of the Nile, so too the greatest part of the fight in Thessaly is no longer about the popularity and fame of Pompey throughout the world or about zeal for war, but rather the pair will be that which ever we have: Freedom and Caesar. With you put to flight, the Senate by dying shows that it fought for itself.

Lucan celebrates the manner of the great one as he leaves the field, his majestic, unbroken nobility in the face of *his* fate. All the time that he salutes the general he also plays along with his egocentric delusions: Pompey now can lay aside the burden of fate, can retreat from ambition, can know what once he was. For his soldiers there is no way out. Yet, amidst the carnage, there is at least the redemption of knowing that there is a cause worthy of support.

As Lucan's address to Pompey moves on, the growing consciousness of this second cause brings with it its own perspective, one radically at odds with that which has gone before. Pompey is put to flight, but the battle continues and will endure as those who fight for liberty take up arms not for another king but for themselves. Lucan's closing *sententia* does not compromise, turns Pompey's point of view on its head as the senators claim for themselves an angry last word: 'the Senate by dying shows that it fought for itself' (*ostendit moriens sibi se pugnasse senatus*), sibilant in its scorn, refutes their former leader's conceits in the terms in which they were expressed, and protests a creed without heroes, without kings.[87]

CONCLUSION

Chapter 1 began with the analysis of a passage, Lucan 7. 185–213, where the poet expresses his intention emotionally to engage his readers and to induce them to cheer for Pompey (*adhuc tibi, Magne, favebunt*). At this point in his narrative, therefore, Lucan seems happy to endorse the conventional Julio-Claudian equation of the Republican

[87] Cf. Cato at Luc. 2. 323, determined to join the Republican cause lest Pompey 'sibi se vicisse putet'.

with the Pompeian cause. The conclusions drawn from the analysis of 7. 647–711 are very different.

The assertion that the readers will cheer for Pompey is problematic from the start. For them to do so, they must be either ignorant of the anxieties expressed by Brutus and Cato as early as Book 2, or unconcerned or willing to suppress concern in the heat of the battle. The evocation of Pompey's perspective and the view from the hill only brings back to prominence and confirms suspicions that it has been possible to harbour throughout. The contrast between the two passages in Book 7 involves inconcinnity but not incoherence.

The reader is invited to watch the battle in company with Pompey. For one accustomed to Lucan's repeated assertion that to watch is to be complicit and that the dissenter must finally engage, Pompey's decision to abandon the spectacle only in order to run away is deeply uncomfortable. Yet what truly undoes the general is the second consequence of watching through his eyes—the awareness of the terrible gap in understanding between Pompey and those who fight on his side.

The *Pharsalia* is too sceptical a poem to have much time for uncritical celebration or exculpation, least of all of Pompey. A serious Republican voice is there to be found, but only if the poem is freed from the false integrations of propaganda and given full scope as a disillusioned, excoriating meditation on the experience of history.

5

Scaeva—Lucan's Exemplary Hero

At the height of his *aristeia*, when apparently overcome at last by his wounds, Caesar's centurion Scaeva pulls one final trick. Feigning surrender, he cries out, 6. 230:

> 'Parcite . . . cives; procul hinc avertite ferrum.'
>
> 'Spare me citizens; turn your swords far away from here.'

With the protest that no more wounds can contribute to his death, he then urges the Pompeians to carry him alive into the camp of their general, adding, 6. 234–5:

> 'Sit Scaeva relicti
> Caesaris exemplum potius quam mortis honestae.'

'Let Scaeva be an example of the abandonment of Caesar rather than of an honourable death.'

This is, of course, a ruse, giving our hero the chance to kill one last Pompeian and to proclaim his warped superiority, 6. 245–6:

> 'Pompei vobis minor est causaeque senatus
> quam mihi mortis amor.'

'You love Pompey and the cause of the Senate less than I love death.'

The arrival of Caesar's cohorts finally rescues Scaeva from retribution, and his own men lead him into their camp, 6. 253–4:

> Ac velut inclusum perfosso in pectore numen
> et vivam magnae speciem Virtutis adorant.

And they worship the divine power which seems shut up in his pierced breast and the living image of great Valour.

However, *virtus* is a traditional Roman Republican military virtue and not one easily attributed to this particular character. He who pretended to be an *exemplum* of the desertion of Caesar, who was then taken by his side for a simple (dis-)embodiment of *virtus*, is finally given a significantly different meaning by the narrator as he closes the episode, 6. 257–62:

Felix hoc nomine famae,
si tibi durus Hiber aut si tibi terga dedisset
Cantaber exiguis aut longis Teutonus armis.
Non tu bellorum spoliis ornare Tonantis
templa potes, non tu laetis ululare triumphis.
Infelix, quanta dominum virtute parasti!

Happy you would be with this claim to repute, had the tough Spaniard or the Cantabrian with his short weapons, the Teuton with his long, retreated before you. You cannot decorate the temples of the Thunderer with the spoils of war, you cannot cry out in joyous triumphs. Unhappy man, with what valour did you procure a master!

This meditation on the concept of *virtus* is fundamental to readings of Scaeva from Rutz to Marti, Conte, Ahl, Johnson, and beyond.[1] This is not surprising, since it is the central concept of the Scaeva episode, one which, in miniature, can encapsulate the approach adopted by Lucan to the description in epic of scenes of civil war in which the conventional evaluations do not apply. In the analysis of different

[1] Rutz (1960) 474 concludes that '"Virtus" ist bei Lucan absolut, gelöst von ihren ethischen Bindungen und daher zum möglichen Bestandteil des Bösen geworden'. This opinion is similar to the judgement offered in Deratani (1970), esp. 145 and to that to be found in Metger (1957) 176. Conte (1974) at 257–62 observes that 'L'impresa eroica del centurione si rivela, alla fine, tutto un "exemplum" negativo: la "virtus" di Sceva è criminale, egli ha agito "fortiter" ma non "bene". Così negargli la possibilità di dedicare le spoglie di guerra è come negare questa sua "virtus" e ogni onorevole riconoscimento ad essa connesso'; while Ahl (1976) 118 quotes Marti (1966) 254: '"Virtus" is here given a precise definition. It is the paradoxical opposite of that highest quality of the Stoics . . . embodied in Cato. Because he is deluded by his ignorance of what is right, Scaeva's valour, ironically, is an evil, the antithesis of what is morally desirable.' Johnson (1987) 57 says of *virtus* in Lucan in general that there is a 'Lucanian epic convention' for 'parodic subversion of the martial arts that entails a radical rejection of the idea of *virtus* on which the epic is founded', and adds *re* Scaeva in particular, p. 59, that '"Species virtutis" is now the sham appearance of virtue, for it is a false virtue that creates *from* itself slavery *for* itself'. Heyke (1970) 153 n. 3 says that Scaeva's *virtus* is 'gepriesen und zugleich gedauert'. Amidst all this consensus, one should also note the eccentric Schnepf (1953), excerpted in Rutz (1970*b*), which recognizes both the drive to death of Scaeva and of the men of Vulteius, also the constant play on exemplarity in the *Pharsalia*, but concludes that all the examples are positive and that (Rutz (1970*b*) 389), 'Diese Todesbejahung ist sache der "virtus".' Most recently, Hardie (1993) 68–9, has offered a more conventional analysis, but one which stresses the inhuman in Scaeva's *virtus*, analysing the elements of the bestial and of the divine in his depiction. For the perversion of *virtus* in a civil-war context, cf. Luc. 1. 667–8, 'scelerique nefando | nomen erit virtus'; Cic. *Off.* 1. 62, 'non modo enim id non virtutis est, sed est potius immanitatis omnem humanitatem repellentis'; and *Anth. Lat.* 460. 19 (SB), 'quod fuerat virtus, factum est scelus'.

aspects of battle narrative in Lucan in the ensuing chapters, therefore, the problem of *virtus* is a recurrent concern. In particular, in this chapter, attention is focused on the specific intellectual context of *virtus*; on the literary forms and customs through which martial values were communicated; on the impact on Lucan's battle narration of the assumption of these various discursive forms and voices. This perspective will also offer a further instance of Lucan's reaction to a Roman literary form or institution centred on the concept of spectacle, and, by extension, reveal some of the strangeness and the black humour of the Scaeva episode.

The title of this chapter stresses the problem of exemplarity. Conte is clearly aware of the significance of this idea, for his notes at, for instance, 6. 196–201 and 257–62, stress the *exemplum* at moments where it might be passed by.[2] At 6. 235, the one explicit reference to the *exemplum*, he cites 3. 730 and 4. 496–9, and emphasizes the quasi-theatrical exhibitionism of the character, the new status of his action as something performed specifically for the benefit of the audience around him, and the close relationship with the exemplary tradition of Valerius Maximus.[3]

Conte's analysis is of the greatest importance, but it requires both extension and refinement. Two tasks in particular present themselves. The first is to classify the different uses made of the *exemplum* in ancient moral and rhetorical education; the second to explore the literary hinterland to which Lucan refers in this episode.

DEFINING THE *EXEMPLUM*

The Latin term *exemplum* is commonly translated with the Greek παράδειγμα, occasionally with the alternative ὑπόδειγμα, and is understood according to the definition offered by Cousin, that is to say as a concrete instance employed to verify an assertion by means of analogy.[4] This sense of 'proof', paralleled in a large number of rhetors, is also that given at Quint. *Inst.* 5. 11. 1:

[2] Conte (1974) ad loc.

[3] Ibid. at 6. 235: 'Si richiami qui quanto si è annotato ai vv. 158–60 e 167 a proposito dell'esibizionismo dei personaggi, che fa di ogni atto un teatrale modello di comportamento (da notare a tal proposito la forma iussiva: 'sit Scaeva . . . exemplum'). L'azione non è più solo in funzione del soggetto-protagonista, ma si fa spettacolo per gli altri che gli stanno intorno e si esaltano all'esibizione di questa o quella 'virtus'. Evidente è il rapporto con la letteratura "paradigmatica" di Valerio Massimo (che appunto aveva fatto dell'aristia di Sceva uno dei suoi "exempla") o degli "exitus virorum illustrium".'

[4] Cousin (1936) 111, 'Genre de preuves fournies par la rhétorique, dont le nom sert à désigner ce qui est fondé sur la comparaison des semblables et l'autorité des faits. Quintilien

Tertium genus, ex iis quae extrinsecus adducuntur in causam, Graeci vocant παράδειγμα, quo nomine et generaliter usi sunt in omni similium adpositione et specialiter in iis quae rerum gestarum auctoritate nituntur.

The third category of those things which are adduced in support of the case from outside is called the 'paradigm' by the Greeks, which name they also use in general for every comparison of like with like and particularly in the case of those things which depend on the authority of deeds performed.

The *exemplum*, *qua* proof, is often discussed in opposition to the *praeceptum*, serving as the particular by which one might illustrate one's abstract *praecepta*.[5] There is, however, a second sense in which the *exemplum* is contrasted with the *praeceptum*, and one in which it is implied that a nation possessed of plentiful moral exemplars can 'do without' fancy abstract precepts. In the Greek world, this notion was closely associated with Sparta, and with the Cynics' celebration of Spartan practical wisdom.[6] Later, however, it came to be considered typical of Roman moral education even by non-Roman writers. In particular, I refer to the creation of a canon of figures and events considered summative of national values and held up to the young as a model to follow.[7] It is to this process that Quintilian refers at *Inst.* 12. 2. 29–30:

Neque ea solum quae talibus disciplinis continentur, sed magis etiam quae sunt tradita antiquitus dicta ac facta praeclare et nosse et animo semper agitare conveniet. Quae profecto nusquam plura maioraque quam in nostrae civitatis monumentis reperientur. An fortitudinem, iustitiam, fidem, continentiam, frugalitatem, contemptum doloris ac mortis melius alii docebunt quam Fabricii,

ne distingue pas la parabole de l'exemple, ni l'exemple de la comparaison. Le sens d'exemple est ancien . . . Le sens de preuve date vraisemblablement de l'époque d'Aristote, ou du moins, il est confirmé à ce moment-là.' Cf. Cousin (1935) 286–92.

[5] For the *exemplum–praeceptum* opposition, see Cic. *Fin.* 4. 5, 'Quam multa non solum praecepta in artibus sed etiam exempla in orationibus bene dicendi reliquerunt'; or Sen. *Marc.* 2. 1, 'Scio a praeceptis incipere omnes, qui monere aliquem volunt, in exemplis desinere', and cf. Prop. 3. 9. 21–2; Sen. *Ot.* 2. 1, *Epp.* 6. 5 and 94. 42. For more on the concept of the *exemplum* in general, see Nicolai (1992) and Mayer (1991).

[6] See Diog. Laert. 6. 11 for a Cynic assertion of the value of deeds over words. Cynics collected moral apophthegms which they dubbed Spartan. These are mentioned at Ar. *Rh.* 1394[b] and collected at Plut. *Mor.* 208 B–236 E, 240 C–242 D etc. See Rawson (1969) 87–8 for discussion. The drawing of exemplary lessons is also typical of the historiography of Ephorus (*FGH* 70 F 42) and later of Polybius. See Walbank (1955) 9–10.

[7] For the maintenance in the Second Sophistic of a canon of classical Greek personalities and events, see Russell (1983) 106–28, but note that Russell only discusses the use of such a canon as a source for rhetorical situations and inventions on a theme, the 'preservation of a sense of pride in the Hellenic inheritance', thus taking a rather more indirect course than that to be seen at Rome.

Curii, Reguli, Decii, Mucii aliique innumerabiles? *Quantum enim Graeci praeceptis valent, tantum Romani, quod est maius, exemplis.*

Nor will it be useful to be acquainted with and ever to contemplate only those things which are contained in such disciplines but rather also those excellent words and deeds which have been handed down from antiquity. These indeed will be found nowhere in greater number or size than in the records of our State. Or will others give better instruction in courage, justice, loyalty, continence, frugality, scorn for pain and death than the Fabricii, the Curii, the Reguli, the Decii, the Mucii and innumerable others? For the strength of the Greeks in precepts is matched by that in examples—which is more—of the Romans.[8]

The above is not an isolated instance of a Roman contrasting his dependence on practical exempla with the faith in abstract conceptions of the Greek, but part of a rich tradition.[9] The sentiment echoes Cic. *De Or.* 3. 137, which observes that 'Just as one should seek examples of valour from the Romans, so one should seek examples of doctrine from the Greeks' (... *Ut virtutis a nostris, sic doctrinae sunt ab illis exempla petenda*), and the practice of teaching by Roman historical example is seen by many as having taken a powerful boost from the influential Augustan moralist Sextius and his followers in the early imperial period.[10] Further, there exists much evidence for the

[8] Cf. Austin (1948) ad loc. for some useful citations. Here, one should also note Habinek (1987), who sees the entire book as attempting to create an exemplary 'perfectus orator', this type both passing on Roman wisdom and embodying its essential, practical nature.

[9] For the particular richness of Rome in terms of *exempla virtutis* on which to draw, cf. Livy, *Pref.* 10–11: 'nulla umquam res publica nec maior nec sanctior nec bonis exemplis ditior fuit'; Sen. *Controv.* 9, *pref.* 3; 'Latronem Porcium declamatoriae virtutis unicum exemplum'; Sen. *Suas.* 6. 2: 'M. Cato ... maxime vivendi moriendique exemplum'; Plin. *HN* 7. 130: 'Gentium in toto orbe praestantissima una omnium virtute haud dubie Romana extitit'; Flor. *De Qualitate Vitae*, 417 in Baehrens (1882–3) iv. 347: 'Sperne mores transmarinos, mille habent offucia. | Cive Romano per orbem nemo vivit rectius; | quippe malim unum Catonem quam trecentos Socratas', this last echoing Cic. *Amic.* 10: '... cave Catoni anteponas ne istum quidem ipsum, quem Apollo ... sapientissimum iudicavit; huius enim facta, illius dicta laudantur'. The discussion of this passage in Seyffert and Müller (1876) is rightly praised by Austin (1948). For a catalogue and discussion of exemplary Romans, see the outstanding Litchfield (1914). Valerius Maximus, it will be noted, divides his *exempla* into Romans and Foreigners, with a preponderance of the former. For a general study of Valerius, see Maslakov (1984).

[10] Cousin (1935) 291–2 observes the prominence in Quintilian of Roman *exempla* from the Republican period, and attributes this to 'l'influence des sextiens et de la diatribe cynico-stoïcienne', citing with approval Oltramare (1926). Ch. 8 of Oltramare, 'L'École Sextienne et les rhéteurs', makes a strong argument for the Romanity of this sect (Sen. *Q. Nat.* 7. 32. 2 talks of 'Sextiorum nova et Romani roboris secta') and for its stress on exemplarity (Fabianus at Sen. *Controv.* 2. 62. 2 asserts 'Nihil est mihi opus

collection in Lucan's period both of works *de viris illustribus* and of *exitus virorum illustrium*.[11] Indeed, the more one reads, the further one goes back, the more one is struck by the central position accorded to the exemplary in education and historiography.

Polybius is remarkable both for the manner in which he uses his narrative as a source of *exempla* for rules which he wishes to draw,[12] and for the description which he gives, as a non-Roman, of the centrality of exemplarity and emulation to aristocratic Roman culture as early as the second century BC. At 6. 52–5, Polybius discusses Rome, beginning with the observation that the Romans are distinguished from the Carthaginians by the use of native infantry rather than mercenaries to fight for their homeland. Polybius then shows how the funeral of a great man is used to engender a spirit of emulation, his corpse kept in standing position as an adult son first eulogizes the dead man himself, then those still alive and gathered at the funeral, moving from oldest to youngest. Further, such occasions are marked by the wearing of the *imagines* of other distinguished dead ancestors, a custom which cannot help but inspire a young man of the proper spirit, 6. 53. 9–10:

οὗ κάλλιον οὐκ εὐμαρὲς ἰδεῖν θέαμα νέωι φιλοδόξωι καὶ φιλαγάθωι· τὸ γὰρ τὰς τῶν ἐπ᾽ ἀρετῆι δεδοξασμένων ἀνδρῶν εἰκόνας ἰδεῖν ὁμοῦ πάσας οἷον εἰ ζώσας καὶ πεπνυμένας τίν᾽ οὐκ ἂν παραστῆσαι; τί δ᾽ ἂν κάλλιον θέαμα τούτου φανείη;

praecipientibus, habeo exemplum'), but is rather eccentric in the assertion that, p. 178: 'Nous sommes amenés à voir dans les Sextiens les premiers diatribistes qui aient utilisé systématiquement l'histoire pour en tirer des leçons de morale'.

11 For a discussion of the collection of the lives of exemplary Romans, see Fairweather (1981) 64–5. Apart from Suetonius, Varro, Santra, Nepos, and Hyginus are all recorded as writing such works, those of Nepos and Hyginus actually entitled *Exempla*. For a discussion of works *de viris illustribus* and of *exitus virorum illustrium*, see the opening pages of Geiger (1979). The latter concept is of obvious relevance to Scaeva, who, at 6. 235, feigns not to want to be an 'exemplum . . . *mortis honestae*'. For the notion of *mors honesta*, see Luc. 3. 134, 10. 539; Livy, 3. 50. 8, 5. 18. 8; Cic. *Quinct.* 49; Cic. *Phil.* 9. 11; Nep. *Chabr.* 4. 3; Curt. 4. 15. 30, 5. 8. 6, 7. 4. 34, 7. 7. 34; Sen. *Epp.* 71. 16, 82. 14 (cf. *Tranq.* 11. 4 and *Ep.* 13. 14); Tac. *Ann.* 1. 70. 4, 12. 51. 2, *Agr.* 33. 6.

12 Polyb. 1. 1. 2 talks of history as a *γυμνασίαν πρὸς τὰς πολιτικὰς πράξεις* and at 2. 61. 3 of his readers as *διορθουμένους ὑπὸ τῶν σπουδαίων καὶ ζηλωτῶν ἔργων ἤπερ ὑπὸ τῶν παρανόμων καὶ φευκτῶν πράξεων*. For an illustration of Polybius' method, see Polyb. 7. 11. 1–4 and the digression on Philip's personal decline, which Polybius justifies as follows, 7. 11. 2: *δοκεῖ γάρ μοι τοῖς καὶ κατὰ βραχὺ βουλομένοις τῶν πραγματικῶν ἀνδρῶν περιποιεῖσθαι τὴν ἐκ τῆς ἱστορίας διόρθωσιν ἐναργέστατον εἶναι τοῦτο παράδειγμα*. Again, at Polyb. 38. 20. 1–3, Scipio gets his audience to gaze on the suppliant Hasdrubal, and comments on how fortune can *παραδειγματίζειν . . . τοὺς ἀλογίστους τῶν ἀνθρώπων*, concluding his remarks with the question, 38. 20. 3: *ἃ τίς οὐκ ἂν ὑπὸ τὴν ὄψιν θεασάμενος ἐν νῶι λάβοι διότι δεῖ μηδέποτε λέγειν μηδὲ πράττειν μηδὲν ὑπερήφανον ἄνθρωπον ὄντα;*

It is not easy for a young man who loves honour and the good to see a fairer sight than this; for whom would it not benefit to see the statues of men who have achieved honour for valour togther, all as if they were living and breathing? What fairer sight than this could be seen?

When such a spirit of emulation is inspired, Romans perform heroic deeds on behalf of the collective, for instance single combat in the sight of and on behalf of the rest of the army, an obvious example being that of Horatius Cocles. After describing his actions, Polybius comments that, 6. 55. 4:

τοιαύτη τις, ὡς ἔοικε, διὰ τῶν παρ' αὐτοῖς ἐθισμῶν ἐγγεννᾶται τοῖς νέοις ὁρμὴ καὶ φιλοτιμία πρὸς τὰ καλὰ τῶν ἔργων.

Some such zeal and ambition to perform fair deeds, it seems, is engendered in the young men by the customs of the country.[13]

Polybius' citation of Cocles as an instance of a particular mentality is close to being a case of the double audience which an *exemplum* narrative can involve. Implicit in Polybius' handling of this story is the notion that Cocles fed on the same spirit of emulation which the subsequent recollection of his story was intended to inspire. At the same time, Polybius is an exemplary historian, and his reporting of the heroic deed also involves a degree of complicity in the casting of Cocles as a model for others to follow. This complicity is much more acute in the case of a historian such as Livy, who has none of Polybius' ethnographic distance, but views himself as a servant of the national purpose. This is made clear at *Pref.* 10, where he suggests the reading of his history with a view to salutary lessons:

Hoc illud est praecipue in cognitione rerum salubre ac frugiferum, omnis te exempli documenta in inlustri posita monumento intueri; inde tibi tuaeque rei publicae quod imitere capias, inde foedum inceptu foedum exitu quod vites.

It is this which is particularly salutary and profitable in the knowledge of history: to look on the records of every exemplary deed as they have been placed in glorious recollection. From this you may discern those things which you should imitate for your own sake and for the sake of your State, from this that which, foul in its inception or foul in its result, you should avoid.

[13] For the *imagines*, see Mayor (1889) at Juv. 8. 1 and Paul (1984) at Sall. *Jug.* 4. 5, 'quom maiorum imagines intuerentur, vehementissime sibi animum ad virtutem accendi'. Maslakov (1984) 445–6 offers a parallel to the *imagines* in the singing of banqueting songs celebrating the deeds of exemplary heroes. For this, see Val. Max. 2. 1. 10; Cic. *Tusc.* 1. 3, 4. 3 = Cato, *Orig.* fr. 118 (Peter) and *Brut.* 75.

One is therefore struck by the inevitable double audience created in so formulaic a narrative as that of the Fabii at Livy 2. 46. 4–47. 1. Here, all three of the Fabii demonstrate the archetypal good general's leading of the charge,[14] and by their action inspire their men. At the beginning of his account, Livy comments, 2. 46. 4:

Inter primores genus Fabium insigne spectaculo exemploque civibus erat
Amongst the leading men, the family of the Fabii offered a noble spectacle and example to the citizens.

At the close, he notes the success of their endeavours, 2. 46. 7:

Sic in primum infensis hastis provolant duo Fabii, totamque moverunt secum aciem.
Thus the two Fabii flew forward with spears levelled to the front and moved the whole army together with them.

The narrative marks the exemplary effect of the heroism of the Fabii on the soldiers immediately present, but one feels that this acts as a cover for the presumed emulative impact of the *exemplum* on the Roman reading audience. They, in short, will read these stories, and will know exactly how to behave when they join the line. A double audience has been created. The constant recurrence of this technique in the Valerian *exemplum virtutis* will not go unremarked.

It is noted that exemplary education is embedded in the narrative of Roman historiography, offering a lead to an age in which, as Livy would have it, 'we can endure neither our vices nor the cure' (*nec vitia nostra nec remedia pati possumus*).[15] The parallel practice of Polybius should discourage talk of an exclusively Roman tendency towards exemplarity, but his ethnographic observations lend weight to the native view that there was something peculiarly Roman about such a strategy. It is important now to show the prominence given to exemplarity in other branches of the Roman education system.

[14] e.g. Q. Fabius at Livy, 2. 46. 4 as 'principem in confertos Veientes euntem' and Caeso Fabius on the need 'ut decet proceres, ut Fabio nomine est dignum, pugnando potius quam adhortando accendamus militum animos'. For a discussion of this heroic ethos in classical generalship, see Wheeler (1991).

[15] Livy, *Pref.* 9. Ogilvie (1965) ad loc. refers to the theme of the usefulness of history first stated at Thuc. 1. 22. 4, and given 'an exclusively moral application' at Polyb. 1. 1. 2, 2. 61. 3; Diod. 1. 1. 4; Sall. *Jug.* 4. 5; Tac. *Ann.* 3. 65. 1, *Agr.* 46. 3.

THE *EXEMPLUM* IN RHETORICAL AND ANECDOTAL EDUCATION

Two fields will here be considered: the rhetorical *controversia* and *suasoria*, which depend on the constant reinvention of stock, exemplary situations; and the collection of exemplary anecdotes of the sort offered by Valerius Maximus. When it is time to consider Lucan's Scaeva narrative, the former will eventually provide the basis for some of its most important thematic reversals. For now, it is important to demonstrate the co-operation of the two forms of the *exemplum*, as citation and model, within the educational programme of the rhetors.

The two senses of the *exemplum* may be said to co-operate in this way. The process of rhetorical persuasion depends largely on leading the audience on from the basis of what they already accept. An *exemplum*, *qua* citation or instantiation of a given point, is not simply pulled from the imagination of the speaker, but from a canonical body of examples which have been shaped into the basic wisdom of speaker and audience. Again, the stock situations bring with them certain fundamental shared assumptions. Debates, for instance, over the right thing to do with a war hero, whether to keep him at home or allow him to fight again, exclude *a priori* certain potential positions, for instance that of the elegist, that war is a folly and the only worthwhile siege that of the beloved's front door. Therefore, a figure imagined speaking within these basic situations, and talking of *exempla* in terms of models for conduct, is liable to offer models which conform to the ideology propounded by the schools.

This marriage of citation and model is not hard to demonstrate. At Seneca, *Controversiae* 1. 8. 9, for instance, it is argued that the *ter fortis* should be held back from further military service because:

> Ad ultimum: utile esse rei publicae ter fortem servari ut sit qui ostendatur iuventuti; iam illum magis posse ornamentum esse quam praesidium.

> Finally: that it was useful for the State for the man thrice a hero to be kept to be shown to the young men; now he could achieve more as an ornament than as a defender

Similarly, at *Controversiae* 8. 5, the hero father of a hero son reflects on the inspiration his heroism has provided to the young. When the latter theme is taken up at 10. 2, the declaimers vie to create good lines on the *exemplum* theme. Thus, Junius Gallio has the son say, *Controv.* 10. 2. 2:

'Vidi patrem iam senem loricam induentem: multum est pugnare cum exemplo'.

'I saw my father putting on a cuirass when he was already an old man: it is a great thing to have an example when fighting'.

Gavius Silo caps this with, *Controv.* 10. 2. 16:

'Solebas mihi, pater, insignium virorum exempla narrare, quaedam etiam domestica; aiebas: "avom fortem virum habuisti; vide ut sis fortior." '

'Father, you used to tell me of the exemplary deeds of famous men, some of them even drawn from our own family; you would say, "Your grandfather was a hero—make sure that you are braver." '

He then adds, *Controv.* 10. 2. 16:

'Contendere me vetabat imperio, iubebat exemplo.'

'By his instructions, he forbade me to compete, by his example he ordered me to.'

Finally, note must be taken of the prominence of the theme in one particular *suasoria* which will return to prominence at the close of this argument, that of the 300 Spartans defending Thermopylae. Thus, at Seneca, *Suas.* 2. 1, Arellius Fuscus Senior opens:

'Non refero opera vestra, non avos, non patres, quorum vobis exemplo ab infantia surgit ingenium.'

'I do not mention your deeds, your grandfathers, your fathers, in emulation of whose example your natural qualities rise from infancy.'

At *Suas.* 2. 2 he continues:

'Ut unum Orthryadem excitem, adnumerare trecentis exempla possum.'

'I need mention only Orthryades in order to provide an example for all three hundred.'

The topic is left alone for a while, but Cestius Pius at 2. 6 returns with:

'O grave maiorum virtutis dedecus: Lacones se numerant, non aestimant!'

'O grave stain on the valour of the ancestors: Spartans count and do not reckon themselves!'

The same speaker then has his Spartans lament the prospect of following a dishonourable Athenian example, *Suas.* 2. 6:

'Adhuc non sum ex ulla parte Atheniensium similis, non muris nec educatione; nihil prius illorum imitabor quam fugam?'

'Hitherto I have borne no likeness to the Athenians, either in defensive walls or in upbringing; will the first thing I imitate in them be flight?'

It is not hard to see from this how the canonical nature of the form acts to lock the speaker within the code of assumptions held by his teachers. The exemplary situations, the exemplary tags rub off, and one is soon ready to head for the battlefield or the forum, a fully moulded Roman citizen. When the declaimers imagine themselves as Spartans convincing each other to hold the line at Thermopylae, when they recall the fundamental import of the *exemplum* to the Spartan mentality, they also offer a map of their own minds.

Valerius Maximus and the Exemplary Anecdote

For now, it is important to turn from the declaimers to a closer consideration of the anecdotal compendium of Valerius Maximus. As has been noted, Conte draws the connection with Valerius, but, like Marti he is essentially concerned with Scaeva as a product of the epic tradition and continues on this basis throughout. Such an approach involves two major difficulties. The first is that Scaeva was a more-or-less historical character cited by a number of writers apart from Lucan,[16] including, of course, Valerius himself. Examination of the various versions of Scaeva reveals the matrix of possible representations in relation to which Lucan's Scaeva could be interpreted. Secondly, Scaeva's appearance in Valerius is in the second chapter of the third book, which is devoted to the listing of examples of the very *virtus* which has been identified as the ideological core of the passage. Therefore, as Valerius has contextualized Scaeva by relating him to the other models of *virtus* which he will cite, so too one can recontextualize Lucan's Scaeva by relating him to the general ideology which emerges from the Valerian whole, and by comparing his individual actions with their specific models within that whole. Beforehand, however, it is necessary to attempt a sketch of Valerius' educational project and with it his attitude to the use of the *exemplum*.

I talk of an educational project and mean just that. For the preface to the third book of Valerius immediately invokes the imagery of upbringing, and with it states the desired end result, *virtus*, the proper state of being a man. The project is defined in these terms, Val. Max. 3, *Pref.*:

[16] Caes. *B. Civ.* 3. 53. 3–5, cf. Val. Max. 3. 2. 23, Suet. *Jul.* 68. 3–4, Flor. *Epit.* 2. 13. 40, Plut. *Caes.* 16. 2–3, App. *B. Civ.* 2. 60. 247–50. Dio Cass. 37. 53. 3 locates Scaeva in Spain and recounts the swimming episode which Valerius places in Britain.

Adtingam quasi cunabula quaedam et elementa virtutis.

I shall touch on certain things that are almost the cradles and the ABC of valour.

It is then given a most apt first example at 3. 1. 1, where the first *vir fortis* is decidedly under-age, and thus a clear spur to a younger audience. Aemilius Lepidus is still a *puer* when:

Progressus in aciem hostem interemit, civem servavit.

Advancing into the line of battle he slew an enemy and saved a citizen.

Aemilius is rewarded by a Senate that:

Iniquum . . . putavit honori nondum tempestivum videri, qui iam virtuti maturus fuisset.

Thought it unjust that a boy should be deemed too young for honour when he had already been old enough for deeds of valour.

Finally, Valerius adds:

Duplicemque laudem e proelio retulit, cuius eum vix spectatorem anni esse patiebantur.

And he won double praise from a battle which his years scarcely permitted him to watch.

The broader question of spectatorship and spectacle may for now be left aside, the simple observation made that Valerius is revealing his pedagogic intent. The boys who read his work will be *spectatores* of past battles, and by their reading will be toughened for the real thing when of age. Thus, at 3. 2. 6, Scipio Aemilianus is made a standard-bearer for the young of the past, the praise of whom is phrased in such a manner as implicitly to upbraid the young of the present:

Sed tunc clarissimus quisque iuvenum *pro amplificanda et tuenda patria* plurimum laboris ac periculi sustinebat, deforme sibi existimans, quos dignitate praestaret, ab his *virtute* superari.

Yet then all the most outstanding youths endured very great toil and danger in order to expand and to defend the homeland, considering it demeaning for them to be bettered in valour by those whom they outdid in dignity of rank.

The young of 3. 2. 6 are then followed by the old of 3. 2. 7, and again by the young at 3. 2. 8. In short, the aim is to educate the minds of the young, to teach them a concept of *virtus* centred on self-sacrifice in the cause of a country presumed united and with a clear imperial purpose.[17] Further to the above, *virtus* is to be inculcated by the use of *exempla*. The term *exemplum* appears almost immediately (3. 2, *Pref.*) in the request to Romulus to allow one example to come before his own (*Sed patere, obsecro, uno te praecurri exemplo*) and its purpose follows soon after in the praise of Cossus (3. 2. 4), who took the *spolia opima* and is admirable 'because he was able to emulate Romulus' (*quod imitari Romulum valuit*). Similarly, recalling that M. Marcellus managed the same feat, Valerius comments, 3. 2. 5:

Ne M. quidem Marcelli memoriam ab his exemplis separare debemus.

I should not even deny a place in these examples to the memory of M. Marcellus.

At 3. 2. 7, the self-sacrifice of the old is the 'example of courage' (*fortitudinis exemplum*) offered by antiquity; at 3. 2. 14, the suicide of Cato is a 'great example to men' (*magnum hominibus documentum*); and when Valerius offers his last and greatest hero, L. Siccius Dentatus, it is with the words, 3. 2. 24:

Sed quod ad proeliatorum excellentem fortitudinem adtinet, merito L. Siccii Dentati commemoratio omnia Romana exempla finierit.

Yet as concerns outstanding courage in warriors, it is right that the recollection of L. Siccius Dentatus should finish all the Roman examples.

Finally, it is important to note how exemplary deeds are shown to have educated those who were immediately present. For instance, at 3. 2. 19, Caesar's bravery sets a crucial example:

Fortitudinem per totum exercitum diffudit labentemque belli fortunam divino animi ardore restituit.

[17] Cf. Sall. *Cat. Pref.* for the distinction between *virtus* and *fortuna*. Here, *virtus* repeatedly sums up the united efforts of the Roman people (see McGushin (1977), introd. to chs. 6–9). This is in conformity with the definition of *virtus* at Lucilius, frr. 1337–8 (Marx): 'commoda praeterea patriai prima putare, | deinde parentum, tertia iam postremaque nostra'. For further uses of *virtus* in this section of Valerius, see 3. 2. 2 'viris puella lumen virtutis praeferendo'; 3. 2. 6: 'eodem et virtutis et pugnae genere usi sunt T. Manlius Torquatus et Valerius Corvinus et Aemilianus Scipio'; 3. 2. 7: 'ceterum ne illo quidem tam misero tamque luctuoso tempore civitas nostra virtutis suae oblita est'; 3. 2. 7 (*fin.*): 'capi ergo virtus nescit'; 3. 2. 19 for Caesar as 'certissimam verae virtutis effigiem'; 3. 2. 20: 'ceterum ut humanae virtutis actum exequamur'; 3. 2. 20: 'spectatores . . . alienae virtutis'; 3. 2. 21 (*init.*): 'quorum virtuti nihil cedit Q. Occius'; 3. 2. 21 (*fin.*) Q. Occius kills 'Pyrresum nobilitate ac virtute omnes Celtiberos praestantem'; 3. 2. 23 for Caesar as 'optimo virtutis aestimatore'.

He spread courage through all the army and restored the tottering fortune of war by the divine fire of his spirit.

Caesar's turning-back of a retreating soldier to face the enemy shows the Romans how to win. At 3. 2. 20, the example of launching one's standard into the enemy leads the army to advance and beats back the hitherto victorious Hannibal.

Valerius, therefore, takes familiar historical stories and retells them in such a way as to draw from them an explicit moral for his reader to ingest. Moreover, he does so according to a set pattern, the structure of which has been outlined by Guerrini.[18] It is striking that it is just this pattern which Lucan reproduces in his account of the corrupt *virtus* of his character. The introduction of Scaeva at 6. 147–8 describes him as:

> Pronus ad omne nefas et qui nesciret in armis
> quam magnum virtus crimen civilibus esset.

Bent on every sinful deed and ignorant how great an indictment could be valour in a civil conflict.

This may be said to function as the analytical exordium, which, after the intervening narrative, is echoed by the analytical conclusion at 6. 257–62, contrasting the *aristeia* of the civil wars and the glory he might have achieved in traditional patriotic conflict and culminating in the exclamation at 6. 262, 'With what valour did you procure a master!' (*Quanta dominum virtute parasti!*)[19]

SUMMARY OF RESULTS—NEW BEGINNINGS

It is time now to bring together the preceding preliminary observations. The first point is that, as many have observed, Lucan's Scaeva talks of himself as an *exemplum*, but is treated by Lucan as an example of the corruption of *virtus* in a civil-war situation. By contrast, the appearance of Scaeva in Valerius Maximus is in the context of a collection of *exempla* explicitly designed to inculcate that very *virtus* in the young. Valerius simply assumes that Scaeva can exemplify the national traditions and patriotic intent he wishes to teach; Lucan assaults the anthologizing principle in order to demonstrate how the truths of

[18] Guerrini (1980).

[19] For a moralizing Livian precedent for the former passage, one might suggest 28. 21. 9 and the verdict on the gladiatorial duelling of Corbis and Orsua: 'cum dirimi ab tanta rabie nequirent, insigne *spectaculum* exercitui praebuere *documentumque quantum cupiditas imperii malum inter mortales esset*'.

virtus collapse in a hostile context. However, if this were all that Lucan did, the recontextualization of Scaeva with reference to Valerius would add relatively little to the understanding of his version and might be left to the whim of the reader with a particular concern for the concept of *exemplum*. One would say that *exemplum* suggested education, but that Lucan reversed the lesson offered. Yet Lucan reacts to exemplary literature far more carefully, and aggressively, than this would suggest and the relationship which emerges is rich with dangerous implications.

SCAEVA IN THE ANTHOLOGY

It is important to begin this section with a caveat. It is dangerous to discuss Valerius Maximus as a specific intertext for Lucan. To talk of a single intended allusion is both reductive and implausible. When Scaeva casts himself as an *exemplum*, he foresees canonization less as a figure in the *Exempla* of Valerius Maximus than in the broader field of literature which this work represents. However, one cannot escape the fact that Valerius offers the only extant full-scale collection of *exempla*, and one, moreover, which gives Scaeva a prominent position. The principle to be followed in this section, therefore, is that just as the whole chapter of Valerius anthologizes examples of military *virtus*, so Scaeva's embodiment of *virtus* implies a relationship with other specific examples apart from his own. He becomes, in effect, a portmanteau of elements from the other *exempla* offered. My primary source of comparisons is Valerius, and it is Valerius who most clearly parallels Lucan's emphasis on the spectacular quality of the *exemplum*, but it is vital also to recall that Valerius is a magpie who lives to plunder and repeat stories and topoi familiar from other writers. In the case of the killing of Aulus, Curtius Rufus may offer a far closer parallel.

It is essential to compare Lucan's Scaeva with the versions offered by the other historians. With a more exact idea of what Lucan omits from previous versions of Scaeva, or what he adds to them, it is possible to see more clearly how he reforms his hero as a monster able to swallow and destroy the rest of Rome's myths as well.

The first example is that of lone resistance. At 6. 130–4, Lucan emphasizes the non-resistance of Scaeva's peers in order to leave him in splendid isolation as he fights:

Nequid victoria ferro
deberet, pavor attonitos confecerat hostes.
Quod solum valuit virtus, iacuere perempti
debuerant quo stare loco. Qui volnera ferrent
iam derant, et nimbus agens tot tela peribat.

Lest victory should owe anything to the sword, fear had done for the dumb-struck foe. Valour could do more: they lay slain where they should have stood. There were no longer men to bear wounds and the storm of so many spears was going to waste.

By contrast, the traditional version of Scaeva stresses his signal deeds amidst the heroic resistance of his cohort. Thus, Caesar, *B. Civ.* 3. 53. 3–5 states:

Sed in castello nemo fuit omnino militum quin vulneraretur, quattuorque ex una cohorte centuriones oculos amiserunt.

Yet in the fort not one of the soldiers was not wounded and four centurions from one cohort lost eyes.

and, while admitting of Scaeva that:

Eius ... opera castellum magna ex parte conservatum esse constabat.

It was generally agreed that the fort had been defended very largely by his efforts.

he records that he:

Cohortem ... postea duplici stipendio, frumento, veste, cibariis militaribusque donis amplissime donavit.

Afterwards rewarded the cohort most lavishly with double pay, corn, clothing, rations and military gifts.[20]

This is also the version of Suetonius, who describes how, *Jul.* 68. 3:

Denique una sextae legionis cohors praeposita castello quattuor Pompei legiones per aliquot horas sustinuit paene omnis confixa multitudine hostilium sagittarum.

Finally, one cohort of the sixth legion which had been put in charge of the fort held up four of Pompey's legions for some hours, though almost all were struck by the mass of enemy arrows.

Appian, *B. Civ.* 2. 60. 249 emphasizes the support offered by Scaeva's commander Minucius. Other writers (Val. Max., 3. 2. 23; Plut. *Caes.* 16. 2–3; Flor. *Epit.* 2. 13. 40) single out Scaeva without mentioning

[20] 'veste, cibariis', cited in the apparatus to du Pontet's OCT, seems preferable to the apparently nonsensical 'vespeciariis'.

his supporters, but none suggests either that he actually fought alone or that the other troops fled. Indeed, the latter idea is utterly alien to the version of Valerius, who uses Scaeva as a demonstration of the discipline in Julius' camp (*in castris divi Iuli disciplina*), in which 'one man with the loss of a hand, another with the loss of an eye, stuck to the enemy' (*alter dextera, alter oculo amisso hostibus haesit*).

Here, therefore, what distinguishes Lucan from previous models is the claim that Scaeva's companions collapsed while he fought alone. The conventional reading of Scaeva argues that this is to be understood in terms of Lucan's representation of the resistance of his hero as an epic *aristeia*. This interpretation is obviously pertinent and helpful, but epic is not the only literary form with a bearing on this figure. Rather, cautiously, it will also be suggested that the isolation of Scaeva acts to bring him into relation with the story of Horatius offered by Valerius at 3. 2. 1.[21]

Horatius, as was seen from Polybius, is a classic model of the heroism and patriotism of early Rome. Finding himself alone on the bridge and repelling the Gauls:

> Unusque duos acerrima pugna consertos exercitus, alterum repellendo, alterum propugnando distraxit.
>
> And one man separated two armies that were locked in the most bitter conflict, driving off the one and defending the other.

Further, in doing so, he makes himself a *spectacle*, and:

> Unus itaque tot civium, tot hostium in se oculos convertit, stupentis illos admiratione, hos inter laetitiam et metum haesitantis.
>
> One man therefore attracted the attention of so many citizens, so many foes, the latter stunned and amazed, the former hesitating between joy and fear.[22]

This concept will be activated later on in the argument, but, for now, it may simply be noted that Scaeva is watched by the 'young men . . .

[21] The parallel between Scaeva and the Livian version of Horatius Cocles is emphasized by Marti (1966) 240 and 243, but without any mention of the fact that Horatius and Scaeva appear in the same book of Valerius in order to exemplify the same *virtus*. Marti also cites Livy 4. 19 (A. Cornelius Cossus, tr. mil.); 4. 38 (Sextus Tempanius, decurion); 22. 50 (P. Sempronius Tuditanus, tr. mil.); 26. 5. 15 (Q. Navius, centurion); 41. 2. 9 (M. Licinius Strabo, tr. mil.); 41. 4 (A. Baeculonius, signifer, and C. Popilius Sabellus) as examples of a Livian pattern of heroic lone resistance by a Roman soldier and posits an Ennian origin for this reformation of the *aristeia*.

[22] For this, cf. Valerius' probable model, Livy 2. 10. 5, esp.: 'insignisque inter conspecta cedentium pugnae terga obversis comminus ad ineundum proelium armis, *ipso miraculo audaciae* obstupefecit hostes'.

marvelling at him and eager to watch' (*mirantes virum atque avidi spectare* . . . | . . . *iuvenes*), who, at the end, 'worship the living image of great Valour' (*vivam magnae speciem Virtutis adorant.*)[23] Thirdly, Horatius, like Scaeva, survives. Many critics have found the reappearance of Scaeva in the tenth book of the *Pharsalia* evidence of an indecent improbability in Lucan's plotting, but it ties him in rather nicely with Horatius:

Cuius fortitudinem dii immortales admirati incolumitatem sinceram ei praestiterunt: nam neque altitudine deiectus quassatus[ve] nec pondere armorum pressus nec ullo verticis circuitu actus, ne telis quidem, quae undique congerebantur, laesus tutum natandi eventum habuit.

The immortal gods, admiring his courage, granted him complete salvation. For neither dismayed by the height nor weighed down by the burden of his armour nor driven by any revolving and whirling of the water, nor hurt even by the weapons, which were showering on him from all sides, he swam off to safety.

Scaeva thus renders grotesque the miraculous *incolumitas* of Horatius. While the latter avoids wounding by the intervention of the gods, Lucan's hero suffers innumerable blows upon blows and still makes it home for supper.[24] The great Roman model of lone resistance, and one of the fundamental figures of exemplary *virtus*, Horatius, is a constant if unacknowledged presence in Lucan's version of Scaeva. The parallels are too close to ignore.

The second instance of absorption and perversion of a Valerian *exemplum* again comes in a part of the Scaeva story for which Lucan is our first extant witness. I refer to the fake surrender and attack on Aulus at 6. 224–39. This episode has been studied more than once over the years, and involves complex problems of source-critcism. My proposal may make them more complicated still.

The nature of the problem is as follows. A century ago, Hosius observed that the Scaeva episode bore a close resemblance to the account of Alexander's assault on the Mallians in Book 9 of Curtius

[23] For this phrase, cf. Sen. *Ep.* 67. 11–13, esp. 67. 12 and the description of Cato as 'virtutis pulcherrimae ac magnificentissimae speciem'.

[24] The improbability of Horatius' escape is alluded to at Livy 2. 10. 11, where he is described as 'rem ausus plus famae habituram ad posteros quam fidei'. It might also be noted that the escape of Horatius by swimming is paralleled by another act of heroism attributed to Scaeva at Val. Max. 3. 2. 23 and Dio Cass. 37. 53. 3, and recorded for an unknown soldier at Plut. *Caes.* 16. 3–4 Valerius recalls that, after the heroic defence of his rock against the Britons, having accumulated a mass of grievous injuries, he leapt into the waves and escaped. It is not impossible that Lucan's reintroduction of Scaeva at 10. 543–6 would have offered a version of this story.

Rufus.[25] Recently, this parallel was discovered anew by Zwierlein, who put particular stress on the tricking of Aulus.[26] For the wounded Alexander is represented as reacting similarly to the attentions of an assailant, Curtius Rufus, 9. 5. 10–11:

Itaque ad spoliandum corpus qui vulneraverat alacer gaudio accurrit. Quem ut inicere corpori suo manus sensit, credo, ultimi dedecoris indignitate commotus, linquentem revocavit animum et nudum hostis latus subiecto mucrone hausit.

Therefore the man who had wounded him ran up eager in his joy to spoil his body. When he sensed that he was laying hands on his body, stirred, I believe, by the indignity of this final disgrace, he summoned once again the spirit that was leaving him and thrust the sword's point up into the unarmed flank of his enemy.

The parallelism is certainly striking, but, sadly, it is not easy to establish a clear relationship between the texts.

The problem may be established by a series of observations:

(i) One obviously missing version of the Scaeva episode is that which must be presumed to have appeared in Livy's account of the civil wars. Livy is probably the single most important source for Valerius Maximus, so the appearance of a detailed account of Scaeva in Valerius is fairly strong circumstantial evidence for his presence in Livy. On the other hand, the absence of the Aulus episode from Valerius may be used as evidence for its absence from Livy as well. I return to the problem of Livy later on.

(ii) There exists a rival version of the Aulus story, in which Scaeva attacks not one but two assailants. This appears in Plut. *Caes.* 16. 2 and App., *B. Civ.* 2. 60. 248 and probably indicates an alternative account of the Scaeva episode dating from some time near the civil-war period and therefore prior to Lucan.[27] On account of the change in the number of victims, one is not tempted to follow Marti and explain Plutarch and Appian in terms of a source in Lucan. Nor is there that

[25] Hosius (1893), esp. 383–92. For a critique of Hosius' reasoning, see Pichon (1912) 254–6.

[26] Zwierlein (1988).

[27] Plut. *Caes.* 16. 2: *τῶι δὲ θυρεῶι βελῶν ἑκατὸν καὶ τριάκοντα πληγὰς ἀναδεδεγμένος, ἐκάλει τοὺς πολεμίους ὡς παραδώσων ἑαυτόν. δυεῖν δὲ προσιόντων, τοῦ μὲν ἀπέκοψε τὸν ὦμον τῆι μαχαίραι, τὸν δὲ κατὰ τοῦ προσώπου πατάξας ἀπέστρεψεν, αὐτὸς δὲ διεσώθη τῶν οἰκείων περισχόντων.* Cf. App. *B. Civ.* 2. 60. 248, where Scaeva first calls on one Pompeian soldier with whom he is familiar, but is then approached by two men, both of whom he assaults: *προσδραμόντων δ᾽ ὡς αὐτομολοῦντι δύο ἀνδρῶν, τὸν μὲν ἔφθασε κτείνας, τοῦ δὲ τὸν ὦμον ἀπέκοψε.*

much to say for the scarcely more plausible hypothesis of an intervening historian embellishing on Lucan.[28]

(iii) Were one to presume from the absence of the Aulus story in Valerius that it was also absent in Livy, a superficially attractive procedure would be to point to the Curtian parallel, and assert a direct imitation of Curtius, or the Alexander tradition in general, by Lucan. However, the existence of the rival version of the Aulus story in Plutarch and Appian would surely testify against Aulus being a Lucanian invention of this sort.

(iv) Anyone wishing to assert that Lucan imitated or responded to Curtius will be rejected out of hand by the sizeable body of scholars who insist that the date of Curtius is considerably later than the reign of Claudius. Recent times may have seen a small majority in favour of the Claudian dating, but there are many who still insist that Curtius wrote under the Flavians or even under Septimius Severus.[29] While there is normally little to say for arguments asserting that an apparent response of Lucan to Curtius is actually the opposite (it is always Lucan who seems to *activate* the relationship between the texts), the problem of dating Curtius may encourage us to think in terms of Lucan's relationship to the broader Alexander tradition.

(v) The resource of the 'broader Alexander tradition' is not to be scorned. A recent article by Fantham likens the mutiny of the troops in Book 5 against Caesar's plans to lead the victorious standards 'into another world' (*alium ... in orbem*) to Alexander in Curtius. While Fantham's caution over attesting a specific relationship in this case is fully justified—the notion of the man who discovered new worlds is much older than Curtius and is exploited in the implicit synkrisis of Alexander and Epicurus in Lucretius, 1. 63–83–the ghost of Alexander permeates the *Pharsalia*, not least in Caesar's re-creation of his deeds.[30]

The difficulties involved in creating a stemma to show Alexander in Curtius as the model for Scaeva in Lucan leave one in some sympathy with Hosius' conclusion that one can do no more than note the possibility, that certainty is out of the question.[31] On the other hand,

[28] Marti (1966) 241–2. It seems much more plausible to see the origin of the Plutarch–Appian version in their customary source, Pollio.

[29] Recent articles asserting a Claudian date include Martin (1983) and Hamilton (1988). For Curtius writing under Septimius Severus, see Fears (1976). Fears (p. 215 n. 7) cites forty different discussions of the dating problem.

[30] See Fantham (1985), and, for Lucretius, Buchheit (1971). The precedent for various of Caesar's deeds in the Alexander tradition is emphasized in Tandoi (1963), Zwierlein (1986), Schrijvers (1990), and Quint (1993) 3–8.

[31] Hosius (1893) 386.

putting aside notions of specific *imitatio* and *aemulatio*, one need have no qualms about asserting that the passages are ideologically related. By this I mean that Alexander's killing of the man who wishes to touch and despoil him is an example of the refusal of ignoble *patientia*. As such, he upholds values close to the heart of the Roman male. Meanwhile, Scaeva, who feigns not just surrender but the wish to desert Caesar, will use any low means to kill one more fellow citizen and feed his hunger for death, *Pharsalia* 6. 236–42:

> Credidit infelix simulatis vocibus Aulus
> nec vidit recto gladium mucrone tenentem,
> membraque captivi pariter laturus et arma
> fulmineum mediis excepit faucibus ensem.
> Incaluit virtus, atque una caede refectus
> 'Solvat' ait 'poenas, Scaevam quicumque subactum
> speravit.'

Unhappy Aulus believed the deceiving speech and did not see him holding his sword with the point ready to thrust, and, just as he was about to lift up together the captive's body and his weaponry, received a thunderous blow in the middle of the throat from the sword. His valour grew hot and, restored by one killing, he said, 'Whoever hoped that Scaeva was beaten, let him pay the penalty.'

Further, the relevance of asserting an ideological relationship between Curtius and Lucan can be seen even more clearly if a third parallel situation is considered. As Scaeva strikes Aulus, 'his valour grew hot' (*incaluit virtus*). Implicitly, this new form of *virtus* can be contrasted with that of Alexander, defined above as a refusal of *patientia*. Explicitly, the *virtus* of Scaeva can be contrasted with that of the old men of Rome at Livy, 5. 39–41 and Valerius Maximus, 3. 2. 7. According to this story, the Romans, besieged by the Gauls and too numerous all to fit into the Capitol, were forced to abandon their old. It is instructive to follow how Valerius partly draws out the moral lesson implicit in Livy, partly uses the story to illustrate the concept of *virtus* to which he adheres.

The first point is that, as with Horatius, this exemplary deed takes the form of a *spectacle*. Thus, Val. Max. 3. 2. 7:

> Ceterum ne illo quidem tam misero tamque luctuoso tempore civitas nostra virtutis suae oblita est: defuncti enim honoribus apertis ianuis in curulibus sellis cum insignibus magistratuum, quos gesserant, sacerdotiumque, quae erant adepti, consederunt, ut et ipsi in occasu suo splendorem et ornamenta praeteritae vitae retinerent.

Yet not even at that so wretched and so grievous time did our State forget its valour: for those who had held office sat down at their open thresholds on their curule seats and with the insignia of the magistracies which they had held and the priesthoods they had obtained, so that even in their last moments they might retain the splendour and the decorations of their past life.

Further, the spectacle of the gesture has an immediate impact on the Gauls:

Venerabilis eorum aspectus primo hostibus fuit et novitate rei et magnificentia cultus et ipso audaciae genere commotis.

The sight of them at first prompted reverence in the enemy, who were stirred by the novelty of the deed and the magnificence of their costume and the very manner of their audacity.

The connection between Scaeva and the spectacular has already been drawn, and here again one can see the connection between this concept and that of the *exemplum*. However, what really unites Scaeva and the old men is the reaction of the audience. Thus, Valerius goes on:

Sed quis dubitaret quin et Galli et victores illam admirationem mox in risum et in omne contumeliae genus conversuri essent?

Yet who could doubt that Gauls, and victorious Gauls at that, would soon turn that admiration into laughter and every type of mockery?

and describes how they go forward to fondle their elderly captives.

At this point, the different accounts of Livy and Valerius might be contrasted. The former writes that, 5. 41. 9:

Ad eos velut ad simulacra versi cum starent, M. Papirius, unus ex iis, dicitur Gallo barbam suam, ut tum omnibus promissa erat, permulcenti scipione eburneo in caput incusso iram movisse, atque ab eo initium caedis ortum, ceteros in sedibus suis trucidatos.

When they turned and stood facing them as if they were statues, M. Papirius, one of the Romans, is said to have provoked their anger by striking the head of the Gaul who was stroking his beard (since he, like all the men of that period, wore it long) with an ivory staff, and that this was the start of the slaughter and that the rest were massacred in their chairs.

Valerius, on the other hand, describes the attentions of the Gaul, and then says the following of the reaction of a different Roman:

Non expectavit igitur hanc iniuriae maturitatem M. Atilius, verum barbam suam permulcenti Gallo scipionem vehementi ictu capiti inflixit eique propter dolorem ad se occidendum ruenti cupidius corpus obtulit. *Capi ergo virtus nescit patientiae dedecus ignorat*, fortunae succumbere omni fato tristius ducit, *nova et speciosa genera interitus* excogitat, si quisquam interit, qui sic extinguitur.

Therefore M. Atilius did not wait for this insult to develop but struck the Gaul who was stroking his beard with a violent blow to the head from his staff, and when the other ran up on account of the pain to kill him, he offered his body with some eagerness. Thus valour cannot be taken prisoner, knows not the disgrace of compliance, considers it worse than any destiny to give in to fortune, devises new and glorious ways to die, if a man dies who is extinguished in this way.[32]

The development of the story is clear: Livy takes time to describe the fashion for beards in archaic Rome, and extracts no explicit moral, while Valerius further expands his conception of *virtus*, adding to courage in war the refusal to take the part of a woman (ignoble *patientia*).

Here then, the ideology implicit in Curtius is made explicit. The noble Roman does not know how to be captured and responds with manly vigour to the insult of being fondled by a foreigner. Scaeva absorbs the model, forming from it an ignoble trick, the consequence of which is to revive his *virtus*, now redefined as a furious taste for blood. The latter would be demeaning in any context, but in a civil war it is indicative of a particularly warped mentality.

Thus, the recontextualization of Scaeva within the educational programme of Valerius gives a deeper understanding of certain aspects of Lucan's description. It also shows how all heroic models fail in a civil-war context. It does not deny the value of Valerius' *exempla* for when Romans are doing what Lucan so often says they should, that is fighting foreigners, but it does attack the anthologizing principle by which the suicide of a Republican Cato can stand side by side with the deeds of a Caesarian lunatic like Scaeva.[33] 'Talis in castris divi Iuli disciplina militares aluit.' Such discipline indeed. There are some disciplines one can do without.

[32] Rutz (1960) 464, who, like Marti, does not refer to Valerius, nevertheless says of Scaeva's attack on Aulus that it is a commonplace that *virtus* knows no surrender: 'Wir begegnen einem allgemein gültigen Kennzeichen der "virtus": der mangelnden Bereitschaft seine Handlungsfreiheit aufzugeben und sich zu ergeben'. To support this, he cites C. Manlius at Sall. *Cat.* 33. 4: 'Libertatem, quam nemo bonus nisi cum anima simul amittit', cf. Dem. 18. 205 and 296, Isoc. 6. 8.

[33] For Lucan's nostalgia for foreign conquest, see Luc. 1. 10–23 cf. 7. 427–31. For this theme, see Jal (1962) and Tandoi (1963) 94–5.

LUCAN AND VALERIUS ON THE *EXEMPLUM* AS SPECTACLE

The second consequence of reading Scaeva in the light of Valerius concerns the concept of spectacle. Here, the essential lines are *Pharsalia* 6. 149–69, in which Scaeva delivers a *paraceleusis* to his troops and urges them to join him in a splendid death, 6. 149–54:

> Hic ubi quaerentis socios iam Marte relicto
> tuta fugae cernit, 'Quo vos pavor inquit adegit
> inpius et cunctis ignotus Caesaris armis?
> Terga datis morti? Cumulo vos desse virorum
> non pudet et bustis interque cadavera quaeri?'

Now, when he saw his comrades abandon the fight and seek safety in flight, 'Where has impious fear, a stranger in all Caesar's army, driven you? Do you retreat in the face of death? Are you not ashamed to be missing from the pile of dead and the pyres and for men to ask where you are amidst the corpses?'

The reaction which he receives is, to say the least, paradoxical, 6. 165–9:

> Movit tantum vox illa furorem,
> quantum non primo succendunt classica cantu,
> mirantesque virum atque avidi spectare secuntur
> scituri iuvenes, numero deprensa locoque
> an plus quam mortem virtus daret.

That speech prompted a greater frenzy than is sparked by the first blast of the battle-trumpets, and the young men followed the man, marvelling at him and eager to watch and find out whether valour outnumbered and in an inferior position might win more than death.

All most peculiar: a *paraceleusis* which produces not allies but an audience.[34] Conte's note at *mirantes . . . spectare* discusses two essential characteristics of the soldiers' reaction. On a general level, he associates the action here with other moments in the *Pharsalia* where the presence of characters acting as spectators exemplifies the collapse of

[34] For an echo of this theme, and thus the sense of its impact on an ancient audience, cf. Stat. *Theb.* 11. 497–8: 'Tunc vero accensae stimulis maioribus irae: | arma placent, versaeque volunt spectare cohortes'. Strangely, Venini has twice noted the Lucanian tone of these lines—Venini (1970) ad loc., cf. Venini (1965) 155–6—but with no reference to the attitude of Scaeva's followers.

epic objectivity, of the world viewed by the narrator from outside, into a mass of conflicting subjective points of view. On a more specific level he observes the paradox that Scaeva's performance of the epic *aristeia* is dependent on the failure of his appeal for active support, on the transformation of his comrades into spectators.[35]

Conte's concern here is to study the position of Scaeva within the traditions of the epic genre. When he states that Lucan's style is not that of epic, the significance of that style is measured in terms of its distance from the genre it rejects. At the same time, however, Scaeva's audience gains a further special significance from its relationship to the other subgenre, the Valerian exemplary narrative, into which the hero has already endeavoured to cast himself. In short, if it is the soldiers' very abandonment of Scaeva which allows him the privilege of the *aristeia*, it is also the fact of their spectatorship which makes and then unmakes Scaeva as a literary *exemplum*.

The importance of visibility to an *exemplum* is common both to Lucan and to Valerius. Thus, a parallel passage to Scaeva is that describing the mass suicide on board the ship of Vulteius in Book 4 of the *Pharsalia*. The gesture which Vulteius contemplates is blessed with the sheer visibility which will allow it the chance to become an *exemplum*, 4. 488–99:

> 'Non tamen in caeca bellorum nube cadendum est
> aut cum permixtas acies sua tela tenebris
> involvent. Conferta iacent cum corpora campo,
> in medium mors omnis abit, *perit obruta virtus*:
> nos in conspicua sociis hostique carina
> constituere dei; praebebunt aequora testes,
> praebebunt terrae, summis dabit insula saxis,
> *spectabunt* geminae diverso litore partes.
> Nescio quod nostris magnum et memorabile fatis
> *exemplum*, Fortuna, paras. Quaecumque per aevum
> exhibuit monimenta fides servataque ferro
> militiae pietas, transisset nostra iuventus.'

'Yet it is not necessary to die in the blind cloud of war or when their own arms shroud the commingled armies in darkness. When the bodies lie thick upon the field, each death becomes part of the mass, valour is buried and goes to waste: the gods have set us on a ship clearly visible to comrade and foe; the sea will provide, the land will provide witnesses, the island with its lofty rocks will give

[35] Conte (1974) ad loc. For spectators in the text, Conte cites 2. 207, 4. 804, 7. 797, and 791. All of these passages are discussed in Ch. 7 and the Epilogue.

them, the two sides will watch from either shore. Fortune, you are preparing some great and memorable example by our death. Whatever records loyalty and military duty preserved by the sword have left through time, our youthful band would have surpassed them.'[36]

For Vulteius, the exemplary quality of a deed is lost without an audience.[37] This is also the impression given by Valerius. The importance of spectacle and spectatorship has already been emphasized in the instances of Aemilius Lepidus, Horatius, and the self-sacrifice of the old. Similarly, at 3. 2. 16, the son of the elder Cato drops his sword in battle, and, though surrounded by the enemy, fights to pick it up with such vigour that:

Quo *spectaculo* adtoniti hostes postero die ad eum supplices pacem petentes venerunt.

Amazed by the spectacle, the enemy came to him the next day to entreat and petition him for peace.

Again, at 3. 2. 20, inspired by the standard-throwing of the Latins, Valerius Flaccus urges his men not to be 'spectators of another's valour' (*spectatores . . . alienae virtutis*) and expresses his intent, 'praying for a death glorious to see' (*speciosam optans mortem*), to rush forward against the foe. Finally, at 3. 2. 21, Q. Occius performs brave and magnanimous deeds 'with both armies looking on' (*utroque exercitu spectante*), and, at 3. 2. 23, Scaeva is apostrophized as follows:

Hinc Romanis, illinc Brittannicis oculis incredibili, nisi cerneris, spectaculo fuisti.

To the eyes of the Romans on one side and of the Britains on the other you provided a spectacle incredible to all but those who saw it.[38]

[36] The problem for Vulteius, of course, is that Luc. 4. 573–81 will recognize the exemplarity of his deed, but interpret it in a rather different light. On this point, see Ch. 7, pp. 259–61. For another hero obsessed with the visual impact of his death, one need look no further than the soliloquy of Pompey prior to his murder in Egypt. Note Luc. 8. 613–21 for Pompey's actions, and particularly 8. 622–7 ('"Saecula Romanos numquam tacitura labores | attendunt, aevumque sequens speculatur ab omni | orbe ratem Phariamque fidem: nunc consule famae. | Fata tibi longae fluxerunt prospera vitae: | ignorant populi, si non in morte probaris, | an scieris adversa pati"') and 8. 632–5 ('"Videt hanc Cornelia caedem | Pompeiusque meus: tanto patientius, oro, | claude, dolor, gemitus; natus coniunxque peremptum, | si mirantur, amant"'). The end of Pompey is coloured by his struggle with heroic expectation. He who shirked death at Pharsalus and would not 'adversa pati', here finally verifies himself by reference to his code. The hero who will be loved by his wife and son only 'si mirantur' is caught in the same trap as Lord Jim after him. In this instance, Lucan's meditation on the heroic code, on exemplarity, transcends burlesque and becomes pathetic.

[37] For a possible parallel to this at Sen. *Ep.* 70. 25–6, see Ch. 7 pp. 260–1.

[38] For parallel Livian *spectacula* inspiring one's peers, see the giant Navius at 26. 5. 15–17 and the leading of the charge by Philip at 31. 24. 11–16.

The connection cannot be denied. An exemplary deed needs an audience or it cannot become an *exemplum*. In this way, Scaeva's spectator allies help give him the status he pursues. It is the same audience, however, which unmakes Scaeva the *exemplum*, which exposes all the flaws in his literary scheme. A further distinction makes this point clear. Aemilius Lepidus, we have observed, performed exemplary deeds when still scarcely old enough to be a *spectator*. For a young boy it is fine to stand by and watch a battle. For a grown man such as Valerius Flaccus, the *exemplum* is an immediate spur to similar deeds of his own. When Scaeva delivers his *paraceleusis*, he believes that his resistance can be an *exemplum* to spur his men to join him in the fight. However, his *spectaculum* instead prompts in the watchers the chill, distanced response of the *spectator*. The *furor* which he breeds in them is that of the schoolboys who take out their notebooks and test in the flesh the reality of the proposition which they have been offered in the classroom, 6. 168–9:

> Scituri iuvenes, numero deprensa locoque
> an plus quam mortem virtus daret.

The young men eager to find out whether valour outnumbered and in an inferior position might win more than death.

Which is, above all, the most splendid joke. Lucan, who came from Rome's most distinguished family of educationalists, who by all accounts was a quite stunningly adept pupil, mercilessly teases the conceits of the Roman school system. The poet himself uses Scaeva as the *exemplum* by which to test the exemplary virtues he has been taught, then treats the soldiers of his cohort as a most disconcerting surrogate for his own analytical attitude.

What Lucan does is to unravel the structuring principles of the Roman exemplary narrative. The use of the double audience meant that the form was never innocent of discursive intent. It set up implicit models for watching and for response to what was seen, the characters acting out their later conduct. In Lucan's version of the form, the behaviour of the audience signalizes a profound dysfunction, one which the poet's framing references to the *virtus* of Scaeva will make explicit. The deformation of the traditional exemplary narrative makes it clear that Lucan's adventures in the grotesque actually serve subtler, more distancing and intellectualizing purposes than simple *Steigerung des Pathos*.

SPARTAN POSTSCRIPT

The examination of Scaeva the *exemplum* is virtually complete. It remains only to suggest a possible exemplification of the abstract situation, 'whether valour outnumbered and in an inferior position might win more than death' (*numero deprensa locoque* | *an plus quam mortem virtus daret*).[39] One could, of course, here return to the example of Horatius Cocles, which answers all the criteria offered. However, the reward for the *virtus* of Horatius has a little too much of the *deus ex machina* about it to exemplify a moral rule. One wants to say, rather, that *virtus* wins one eternal glory even after death.[40] Further, the same work which offers Lucan so much material for his Scaeva episode, that of Valerius Maximus on *virtus*,[41] provides an excellent alternative example in the case of Leonidas and the 300 at Thermopylae. Outnumbered to the tune of a few hundred thousand, after betrayal they were also 'deprived of the advantage in position' (*opportunitate loci spoliati*.) Of course their sacrifice led to their deaths, but it also rendered them immortal.[42] There are also two further compelling reasons to look to the Spartans for the model.

One is the close association of the Spartans as a nation with the concept of the practical *exemplum*. The other is the very terminology in which it was customary for the declaimers to make the Spartans express their refusal to retreat. Like Scaeva, quite simply, a Spartan soldier was his country's walls. The connection between Lucan and this declamatory commonplace is noted by Bonner,[43] who considers the rhetorical origins of the pairing of Scaeva vs. *bellum* and cites a parallel from Polemo for 'he stands an unbreakable wall for Caesar' (*stat non fragilis pro Caesare murus*):

ἔνθα πολλὰ μὲν βελῶν καὶ κοντῶν καὶ ξιφῶν καὶ παντοδαπῶν βλημάτων ὑπεδέξατο, πάσας δὲ αὐτῶν ὑπέμεινε τὰς προσβόλας ὥσπερ ἐξ ἀδάμαντος ὢν πύργος ἢ τεῖχος ἄρρηκτον.

[39] Luc., 6. 168–9.

[40] The situation is also Caesarian, e.g. *B. Gall.* 7. 50. 1, where 'Cum acerrime comminus pugnaretur, hostes loco et numero, nostri virtute confiderent'.

[41] Val. Max. 3. 2. *Ext.* 3.

[42] For another outnumbered and self-sacrificing Roman, see Cato, *Orig.* fr. 83 (Peter), for Q. Caedicius, a *tribunus militum*: 'Leonides Laco quidem simile apud Thermopylas fecit, propter eius virtutes omnis Graecia gloriam atque gratiam praecipuam claritudinis inclitissimae decoravere monumentis: signis, statuis, elogiis, historiis, aliisque rebus gratissimum id eius factum habuere; at tribuno militum parva laus pro factis relicta, qui idem fecerat atque rem servaverat'.

[43] Bonner (1966) 283, incl. n. 68.

Then he was hit by many spears and pikes and swords and missiles of all kinds, but he withstood all their attacks as if he were a tower made of adamant or an unbreakable wall.

However, Bonner does not see, as do Marti and Saylor, the centrality of the image of Scaeva as wall, and therefore does not follow through this most important point. Yet one of the most significant aspects to emerge from the previous interpretations of this episode is the emphasis put on how Scaeva, who is gradually dehumanized by the range of wounds which he suffers, thus comes to represent the very wall, the breaching of which he resists.[44] This is given its strongest expression at 6. 198–202:

Hunc aut tortilibus vibrata falarica nervis
obruat aut vasti muralia pondera saxi,
hunc aries ferro ballistaque limine portae
promoveat. Stat non fragilis pro Caesare murus
Pompeiumque tenet.

Let a missile sent whirring by twisted cords overwhelm this man or the wall-breaking weight of a huge stone, let the battering-ram with its steel and the catapult shift him from the entrance to the gate. He stands an unbreakable wall for Caesar and holds Pompey up.[45]

Conte here connects the image of the wall to the epic tradition, citing a number of passages from Homer, Ovid, and finally the *Troades* of Seneca.[46] Yet here again, there are good grounds for looking beyond epic for the sources of Lucan's inspiration. For, of all these citations, it

[44] e.g. Marti (1966) and Saylor (1978). Looking at this passage in the terms of Masters (1992), one might also say that the walls overtop all other epics in their monumentality, thus miming the achievement of Lucan's poem, 6. 48–54: 'Nunc vetus Iliacos attollat fabula muros | ascribatque deis; fragili circumdata testa | moenia mirentur refugi Babylonia Parthi. | En, quantum Tigris, quantum celer ambit Orontes, | Assyriis quantum populis telluris Eoae | sufficit in regnum, subitum bellique tumultu | raptum clausit opus'. For the further metaliterary function of the walls and Scaeva as *belli mora*, see below.

[45] Marti (1966) 247 cites other choice pieces of wall imagery, for instance 6. 185 'vallatus bello', cf. 6. 189 'illum tota premit moles, illum omnia tela', cf. (my favourite) 6. 224–5 'stetit imbre cruento | informis facies'. For 6. 198–202 and the allusion to Bitias at Verg. *Aen.* 9. 703–9, see Conte (1974) ad loc.

[46] Conte gives Hom. *Il.* 1. 283–4 (μέγα πᾶσιν | ἕρκος Ἀχαιοῖσιν . . . πολέμοιο κακοῖο), 3. 229 and 4. 299, *Hymn. Hom. Mart.* 3 (ἕρκος Ὀλύμπου); Ov. *Met.* 13. 281 (*Graium murus, Achilles*); and Sen. *Tro.* 126 (to Hector, *tu murus eras*). Cf. Hom. *Od.* 11. 556; Aesch. *Ag.* 1437; Eur. *Alc.* 311, *Med.* 390; Sil. *Pun.* 16. 68; Stat. *Theb.* 3. 356; Claud. *Carm.* 3. 264–5 (Hall), 8. 109 (Hall), 8. 432–3 (Hall), Venant. Fort. 7. 12. 11. I have plundered most of this more extensive list from Erbig (1931). See also Fantham (1982) at Sen. *Tro.* 126.

is that from Seneca which is the most pertinent. At *Troades* 124–6, Hecuba expresses her lament for Hector in these terms:

> Columen patriae, *mora fatorum*,
> tu praesidium Phrygibus fessis,
> tu *murus* eras.

Pillar of the fatherland, delayer of destiny, you were the defence of the weary Phrygians, you were their wall.

There are two good reasons to emphasize these lines of Seneca. The first is the all-important reference to *mora*. Masters has shown how Lucan uses this term to encapsulate the principle of retardation which characterizes his narrative.[47] Here, Caesar's walls, and with them the man-wall Scaeva, act as a *belli mora*, first in the amount of time which it takes for the poet to describe them, second in their ability, while providing one of Lucan's few genuine battle-scenes, effectively to separate the armies. All combine to delay the battle of Dyrrachium, and then Pharsalus itself.

Mora is already used in Seneca to denote the principle which restrains the force necessary to unleash disaster and create the tragedy.[48] It is very likely that the lament of Hecuba in the *Troades* was in Lucan's mind when he wrote. However—and here emerges the second reason to emphasize the *Troades*—it is also very likely that both he and his uncle were aware of another Senecan association of the man-wall with *mora*, and this time in the very context of Thermopylae which I take as the underlying model for this scene.

At *Suasoria* 2. 19, the elder Seneca quotes two lines of Abronius Silo:

> 'Ite agite, o Danai, magnum paeana canentes,
> ite triumphantes: *belli mora* concidit Hector.'

'Yes go, O Danaans, singing the great paean, go in triumph: Hector the delayer of war has fallen.'

Yet these lines are said to be only a pollution (*polluit*) of the apophthegm of Porcius Latro, urging his fellow *suasoria* Spartans to stay at Thermopylae, *Suas.* 2. 19:

'Si nihil aliud, erimus certe *belli mora*.'

'If nothing else, we will certainly delay the war.'

The second good reason to emphasize the passage from the *Troades*, therefore, is its use of language which can be paralleled in the Laconizing

[47] Masters (1992) 3–10, 43, 54–5, 60, 95–6, 119–22, 183.

[48] See Sen. *Ag.* 130–1 and Tarrant (1976) ad loc. and cf. Sen. *Med.* 54 and 1015.

show-speeches of the schoolroom. The Spartans of Seneca, it has been noted, like the Spartans of so much ancient literature, are celebrated as their country's walls. Instances of this connection are not hard to find. According to the historical tradition, Lycurgus had forbidden the creation of walls to defend Sparta and had asserted that the nation's warriors sufficed for this role.[49] The influence of this tradition is clear in the contrast often made in Greek poetry between the walls or tower of a city, the body of a boat, and its inhabitants. This emerges in the assertion at Alcaeus, fr. 112. 10 (Lobel-Page) that 'men are the mighty tower of a city' (ἄνδρες γὰρ πόλ(ιος πύργος ἀρευί)ος) and is reflected in a number of writers.[50] More importantly, however, the question of whether or not the Spartans should build a wall became a common topic in rhetorical education, as we see from Philostratus, *Vit. Soph.* 514:

τοὺς μὲν γὰρ Λακεδαιμονίους ἀγωνιζόμενος τοὺς βουλευομένους περὶ τοῦ τείχους ἀπὸ τῶν Ὁμήρου ἐβραχυλόγησε τοσοῦτον· ἀσπὶς ἄρ' ἀσπίδ' ἔρειδε, κόρυς κόρυν, ἀνέρα δ' ἀνήρ. οὕτω στῆτέ μοι, Λακεδαιμόνιοι, καὶ τετειχίσμεθα.

For, when addressing the Spartans as they took counsel on the question of building a wall, he summed up his argument with the following quotation from Homer: '"Shield pressed shield, helmet helmet, man man": stand like this for me, Spartans, and we have a wall.'

This example from Greek rhetorical practice is echoed in a quotation from the declaimer Damas, who tried: 'whither will you flee, hoplites, walls?' ('ποῖ φεύξεσθε, ὁπλῖται, τείχη;') What is significant here is not

[49] Plut. *Mor.* 228 E: καὶ πάλιν ἐπιζητούντων περὶ τειχῶν, οὐκ ἔφη πόλιν εἶναι ἀτείχιστον, ἥτις ἀνδράσι καὶ οὐ πλίνθοις ἐστεφάνωται. Cf. Plut. *Lyc.* 19. 4 for the same words and Plut. *Mor.* 210 E and 217 E for Agesilaus: ταῦτά ἐστιν . . . τὰ Λακεδαιμονίων τείχη cf. τείχη δὲ ἔλεγεν εἶναι τῆς Σπάρτης τοὺς νέους, ὅρια δὲ τὰς ἐπιδορατίδας. This is reflected at Pl. *Leg.* 778 D, περὶ δὲ τειχῶν, ὦ Μέγιλλε, ἔγωγ' ἂν τῆι Σπάρτηι ξυμφεροίμην τὸ καθεύδειν ἐᾶν ἐν τῆι γῆι κατακείμενα τὰ τείχη καὶ μὴ ἐπανιστάναι, a sentiment which is implicitly rebuked at Ar. *Pol.* 1330^{b} 32–3: περὶ δὲ τειχῶν, οἱ μὴ φάσκοντες δεῖν ἔχειν τὰς τῆς ἀρετῆς ἀντιποιουμένας πόλεις λίαν ἀρχαίως ὑπολαμβάνουσιν, καὶ ταῦθ' ὁρῶντες ἐλεγχομένας ἔργωι τὰς ἐκείνως καλλωπισαμένας. For a Roman version of this tradition, cf. Livy, 39. 37. 1–3: '"At enim illa certe vestra sunt, Achaei, quod leges disciplinamque vetustissimam Lycurgi sustulistis, quod muros diruistis. Quae utraque ab iisdem obici qui possunt, cum muri Lacedaemonis non ab Lycurgo, sed paucos ante annos ad dissolvendam Lycurgi disciplinam exstructi sunt? Tyranni enim nuper eos arcem et munimentum sibi, non civitati paraverunt; et si exsistat hodie ab inferis Lycurgus, gaudeat ruinis eorum, et nunc se patriam et Spartam antiquam agnoscere dicat"'. Cato, *Orig.* frr. 50–1 (Peter) and Cn. Gellius, fr. 10 (Peter) claim that the Sabines are descended from the Spartan Sabus and emphasize the unwalled settlements of the tribe.

[50] Aesch. *Pers.* 349; Soph. *O.T.* 56–7; Thuc. 7. 77. 7; Dem. 18. 299.

so much the evidence that this was a regular debating issue as quite how close to Lucan's home is the provenance of this last example. For, Damas, like Latro, is cited at Seneca, *Suasoria* 2. 14, which deals with the 300 at Thermopylae. Bonner notes this usage, but, disregarding Lucan's wall motif, makes little of it. However, it is essential to underline the presence both of this tag and of a succession of others on the same theme in the same context. Thus, at 2. 1, Arellius Fuscus offers:

'Et nunc produntur condita sine moenibus templa?'

'And are the temples built without walls now betrayed?'

At 2. 3, Triarius:

'Ne sit Sparta lapidibus circumdata: ibi muros habet ubi viros.'

'Let not Sparta be surrounded with stone: there has she walls where she has men.'

At 2. 5, Cestius:

'Ideo muri nostri arma sunt.'

'For that reason weapons are our walls.'

And at 2. 6:

'Adhuc non sum ex ulla parte Atheniensium similis, non muris nec educatione.'

'Hitherto I have borne no likeness to the Athenians, either in defensive walls or in upbringing.'

And finally, at 2. 16, Catius Crispus the tasteless:

'Aliud ceteros, aliud Laconas decet; nos sine deliciis educamur, sine muris vivimus, sine vita vincimus.'

'One thing is fitting for the rest, another for the Spartans; we are brought up without luxuries, we live without walls, we win without surviving.'

This is the practical instance sought. When the soldiers sit down to test through Scaeva the 'reality' of their notoriously unreal debating formulae, the particular problem which Scaeva represents is that of the men-wall Spartans of Thermopylae, one of the favourite themes of his own grandfather. When Bonner points to the similarity between the *murus* of Lucan's Scaeva and that of Polemo's Callimachus, he recognizes an important poetic image. Yet, when he notes the hoplites of Damas, he touches on a much more significant tradition. For, in the

Greek world, it is Sparta which is classically associated both with the notion of men as walls and with the practical *exemplum* as the centrepiece of a moral education. At Rome, in the Sabine Cato's fantasies of Spartan descent, Sparta is celebrated as the great military state, the state Rome 'is' or should be. And yet it is that very military state—and with it the *exempla* that embody its wisdom—which Lucan is concerned to portray in collapse.

6

The Crazy Gang—Watching Caesar's Centurions

This chapter extends the investigation of Lucan's distanced and perhaps comic or burlesque modes of narration centred on the concepts of spectacle and spectatorship. In particular, it examines Lucan's reflection of the theme in Caesar's Commentaries of the deep loyalty of the centurions to their general and of their desire to fight in his sight. In Lucan, it is argued, this ambition is indicative not just of loyalty but of a closed and insane community, at one in its perversion of traditional military values.[1] This perversion is most evident in the distortion of inherited attitudes to the body, to the proper stance of the warrior, and to honour and dishonour in wounding. It is finally exemplified in Scaeva's reproduction of a second traditional mode of spectacular display—and one closely associated with the Marian tradition Caesar inherited—that is, the display of scars and wounds to the breast. In this display, it is possible to measure the distance at which Caesar's men stand from Roman tradition, and the alienation which such a stance must provoke.

CENTURIONS IN CAESAR AND LUCAN

In the discussion of exemplarity in Lucan, it was noted that the centurion Scaeva was not a fictional creation of Lucan, but a historical figure first reported by Caesar at *B. Civ.* 3. 53. 3–5. Here, he is

[1] The emphasis of this chapter is entirely on Caesar and his men. Other minor characters are notable for their devotion to Pompey, most notably Domitius in Books 2 and 7, Cordus in 8, and the Cilician Tarcondimotus at 9. 215–93. In the case of the first, loyalty to Pompey goes hand in hand with loyalty to Republican institutions, in that of the last it does not. On at least one occasion, obedience to a Republican general leads to the sort of criminal display to be discussed here—Luc. 4. 243–52 describes the soldiers' reaction to the speech of Petreius, for which see esp. 4. 250–2, 'Fervent iam castra tumultu, | ac, velut occultum pereat scelus, omnia monstra | in facie posuere ducum: iuvat esse nocentis'.

described as leading the defence of his fort at Dyrrachium and receiving promotion as a reward:[2]

Quem Caesar, ut erat de se meritus et de re publica, donatum milibus CC collaudatumque ab octavis ordinibus ad primipilum se traducere pronuntiavit.

Since he had served him and the State well, Caesar announced that he was granting him two hundred thousand sesterces and was promoting him with special commendation from the eighth rank to the first centurionate.[3]

Similarly, the Crastinus whom Lucan curses at 7. 470–3 for casting the first weapon at Pharsalus[4] is represented quite differently at *B. Civ.* 3. 91:

Erat C. Crastinus evocatus in exercitu Caesaris, qui superiore anno apud eum primum pilum in legione X duxerat, vir singulari virtute. Hic signo dato 'Sequimini me', inquit, 'manipulares mei qui fuistis, et vestro imperatori quam constituistis operam date. Unum hoc proelium superest; quo confecto et ille suam dignitatem et nos nostram libertatem recuperabimus'. Simul respiciens Caesarem, 'Faciam', inquit, 'hodie, imperator, ut aut vivo mihi aut mortuo gratias agas'. Haec cum dixisset, primus ex dextro cornu procucurrit atque eum electi milites circiter CXX voluntarii eiusdem cohortis sunt prosecuti.

There was a certain recalled veteran, C. Crastinus, in Caesar's army, who in his service the year before had held the rank of first centurion in the tenth legion, a man of outstanding valour. When the signal was given, he said 'Follow me, you who were in my company of old, and grant your general the service you have promised. This one battle remains; when it is over, he will recover his position of respect, and we our freedom.' At the same time, looking back at Caesar, he said, 'I shall today ensure, general, that you thank me whether I am alive or dead.' When he had said these words, he ran forward from the right wing before the rest and around one hundred and twenty chosen volunteer soldiers from the same cohort followed him.[5]

Again, at the close of the battle, Caesar's account of losses makes special reference to Crastinus, Caes. *B. Civ.* 3. 99. 1–3:

In eo proelio non amplius CC milites desideravit, sed centuriones, fortis viros,

[2] The promotion of Scaeva seems to cease here—*ILLRP* 498 and 1116a would suggest that Scaeva was still a centurion at the time of the Perusine War.

[3] 'collaudatumque' Dinter. Du Pontet's OCT reads '[atque]', which is evidently corrupt. While it is my policy in this study wherever possible to follow the OCT, the text of Caesar in particular is often more readily comprehensible in later editions.

[4] Luc. 7. 470–3: 'Di tibi non mortem, quae cunctis poena paratur, | sed sensum post fata tuae dent, Crastine, morti, | cuius torta manu commisit lancea bellum | primaque Thessaliam Romano sanguine tinxit'.

[5] 'cohortis' Peskett, 'centuriae' MSS and Du Pontet.

circiter XXX amisit. Interfectus est etiam fortissime pugnans Crastinus, cuius mentionem supra fecimus, gladio in os adversum coniecto. Neque id fuit falsum quod ille in pugnam proficiscens dixerat. Sic enim Caesar existimabat eo proelio excellentissimam virtutem Crastini fuisse optimeque de se meritum iudicabat.

In this battle no more than two hundred of his soldiers were killed but he lost around thirty centurions, heroic men. Crastinus too, whom I mentioned earlier, was killed while fighting with the utmost courage, a sword thrust full in his face. Nor were the words he uttered as he set off to fight proved false. For Caesar considered the valour of Crastinus in this battle to have been quite outstanding and held him to have done him excellent service.[6]

Here are two Caesarian centurions recalled by Lucan. To these examples of the loyal subordinate should be added the probably invented centurion Laelius of Book 1[7] and the *tribunus militum* Vulteius of Book 4.[8] In the case of Vulteius, there is no reference to his career in Caesar's Commentaries, but comparison of the evidence in Florus, Livy, and the *Commenta Bernensia* provides an intriguing picture. Of these three accounts, those of Livy and Florus are the least helpful, Livy adding to the evidence in Lucan only that the Opitergini were Transpadanes, Florus that Vulteius held the rank of *tribunus militum*. The latter, moreover, often reveals his own direct dependence on the *Pharsalia* for his information.[9] The note given by the *Commenta Bernensia* at 4. 462, however, quite apart from including the information that six men survived, also reveals both the rank of Vulteius and the assiduous care of Caesar to cultivate his Transpadane supporters:

[6] For more on Crastinus in Livy, Plutarch, and Appian, see Ch. 4, pp. 140–2. See also Heyke (1970) 81–4. Quint (1993) 148–9 makes an observation of some pertinence to the concerns of this chapter. When Lucan cries out 'O praeceps rabies' at 7. 474, he grants to the centurion Crastinus the one epithet most characteristic of his general's headlong progress through the epic—cf. 2. 656, 3. 50–1, 9. 47–8, 10. 507–8.

[7] Luc. 1. 356–88.

[8] Luc. 4. 402–581.

[9] Liv., *Per.* 110: 'C. Antonius, legatus Caesaris, male adversus Pompeianos in Illyrico rebus gestis captus est; in quo bello Opitergini Transpadani, Caesaris auxiliares, rate sua ab hostilibus navibus clusa, potius quam in potestatem hostium venirent, inter se concurrentes occubuerunt.' Flor. *Epit.* 2. 13. 32–3 may be annotated so as to reveal its indebtedness to Lucan: 'Missae quoque a Basilo [Luc. 4. 416] in auxilium eius rates, quales inopia navium fecerat, nova Pompeianorum arte Cilicum [Luc. 4. 448–9] actis sub mari funibus captae quasi per indaginem. Duas tamen aestus explicuit [Luc. 4. 452–4]. Una, quae Opiterginos ferebat, in vadis haesit [Luc. 4. 454] memorandumque posteris exemplum [Luc. 4. 496–7, cf. 4. 575–6] dedit. Quippe vix mille iuvenum manus circumfusi undique exercitus per totum diem tela sustinuit, et cum exitum virtus non haberet, tandem, ne in deditionem veniret, hortante tribuno Vulteio mutuis ictibus inter se concurrit.'

Opitergium oppidum est, quod cum Caesare sentiebat contra Pompeium. In qua nave erat C. Vulteius Capito tribunus militum. Qui primum suos hortatus est ut fortiter dimicarent, deinde cum ad deditionem vocarentur, exceptis sex invicem se occiderunt. Propter quod Caesar in solacium Opiterginis in annos xx vacationem militiae dedit finesque eorum trecentis centuriis ampliavit.

Opitergium is a town which supported Caesar against Pompey. On the ship mentioned was C. Vulteius Capito, a military tribune. At first he ordered his men to fight courageously, then, when they were being invited to surrender, all but six of them killed each other. In response to this and to console the people of Opitergium, Caesar granted them twenty years' dispensation from military service and enlarged their boundaries by three hundred centuries.[10]

This concentration of figures would suggest that the Italian junior officer, centurion or *tribunus militum*, holds a central position in Caesar's ideology and in Lucan's engagement with it. Closer examination of the two authors demonstrates that the above is true and that the corrupt heroism of the Caesarian centurion becomes one of the prime loci for Lucan's demonstration of the perversion of more traditional national values in battle.

Historians have often represented Caesar's cultivation of the Italian *municipia* as a continuation of the Marian political tradition.[11] It may have been Pompey's father who gained Latin rights for Transpadane communities such as Opitergium, but it was Caesar who came increasingly to represent their interests.[12] The scandalous treatment meted out in 50 BC to the delegation from Novum Comum by Pompey's ally, the arch-optimate Marcellus, can only have contrasted with Caesar's conscious cultivation of the towns of northern Italy and protection of them from Gallic raids.

The most significant aspect of the Marian ideology in this context is the assertion that true nobility is not the product of high birth but of deeds of *virtus* in defence of the State.[13] This assertion supports the

[10] For Opitergium, see Smith (1870) ii. 485.

[11] e.g. Syme (1939) 65, 89–90, 94.

[12] Ibid. 74.

[13] See Sall. *Jug.* 85. The speech is used as an example of the rhetoric of the *novus homo* in Earl (1967) 44–53. The theme is taken up at Juv. 8, for which see the introd. to Courtney (1980) and the excellent discussion and citations offered by Braund (1988) ch. 3. See also Cic. *Leg. Agr.* 2. 100 for the distinction between those attaining glory 'in cunabulis' and those 'in campo'. Cicero notes that as a 'novus homo', he has 'nulli ... maiores', 'nulli ... auctores generis', and 'nullae ... imagines' to commend him. For other Ciceronian reflections on the theme, cf. *Mur.* 17, *Verr.* 2. 3. 7 and 2. 5. 180, and *Sest.* 136. Detailed discussions of *virtus* and the ideology of *novitas* are to be found in Roloff (1936) 10–22; Hellegouarc'h (1963) 476–83; Woodman (1977) 255–63; Wiseman (1971) 107–16. For the currency of the idea in Lucan's time and immediate circle, one might note Tac. *Ann.* 14. 53, where Seneca is represented as asking Nero: 'Inter nobilis et longa decora

demands of those from outside the traditionally empowered Roman families for a share in political power.[14] It is evident that Julius Caesar involved himself in a political programme very much in the spirit of this contention and that he treated his army as a vehicle for social change. Dio, for instance, reports the enrolment of former centurions into the Senate in 47 and 45 BC, an allegation confirmed by Cicero.[15] While the only centurion-senator who can be identified with certainty is C. Fuficius Fango, later governor of Africa for Octavian in 41 BC, a strong case has been made for the participation of L. Decidius Saxa and his associate Cafo in the land commission set up after the bill of June 44 BC of M. Antonius and P. Cornelius Dolabella, while a reference in Cicero's letters to the *Tebassos Scaevas Fangones* implies the central position of the centurion in Caesar's party.[16]

It is surely in this context that the peculiar emphasis in the Commentaries on Caesar's use of his legions— he demanded heroic endeavour from his troops and offered strong upward mobility to those who served him well—should be explained. In Caesar's narrative this manifests itself most strongly in his profound affection for the Italian centurion class. Occasionally this is at the expense of urban cissies;[17] more

praeferentis novitas mea enituit?' For the rhetoric of *virtus* vs. *genus*, see Sen. *Her. F.* 337–41, and the note ad loc. in Fitch (1987).

14 It should be noted that Morford (1966) talks about the Marian tradition in the sense of the specific biographical tradition relating to Marius, and does not touch on the issues raised here.

15 Dio Cass., 42. 51. 5 and 43. 47. 3 cf. Cic. *Div.* 2. 23 and Syme (1937) 127 and (1938) 12–18. Also significant is the speech of counsel to Augustus given to Maecenas at Dio Cass., 52. 25. 6, where the Emperor is warned not to introduce to the Senate officers who have risen from the lower ranks.

16 For Fango, see Dio Cass., 48. 22. 3, *ἔν τε γὰρ τῶι μισθοφορικῶι ἐστράτευτο· πολλοὶ γὰρ καὶ τῶν τοιούτων ἐς τὸ βουλευτήριον, ὥσπερ εἴρηται μοι, κατελελέχατο*. For L. Decidius Saxa, see Caes. *B. Civ.* 1. 66 and cf. the insults of Cicero at *Phil.* 11. 12, 13. 27, 14. 10 with Syme (1937) 132–6. Decidius and Cafo are connected at *Phil.* 8. 26, where Cicero represents them as dependents of Antony: 'Cafoni etiam et Saxae cavet, quos centuriones pugnacis et lacertosos inter mimorum et mimarum greges conlocavit', and again at *Phil.* 10. 22, 'et sollicitant homines imperitos Saxae et Cafones, ipsi rustici atque agrestes'. At *Phil.* 11. 12 Cicero talks of 'veteranus Cafo, quo neminem veterani peius oderunt'. Cic. *Att.* 14. 10. 2 complains of three Caesarians—'redeo ad Tebassos Scaevas Fangones: hos tu existimas confidere se illa habituros stantibus nobis?' Syme (1937) 128 and (1938) 13 is sceptical of Münzer's deduction that these men were all senators but does see them as all classic Caesarian types, observing the Sabine ring of the name Tebassus and describing Scaeva as 'a Caesarian centurion proverbial for valour and the type of his class'.

17 e.g. Caes. *B. Gall.* 1. 39. 2. Great fear about fighting the Germans first hits urban types: 'Hic primum ortus est a tribunis militum, praefectis reliquisque, qui ex urbe amicitiae causa Caesarem secuti non magnum in re militari usum habebant'. Cf. 1. 39. 5, 'Horum

often, as with Crastinus, he simply praises their *virtus*, or, as with Scaeva, recounts their promotion through the ranks.[18]

For Caesar, *virtus* is an entirely martial quality. Both Gauls and Romans have to recall their 'antique valour' (*pristina virtus*),[19] which is often 'outstanding' (*egregia*) or 'remarkable' (*singularis*).[20] The type of the man of *virtus* is most clearly the centurion, hence the peculiar aptness of Lucan's Scaeva scene. This aspect to the Caesarian centurion emerges at *B. Gall.* 5. 44 and the account of the rivalry between the 'men of the greatest courage, centurions, who were approaching the first rank' (*fortissimi viri, centuriones, qui primis ordinibus appropinquarent*), Titus Pullo and Lucius Vorenus. We are told that these men engaged in constant disputes with each other and the challenge of Pullo makes clear the nature of their fight, 5. 44. 3:

'Quid dubitas', inquit, 'Vorene? aut quem locum tuae probandae virtutis exspectas? Hic dies de nostris controversiis iudicabit'.

'Why do you hesitate, Vorenus?', he said. 'And what chance are you waiting for to prove your valour? This day will decide our disputes.'[21]

Finally, after the narrative has shown this competition to be entirely salutary in its effect, and both centurions have returned safely to the camp, Caesar concludes, 5. 44. 13:

Sic fortuna in contentione et certamine utrumque versavit, ut alter alteri inimicus auxilio salutique esset neque diiudicari posset, uter utri virtute anteferendus videretur.

Fortune so exercised them both in competition and struggle that the one, by rivalry with the other, brought him aid and salvation and it was impossible to judge which seemed of superior valour to the other.

vocibus ac timore paulatim etiam ei qui magnum in castris usum habebant, milites centurionesque quique equitatui praeerant, perturbabantur'. Cf. 1. 40, where Caesar attacks the centurions for despairing 'de sua virtute'.

[18] Various scholars have made passing allusion to the love-affair between Caesar and his soldiers, particularly the centurions: see Harmand (1967) 453 and nn. 92–3; Yavetz (1983) 162–3; Stevens (1952) 7–8; Syme (1939) 70; and particularly La Penna (1952) 203–5, esp. 204: 'Cesare ricambia l'attaccamento dei suoi soldati con un amore che è il sentimento il più sincero nella sua opera. La vittoria appare frutto non tanto dell'abilità del generale quanto del valore dei soldati. Come nel *Bellum Gallicum* così nel *Bellum Civile* Cesare ama riferire i singoli episodi di valore, come ad iscrivere i soldati più valorosi nel ricordo della posterità'. This article is important both for the stress placed on Crastinus and Scaeva, and for La Penna's awareness of the democratic quality of Caesar's army.

[19] Caes. *B. Gall.* 1. 13. 4, cf. 2. 21. 2, 5. 48. 6, 7. 62. 2, 7. 77. 4, *B. Civ.* 3. 28. 5; Sall. *Cat.* 60. 3 for an intriguing echo in a civil-war situation.

[20] Caes. *B. Gall.* 1. 28. 5, cf. 2. 24. 4, 7. 22. 1, 8. 8. 2, 8. 48. 2, *B. Civ.* 3. 59. 1, 3. 91. 1.

[21] 'probandae virtutis exspectas' Peskett, 'pro laude virtutis spectas' Du Pontet.

Similarly, at *B. Gall.* 6. 39, a returning forage party is surrounded and, in shock, looks to the centurions for leadership.[22] This is forthcoming, and 6. 40. 4 depicts the exemplary unity and inspiration of the old hands:

Hoc veteres non probant milites, quos sub vexillo una profectos docuimus. Itaque inter se cohortati duce Gaio Trebonio, equite Romano, qui eis erat praepositus, per medios hostis perrumpunt incolumesque ad unum omnes in castra perveniunt.

The veterans, who I said set off together under the standard, did not approve of this. Therefore, led by Gaius Trebonius, a Roman knight who had been put in charge of them, they exhorted each other and burst through the midst of the foe and all of them to a man arrived unharmed at the camp.

The camp followers and cavalry are saved 'by the valour of the troops' (*militum virtute*). Meanwhile, others, caught on top of a hill and in a useless situation, are given some leadership and help by their heroic centurions, 6. 40. 7:

Centuriones, quorum nonnulli ex inferioribus ordinibus reliquarum legionum virtutis causa in superiores erant ordines huius legionis traducti, ne ante partam rei militaris laudem amitterent fortissime pugnantes conciderunt. Militum pars, horum virtute summotis hostibus, praeter spem incolumis in castra pervenit, pars a barbaris circumventa periit.

The centurions, some of whom on account of their valour had been promoted from the lower ranks of the other legions to the higher ranks of this legion, died fighting with the utmost courage lest they should lose the glorious military reputation they had won before. Some of the soldiers, where the foe had been dislodged by the valour of these men, made it unexpectedly to the camp, others were surrounded by the barbarians and slain.

The reward for such outstanding bravery is promotion through the ranks. It is apparently in Caesar's army that the rank of *primipilaris* is first introduced and one explanation of this phenomenon is that it acts as a bridge for the previously absolute gap between the centurionate and the *militia equestris*. While there is no firm evidence in the reference to figures such as Crastinus, Titus Balventius, and P. Sextius Baculus who *had held* the *primus pilus*, the first certain instances of former centurions becoming military tribunes are suspiciously close to

[22] Caes. *B. Gall.* 6. 39. 2: 'Hic vero nulla munitio est quae perterritos recipiat: modo conscripti atque usus militaris imperiti, ad tribunum militum centurionesque ora convertunt; quid ab his praecipiatur exspectant. Nemo est tam fortis quin rei novitate perturbetur.'

the time of Caesar.[23] Thus, many centurions are marked, like Scaeva, Crastinus, and those just cited, by their upward mobility, for instance Q. Fulginius at *B. Civ.* 1. 46. 4:

Ex primo hastato legionis XIIII, qui propter eximiam virtutem ex inferioribus ordinibus in eum locum pervenerat.

[A man] from the first line of the fourteenth legion, who had risen from the lower ranks to this position on account of his outstanding valour.

This upward mobility is also visible in the case of non-centurions such as the Gaul Viridomarus at *B. Gall.* 7. 39. 1:

Quem Caesar ab Diviciaco sibi traditum ex humili loco ad summam dignitatem perduxerat.

Whom Diviciacus had handed over to Caesar and the latter had promoted from a lowly position to one of the highest respect.

The same is true of the Gallic brothers at *B. Civ.* 3. 59, who are *singulari virtute* and, *propter virtutem*, dear to the army, 3. 59. 2:

His domi ob has causas amplissimos magistratus mandaverat atque eos extra ordinem in senatum legendos curaverat agrosque in Gallia ex hostibus captos praemiaque rei pecuniariae magna tribuerat locupletesque ex egentibus fecerat.

For these reasons he had granted these men magistracies of the highest rank in their native communities and had taken care specially to enrol them to the Senate and had granted them land in Gaul that had been captured from the foe and substantial financial rewards and had made them rich where once they were poor.

It is Caesar who rewards and who punishes,[24] and it is hard to ignore the bonds of loyalty which Caesar creates between himself and his troops, particularly his junior officers and NCOs. An important example comes from the Spanish campaign of the civil wars, where

[23] Caes. *B. Civ.* 3. 91. 1 and *B. Gall.* 5. 35. 6 refer to Crastinus and Balventius having been *primipilares* 'in the previous year'. Caes. *B. Gall.* 6. 38. 1 makes a similar claim for Sextius. Harmand (1967) 330–5 sees this as implying subsequent promotion to the *militia equestris* but another possibility is that of return to the rank of ordinary centurion. The first former centurion to reach the rank of military tribune may be Pompey's assassin Septimius, whom Caes. *B. Civ.*. 3. 104. 3 and Luc. 8. 598 both describe as a former centurion of Pompey but whom Caes. *B. Civ.* 3. 104. 2 now describes as *tribunus militum*. More certain instances are those of L. Firmius from the triumviral period (see *ILS* 2226) and T. Marius from Urvinum under Augustus (see Val. Max. 7. 8. 6, 'ab infimo militiae loco beneficiis divi Augusti imperatoris ad summos castrensis honores perductus'). On this problem, see also Dobson (1974).

[24] Cf. Caes. *B. Civ.* 3. 74. 1: 'Hac habita contione nonnullos signiferos ignominia notavit ac loco movit'.

Caesar's borrowing of money from tribunes and centurions to pay his troops binds both classes to him, Caes. *B. Civ.* 1. 39. 3:

Simul a tribunis militum centurionibusque mutuas pecunias sumpsit; has exercitui distribuit. Quo facto duas res consecutus est, quod pignore animos centurionum devinxit et largitione militum voluntates redemit.

At the same time, he borrowed money from the military tribunes and the centurions and distributed it to the army. By doing this he achieved two aims, in that he secured the loyalty of the centurions with this security and won the good will of the soldiers by his generosity.[25]

The most significant reflection, however, of this relationship of loyalty and intimacy connects to the concern shown in the previous chapter for the line of vision, and is clearly echoed in Lucan's portrait of the centurion.[26] I think in particular of *Pharsalia* 6. 158–60, lines which also have a resonance for Scaeva the gladiator performing under the eyes of the emperor:

'Peterem felicior umbras
Caesaris in voltu: testem hunc fortuna negavit:
Pompeio laudante cadam.'

I would sooner die under the gaze of Caesar: fortune has denied me this witness—let Pompey praise me as I fall.'

Scaeva exemplifies the Caesarian soldier who fights with particular zeal in the knowledge that he is watched by his general. Later, the witness whom he is here denied himself emphasizes his role as observer of the deeds of each one of his men in the Gallic campaigns, 7. 285–92:

[25] The financial rewards which can bind the loyalty of the centurion are emphasized in Campbell (1984) 101–9, though the author has nothing to say of the change in the relationship of centurion to general engineered by Caesar himself.

[26] My view of the relationship of Scaeva to Caesar stresses the position of the centurion in historical writing. A different assessment is to be found in Hardie (1993) 35, who considers Scaeva in terms of surrogacy and substitution: 'When a human actor repeats or imitates a personal model by entering into the latter's substance (impersonation) or by being invaded by the prior person (possession), then we may say that the drives towards totalisation and continuation coincide, through an act of appropriation. Yet the resulting personal totality is always in a relation of dependence, and hence incompleteness, in regard to the prior person. For example, Lucan's hyperbolic parody of the epic "unus homo", Scaeva, achieves his unique status as the result of a chain of substitutions: Scaeva stands in for Caesar, who in turn stands for the multitude of soldiers under his command. But Scaeva has no justification for his existence except as an "alter Caesar".' I feel that this view of Scaeva is vitiated by its application of purely epic criteria. Lucan is not just the successor of Vergil.

'Sed me fortuna meorum
commisit manibus, *quarum me Gallia testem*
tot fecit bellis. Cuius non militis ensem
agnoscam? Caelumque tremens cum lancea transit,
dicere non fallar quo sit vibrata lacerto.
Quod si, signa ducem numquam fallentia vestrum,
conspicio faciesque truces oculosque minaces,
vicistis.'

'But fortune has entrusted me to the hands of my men, to which Gaul made m witness in so many campaigns. Which soldier's sword will I not recognize? An when the quivering lance travels through the sky, I will make no error when say by which arm it was cast. But if I see the signs which never deceive you general, ferocious expressions and menacing eyes, you have won.'[27]

The effect of an audience is a recurrent theme in Caesar's battl narrative. The inspiration offered by the presence of the general a spectator has been remarked by La Penna,[28] and it is on this them that discussion here will concentrate, but different sorts of audienc can have a similar effect. For instance, at *B. Gall.* 1. 52. 1, Caesar put legates and a quaestor in charge of each legion 'so that each mar might have them as witnesses to his valour' (*uti eos testis suae quisqu virtutis haberet*), and at both *B. Gall.* 7. 80. 2–5 and 8. 42. 3–5 the moti vating factor is the audience provided by the rest of the army lookin up or down at the action.[29] Moreover, the idea at *B. Gall.* 7. 80. 5 o being unable to disguise any 'foul deed' (*turpiter factum*) is given a crue twist at *Pharsalia* 7. 626–30, where Lucan will not ask:

Quis pectora fratris
caedat et, ut notum possit spoliare cadaver,
abscisum longe mittat caput, ora parentis

[27] The confidence of Caesar in his troops is also apparent at 5. 492–4, where h anticipates a zeal as suicidal as his own: 'Ne retine dubium cupientis ire per aequor: | s bene nota mihi est, ad Caesaris arma iuventus | naufragio venisse volet'. Caesar' inspection of his men's swords at 7. 560–5 seems to repeat at Pharsalus the role he claim for himself in Gaul.

[28] La Penna (1979) 162 talks of 'l'impressione viva dello spirito agonistico che anima centurioni, soldati, *specialmente se combattono sotto gli occhi del loro generale*'.

[29] Caes. *B. Gall.* 7. 80. 2 and 5: 'Erat ex omnibus castris, quae summum undique iugum tenebant, despectus, atque omnes milites intenti pugnae proventum exspectabant .. *Quod in conspectu omnium res gerebatur neque recte ac turpiter factum celari poterat, utrosque e laudis cupiditas et timor ignominiae ad virtutem excitabat*'. Cf. *B. Gall.* 8. 42. 3–5: 'Milites contra nostri, quamquam periculoso genere proeli locoque iniquo premebantur, tamen omnia fortissimo sustinebant animo. Res enim gerebatur *et excelso loco et in conspectu exerci tus nostri*, magnusque utrimque clamor oriebatur. Ita quam quisque poterat *maxime insig nis*, quo *notior testatiorque virtus* esset eius, telis hostium flammaeque se offerebat.'

quis laceret nimiaque probet spectantibus ira
quem iugulat non esse patrem.

Who strikes the breast of his brother and, that he may despoil a corpse he knows, throws far away the severed head; who lacerates the face of a parent and by excess of anger demonstrates to the watchers that the man he slays is not his father.

However, the spectator who really matters is Caesar, and the Commentaries offer a number of striking parallels for the mentality displayed by Scaeva.[30] A famous example is that of Caesar's exemplary charge against the Nervii at *B. Gall.* 2. 25. With all the centurions dead, wounded or fled, Caesar, 2. 25. 2–3:

Scuto ab novissimis uni militi detracto, quod ipse eo sine scuto venerat, in primam aciem processit centurionibusque nominatim appellatis, reliquos cohortatus milites, signa inferre et manipulos laxare iussit, quo facilius gladiis uti possent. Cuius adventu spe inlata militibus ac redintegrato animo, cum pro se quisque *in conspectu imperatoris* etiam in extremis suis rebus operam novare cuperet, paulum hostium impetus tardatus est.

Taking a shield away from one of the soldiers in the back line (for he himself had come there without a shield), he advanced to the front line, called on each of the centurions by name, exhorted the rest of the troops and ordered them to advance the standards and spread out the maniples so that they might the more easily use their swords. The soldiers grew more optimistic at his arrival and had their spirit restored (for each man for his own sake wished to renew his efforts even in the direst circumstances when he was fighting under the eyes of the general) and the assault of the enemy was held up for a while.[31]

Again, at *B. Gall.* 3. 14, the cliffs looking down on the sea battle form a natural theatre, and Caesar is there to look on, 3. 14. 8–9:

Reliquum erat certamen positum in virtute, qua nostri milites facile superabant, atque *eo magis quod in conspectu Caesaris atque omnis exercitus res gerebatur, ut nullum paulo fortius factum latere posset: omnes enim colles ac loca superiora unde erat propinquus despectus in mare, ab exercitu tenebantur.*

[30] Apart from the Commentaries, see also Plut. *Caes.* 16, which emphasizes Caesar's special relationship with his troops and esp. 16. 3, where the heroic deed attributed at Val. Max. 3. 2. 23 to Scaeva is said to be performed Καίσαρος αὐτοῦ τὴν μάχην ἐφορῶντος.

[31] Cf. Caes. *B. Civ.* 3. 69. 4, where it is a measure of the panic that not even the example of Caesar can halt the retreat: 'omniaque erant tumultus, timoris, fugae plena adeo ut, cum Caesar signa fugientium manu prenderet et consistere iuberet, alii admissis equis eodem cursu confugerent, alii metu etiam signa dimitterent, neque quisquam omnino consisteret.' 'admissis', 'metu', 'eodem cursu' Peskett; 'dimissis', 'ex metu', 'eundem cursum' Du Pontet.

The rest of the fight was about valour, in which our men were easily superior and this all the more because the matter was being acted out before the eyes of Caesar and of all the army, with the result that no act even a little braver than the norm could pass unseen; for all the hills and the higher places from which there was a close view of the sea below were held by the army.

One might compare the natural theatre of *B. Gall.* 3. 14 with that of Vulteius in Book 4.[32] For, while Caesar is unable physically to be present at the suicide, he is clearly there in the heart of his loyal skipper. Vulteius is determined on a show of devotion and he feels close enough to Caesar to address him directly as he communicates his resolve, 4. 497–502:

> 'Quaecumque per aevum
> exhibuit monimenta fides servataque ferro
> militiae pietas, transisset nostra iuventus.
> Namque suis pro te gladiis incumbere, Caesar,
> esse parum scimus; sed non maiora supersunt
> obsessis tanti quae pignora demus amoris.'

'Whatever records loyalty and military duty preserved by the sword have left through time, our youthful band would have surpassed them. For, Caesar, we know that it is insufficient to fall on our swords for you; but there remain to us in this state of siege no greater proofs of our so great love to give.'[33]

Again, at 4. 512–14, the purpose of the gesture is to make the absent Caesar feel the loss he has suffered:

> 'Magna virtute merendum est,
> Caesar ut amissis inter tot milia paucis
> hoc damnum clademque vocet.'

'We must by great valour ensure that, when a few men perish among so many thousands, Caesar calls this a loss and a disaster.'[34]

Further, at 6. 162–5, this sense, of enduring so much that the absent Caesar cannot fail to notice, compensates Scaeva for the lack of the general's personal audience:

[32] For more on this theme, see esp. Ch. 7, pp. 259–64.

[33] For *amor* as amorous attachment between general and troops, see my discussion of Laelius, pp. 204–6.

[34] I note that Ahl (1976) 120 draws the comparison with 6. 158–9 and remarks that 'Like Scaeva he wishes to die with the active approval of his lord'. For further similarities between my approach and that of Ahl, see my discussion of Laelius. Since Vulteius and his men show such zeal to serve their leader, it is worth wondering whether the *dux* referred to at 4. 572–3 is not Vulteius (though cf. 4. 466, 'dux erat ille ratis') but rather Caesar ('ducibus mirantibus, ulli | esse ducem tanti').

> 'Iam longinqua petit pulvis sonitusque ruinae,
> securasque fragor concussit Caesaris aures.
> Vincimus, o socii: veniet qui vindicet arces
> dum morimur.'

Now the dust-cloud and the sound of destruction reach far off and the din has shaken Caesar's unconcerned ears. We are winning, comrades: he will come to claim the citadel as we die.'

Nor should this rather perverse concern even for an absent Caesar be regarded as something purely Lucanian. For, on two occasions in the *Bellum Gallicum*, a *paraceleusis* of Labienus is reported as urging the troops to imagine the presence of Caesar as they fight. The first is Caes. *B. Gall.* 6. 8. 4:

'Habetis,' inquit, 'milites, quam petistis facultatem: hostem impedito atque iniquo loco tenetis: *praestate eandem nobis ducibus virtutem, quam saepe numero imperatori praestitistis, atque illum adesse et haec coram cernere existimate.*'

'Soldiers,' he said, 'you have the chance you sought: you hold the foe on difficult and unfavourable ground; show me as your leader the same valour you have often shown to your general and imagine him to be present and to be looking directly at these events.'

The second is Caes. *B. Gall.* 7. 62. 2:

Atque ipsum Caesarem, cuius ductu saepe numero hostis superassent, *praesentem adesse existimarent.*

And they should imagine Caesar himself, under whose command they had often beaten the foe, to be present and on the spot.[35]

Lucan finds in Caesar a loyalty between general and troops, particularly centurions, which is already so extreme as to require only a small amount of rewriting before it will fit his poem perfectly. Crastinus, who in Caesar typifies the centurion, is not burlesqued, merely condemned,

35 See also Caes. *B. Civ.* 1. 57. 4. Barton (1992) 20 n. 32 cites Minucius Felix, *Octavius* 37. 2, where the Christian resisting in the knowledge that God is looking on is likened to the good soldier: 'Quis non miles sub oculis imperatoris audacius periculum provocet?' For further instances, cf. Harnack (1981) 60. At Plut. *Otho* 10. 1, the general's absence from the Battle of Bedriacum is detrimental not least because τὴν ἐν ὀφθαλμοῖς αὐτοῦ παρόντος αἰδῶ καὶ φιλοτιμίαν ἀφεῖλε τῶν ἀγωνιζομένων. At Livy, 3. 12. 3–4, the testimonial of T. Quinctius Capitolinus for Caeso Quinctius concludes, 'suum primum militem fuisse, se saepe vidente pugnasse in hostem'. See also Curt. 3. 11. 9 for the warriors of Darius at the Battle of Issus, '*ante oculos regis* egregia morte defuncti, omnes in ora proni, sicut dimicantes procubuerant, adverso corpore vulneribus acceptis', and 4. 15. 24–5 for the attitude of the men of both Alexander and Darius at Arbela, 'utrumque delecti tuebantur, sui immemores; quippe amisso rege nec volebant salvi esse nec poterant. *Ante oculos sui* quisque *regis* mortem occumbere ducebat egregium.'

but it would perhaps be alien to the general pathetic tone of Lucan' Pharsalus narrative for him to play the comic-grotesque role of Scaeva or a Vulteius. One centurion, however, who does share number of the qualities of these two is the oddly neglected figure c Laelius in Book 1 of the *Pharsalia*. I intend to discuss Laelius for hi anticipation first of the absolute loyalty of the other Caesarians, secon of their perversion of traditional Roman notions of the good death in battle.

The first thing to say of Laelius is that his appearance so early in the narrative is programmatic for the significance to be attached to the figure of the centurion. Thus, he is introduced at 1. 356–8 as:

> Summi tum munera pili
> Laelius emeritique gerens insignia doni,
> servati civis referentem praemia quercum.

Then Laelius, who held the rank of first centurion and the insignia of the awar he had won, the oak which indicates the reward for saving a citizen.

In other words, he holds the rank of chief centurion and has bee awarded the *corona civica*, the prize given to those who have rescue another citizen in battle. For a soldier who will go on to ask, 1. 366:

> 'Usque adeo miserum est civili vincere bello?'

'Is it so very wretched to conquer in a civil war?'[36]

and to proclaim, 1. 373–4:

> 'Nec civis meus est, in quem tua classica, Caesar,
> audiero.'

'Nor is he my fellow citizen, Caesar, against whom I hear your battle-trumpets.

this is an obviously ironic award,[37] and an early instance of the way tha values consensual in imperial warfare break down when applied in civi conflict.

Next, it should be observed that Laelius maintains a considerabl degree of intimacy with Caesar. In a *suasoria*-style speech such as this the repeated direct address to Caesar as *tu* should perhaps no

[36] The effect of this question is, of course, heightened by the recollection of the dignified 'Usque adeone mori miserum est?' of Turnus at Verg. *Aen.* 12. 646.

[37] Ahl (1976) 201 remarks that 'It is grimly ironic that Laelius should be wearing, as he speaks, the "quercus civilis", the soldier's highest honor, awarded for saving the life of a fellow-citizen in battle'. For the conditions for the award of the *corona civica*, see Plin. *HN* 16. 12–13 and Gell. *NA* 5. 6. 11–15. The most authoritative modern discussion of the crown is to be found in Maxfield (1981), esp. 70–4.

occasion undue surprise,[38] but it is certainly true that this is a speech of loyalty less marked by deference than by reference to the relationship between speaker and addressee. 'Deratne tibi fiducia nostri?' Did you not trust us? Did you not trust me? Laelius adopts the tone of the injured lover.[39] Similarly, at 1. 367–72, he uses a military topos which had been substantially recast by the Roman elegists:

> 'Duc age per Scythiae populos, per inhospita Syrtis
> litora, per calidas Libyae sitientis harenas:
> haec manus, ut victum post terga relinqueret orbem,
> Oceani tumidas remo compescuit undas
> fregit et Arcto spumantem vertice Rhenum:
> iussa sequi tam posse mihi quam velle necesse est.'

'Lead me, I bid you, through the peoples of Scythia, through the inhospitable shores of the Syrtes, through the hot sands of thirsty Libya: this band, that it might leave a conquered world behind it, quelled with the oar the swelling waters of the Ocean and broke the foaming northern Rhine: it is as needful for me to be able to follow your orders as it is to want to.'

The readiness to endure any geography in pursuit of the addressee may echo the terminology of the military *sacramentum*,[40] but it is also used for the devoted loyalty of friends,[41] in a *propempticon*,[42] in an *epicedion*,[43] and, most frequently, to express the devotion of one lover, often an elegist, for another.[44] Moreover, it should be noted that

[38] Luc. 1. 361 'tuas', cf. 362 'tibi', 373 'tua', 375 'tuos', 383 'tu'.

[39] Luc. 1. 362. Fantham (1985) 131 analyses the speech of the troops distressed at Caesar's night voyage in much the same way, and points to the tendency of the Alexander tradition to represent the great general's soldiers as his ἐραστάι. For repetition of *tu* in elegy, see Prop. 1. 8. 1–8, 'tune . . . te . . . tibi . . . tibi . . . tune . . . tu . . . tu' and cf. Gallus at Verg. *Ecl.* 10. 46–9, 'tu . . . te . . . tibi'. However, it should also be noted that Fedeli (1980) at Prop. 1. 8. 5–8 sees the repetition of *tu* as typical of hymnic *Du-Stil.*

[40] See Nisbet and Hubbard (1970) at Hor. *Carm.* 1. 22. 5–8, and (1978) at 2. 6. 1 and 2. 17. 10. See also Nisbet (1978) 95, Headlam (1922) at Herod. 5. 43, and Harrison (1991) at Verg. *Aen.* 10. 672, who points to Walbank (1957–79) at Polyb. 6. 21. 1–3. Walbank cites Dion. Hal. *Ant. Rom.* 10. 18 and 11. 43. Barton (1992) 15 n. 14 gives Livy 28. 27 and Arr. *Epict. Diss.* 1. 14.

[41] See Catull. 11. 1–14 for Furius and Aurelius and Hor. *Epod.* 1. 11–14 for the poet following Maecenas.

[42] See Prop. 1. 6. 3–4 and Cairns (1972) 99.

[43] Stat. *Silv.* 5. 1. 127–134.

[44] See Verg. *Ecl.* 10. 44–9 and 64–8 for Gallus and Lycoris and cf. Ov. *Am.* 1. 9. 9–14, and the excellent note ad loc. in McKeown (1989), Ov. *Am.* 2. 16. 15–32, *Ars Am.* 2. 229–32, and Sen. *Phaed.* 609–16. This last instance typifies the problem of defining this topos as either military or amorous. Apart from the common borrowing of military themes by the elegists to express their condition (and here we see Phaedra invoke the 'servitium amoris'), there is also the problem that Phaedra, in order to render herself attractive to the sporty Hippolytus, takes on a number of typically macho roles: hunting, dying by the sword, etc.

Catullus and his companions will visit the monuments of Caesar a they cross the Alps in order to leave Italy, while Laelius and his peer have just followed their general back across the Alps in order to invad their homeland.[45]

The expression of loyalty through geography, I would argue, canno easily be dissociated from the passionate applications which it ha received. Laelius, who casts himself as Caesar's ἐραστής, exemplifies kinship between general and troops which, as Caesar's own Com mentaries testify, is well beyond the norm. And the most obvious con sequence of this is the willingness of the troops to do absolutel anything for their general, a theme on which Laelius now elaborates.

LAELIUS AND THE GOOD DEATH

The elaboration is worthy of some closer attention. Caesar's Com mentaries, especially those on the Gallic wars, are an apologia to th extent that they create an image of collective, patriotic endeavour o the part of Caesar and his troops. In Lucan, the image which they pro duce can be used to signify the absence or impossibility of patrioti endeavour, for instance at 1. 514–20.[46] Alternatively, as was signalize by the *corona civica* image, the Caesarians become the bearers of th images of patriotism, now hopelessly distorted. These images ma spring from inside the Commentaries, but they also see Lucan draw o a range of other patriotic writings. It is a technique which can be exem plified with reference to the ideology of the body in battle.

At *Pharsalia* 1. 374–86, Laelius expresses his devotion to Caesar i the following terms:

> 'Per signa decem felicia castris
> perque tuos iuro quocumque ex hoste triumphos,
> pectore si fratris gladium iuguloque parentis
> condere me iubeas plenaeque in viscera partu
> coniugis, invita peragam tamen omnia dextra;
> si spoliare deos ignemque inmittere templis,
> numina miscebit castrensis flamma monetae;

[45] See Luc. 1. 183: 'Iam gelidas Caesar cursu superaverat Alpes'.

[46] Where the abandonment of Rome in the face of a Roman enemy is compared to th staunch resistance to foreign foes when protected by only the flimsiest rampart: 'Cur pressus ab hoste | clauditur externis miles Romanus in oris, | effugit exiguo nocturn pericula vallo, | et subitus rapti munimine caespitis agger | praebet securos intra tentori somnos: | tu tantum audito bellorum nomine, Roma, | desereris; nox una tuis non credit muris'.

castra super Tusci si ponere Thybridis undas,
Hesperios audax veniam metator in agros.
Tu quoscumque voles in planum effundere muros,
his aries actus disperget saxa lacertis,
illa licet, penitus tolli quam iusseris urbem,
Roma sit.'

'I swear by ten years' happy service in your camp and by your triumphs over each and every foe, if you order me to bury my sword in the breast of my brother or the throat of my father or the womb of my pregnant wife, I will still do it all, however reluctant my hand; if you bid me rob the gods and fire the temples, the flame of the military mint will melt the statues of the gods; if you bid me make camp by the waters of the Etruscan Tiber, I will dare to come to the fields of Italy and measure out the lines. Whichever walls you wish to level to the ground, these arms will drive the battering ram that scatters the stones, even if the city that you bid us utterly destroy be Rome.'

The soldiers of the civil war are characterized by obsessive loyalty and pride in their role. The highly stylized terms of this oath betray various characteristics of this mentality apparent elsewhere in the epic. An important instance is the manner in which the oath by Caesar's triumphs 'over each and every foe' (*quocumque ex hoste*) obviously balances lines 373–4:

'Nec civis meus est, in quem tua classica, Caesar,
audiero.'

'Nor is he my fellow citizen, Caesar, against whom I hear your battle-trumpets.'

At 5. 357–8, Caesar will turn angrily on the mutineers and mock:

'Discedite castris,
tradite nostra viris ignavi signa *Quirites*.'

'Quit the camp, hand over our standards to men, cowardly Citizens.'

In the instance of the mutiny, the soldiers are mocked as citizens in the particular sense of being civilians.[47] Here, the language of citizenship echoes the constitutional crisis surrounding the execution of citizens at the height of the Catilinarian conspiracy. Yet, in comparison to Cicero's desperate concern to prove that a *civis* making war on the State is actually a *hostis*,[48] Laelius simply presumes that anyone

[47] Cf. Luc. 5. 333–4, 'Vos despecta senes exhaustaque sanguine turba | cernetis nostros iam plebs Romana triumphos'. The theme of the soldiers of the civil war contemptuous of the tawdry world of the civilian is discussed at Jal (1963) 484, comparing Suet. *Jul.* 70. 2 and App. *B. Civ.* 2. 93. 392.

[48] Cic. *Cat.* 4: 10: 'qui autem rei publicae sit hostis eum civem esse nullo modo posse'.

opposing his Caesar is an enemy and not a citizen. He is set apart from the Rome he first enlisted to serve, will sack even Rome to show his loyalty to the general, and, if a little reluctantly, will do to his own kin what it is horrifying to hear Agamemnon wish to do to the enemy.[49] It is typical of the state of mind to be investigated in this chapter that what Laelius here states he is willing to do for Caesar is what his general, at the height of the mutiny, will be represented as ready to permit to his soldiers, 5. 305–9:

> Non illis urbes spoliandaque templa negasset
> Tarpeiamque Iovis sedem matresque senatus
> passurasque infanda nurus. Vult omnia certe
> a se saeva peti, vult praemia Martis amari;
> militis indomiti tantum mens sana timetur.

He would not have refused them cities and temples to rob and the Tarpeian seat of Jupiter or the mothers and daughters of the senators to rape. He certainly wishes to be asked the right to commit any savage act, wishes the rewards of war to be their desire; the only thing he fears is that the doughty soldiers may grow sane.

Caesar is the titular commander of this army but the relationship of soldiers to general transcends the conventional concept of loyalty. As important as the spiritual inseparability of commander and troops, moreover, is the distance at which this force stands from the traditional values of the nation they once served and now invade. This is most evident in the lines on which I wish to concentrate, 1. 376–7:

> 'Pectore si fratris gladium iuguloque parentis
> condere me iubeas . . .'

'If you order me to bury my sword in the breast of my brother or the throat of my father . . .'

[49] For slaughtering the unborn child in the womb, cf. Hom. *Il.* 6. 57–60. In general, here, cf. Ahl (1976) 200–1: 'The soldiers who follow Caesar place loyalty to him above all considerations of civilised behaviour . . . To Laelius there are no deities save the victories of Caesar; there is no loyalty, no "pietas", to family, to religion or city. What motivates him is precisely what motivates both Scaeva and Vulteius: "militiae pietas". They have given themselves to Caesar, body and soul. The only vestige of traditional values to be found in Laelius is the suggestion that his right hand may be unwilling to respond to the order to commit parricide. Yet he does not doubt that he can overcome the instinctive piety of a mere limb. Laelius, like the rest of Caesar's army, hesitates at the thought of an invasion of his homeland . . . but counterbalancing and finally overswaying such considerations is love of warfare and fear of their leader: "sed diro ferri revocantur amore | ductorisque metu" (1. 355–6).'

These lines are particularly resonant because they refer to a fundamental opposition structuring much ancient, and particularly Roman, battle literature. As such, they are consonant with the suicidal image of Lucan's proem where the civil war sees:

> Populumque potentem
> in sua victrici conversum viscera dextra.

[And] a mighty people that turned against its own guts with a victorious right hand.[50]

and where the consequence is:

> Infestisque obvia signis
> signa, pares aquilas et pila minantia pilis.

Standards meeting hostile standards, matched eagles and spears menacing spears.[51]

The *aquilifer* is expected to lead the charge. As such, he becomes a hero-figure in Caesar's Commentaries.[52] It is surprising to see the *aquilifer* behind one,[53] and obviously surprising to see him face to face. Similarly, the physical reality of battle is reflected in the often ethically weighted terms used to describe it. The *adversi* are not only the enemy, but also those facing. A wound taken while attacking them is liable to be taken in the *pectus* or *iugulum* and not the *tergum*. Standard terms for retreat are *terga dare*, *terga vertere*, or *tergiversari*. Things behind one are *a/ab tergo*. On these simple grounds, therefore, the courageous death or wound is that in the chest or the throat.[54] Further, it is clear that Laelius and his peers require a new sort of courage if they are to face and recognize fathers or brothers as *adversi* and still strike. It is this sense which recurs at *Pharsalia* 7. 181–3, where Lucan describes:

[50] Luc. 1. 2–3. It is an important aspect of Caesar's actions at Pharsalus that his assault on the body of the Roman people should enact the proem. Note 7. 490–1, 'odiis solus civilibus ensis | sufficit, et dextras Romana in viscera ducit'; 7. 579, 'scit cruor imperii qui sit, quae viscera rerum'; 7. 619–20, 'letiferum per cuius viscera volnus | exierit'; 7. 721–2, 'Tu, Caesar, in alto | caedis adhuc cumulo patriae per viscera vadis'.

[51] Luc. 1. 6–7.

[52] See Caes. *B. Gall.* 4. 25. 2–6 for the *signifer* of the 10th legion landing in Britain; 5. 37. 5 for the heroics of the *aquilifer* Lucius Petrosidius; cf. *B. Civ.* 1. 57 for the élite soldiery of the *antesignani* and *B. Civ.* 3. 74. 1 for the *signiferi* punished for the disaster of Dyrrachium.

[53] See Stat. *Theb.* 7. 622–3 for the men rushing to war so fast as to leave 'vexilla tubaeque' behind them.

[54] For the connection between these basic terms of spatialization and the evaluation of action in battle, see Bettini (1991) 165–6. A similar methodology is applied to the obligation to hold one's place in the line in Borghini (1979). The military reality which spawned Borghini's code is impressively evoked in Rosenstein (1990) 95–8.

Voti turba nefandi
conscia, quae patrum iugulos, quae pectora fratrum
sperabat.

The band cherishing a sinful prayer, which hoped for the throats of fathers, the breasts of brothers.[55]

The same is also true for 7. 320–2, where the *paraceleusis* of Caesar shows his oneness with the mentality of his troops:

'Non vos pietatis imago
ulla nec adversa conspecti fronte parentes
commoveant; voltus gladio turbate verendos.'

'Be not moved by any image of affection, or by the sight of parents looking straight at you; mangle with the sword the faces you ought to revere.'[56]

The recurrence of the motif is striking and suggests that Lucan is doing more than simply playing on an implicit, natural expectation. Rather, the Caesarians can be shown to reverse terms which are 'weighted' in the sense that they have long served as the literary distillation of the experience of battle, and which have been treated as forming an ethical test to determine the good soldier from the bad. Just as there exists a chill distance between Scaeva's conscious self-figuration as an *exemplum*, and the necessary conditions of true exemplarity, so here the Caesarians' obsession with heroism can only be read with a constant awareness of the distortion wrought on traditional values by zealots of a civil war. The consequence of this is an epic attuned less to pathos than to satire.

EVIDENCE FOR THE GOOD DEATH: EPIC AND LYRIC

The association of the good warrior with a wound in the breast is apparent in the paean delivered by Idomeneus to Meriones at *Il.* 13. 275–94. No one could mock the μένος καὶ χεῖρας of Meriones, *Il.* 13. 288–91:

[55] My use of this passage will often bring it into contact with an ideology expressed clearly only on the Caesarian side. On the other hand, it, like 7. 626–30, is applicable to Pompeians as well as Caesarians. Cf. also 7. 58–9: 'Hoc placet, o superi, cum vobis vertere cuncta | propositum, nostris erroribus addere crimen?'

[56] Fantham (1992*b*) 101–3 and n. 12 stresses the 'abomination' faced by the 'parent-killers' at Pharsalus and repeatedly evoked by the term *adversus*. However, Fantham sees only an allusion to Orestes as Perseus in Aeschylus and Euripides and does not note that at least some of this emphasis derives from the tradition that for this particular battle Caesar delivered the order 'faciem feri'. For this, see Ch. 3, p. 105 and n. 53.

> 'εἴ περ γάρ κε βλεῖο πονεύμενος ἠὲ τυπείης,
> οὐκ ἂν ἐν αὐχέν' ὄπισθε πέσοι βέλος οὐδ' ἐνὶ νώτωι,
> ἀλλά κεν ἢ στέρνων ἢ νηδύος ἀντιάσειε
> πρόσσω ἱεμένοιο μετὰ προμάχων ὀαριστύν.'

For if you were struck or hit while fighting, the dart would not fall behind in your neck or your back, but would hit your breast or your belly as you charged forward into the ruck of the front-fighters.'[57]

The wound in the back is emblematic for Idomeneus of the death of the coward, caught retreating from the enemy. It is clear that this is also the value of Diomedes in his angry challenge to Odysseus at *Il.* 8. 93–5:

> 'διογενὲς Λαερτιάδη, πολυμήχαν' Ὀδυσσεῦ,
> πῇ φεύγεις μετὰ νῶτα βαλών, κακὸς ὣς ἐν ὁμίλωι;
> μή τίς τοι φεύγοντι μεταφρένωι ἐν δόρυ πήξηι.'

'God-descended son of Laertes, many-wiled Odysseus, whither do you flee, turning your back like a coward in the fight? Let no one stick a spear in your back as you flee.'

The opposition is present in Homeric epic, but takes on a far greater prominence in the hoplite poetry of Tyrtaeus. Thus, at fr. 11 (West) 17–24, he writes:

> ἀργαλέον γὰρ ὄπισθε μετάφρενόν ἐστι δαΐζειν
> ἀνδρὸς φεύγοντος δηΐωι ἐν πολέμωι·
> αἰσχηρὸς δ' ἐστὶ νέκυς κατακείμενος ἐν κονίηισι
> νῶτον ὄπισθ' αἰχμῆι δουρὸς ἐληλάμενος.
> ἀλλά τις εὖ διαβὰς μενέτω ποσὶν ἀμφοτέροισι
> στηριχθεὶς ἐπὶ γῆς, χεῖλος ὀδοῦσι δακών,
> μηρούς τε κνήμας τε κάτω καὶ στέρνα καὶ ὤμους
> ἀσπίδος εὐρείης γαστρὶ καλυψάμενος.

For it is dire to strike behind at the back of a man fleeing in terrible war. A corpse lying in the dust driven behind in the back with the steel of a spear is shameful. But let each man plant himself firmly and hold his place, pressing the ground with both feet, biting his lip with his teeth, guarding his thighs and his shins below, his breast and his shoulders with the round of his broad shield.

Later in the poem, at 31–4, Tyrtaeus stresses that the men must fight

[57] The T Scholion here cites Lysias, fr. 47 (Thalheim), τὸν Ἰφικράτην ποιεῖ λέγοντα τραύματα ἔχων οὐχ ἑτέρων ἐπ' ἐμὲ ἐρχομένων, ἀλλ' αὐτὸς ἐπιών and TrGF ii. 450 = Eupolis fr. 41 (Kock) = Men. fr. 942 (Koerte), ὀλίγα τραύματ' ἐξόπισθ' ἔχων, τῆς δειλίας σημεῖα κοὐχὶ τοῦ θράσους cf. Aesch fr. 362 (Radt) = *TrGF* iii. 362, πολλὰ τραύματ' ἐν στέρνοις λαβών.

'standing side by side' (πόδα πὰρ' ποδὶ θεὶς) and 'joining breast to breast' (στέρνον στέρνωι πεπλημένος), and in fr. 12 (West) 21–6, there follows another description of the good man and his death:

αἶψα δὲ δυσμενέων ἀνδρῶν ἔτρεψε φάλαγγας
  τρηχείας· σπουδῆι δ' ἔσχεθε κῦμα μάχης,
αὐτὸς δ' ἐν προμάχοισι πεσὼν φίλον ὤλεσε θυμόν,
  ἄστύ τε καὶ λαοὺς καὶ πατέρ' εὐκλεΐσας,
πολλὰ διὰ στέρνοιο καὶ ἀσπίδος ὀμφαλοέσσης
  καὶ διὰ θώρηκος πρόσθεν ἐληλάμενος.

Immediately he turns the rough phalanxes of the enemy and holds the wave of battle, and he dies falling amidst the front-fighters, granting fair fame to his city and people and father, struck many times from the front through the breast and the round shield and the cuirass.

The instance of Tyrtaeus now presents an important paradox. For, while the major studies of 'la belle mort' in Homer and Tyrtaeus, those of Müller, Loraux, and Vernant,[58] make almost no mention of the breast or the back (στέρνον, στῆθος, νῶτον, or μετάφρενον) and instead concentrate on issues such as ῥιψασπία and the fetishization of the shield (cf. Archilochus, frr. 5 and 139 West), the obsession with mutilating and denying burial to one's enemy, and the *noblesse oblige* of life in the front line, the story of his reception at Rome is rather different. Thus, Horace, *Carm.* 3. 2. 13–16, evidently Tyrtaean in tone, urges 'la belle mort' and condemns flight:

Dulce et decorum est pro patria mori:
mors et *fugacem* persequitur virum,
nec parcit imbellis iuventae
poplitibus *timidovue tergo*.

It is sweet and fitting to die for one's country: death follows even the man who runs away and does not spare the knees or the fearful back of cowardly youths.

[58] Müller (1989) cf. Loraux (1977) and Vernant (1982). Of these, only Loraux comments on Tyrtaeus' inclusion in the category of τρέσαντες of those who have suffered a wound in the back, speaking of an 'attitude maximaliste que ne suivent pas ses successeurs'. Perhaps even more striking is the absence of comment on specific parts of the body in the passages I have cited in the otherwise excellent commentary of Prato (1969). He breaks his silence only at fr. 11 (West), 17 (ἀργαλέον γὰρ ὄπισθε μετάφρενον ἐστι δαΐζειν), defending ἀργαλέον over ἀρπαλέον with the observation that 'ci conserva una preziosa traccia dell'antica aversione spartana per un accanito inseguimento del nemico in fuga' and cites Thuc. 5. 73. 4 and Plut. *Lyc.* 22. 5, τρεψάμενοι δὲ καὶ νικήσαντες ἐδίωκον ὅσον ἐκβεβαιώσασθαι τὸ νίκημα τῆι φυγῆι τῶν πολεμίων, εἶτα εὐθὺς ἀνεχώρουν, οὔτε γενναῖον οὔτε Ἑλληνικὸν ἡγούμενοι κόπτειν καὶ φονεύειν ἀπολεγομένους καὶ παρακεχωρηκότας.

Horace reflects a central Roman opposition. The obligation to stand one's ground and face the enemy is evident in the *Periocha* of Livy, 13:

Post id proelium cum corpora Romanorum qui in acie ceciderant Pyrrhus inspiceret, *omnia versa in hostem* invenit.

After this battle, when Pyrrhus was inspecting the bodies of the Romans who had fallen in combat, he found all of them turned to face the enemy.[59]

So too in Ennius' depiction of the immovable centurion at *Annals* 391–4 (Skutsch)[60] and in the fragmentary speech at *Scaenica* 254–7 (Jocelyn).[61] The opposition operates at a deep level of consciousness and provides an implicit evaluation of a succession of events in Roman epic, from the recollection of Hector in Turnus' rebuttal of the slurs of Drances and final fatal resolve,[62] to the devotion to heroic etiquette of Mezentius.[63]

[59] This refers to the famous defeat of P. Valerius Laevinus at Heracleia in 280 BC. For more on this, see Volkmann at *RE*, 2nd ser. viii. A. 1. 50–1.

[60] 'Undique conveniunt velut imber tela tribuno: | configunt parmam, tinnit hastilibus umbo, | aerato sonitu galeae, sed nec pote quisquam | undique nitendo corpus discerpere ferro.' Cf. Ennius, *Annals* 356 (Skutsch), 'Missaque per pectus dum transit striderat hasta'.

[61] 'Sed virum vera virtute vivere animatum addecet | fortiterque innoxium stare adversum adversarios. | Ea libertas est qui pectus purum et firmum gestitat; | aliae res obnoxiosae nocte in obscura latent.' 'Animatum addecet' is the proposal of Carrio. Jocelyn prints 'animatum adiecit' *in crucibus* and offers Carrio in the apparatus. He also prints 'innoxium vocare' (as does Vahlen), again offering Bentley's 'innoxium stare' in the apparatus. Here, I take *pectus* as having both a figurative value as the location of courage and virtue, and an implied physical position from the immediately preceding 'stare adversum adversarios'. Note how the physical positioning of the *pectus* in the line of battle is associated with two Republican virtues, those of *virtus* and *libertas*.

[62] For the rebuttal of Drances, see *Aen.* 11. 389–91, 'Imus in adversos—quid cessas? An tibi Mavors | ventosa in lingua pedibusque fugacibus istis | semper erit?' The concern to prove Drances wrong returns at *Aen.* 12. 643–6, 'Exscindine domos (id rebus defuit unum) | perpetiar, dextra nec Drancis dicta refellam? | Terga dabo et Turnum fugientem haec terra videbit? | Usque adeone mori miserum est?' Turnus here echoes Hector's conflict with Polydamas and his final challenge to Achilles at Hom. *Il.* 22. 250–3 and 283–6. There is an excellent discussion of the Homeric background to the conflict of Turnus and Drances in Burke Jr. (1978). Other instances of the devotion of Turnus to this opposition are apparent at *Aen.* 9. 756–61 (though note Bentley's emendation of 'aversos' for 'adversos' at 9. 761) and 9. 792–8.

[63] Vergil's capacity to identify a heroic quality in Mezentius is apparent at *Aen.* 10. 729–36, 'Sic ruit in densos alacer Mezentius hostis, || . . . atque idem fugientem haud est dignatus Oroden | sternere nec iacta caecum dare cuspide vulnus; | obvius adversoque occurrit seque viro vir | contulit, haud furto melior sed fortibus armis.' Note that these lines are imitated at Stat. *Theb.* 10. 257–9 to describe another villain and 'contemptor divum' still devoted to a martial ideal, Capaneus. For further similarities between Mezentius and Capaneus, compare Verg. *Aen.* 10. 773–4 and Stat. *Theb.* 9. 548–50 with Dewar (1991) ad loc.; for Capaneus and the heroic ideal, see also Stat. *Theb.* 10. 482–6. There are sympathetic discussions of the development of the character of Mezentius in Thome (1979) and La Penna (1980).

Flavian epic differs very little from Vergil in this respect, whether one thinks of the description in Silius of the admiration of Hannibal for the dead Sychaeus, *Punica* 5. 594–8:

> 'Cerno' ait 'adverso pulchrum sub pectore vulnus
> cuspidis Iliacae. Dignus Carthagine, dignus
> Hasdrubale ad manes ibis, nec te optima mater
> dissimilem lugebit avis, Stygiave sub umbra
> degenerem cernens noster vitabit Hamilcar.'

'I see', he said, 'the fair wound of the Trojan spear underneath the breast turned to face the foe. Worthy of Carthage, worthy of Hasdrubal, you will go to the shades below, nor will your excellent mother grieve that you are unlike your grandfathers, nor will my Hamilcar shun you as degenerate when he sees you in the shadowy world of the Styx.'[64]

or of the direct imitation in Valerius of Vergil's Elysium, 1. 836–40:

> Rara et sponte patet, *siquando pectore ductor*
> *vulnera nota gerens*, galeis praefixa rotisque
> cui domus aut studium mortales pellere curas,
> culta fides, longe metus atque ignota cupido,
> seu venit in vittis castaque in veste sacerdos.

It [the gate] opens rarely but of its own accord, when there comes a general who bears famous wounds on his breast, whose home is decorated with helmets and wheels, or one whose aim was to dispel the cares of mortals, who practised loyalty, who kept fear at a distance and knew no desire, or a priest dressed in fillets and holy garb.[65]

This survey of the poetic evidence demonstrates the pathetic significance of the *pectus–tergum* opposition. This should be emphasized.

[64] An interesting parallel for the praise of Sychaeus is offered at App. *Hann*. 50. 216–17 where Marcellus *ἐμάχετο γενναίως, μέχρι κατακοντισθεὶς ἀπέθανε* and *καὶ αὐτοῦ τῷ σώματι ὁ Ἀννίβας ἐπιστάς, ὡς εἶδε τὰ τραύματα πάντα ἐπὶ τῶν στέρνων, ἐπῄνεσε μὲν ὡς στρατιώτην, ἐπέσκωψε δὲ ὡς στρατηγόν*. For Hannibal's hatred of turning the back in retreat, see Sil. *Pun.* 12. 206–9, 289, 291–2, 677–8 and cf. 12. 277–8. For other instances in Silius, see 4. 193–4, 4. 329, 5. 638–43, 7. 680, 10. 62–5, 10. 215–7, 10. 278–9, 10. 286–8, 10. 654–5, 11. 157, 11. 170–1, 12. 593–4, 13. 376, 13. 657, 17. 484–5.

[65] Cf. Verg. *Aen*. 6. 660–5: 'Hic manus ob patriam pugnando vulnera passi, | quique sacerdotes casti, dum vita manebat, | quique pii vates et Phoebo digna locuti, | inventas aut qui vitam excoluere per artis, | quique sui memores alios fecere merendo: | omnibus his nivea cinguntur tempora vitta.' For further instances in Valerius, see Val. Flacc. *Arg.* 1. 432, 435, 438–9; 2. 656–8; 3. 135–6, 268–9, 287, 644; 6. 207–8, 520–1, 552, 572–4, 652–5. Statius, who often copies the civil-war paradoxes of the *Pharsalia*, also offers conventional variations on the theme, for instance the description of Hypseus by Antigone at *Theb.* 7. 311–12: 'ter insuto servantur pectora ferro, | pectora: nam tergo numquam metus'. See also Amphion at 7. 280–1, Menalcas the Spartan at 8. 432–6, the Argives at 10. 541–3, and the three brothers slain by Theseus at 12. 745–6.

It is evident that the greatness to be won by challenging one's *adversi* face-on carries with it the balancing acceptance of receiving a wound in the chest oneself. Later, the evidence from history and rhetoric will show that a survivor often cherishes and adores his own wounds. However, what matters for epic is the willingness of the warrior to suffer for his troops, his citizens, whatever his fears. Drances, for instance, a man who never fights, charges Turnus with causing the Latins to die for his selfish love. This slur is then reversed, as Turnus, through whose perspective so much of *Aeneid* 12 is told, goes out to engage in an honourable combat which he has no hope of surviving. To be pathetic, Turnus must, like those he defends, truly wish to live. Then, his death is a sacrifice and not a stunt or a thrill. Yet, to be pathetic, he must also be willing to die, and to die decently. 'La belle mort' is not that of the spear in the back of the man caught running away.

LUCAN'S CAESARIANS AND THE GOOD DEATH IN CIVIL CONFLICT

The accounts of the charge to death of Crastinus in Appian, Plutarch, and Caesar have already been examined, first for the suggestion of his self-devotion, second as evidence for the mutual attachment of Caesar and his centurions. A final account, that dependent on Livy, 111 provided by the *Commenta Bernensia* note at Lucan 7. 470, offers a construction most suggestive for the argument to be advanced in this section:

Crastinus dictus est hic qui primus iaculatus in Pompei aciem bella commisit, qui, ut historia refert, adacto in os gladio,—sic inter cadavera repertus est,—libidinem ac rabiem qua pugnaverat ipsa novitate vulneris praeferebat. De quo Titus Livius dicit 'tunc fuisse evocatum, proximo anno deduxisse primum pilum Gaium Crastinum qui a parte Caesaris primus lanceam misit.'

The Crastinus mentioned is the one who started the battle by throwing the first spear against Pompey's line, who, as history relates, had a sword thrust into his face—this is how he was found amidst the corpses—and displayed by the very novelty of the wound the zeal and frenzy with which he had fought. Titus Livius says of this man, 'Gaius Crastinus, who was the first to cast a spear on Caesar's side, had then been recalled to the ranks and had served as first centurion the year before.'

That Crastinus was struck by a sword-stroke to the mouth is familiar from Caesar, that he was subject to a form of madness or possession, from the version in Plutarch and Appian attributed to Pollio. What is striking about this account is that the wound to the mouth is marked as both novel and, in its novelty, as itself indicative of the madness of the centurion. The construction here placed on the death of Crastinus reveals that somebody, very possibly Livy, injected into the narrative of civil war an association between the frenzied loyalty of the troops of Caesar and a process of innovation, of deformation in the wounds suffered by the soldiers of Rome. The paradigm established in the previous section is menaced, loses sense in the new world of civil war. Lucan's Caesarians are its most ferocious assailants.

The assault is conducted on a number of levels. The first level has already been isolated and discussed above. Laelius at 1. 376–8 expresses a reluctant willingness to do what at 7. 181–3[66] the troops yearn to do: to commit a ghastly crime. A similar double consciousness is then visible in a section of Caesar's *paraceleusis*, part of which has already been cited as an illustration of the dilemma facing Roman soldiers in a civil war, 7. 318–25:

> 'Vos tamen hoc oro, iuvenes, ne caedere quisquam
> hostis terga velit: civis qui fugerit esto.
> Sed, dum tela micant, non vos pietatis imago
> ulla nec adversa conspecti fronte parentes
> commoveant; voltus gladio turbate verendos.
> Sive quis infesto cognata in pectora ferro
> ibit, seu nullum violarit volnere pignus,
> ignoti iugulum tamquam scelus inputet hostis.'

'Yet I beg this of you, young men, that no man wish to strike the foe in the back: all those that flee, let them be citizens. But while the weapons gleam, be not moved by any image of affection or by the sight of parents looking straight at you; mangle with the sword the faces you ought to revere. Whether one of you attacks with hostile steel the breast of a relative or violates no bond of loyalty by the wound, let him count the killing of an unknown enemy as a crime [i.e. to be praised by me].'

This passage illustrates impressively Lucan's complication of the historical tradition. The first two lines open with an order later marked as one of the saving graces of Caesar's conduct in the civil war: the instruction to restrict all killing to the battlefield itself.[67] Yet what others can represent as simply admirable, in Lucan becomes symptomatic of a

[66] See above, p. 210 n. 55, for some cautionary remarks about these lines.

[67] For praise of Caesar's restriction of killing to those on the battlefield, see Cic. *Marc.* 6. 17, *Deiot.* 11. 33–4, Sen. *Ben.* 5. 16. 5, Suet. *Jul.* 75. 3, Flor. 2. 13. 90, Dio Cass. 43. 12.

perversely aestheticized etiquette. At 4. 165–6, for instance, Caesar has his men take the long route round in order to cut off the flight of the enemy and ensure not just that they die, but that they die like men:

> 'Nec liceat pavidis ignava occumbere morte:
> excipiant recto fugientes pectore ferrum.'

'And let not the tremblers die a coward's death: though they flee, let them take the blow of the sword to the front and in the breast.'

Later, at Pharsalus, as the battle progresses, Caesar's leniency to the backs of those in retreat contrasts with the fevered determination of his men to attack the breasts of those resisting them even at the expense of convenience, 7. 498–501:

> Qua torta graves lorica catenas
> opponit tutoque latet sub tegmine pectus,
> hac quoque perventum est ad viscera, totque per arma
> extremum est quod quisque ferit.

Where the twisted cuirass opposes its heavy chain-mail and where the breast lies hidden under its safe covering, even this way they took to get to the guts, and it is at that last point at the end of so many layers of armour that each man thrusts.

The significant point is that the mentality implied in this description is one which has already been communicated in the development of the clement Caesar's sentiments at 7. 318–25. While those who flee are allowed to be citizens, the soldiers are urged to abjure *pietas* when confronted with those who stand and fight. In the closing lines, moreover, Caesar actually goes beyond the formulation offered by Laelius, that any citizen (*civis*) who opposes him must be an enemy (*hostis*), and offers criminality as the one measure of achievement. The soldiers must assault the breast (*pectus*) and the throat (*iugulum*)—orders which, as we have seen, they enthusiastically obey—and they must have no qualms if the victim they see facing them is *not* a relative but only a stranger; for this too is crime (*scelus*) and is therefore certain to win the general's esteem.

Caesar also offers the lead to a further category of deformation of the traditional paradigm, that is its use to express the suicidal quality of civil war. The lion simile applied to Turnus at *Aen.* 9. 792–8 shows both a conditioned inability to retreat and a recognition of the fatal consequences of attack.[68] By contrast, and here surely must be seen an

[68] e.g. Verg. *Aen.* 9. 795–6, 'nec tendere contra | ille quidem hoc cupiens potis est per tela virosque'.

element of programme, the lion simile for Caesar at 1. 205–12 stresses a simply suicidal valour:

> Sicut squalentibus arvis
> aestiferae Libyes viso leo comminus hoste
> subsedit dubius, totam dum colligit iram;
> mox, ubi se saevae stimulavit verbere caudae
> erexitque iubam et vasto grave murmur hiatu
> infremuit, tum torta levis si lancea Mauri
> haereat aut latum subeant venabula pectus,
> per ferrum tanti securus volneris exit.

In like manner, in the untilled fields of torrid Libya a lion seeing the enemy close at hand crouches down hesitating while it gathers all its anger; soon, when it has aroused itself with lashes from its savage tail and made its mane to stand and bellowed with a great roar from its gaping jaw, then, should the twisted lance of the agile Moor stick or the spears pierce its broad breast, it runs through the steel unconcerned by so great a wound.[69]

The suicidal impulse is first associated with the general, then finds its richest expression in the actions of his hyper-loyal followers on the ship of Vulteius. They have no other way to express their devotion to Caesar or to make him feel their loss than to kill themselves, and the manner of their death at once conforms to, reverses, and denies the paradigm, 4. 556–62:

> Sic mutua pacti
> fata cadunt iuvenes, minimumque in morte virorum
> mors virtutis habet. Pariter sternuntque caduntque
> volnere letali, nec quemquam dextra fefellit
> cum feriat moriente manu. Nec volnus adactis
> debetur gladiis: percussum est pectore ferrum
> et iuguli pressere manum.

So fell the young men who had pledged to slay one another, and in the death of the men death itself required the smallest part of valour. They slew and fell

[69] Masters (1992) 2 n. 5 assesses the claims by different scholars for various Vergilian and Homeric lion similes to be the model for this passage of Lucan, and then adds: 'All the commentators have missed the obvious point that Lucan's lion, inasmuch as he runs himself through by leaping at the hunters' spears, is pointing up Caesar's *suicide*.' Masters's point is correct, but it should be supported by reference to an important parallel. For, the reference to the 'venabula' at Luc. 1. 211 should remind us both of Scaeva as a leopard who leaps 'per summa . . . venabula' at 6. 183 (again centurion and general are as one) and, most importantly, of Helenor at Verg. *Aen.* 9. 551–2, where his suicidal death-rush is compared to that of a 'fera' who 'seseque haud nescia morti | inicit et saltu supra venabula fertur'. There is only one other reference to the *venabulum* in the *Aeneid.* For the similarities between Luc. 1. 205–12 and Ov. *Fast.* 2. 205–13, see above, p. 109 n. 69.

together with fatal wounds, nor did any man's aim let him down as he struck with dying hand. Nor did wounding require a thrust from the sword: the steel was struck by the breast and throats pressed the hand.

On the one hand, the conventional association of *virtus* with the assault on the breast is acknowledged in order to be denied. In this case, no skill or courage is required because the victim does not resist. On the other, suicide reverses the conventional relationship of weapon to body, of active to passive. This formula is recognized by Hübner in his study of hypallage in Lucan.[70] The process of exchange by which the logical object of a sentence becomes its subject is analysed for the arresting quality which it can give to an expression and for the intellectualizing demands which it makes on the reader,[71] and is exemplified with particular reference to the relationship of the weapon to the body. The emphasis on the interpretative activity of the reader is just. For the establishment of a paradigm for conventional representation of the *pectus* and the *tergum* demonstrates the expectations which an ancient reader might have brought to the use of such terms. The hypallage deforms those terms. At the same time, one is aware of the military context in which the conventional representation is grounded. That context also gives the conventional understanding of *virtus*. All of this is reversed in a civil-war situation, and it is the function of the hypallage to make the reader consider the special nature of a civil war.

Hübner is therefore on better ground when he emphasizes the 'senseless perversity of the war'[72] than when he explains the phenomenon in terms of the *aemulatio* of the Silver Age poet faced with predecessors such as Vergil and Ovid.[73] There is a considerable difference between making something new simply in the name of novelty and doing the same in order to force into the reader's consciousness how that thing really is. It is therefore striking that Lucan should extend his use of the suicidal hypallage beyond his one bona fide suicide theme, and use it to represent the nature of civil war in general. This is apparent at 7. 621–4, where Lucan refuses to ask 'who stood face to face and with his dying breath drove out the sword thrust down his throat' (*ore quis adverso demissum faucibus ensem | expulerit moriens anima*), or 'which men sent the weapons through them with their

70 Hübner (1972).

71 Ibid. 577: 'Ein solcher Stil erfordert eine ganz besondere Umstellung des Lesers, insofern er ständig zum Mitdenken und Deuten aufgefordert ist.'

72 Ibid. 580.

73 Ibid. 582 on poets who 'stehen unter dem Zwang, sich mit anerkannten Vorgängern wie Vergil und Ovid auseinandersetzen zu müssen'.

breasts' (*qui pectore tela | transmittant*), and most strikingly in the command of Scaeva at 6. 160–1. Just after referring to the spectatorship of Caesar, the centurion cries out:

> 'Confringite tela
> pectoris inpulsu iugulisque retundite ferrum.'

'Shatter the spears with the attack of your breast and blunt the steel with your throats.'

The man who needs the eyes of Caesar to make sense of his actions for him displays an uncanny ideological resemblance to his general's suicidal lion at 1. 205–12. He is also the character who most completely reverses the relationship of body to weapon, throwing away his shield for fear of cowardice, and then bizarrely using the forest of spears already in his guts as protection against further wounding. Thus, at 6. 202–6, Scaeva is depicted in these terms:

> Iam pectora non tegit armis,
> ac veritus credi clipeo laevaque vacasse
> aut culpa vixisse sua tot volnera belli
> solus obit densamque ferens in pectore silvam
> iam gradibus fessis, in quem cadat, eligit hostem.

No longer does he cover his breast with his armour and, fearing to depend on his shield and to do nothing with his left hand or by his own fault to have survived, he faces alone so many wounds of war and, bearing a thick forest in his breast, now with weary steps chooses which enemy to fall on.[74]

And at 6. 208–13 he is described by a grotesque contrast simile:

> Sic Libycus densis elephans oppressus ab armis
> omne repercussum squalenti missile tergo
> frangit et haerentis mota cute discutit hastas:
> viscera tuta latent penitus, citraque cruorem
> confixae stant tela ferae: tot facta sagittis,
> tot iaculis unam non explent volnera mortem.

In like manner a Libyan elephant attacked by a shower of arms breaks every missile that bounces off its scaly back and knocks off those spears that stick with a shake of its hide: deep down the guts lie hidden and safe, the weapons do not reach the blood of the pierced beast: so many wounds from arrows, so many wounds from darts do not suffice to cause one death.[75]

[74] For the interpretation of 'credi' at Luc. 6. 203, see Conte (1974) ad loc.

[75] This is a parody of Verg. *Aen.* 10. 707–18, esp. 717–18, where Mezentius is likened to a boar at bay, which 'tergo decutit hastas'. For Scaliger's transposition of 717–18 to follow 713, see Harrison (1991) ad loc.

SCAEVA'S WOUNDS AND THE CULTURE OF DISPLAY

Once again, it is hard not to regard Scaeva's words and actions as encapsulating Lucan's vision of the civil war. All the distortions and perversions are there in this figure. The lines just quoted, moreover, carry further resonances, exemplifying one final aspect to this process—and an aspect peculiarly resonant of the Marian tradition from which I began. The analysis of this question forms the final section of this chapter. First, however, it is essential to draw together the various contentions that have so far been advanced.

The first contention was that Lucan developed a range of minor characters who conformed to the type of the Caesarian centurion. This type was shown to be the principal focus of Caesar's admiration and Marian ideology in the Commentaries, and the relationship of kinship between centurion and general in Caesar was described. This was exemplified by the striking manner in which centurions in both Caesar and Lucan yearned for or responded to Caesar as a spectator of their deeds. The sense that in Lucan this spectatorship involved the general's understanding and endorsement of his soldiers' bizarre military ethics was enforced by the identification of the constant deformation of a simple military paradigm on the part of both Caesar and his followers. While the reader could engage with their mentality only across the awareness of the distortion practised, they appeared to be part of a peculiar ethical community of their own.

Scaeva has previously been described as casting himself as an *exemplum virtutis* when the civil-war context of his actions admits only of a perversion of *virtus*. Here, it should be added that the deliberate courting of wounds at 6. 202–6 sees another flawed attempt to cast himself as a traditional figure of patriotism, that is the proudly cicatrized warrior. This is just how he is treated at 6. 251–4:

> Labentem turba suorum
> excipit atque umeris defectum inponere gaudet;
> ac velut inclusum perfosso in pectore numen
> et vivam magnae speciem Virtutis adorant.

A band of his men pick him up as he falls and rejoice to put him fainting on their shoulders; and they worship the divine power which seems shut up in his pierced breast and the living image of great Valour.

In Greek literature, the scar features most famously in the recognition scenes at Homer, *Odyssey* 19. 392–466 and Euripides, *Electra*

573–4, and two recent studies have argued convincingly that the memory of Odysseus' wound endured while hunting the boar of Parnassus highlights the childish or unheroic nature of Orestes' fall while chasing a fawn inside the palace of Agamemnon.[76] There are also examples of the Greek soldier showing pride in his wounds. Wheeler[77] cites Xenophon, *Agesilaus* 6. 2 for his wounds as 'clear signs of having fought with spirit' (σαφῆ . . . σημεῖα . . . τοῦ θυμῷ μάχεσθαι),[78] while the *Memorabilia* also feature the lament of Nicomachides, who resents his defeat at the polls by men with no military experience, when 'I have so many wounds suffered at the hands of the enemy' (τραύματα ὑπὸ τῶν πολεμίων τοσαῦτα ἔχω), and, to prove the point, promptly strips (ἅμα δὲ τὰς οὐλὰς τῶν τραυμάτων ἀπογυμνούμενος ἐπεδείκνυεν).[79] Further, one suspects that, in the story told at Plutarch, *Moralia* 187 C and *Pelopidas* 2. 3 of Timotheus' chiding of Chares for displaying his wounds, the high-mindedness of the former is the more marked for the conventionality of the latter's conduct.[80] Certainly, one should not overlook the catalogue of the wounds of Alexander at Plutarch, *Moralia* 327 A–B or the consolation to the wounded Philip at *Moralia* 331 B–C:

'θάρρει, πάτερ, . . . καὶ πρόιθι φαιδρῶς, ἵνα τῆς ἀρετῆς κατὰ βῆμα μνημονεύῃς.'

'Cheer up, father, and go forth happily, so that with each step you may recall your courage.'

Note also Plutarch's ensuing reflection on this and on the mentality of Alexander himself:

πῶς γὰρ αὐτὸν οἴει τοῖς ἰδίοις ἀγάλλεσθαι τραύμασι, καθ' ἕκαστον μέρος ἔθνους μνημονεύοντα καὶ νίκης καὶ πόλεων ἁλισκομένων καὶ

[76] Tarkow (1981) and Goff (1991). Goff's argument is a more sophisticated version of that offered by Tarkow, but does not really take up Tarkow's suggestion that (p. 147) the meaning of the scar to late 5th-c. Greeks is 'a topic which is in need of considerably more investigation than it has heretofore received'.

[77] Wheeler (1991) 146.

[78] Cf. Plut. *Ages.* 36. 2, ὑπὸ τραυμάτων τὸ σῶμα κατακεκομμένος.

[79] Xen. *Mem.* 3. 4. 1.

[80] There is some suggestion that the soldier boasting of his battles and scars is a stereotype of Greek comedy. The best evidence for this is Phoenicides, fr. 4. 4–7 (Kassel-Austin), esp. 6, ἐδείκνυ ἅμα λέγων τὰ τραύματα. For this, cf. Menander, fr. 745 (Koerte) and the discussion in Brown (1992) 91–4. In Roman comedy, Plaut. *Curc.* 392–400 has Curculio pretend to have lost an eye in battle, but the *locus classicus* is Ter. *Eun.* 482–3, 'neque pugnas narrat neque cicatrices suas | ostentat'. I would like to thank Peter Brown for his help on this point.

βασιλέων παραδιδόντων, οὐκ ἐγκαλυπτόμενον οὐδὲ κατακρύπτοντα τὰς οὐλάς, ἀλλ᾽ ὥσπερ εἰκόνας ἐγκεχαραγμένας ἀρετῆς καὶ ἀνδραγαθίας περιφέροντα;

For how do you think he rejoiced in his own wounds, in each part recalling a nation, a victory, captured cities and surrendering kings, not covering himself up or hiding away the scars but carrying them around as if as inscribed images of courage and bravery?[81]

However, as with the *exemplum virtutis*, the display of scars on the chest as evidence of patriotic valour and as a model to the young is so remarkably prevalent a custom among the Romans as almost to seem a national peculiarity. The existence of Greek parallels must be balanced against the sheer volume of instances among the Romans.

The military values encoded in the linguistic opposition of front and back, and exemplified in the battle narratives of the epicists, find physical expression in the public display of scars and wounds to the breast. This is clearly exemplified in Ovid's marriage of epic and rhetoric in the speech of Ulysses demanding the arms of Achilles, Ov. *Met.* 13. 262–7:

'Sunt et mihi vulnera, cives,
ipso pulchra loco: nec vanis credite verbis.
Adspicite en!' vestemque manu diduxit et 'haec sunt
pectora semper' ait 'vestris exercita rebus
at nil inpendit per tot Telamonius annos
sanguinis in socios et habet sine vulnere corpus.'

'I too, citizens, have fair wounds in the proper place. And do not believe empty words. Look, Lo!' and he drew apart his garment with his hand and said, 'This breast has ever been exercised on your behalf! Yet the Telamonian through all these years has spent not one drop of blood for his comrades and has an unwounded body!'

Many have identified this as a parody of a schoolboy's rhetorical exercise.[82] It certainly conforms to the sort of declamatory fantasy

[81] Note that this account differs in no significant detail from that given at Cic. *De Or.* 2. 249 of the attitude of the mother of Sp. Carvilius to the embarrassment of her wounded son: 'Nam quod Sp. Carvilio graviter claudicanti ex volnere ob rem publicam accepto et ob eam causam verecundanti in publicum prodire mater dixit: "Quin prodis, mi Spuri? Quotienscumque gradum facies, totiens tibi tuarum virtutum veniat in mentem".' For other instances of the topos, see Callim. *Aet.* fr. 107 Pfeiffer; Plut. *Mor.* 241 E; Stob. *Flor.* 3. 7. 28 Hense.

[82] Solodow (1988) 19 talks of this passage as 'a brilliant example of forensic oratory'. Cf. Otis (1970) 282 on 'the clever "controversia" between Ajax and Achilles'. Bömer (1969–86) vi. 197 says that the 'iudicium armorum' was 'ein beliebtes Thema . . . der

deplored at the opening of the *Satyricon*:[83]

'Num alio genere Furiarum declamatores inquietantur, qui clamant: "Haec vulnera pro libertate publica excepi; hunc oculum pro vobis impendi: date mihi ducem, qui me ducat ad liberos meos, nam succisi poplites membra non sustinent"?'

'Surely the declaimers are driven by no different sort of Furies who cry out, "These wounds I suffered for the freedom of the State; this eye I lost for you; give me a guide to take me to my children, for my tottering knees do not support my limbs"?'

Further, Ulysses' emphasis on the wound is paralleled by a number of passages from the elder Seneca, a writer who would surely provide more material were his text intact.[84] An important example is *Controversiae* 1. 8, the case of the man thrice a hero whose father wishes to restrain him from further combat, and who asserts that such a figure should be kept behind in order to reproduce himself, 1. 8. 3:

Erubescit res publica tam cicatricoso milite uti. Non oportet tantam virtutem sine successore concidere: ducenda uxor est; sed iam nunc te admoneo ne unum tollas.

The State blushes to use so cicatrized a soldier. Such great valour should not fall without an heir: he should take a wife; but now I warn you—do not raise a single son.

Warming to the theme, Cornelius Hispanus then offers a *color* worthy of Scaeva, arguing that the hero can be wounded only through existing scars,[85] and the son is then depicted as replying with the claim that he

Rhetorenschulen in Rom'. However, many of the examples which he cites ([Cic.] *Her.* 1.18, 1. 27, 2. 28; *Inv. Rhet.* 1. 92; Quint. *Inst.* 4. 2. 12–13, 5. 10. 41) involve a presumed murder trial for Odysseus consequent on the suicide of Ajax. On the other hand, one cannot help but be struck by the suggestion at Sen. *Controv.* 2. 2. 8 that *Met.* 13. 121–2 began as a *sententia* of Latro which Ovid versified while speaking the part of Ajax at the school of Arellius Fuscus. For other apparent references to school versions of the *iudicium*, see Juv. 7. 115–18 and 10. 83–5, and the notes of Duff (1970) and Courtney (1980) ad loc. It should be added that the disrobing of Ulysses in this debate is also very similar to that performed by Cleonnis, the hero of the First Messenian War whose κρίσις ἀριστείου with Aristomenes is recorded at Diod. 8. 12.

[83] Petron. 1.

[84] For instance, the 'vir fortis sine manibus' case of *Controv.* 1. 4 is reported with concern for the *colores* and *divisio*, while the traditional *narratio* elements are absent, though marked. Thus, at 1. 4. 2, we have the heading 'descriptio pugnantis viri fortis' and at 1. 4. 12, 'cum pugnantem se acie descripsisset'.

[85] Sen. *Controv.* 1. 8. 3: 'Non ante te retinere coepi quam dimisit res publica. Nullum iam tibi vulnus nisi per cicatricem inprimi potest. Adhuc diutius fuisti cum hoste quam apud patrem: domi tantum sanatus es'.

only obeyed the commands of his father, the greatest admirer of his wounds.[86] Finally, it should be noted that at 1. 8. 9 the argument from exemplarity can be advanced in order to keep the son out of battle and thus a living model to the young:

Ad ultimum: utile esse rei publicae ter fortem servari ut sit qui ostendatur iuventuti; iam illum magis posse ornamentum esse quam praesidium.

Finally: that it was useful for the State for the man thrice a hero to be kept to be shown to the young men; now he could achieve more as an ornament than as a defender.[87]

In this context, an important parallel is furnished by the Third Major Oration attributed to Quintilian, in which counsel for the *miles Marianus* justifies the killing of a senior officer to the general, pleading provocation on the grounds of sexual harassment.[88] Here, the theme of *virtus* becomes an insistent leitmotiv, constantly associated with the name of the judge[89] in order to win him over to the side of a brave man[90] who will not compromise himself sexually and take the part of a woman.[91] In this context, the scar and the wound become the mark both of the soldier's patriotism and of his masculinity.[92] The theme first appears as metaphor at 3. 1 as counsel for the defence expresses his client's indifference to the verdict (*neque est tam inbellis, ut non forti pectore adversa, dum non inhonesta, toleret*) and returns at 3. 6

[86] Ibid. 1. 8. 4–5: 'Pareo tibi, pater, qui gloria nos inmortales fieri dicebas, qui ex acie redeuntis vulnera osculabaris'.

[87] For other conflicts between hero-father and hero-son, see ibid. 8. 5 and 10. 2, esp. 10. 2. 5, 'vulneribus me senem feci'.

[88] This case is recorded at Val. Max. 6. 1. 12 and Plut. *Mar.* 14. 3–5, and is frequently mentioned as a topos of rhetoric, e.g. Cic. *Inv. Rhet.* 2. 124, *Mil.* 9; Quint. *Inst.* 3. 11. 14.

[89] e.g. 3. 2, 'tua . . . divina virtus'; cf 3. 4, 'ad unicum, C. Mari, cum virtutis tuae, tum sanctitatis severitatisque praesidium confugimus' and 3. 18, 'fulgentes virtutes tuas' and 'ex ipsa stirpe virtutum'.

[90] 3. 10, 'Hunc mirabitur sola virtutium incorrupta testis vetustas' cf. 3. 19 on the 'nuda virtus' of the youth.

[91] 3. 3, 'At ego, si qua est fides, pudicitiam in milite etiam laudare erubesco: feminarum est ista virtus', cf. 3. 16, 'quidquid in pugna patimur, virorum est' and 'saeviat denique in terga verberibus, exigat servilem plagarum patientiam', where what the soldier will endure is implicitly contrasted to the *muliebria pati* which he shuns.

[92] For another example of pride in one's wounds, see ps.-Quintilian 4. 8, where the 'vir fortis' who constantly sought death in battle still observes: 'Quotiens mehercule haec vulnera et rorantia hostili cruore arma conspexi, animum supra necessitates erigo, supra fatum pono'. Further, at 4. 11, in support of his wish to commit suicide, the hero expresses what one rather suspects, that veterans constantly baring their scars were a bit of a bore: 'Quam miserum, quam deforme est meminisse quod fueris, referre cicatricum tuarum redundationes et frigidam praeteritorum memoriam, cum iam fidem membra non habeant, supra sua facta rideri'.

with the paradox that the officer should be attracted to one who is marked as a man by the very ruination of his body.[93] The closing *sententia* emphasizes the wound:[94]

Vulgaria inritamenta sunt cupiditatis forma, aetas; singularis res est fortis concubinus: *illas cicatrices, illa vulnera*, illa tot eximiae decora militiae—quid exequar ultra, imperator?

Beauty and youth are commonplace incitements to desire; a courageous concubine is an unusual affair: those scars, those wounds, those so many decorations for military excellence—General, why should I go on?

However, the collection and display of wounds is not just a game from the schoolboy's rhetorical manuals. Seneca's philosophy puts great emphasis on the association of the good soldier with his wounds. *De Vita Beata* 15. 5 connects this theme with that of falling before one's general:

Ut bonus miles feret volnera, numerabit cicatrices, et transverberatus telis moriens amabit eum pro quo cadet imperatorem . . .

As a good soldier will endure wounds, will count his scars, and pierced through with weapons will love the general for whom he falls as he dies . . .

More importantly still, *De Providentia* 4. 4 marks those same scars and wounds as a thing to be displayed, the material of spectacle:

Avida est periculi virtus et quo tendat, non quid passura sit cogitat, quoniam etiam quod passura est gloriae pars est. Militares viri gloriantur vulneribus, laeti fluentem meliori casu sanguinem ostentant: idem licet fecerint qui integri revertuntur ex acie, *magis spectatur qui saucius redit*.

Courage is eager for risk and considers where it is heading, not what it will suffer, since even what it will suffer is a part of glory. Soldiers glory in wounds, happily show off the blood that flowed to no ill effect: though they may have done the same things who return from the line unharmed, people look up more to the wounded soldier.

The admiring gaze attracted by Seneca's wounded warrior points to the prime significance of the scar in Roman life, that is as an object for public display. This emerges in the rhetorical theorists' assertion of the

[93] 3. 6 'hoc ipsum, quod primus ante signa procurrit, quod veteranos tiro praecedit, quod redit pulvere et cruore concretus, istud, istud, quod tam vir est.'

[94] Cf. 3. 7 for jokes at the expense of the officer rushing 'per vulnera' in order to embrace the soldier; 3. 9, where the officer's lustful hands compromise the wounds which testify to the soldier's manhood; 3. 16, where the soldiers who will not 'muliebria pati' proclaim that 'fortiter ancipites inibimus pugnas, vulnera laude pensabimus'.

usefulness of displaying one's wounds in court. Repeated reference is made, for instance, to the notorious acquittal of M'. Aquilius acquired by M. Antonius in 99 BC, when the defendant's manifest guilt allowed only the final resort of tearing his clothing in order to reveal the honourable scars on his chest,[95] and there is clear evidence that Cicero adopted the tactic himself. Thus, Quintilian, *Inst.* 6. 1. 21 counsels:

Periclitantem vero commendat dignitas et studia fortia et susceptae bello cicatrices et nobilitas et merita maiorum. Hoc quod proxime dixi Cicero atque Asinius certatim sunt usi, pro Scauro patre hic, ille pro filio.

Dignity and brave deeds and scars endured in war and nobility and the achievements of ancestors truly commend a defendant. As I mentioned earlier, Cicero and Asinius used this strategy as if in rivalry with one another, the former for Scaurus the father, the latter for the son.[96]

And a second instance of this practice is offered by the fragmentary close to the *Pro Rabirio*:[97]

Qui hasce ore adverso pro re publica cicatrices ac notas virtutis accepit, is ne quod accipiat famae volnus perhorrescit; quem numquam incursiones hostium loco movere potuerunt, is nunc impetum civium, cui necessario cedendum est, perhorrescit.

He who suffered these scars and marks of valour on the front of his face in the name of the State now shudders lest he should receive a wound to his reputation. He whom the attacks of the enemy never moved from his post now shudders at the assault of the citizens, to which he must of necessity give way.[98]

95 Cic. *De Or.* 2. 124, 'iudicibus cicatrices adversas senis imperatoris ostendere' and 195, 'ut discinderem tunicam, ut cicatrices ostenderem'; cf. Cic. *Verr.* 2. 5. 3, 'arripuit M'. Aquilium constituitque in conspectu omnium tunicamque eius a pectore abscidit, ut cicatrices populus Romanus iudicesque aspicerent adverso corpore exceptas; simul et de illo vulnere quod ille in capite ab hostium duce acceperat multa dixit'; Quint. *Inst.* 2. 15. 7, 'scissa veste cicatrices quas is pro patria pectore adverso suscepisset ostendit'; and Livy, *Per.* 70. 1, 'Cum M'. Aquilius de pecuniis repetundis causam diceret, ipse iudices rogare noluit. M. Antonius qui pro eo perorabat, tunicam a pectore discidit, ut honestas cicatrices ostenderet, et indubitate absolutus est. Cicero eius rei solus auctor'. It is striking that Livy should have devoted one of his source-critical discussions to the question of the scars of Antonius. Evidently, there has here been lost a significant discussion of the gesture. Compare also the hilarious return to the theme at Cic. *Verr.* 2. 5. 32: 'Hic scilicet est metuendum ne ad exitum defensionis tuae vetus illa Antoniana dicendi ratio atque auctoritas proferatur, ne excitetur Verres, ne denudetur a pectore, ne cicatrices populus Romanus aspiciat, ex mulierum morsu vestigia libidinis atque nequitiae.'

96 While the extant fragments of Cic. *Scaur.* contain no references to scars, it is worth noting in this context that Cic. *Scaur.* fr. 1. 4 seems to celebrate the father of Scaurus and that Quint. *Inst.* 4. 1. 69 refers to a separate lost speech on the charge of 'ambitus'.

97 Cic. *Rab. Perd.* 36.

98 The practice of Cicero is paralleled in that of his great rival Hortensius. Malcovati

To these Ciceronian examples may be added a number of instances of the gesture in the historians, predominantly performed by irate soldiers, serving or recently retired. Livy, for instance, retrojects the tradition to the early years of the Republic. At 2. 23. 4, an old man enters the forum in protest and:

Testes honestarum aliquot locis pugnarum cicatrices adverso pectore ostentabat.

He displayed the scars on his breast which bore testimony to his honourable service in various battles.

This form of protest is repeated almost immediately at 2. 27. 2 by the veterans of Servilius.[99] Again, at 4. 58. 13, soldiers use their wounds, the sign of their loyalty to the State, to demand the loyalty of the State in return,[100] and, at 6. 14. 6, when the revolutionary Marcus Manlius pays off the debts of a centurion fallen victim to the evils of usury, the soldier uses his scars to verify his patriotism and whip up the crowd.[101] Moreover, at 6. 20. 7–10, Manlius lists his achievements, the demonstration of scars coming after various military crowns and second only to an appeal to the gods, but the stress here placed on scars is nothing to that of M. Servilius Pulex Geminus.[102] Faced with the crushing self-regard of this warrior, one can only be grateful for the bathos of his *tumor inguinum*.[103]

(1955) i. 92. 35 quotes 'Q. Hortensius Hortalus Pro C. Rabirio contra T. Labienum' as referring to 'cicatricum mearum'.

[99] Livy, 2. 27. 2: 'Concursus ad Servilium fiebat; illius promissa iactabant; illi exprobrabant sua quisque belli merita cicatricesque acceptas'.

[100] Livy, 4. 58. 13: 'Prensantesque veteranos stipendia cuiusque et volnera ac cicatrices numerabant; quid iam integri esset in corpore loci ad nova volnera accipienda, quid super sanguinis quod dari pro re publica posset rogitantes'.

[101] Livy, 6. 14. 6: 'Acceptus extemplo in tumultuosam turbam et ipse tumultum augebat, cicatrices acceptas Veienti Gallico aliisque deinceps bellis ostentans'.

[102] Livy, 45. 39. 17–18: 'Nudasse deinde se dicitur et, quo quaeque bello volnera accepta essent, rettulisse. Quae dum ostentat, adapertis forte, quae velanda erant, tumor inguinum proximis risum movit. Tum "hoc quoque, quod ridetis", inquit, "in equo dies noctesque persedendo habeo, nec magis me eius quam cicatricum harum pudet paenitetque, quando numquam mihi impedimento ad rem publicam bene gerendam domi militiaeque fuit."' For this story, cf. Plut. *Aem.* 31. 5–6, and Servilius' description of the Romans as ἡμᾶς τοὺς τοσούτοις τραύμασι πεπαιδευμένους ἀρετὰς καὶ κακίας κρίνειν στρατηγῶν.

[103] For a Julio-Claudian example, see Tac. *Ann.* 1. 35. 1 and the mutiny of the German legions; cf. *Ann.* 1. 49. 3 where, at the close of the mutiny, the soldiers resolve that they cannot placate the ghosts of their peers until 'pectoribus impiis honesta vulnera accepissent'. Rosenstein (1990) 132 n. 68 also offers Dio Cass. 54. 14. 3 for the display in 18 BC of scars by a senator purged by Augustus and protesting his worth.

It is this category of the disgruntled soldiery that is the most significant. For the display of scars on the chest is most closely identified with the rhetoric of the very Marian tradition with which, at the start of this chapter, it was asserted that Caesar associated himself. Here, the *locus classicus* is Sallust, *Bellum Jugurthinum* 85. 29–30, in which the *novus homo* Marius uses the evidence of wounds sustained in the defence of the State to claim for himself a stake in that very State which his aristocratic detractors, by recitation of lineage and family achievement, can claim for their own:

'Non possum fidei causa imagines neque triumphos aut consulatus maiorum meorum ostentare, at, si res postulet, hastas, vexillum, phaleras, alia militaria dona, praeterea cicatrices advorso corpore. Hae sunt meae imagines, haec nobilitas, non hereditate relicta, ut illa illis, sed quae egomet plurumis laboribus et periculis quaesivi.'

'I cannot show off in evidence the portraits or the triumphs or the consulates of my ancestors, but, should it be required, spears, a standard, breastplates, other military awards, and, besides, the scars on the front of my body. These are my portraits, this is my nobility, not left like theirs as an inheritance but which I personally have obtained through countless toils and dangers.'

The denial of outward nobility (εὐγένεια) is a Stoic,[104] but more particularly a Cynic theme,[105] and there is a definite Cynic tone to much of this speech.[106] However, the specific contrast between *imagines* and scars as evidence of nobility is not so much Cynic or Stoic as classically Marian. Skard suspects that his original inspiration in this is the elder Cato,[107] but the theme comes to be no less closely associated with Marius than with Cato.[108] This is most evident in the similarities between the portraits of Marius and Sertorius in both Sallust and Plutarch, a similarity generally explained in terms of the inheritance by Sertorius of the rhetoric and tradition of Marianism.[109]

104 Hor. *Sat.* 1. 6. 8 with Heinze and Kiessling (1957) ad loc. and Sen. *Ep.* 44.

105 Diog. Laert. 6. 10.

106 See Skard (1941).

107 Skard (1956) 97 compares Sall. *Jug.* 85. 29 to Plut. *Cato Mai.* 1. 5, which he suspects to be reproducing Cato's own words: ἔτι μειράκιον ὢν τραυμάτων τὸ σῶμα μεστὸν ἐναντίων εἶχε. Leigh (1995) finds support for Skard's hypothesis in a close analysis of the speculation at Plut. *Mor.* 276 C–D = Cato, *Orig.* fr. 112 (Peter) that old-time Roman politicians used to leave off their tunics when canvassing in order to display the scars they had suffered in the line of battle.

108 Caviglia (1966) 156–7 notes the undeniable parallel between Sall. *Jug.* 85. 29 and Plut. *Mar.* 9. 2, and endorses the view of Passerini (1934) 21, arguing that 'Il discorso di Mario poteva fornire un ricco materiale per la caratterizzazione di "homines novi", quali appunto Mario o Sertorio, materiale da cui dovette attingere Plutarco o l'ipotetica biografia che gli servì da modello'.

109 See Gell. *NA* 2. 27 = Sall. *H.* fr. i. 88 (Maurenbrecher), where Sertorius' pride in his

Not every instance of pride in scars is associated with the anti-aristocratic tradition. When the display of scars in electoral canvassing is mentioned in Plutarch's *Coriolanus*, it is more as an ancestral proof of the *virtus* and worth of the candidate.[110] As a balance to this, however, must be noted Coriolanus' use of the disrobing gesture in Dionysius specifically in order to win the sympathy of the common people.[111] To this should be connected the further phenomenon of the development of a canon of *popularis* exemplars to match the traditional aristocratic body of heroes. It is to this movement, particularly to the efforts of the late-Republican Licinius Macer, that the fame of L. Siccius Dentatus should be attributed.[112] Valerius Maximus, the elder Pliny, and Aulus Gellius all award to Dentatus the palm as Rome's greatest warrior, and, quoting Varro, record that he:

wounds is contrasted with the Romans' failure to give credit for his deeds 'primo per ignobilitatem, deinde per invidiam scriptorum'. Caviglia (1966) notes the similar phrasing of Plut. *Sert.* 4. 2 and attributes both passages to the influence of Marianism. Cf. La Penna (1963) 223: 'Quando Sallustio richiama la carriera gloriosa di Sertorio come tribuno militare in Ispagna e poi nel *bellum Marsicum*, egli esplicitamente si contrappone alla storiografia filoaristocratica'.

[110] See Plut. *Cor.* 14. 1, where candidates standing for consul would enter the forum without a tunic, either to demonstrate their temperance or *δεικνύντας οἷς ἦσαν ὠτειλαὶ προφανῆ τὰ σύμβολα τῆς ἀνδρείας*.

[111] See Dion. Hal. *Ant. Rom.* 7. 62. 2–3. For more on this as the turning of the rhetoric of the people on the people, see Leigh (1995).

[112] Val. Max. 3. 2. 24 cf. Plin. *HN* 7. 101–3, who describes the hero as 'quadraginta quinque cicatricibus adverso corpore insignis, nulla in tergo' and parallels the case with that of Manlius Capitolinus who 'XXIII cicatrices adverso corpore exceperat'; cf. Gell. *NA* 2. 11. 2, who reports that he 'cicatricem aversam nullam, adversas quinque et quadraginta tulisse'. For very similar versions of the story, see Dion. Hal. *Ant. Rom.* 10. 36–49, Festus, 208. 19 (Lindsay), Fulgentius, *Serm. Ant.* 113. 9 (Helm). Fulgentius attributes the story to Varro. Holford-Strevens (1971) would seem to support the connection between the celebration of *virtus* and the anti-aristocratic ideology, when he comments that 'It is possible that Siccius was at least built up, if not actually invented, as a plebeian counterpart to the patrician Sergius, particularly if the source of our accounts be Licinius Macer.' On this point, see Klotz (1940). While the scepticism towards Klotz of Ogilvie (1965) at Livy 3. 43 is misplaced, the latter does offer an acute observation when he suggests that the conventional pairing of Siccius with M. Sergius Silus induces Livy to represent the death of the former in terms similar to those in which Sallust depicted that of the latter's descendant L. Sergius Catilina: Livy 3. 43. 6, 'Sicciumque in medio iacentem armatum omnibus in eum versis corporibus videre'. The treatment of Dentatus as a plebeian hero is most evident in Dionysius of Halicarnassus, where he is depicted as speaking in favour of agrarian reform, and applying all the classic Marian arguments concerning *virtus*. Thus, at 10. 37. 2, he proclaims that *τραύματα δὲ πέντε καὶ τετταράκοντα εἴληφα καὶ πάντα ἐμπρόσθια, κατὰ νώτου δ' οὐθέν*, and then, at 10. 37. 5, complains *ὁπότε δ' οὐθὲν ἔχοντες ἐπιδείξασθαι μέγα καὶ νεανικὸν ἔργον ἀνθ' οὗ τὰ ἡμέτερα βίαι κατέσχον, ἀναισχυντοῦσι καὶ οὐδ' ἐξελεγχόμενοι μεθίενται αὐτῶν, τίς ἂν ἀνάσχοιτο;* Later, at 10. 38. 1, he challenges the aristocrats to *ἐπιφανεῖς καὶ καλὰς πράξεις*, asking which of them, for instance, is *τραύματα πλείω λαβὼν*.

V et XL vulnera pectore excepisse, tergo cicatricibus vacuo.

Took forty-five wounds to the breast while his back was bare of scars.[113]

Once again, the scar sustained in defence of the State takes pride of place in the rhetoric of anti-aristocratic politicians and historians.

CONCLUSION

The loyal centurion has already been shown to be a central figure in Caesar's Marian or *popularis* ideology. Now, there appears a further, more surprising way in which this is true. Scaeva throws away his shield and invites wounding; a forest of spears sticks in his guts, but he survives. The young men who form his audience carry him back to the camp and, 6. 253–4:

> Velut inclusum perfosso in pectore numen
> et vivam magnae speciem Virtutis adorant.

They worship the divine power which seems shut up in his pierced breast and the living image of great Valour.

Scaeva is now the noble cicatrized hero, the Roman who has lived according to the rules of public morality and has the marks to prove it. And yet it is not so easy to go along. Something is not quite right. What it is that has gone wrong may be stated in these terms.

The obvious first point is that made earlier concerning the suicidal zeal of the Caesarians. The traditional admiration for the epic hero unafraid to be wounded in the breast is underpinned by the presumption that he no more yearns to die than his reader. Otherwise, the nobility of the sacrifice is rather tarnished. Scaeva and his peers are set apart by their *amor mortis*, a desire which extends beyond killing to dying as well. The emotional discontinuity between reader and character is alienating.

Second, the scar as emblem of *virtus* is undermined by its civil-war context in the same way as the *exemplum* discussed in the previous chapter. The catalogue of scar-gestures offered here consists entirely of wounds honourably sustained fighting for the unified Roman State against overseas enemies. Important in this context must be Horace, *Carm.* 1. 35. 33–4, and the lament:

113 The scars of Dentatus are given their proper importance by Oakley (1985), esp. 408–10. 409 n. 145 also offers a useful catalogue of scar-displays.

> Heu heu, cicatricum et sceleris pudet
> fratrumque.

Alas, alas, we are ashamed of our scars, our crimes and the brothers we slew.

The implicit civil-war quality of the bad scars is made clear by the paradigmatic reference to the conflict of brothers, of Romulus and Remus, of Eteocles and Polynices, of Caesar and Pompey.[114] This is then opposed to the need for a new imperial purpose in which, one presumes, the scar will once again be a mark of honour, 1. 35. 38–40:

> O utinam nova
> incude diffingas retusum in
> Massagetas Arabasque ferrum!

O would that on a new anvil you might remodel the blunted steel and turn it against the Massagetae and the Arabs!

Scaeva's readers must assess his wounds in the light of the same opposition.

Finally, one must stress the peculiar status of the display of scars. The rhetoricians clearly regard this visual effect as far more eloquent than any wordy disquisition on the *virtus* of the defendant. Just as the scar is sustained in the defence of the whole community, so its interpretation is immediate and uniform for all those watching. In the previous chapter, the idea was outlined that the creation of an internal audience within the action co-operated with the reading public to re-create the double audience characteristic of Roman exemplary narratives. On the other hand, Scaeva's 'exemplary behaviour' was presumed to repel the reading public and, comically, only to fascinate his youthful colleagues. Now, there is a different dysfunction. The youthful audience which did not fight for Scaeva still adores his wounded breast, while the reading public can be presumed to take the attitude of a Horace. In this is captured the essence of the deformation of the traditional attitude to the *pectus* and the *tergum* consistently shown by Lucan's Caesarians. Scaeva and Vulteius yearn for Caesar to see their actions because only Caesar and the Caesarians can properly make sense of their attitudes. They are marked as an isolated community, isolated in particular from the conventional Romans reading the epic. The mute eloquence of Scaeva's wound bespeaks a courage as

[114] See Conte (1966) and Nisbet and Hubbard (1970) ad loc., who cite Hor. *Epod.* 7. 17–20; Verg. *G.* 2. 510; Luc. 2. 148–51; and *Anth. Lat.* 460–1 (SB) for Maevius killing his brother at Actium ('fratribus, heu, fratres, patribus concurrere natos | impia sors belli fataque saeva iubent'). See also Petron. 80. 3.

ıatural to them and alien to others as is the suicidal courting of disas-er or the willingness to kill even one's family members in the name of Caesar. The double audience is a divided audience: divided in its eaction to the same event, with both sides bemused the one by the other. Lucan's ideal reader must presume that the Caesarians, granted he same chance to stare at him that he has to stare at them, would ind his values as bizarre as he does theirs.

7
A View To a Kill—Lucan's Amphitheatrical Audience

Ἀλλ’, ἦν δ’ ἐγώ, ποτὲ ἀκούσας τι πιστεύω τούτωι· ὡς ἄρα Λεόντιος ὁ Ἀγλαΐωνος ἀνιὼν ἐκ Πειραιῶς ὑπὸ τὸ βόρειον τεῖχος ἐκτός, αἰσθόμενος νεκροὺς παρὰ τῶι δημίωι κειμένους, ἅμα μὲν ἰδεῖν ἐπιθυμοῖ, ἅμα δ’ αὖ δυσχεραίνοι καὶ ἀποτρέποι ἑαυτόν, καὶ τέως μαχοιτό τε καὶ παρακαλύπτοιτο, κρατούμενος δ οὖν ὑπὸ τῆς ἐπιθυμίας, διελκύσας τοὺς ὀφθαλμούς, προσδραμὼν πρὸς τοὺς νεκρούς, “ἰδοὺ ὑμῖν,” ἔφη, “ὦ κακοδαίμονες, ἐμπλήσθητε τοῦ καλοῦ θεάματος.”

Yet, said I, I have more confidence in this story I once heard, about how Leontios, son of Aglaion, when he was going up from the Piraeus outside the north wall, saw some corpses lying near the public executioner and at once both desired to see them and also was disgusted and turned away, and struggled for a while and covered his eyes, but then finally was overcome by desire, opened his eyes, ran up to the corpses, and cried, 'Go on then, wretches, feast yourselves on the lovely sight.'

Plato, *Republic* 439 E–F

In the previous two chapters, different modes of spectacle have been investigated—modes which traditionally serve to communicate a shared and stable ideology but which civil war leaves fractured and dysfunctional. Whether the issue is the collection of scars, battle under the eyes of the general, or the exemplary display of *virtus*, Lucan's Scaeva scene has a central position. In particular, the bizarre reformation of an *exemplum virtutis* narrative was most strikingly apparent in the reaction of the audience at 6. 165–9:

> Movit tantum vox illa furorem,
> quantum non primo succendunt classica cantu,
> *mirantesque* virum atque avidi *spectare* secuntur
> scituri iuvenes, numero deprensa locoque
> an plus quam mortem virtus daret.

'hat speech prompted a greater frenzy than is sparked by the first blast of the attle-trumpets, and the young men followed the man, marvelling at him and ager to watch and find out whether valour outnumbered and in an inferior osition might win more than death.

The argument to be advanced in this chapter takes these lines as its tarting-point, but draws a deeper significance from them, one which onnects them to other passages in the *Pharsalia* where Lucan arodies traditional Roman battle narrative; and which engages more adically with the sense emerging in the last chapter that what is here t issue is a peculiarly Caesarian form of display. In short, the Scaeva pisode will be shown to stand as Lucan's gladiatorial combat; the sea attle off Massilia in Book 3 and the suicide of the crew of Vulteius in 3ook 4 as his *naumachiae*; and the episode of the snakes of Libya in 3ook 9 as his *venatio*. This will be established by the demonstration of number of gladiatorial terms and images in each passage, and continuously by the presence in all of the passages of the terms of spectatorship marked above. Finally, it will be argued that the use of these erms to suggest a writing and reading strategy in which civil war is, mong other things, as enjoyable to watch as the slaughter of the mphitheatre, provides an uncomfortable and challenging rejoinder to ucan's customary voice of lamentation. This theory of amphitheatricalty in Lucan is also a deliberately Neronian and modern challenge to hose ritualists who wish to explain all such imagery in his work as refering to the antiquarian conception of the gladiatorial *munus* as propitiaion of the dead by human sacrifice. Shamanism is not on the agenda.

It has long been known that the amphitheatre features prominently s a metaphor in Roman accounts of civil war and that Lucan is a otable exponent of this technique.[1] My studies of the Massilia, 'ulteius, and Scaeva episodes all build on suggestions made by preious scholars. As early as Haskins,[2] commentators were remarking on he use of the gladiatorial pair as an image for what Jupiter impassively bserved in the civil war, and terms such as *par* and *harena* have been nalysed particularly well by Ahl[3] and Masters.[4] This study, however, is

[1] For the idea of civil war in general, see esp. Jal (1963) 341–3. Some of Jal's assertions vith regard to single combat are not endorsed here, but his basic collection of material is xtremely useful.

[2] See Haskins (1887) at Luc. 6. 3, 6. 191, 7. 695, cf. Haskins at 7. 447, '"spectabit": a netaphor from the gladiatorial contests'.

[3] Ahl (1976) 86–8.

[4] Masters (1992) 35, 44, 109–10, 155. Jal (1963) 341 shows the prominence of *par* in other writers, e.g. Petron. 80. 3; Sen. *Prov.* 2. 9; Flor. *Epit.* 2. 13. 35, and of *harena* at Aug. De *Civ. D.* 3. 4; Flor. *Epit.* 2. 9. 1, 2. 13. 18, 2. 17. 6.

characterized by the new terms which it adds to the equation, giving particular prominence to those words centred on the concepts of *mirari* and *spectare*. These, it is asserted, can always bear the general connotation and often demand the specific denotation of the experience of amphitheatrical spectatorship.[5]

If this argument seems to involve a rather serious jump from the assertion in Chapter 5 that the concept of *spectaculum* was central to a Roman *exemplum virtutis*, it must be stated that the categories under consideration are not entirely discrete. For instance, an *exemplum virtutis* is always the act of an individual, and can thus often centre on actions such as single combat by *provocatio*.[6] This is evident from the emphasis placed on single combat in Valerius Maximus,[7] but it is a theme which can be traced back to the annalists and which is prominent in Livy. Thus, at Livy, 7. 33. 11–12, the consul Valerius, whose cheery oneness with his troops has marked him as the type of the good general (7. 33. 1–4), leads the charge, and, by his success in single combat, inspires the others to advance:

> Primus omnium consul invadit hostem et cum quo forte contulit gradum obtruncat. Hoc spectaculo accensi dextra laevaque ante se quisque memorandum proelium cient; stant obnixi Samnites, quamquam plura accipiunt quam inferunt volnera.
>
> The consul led everyone in the attack on the enemy and slew the first man he met. Fired by this spectacle, each man to left and right before him began to fight a memorable fight; the Samnites stood firm in resistance though they were suffering more wounds than they were dealing.

At the same time, Livy repeatedly notes that the character of that same single combat is very similar to that of a gladiatorial duel, and uses the same term *spectaculum* to make his point. For instance, Hardie,[8] in examining the gladiatorial element in the duel of Turnus and Aeneas, cites Livy, 7. 10. 6 for the duel of Manlius Torquatus with the Gaul:

[5] The amphitheatrical denotation arises from the presence of other relevant terms. Many areas of Roman life are described in terms of spectacle, as the following catalogue from Livy and Seneca alone will suggest: battle, Livy, 1. 28. 1, 3. 22. 8, 4. 27. 11, 6. 23. 12; duels, Livy, 1. 25. 1–2, 6. 24. 5–6, 7. 9. 7–10. 14, 8. 7. 9 (see below); triumphs, Livy, 4. 20. 1–2; Sen. *Tranq.* 11. 12; execution, Livy, 1. 26. 10, 1. 28. 11, 2. 5. 5–8; Sen. *Vit. Beat.* 19. 3; boxing, wrestling, games, Livy, 1. 35. 7–9, 2. 31. 3, 4. 35. 4, 9. 40. 17, 10. 47. 3; Sen. *Brev.* 12. 2; dancing, Sen. *Tranq.* 17. 4; theatres, Livy, 7. 2. 3–7; dinner parties, Sen. *Vit. Beat.* 11. 4, *Tranq.* 1. 8–9 and 7. 1–2; libraries, Sen. *Tranq.* 9. 4–5; natural phenomena, Sen. *Ot.* 5. 2–4.

[6] For *provocatio* in Book 9, see below, p. 274 n. 104.

[7] e.g. Val. Max. 3. 2. 21 for Q. Occius fighting Pyrresus and 3. 2. 24 for L. Siccius Dentatus, for whom see above pp. 230–1 and n. 112.

[8] Hardie (1986) 151–4.

:t duo in medio armati spectaculi magis more quam lege belli destituuntur, equaquam visu ac specie aestimantibus pares.

and the two men took their place in the middle in a manner more akin to a ladiatorial spectacle than to the laws of war, seeming in no way equally natched to those who judged by look and outward appearance.

)f this Hardie comments that Livy is giving the 'contemporary Roman reader' a 'stage direction' as to how to approach the scene, nd then adds that: 'For a Roman of the time of Augustus it was ertainly the wounded gladiator who provided the most accessible pectacle of death in arms, and there is a strong feeling of the ;ladiatorial about the death of Turnus: *the sense that these two awesome warriors are fighting for their lives in total isolation, despite and because of the iuge audience of spectators* [my italics]'.[9] Hardie next analyses gladia-orial language in *Aeneid* 12 and leaves Livy behind. However, closer xamination of the historian reveals a number of parallel cases, for nstance at 1. 25. 2, where three Romans duel with three Albans as he other soldiers look on:

taque ergo erecti suspensique in minime gratum *spectaculum* animo intenluntur.

'or this reason then, excited and in suspense they turned their attention to the nost unpleasant spectacle.[10]

Much the same thing is then seen at 8. 7. 9 for the duel of the Roman Titus Manlius and the Tusculan Geminus Maecius,[11] and at

[9] Ibid. 152. Livy's emphasis on the disparity between the fighters recalls the tradition of pitting different types of gladiator against one another. For disparity in the pair cf. ,ivy, 1. 25. 7 'nequaquam par', Luc. 1. 129 'nec coiere pares', and Sen. *Brev.* 13. 7 'cum ellum inter tam disparia animalia committeret'. The emphasis on the audience of pectators predates Livy's account of the duel, figuring prominently in his model, the nnalist Claudius Quadrigarius (fr. 10b (Peter) = Gell. *NA* 9. 13), who writes 'metu nagno ea congressio in ipso ponti utroque exercitu inspectante facta est'. Both Livy and Claudius are discussed, though with reference only to tragic history, at Borzsák 1973) 60.

[10] Compare the continuation at 1. 25. 5: 'Consertis deinde manibus cum iam non notus tantum corporum agitatioque anceps telorum armorumque sed *volnera quoque et anguis spectaculo essent,* duo Romani super alium alius, vulneratis tribus Albanis, xspirantes corruerunt.' Note that other elements of the 1. 25 narrative are strongly ;ladiatorial, esp. 1. 25. 7 for one unwounded Roman vs. three wounded Curiatii as nequaquam par' and 1. 25. 12 for the mixture of gladiatorial and epic in the mode of lispatch, 'male sustinenti arma gladium superne iugulo defigit, iacentem spoliat'.

[11] Livy, 8. 7. 9, 'Equitibus ceteris velut ad *spectaculum* submotis, spatio, quod vacui nteriacebat campi, adversos concitant equos'. Again, at 8. 7. 11, a gladiatorial tone is rovided by the mode of dispatch, where Manlius strikes his opponent 'ab iugulo'.

23. 47. 3 for the duel of the Campanian Cerrinus Vibellius Taurea and the Roman Claudius Asellus.[12]

Men in single combat are like gladiators, men who watch a battle and do not fight are like spectators.[13] In all this, it is possible to agree with Hardie. However, it is harder to accept unconditionally his final observation, namely that: 'the gladiatorial arena sees the final reduction of the fighter to a non-person, whose moment of violent action exists only to supply a passing spectacle for others'.[14] Modern scholars tend to stress the Roman conception that gladiators were either worthless or dangerous people whose extinction was for the public good, whose suffering did not matter.[15] This view is well supported by the literary evidence, and the concept of an emotionally distanced audience is certainly of the essence in the analysis of the episodes to be examined in this chapter, but it is not the whole story, even for Lucan. For the *spectaculum* element of an *exemplum* and that of the gladiatorial games are seen to be even less discrete categories when one considers the role asserted for the latter in the exemplary education of a warlike people. This is the aim of Hannibal at Livy, 21. 42. 1–43. 2, where first the general:

> Rebus prius quam verbis adhortandos milites ratus, circumdato ad *spectaculum* exercitu captivos montanos vinctos in medio statuit.

Considering that the soldiers would better be spurred by deeds than words, he drew up the army in a circle for a show and placed in the middle some chained captives from the men of the mountains.

[12] Livy, 23. 47. 3, 'Hinc Romani ad *spectaculum* pugnae eius frequentes exierant, et Campani non vallum modo castrorum sed moenia etiam urbis prospectantes repleverunt'. Some of these examples may be said to derive from a civil-war context (e.g. Livy, 1. 25), but not all. It is therefore difficult to regard single combat under the eyes of the army, as Jal does, as the peculiar property of civil war. However, there is a strong gladiatorial element in the examples which he discusses: Verg. *Aen.* 12. 131–3, Livy, 1. 25, Dion. Hal. *Ant. Rom.* 3. 18. 2, Caes. *B. Hisp.* 25. 3–7. Closely related is the combat of the two praetorian guards of Antony and Octavian at Modena at App. *B. Civ.* 3. 68. 279–81. One reason why civil war should so often remind Romans of gladiatorial combat is suggested at Sen. *Ira* 2. 8. 2–3, 'Non alia quam in ludo gladiatorio vita est *cum isdem viventium pugnantiumque*. Ferarum est iste conventus, nisi quod illae inter se placidae sunt morsuque similium abstinent, hi mutua laceratione satiantur.'

[13] e.g. Livy, 28. 33. 16, 'Tertia pars, quae in colle ad *spectaculum* magis tutum quam ad partem pugnae capessendam steterat, et locum et tempus ad fugiendum habuit'. cf. Livy 33. 9. 4, 'Media acies, quae propior dextrum cornu erat, stabat spectaculo velut nihil ad se pertinentis pugnae intenta'.

[14] Hardie (1986) 154.

[15] See Ville (1981) ch. 6, 'L'Idéologie et l'arène: Contestations et morale du munus', Coleman (1990), and Barton (1991) ch. 1. It should, however, be noted that other parts of Ville's work put emphasis on the prestige and sexual status of the gladiator. At p. 344, he concludes with the assertion that the gladiator is treated with both 'honneur et mépris' and that individual Romans entertained 'sentiments contradictoires' towards him. This ambivalence is at the centre of Barton's concerns.

He then offers the prisoners freedom should they be willing to fight each other as gladiators. This is designed to deter Hannibal's men from defeat or capture, a point made explicitly by their leader at 21. 43. 2:

'Si, quem animum in alienae sortis *exemplo* paulo ante habuistis, eundem mox in aestimanda fortuna vestra habueritis, vicimus, milites; *neque enim spectaculum modo illud sed quaedam veluti imago vestrae condicionis erat.*'

'Soldiers, if soon you show the same spirit in contemplating your own fortune as just lately you showed in the case of the lot of others, then we have won. For that was not just a spectacle but by way of being a representation of your own condition.'

In this case, the gladiators exemplify the condition which the men wish to avoid, but it is frequently the case that the warlike skills of the gladiator are the model to which Roman youth are intended to aspire. This is seen at Livy, 41. 20. 10–12, where the importation by Antiochus of the gladiatorial show from Rome finally offers both edification to the audience and inspiration to the young, 41. 20. 11–12:

Gladiatorum munus Romanae consuetudinis primo maiore cum terrore hominum insuetorum ad tale *spectaculum* quam *voluptate* dedit; deinde saepius dando et modo volneribus tenus, modo sine missione, etiam familiare oculis gratumque id *spectaculum* fecit, *et armorum studium plerisque iuvenum accendit.*

He gave a gladiatorial games as is the Roman custom, at first provoking more terror amongst the men, who were unused to such a spectacle, than pleasure; later, when he repeatedly gave the games–sometimes stopping at wounding, sometimes fighting to the death–he even accustomed their eyes to the spectacle and made it pleasing, and roused an enthusiasm for arms in most of the young men.

Nor need one stick to examples of Roman practice abroad, but might also cite the defence from educational value offered for the games at Pliny, *Panegyric* 33. 1:

Visum est spectaculum inde non enerve nec fluxum, nec quod animos virorum molliret et frangeret, sed quod ad pulchra vulnera contemptumque mortis accenderet, cum in servorum etiam noxiorumque corporibus amor laudis et cupido victoriae cerneretur.

Then there was seen a spectacle neither feeble nor dissolute nor likely to soften and break the spirit of men, but one to rouse them to fair wounds and scorn for death, when the love of praise and the desire for victory was visible even in the bodies of slaves and criminals.

Lastly, one should note Appian, *B. Civ.* 3. 68. 279–81, where the combat between the praetorian guards of Antony and Octavian is described through the recurrent metaphor of athletic training: the men, who 'fought at close quarters with their swords as if in a wrestling match' (τοῖς ξίφεσιν ὡς ἐν πάλῃι συνεπλέκοντο), and only rested very briefly 'as if in gymnastic games' (ὥσπερ ἐν τοῖς γυμνικοῖς), finally, like Scaeva, attract an audience of youths, 3. 68. 281:

θάμβος τε ἦν τοῖς νεήλυσιν ἐπελθοῦσι, τοιάδε ἔργα σὺν εὐταξίαι καὶ σιωπῆι γιγνόμενα ἐφορῶσι.

And the new-comers were amazed when they arrived to see such deeds being performed with discipline and in silence.[16]

In short, the *exemplum* and the *gladiatorum munus* are not at all separate entities and must be studied together.[17] In the cases of Scaeva and Vulteius, where one may wish to argue that both elements are present, it is possible simply to rephrase the question and wonder exactly what lessons the gladiators are offering today. In other cases, one may wonder how far the figure of the gladiator as exemplar of Stoic resistance to denigration finds his role only in the context of his public's tainted spectatorship.

It has been shown how the categories can merge. It is also necessary to show how they divide. It will be recalled, for instance, that a Valerian *exemplum virtutis* narrative often involved the reaction to the *exemplum* by secondary characters on the field of battle who were inspired to valorous deeds of their own. This gave the *exemplum* a double audience, and the reading audience a double model later to emulate. On the other hand, there is no sense in which the bravery of a

[16] See also Val. Max. 2. 3. 2 for P. Rutilius Rufus, consul in 105 BC, giving his soldiers gladiatorial training and 2. 4. 1 for gladiatorial combat as the closest thing to war.

[17] In this context, one should also note Cic. *Tusc.* 2. 41, where the ability of the gladiator to withstand pain and keep his dignity is praised. If he can do it, 'vir natus ad gloriam ullam partem animi tam mollem habebit, quam non meditatione et ratione conroboret? Crudele gladiatorum spectaculum et inhumanum non nullis videri solet, et haud scio an ita sit, ut nunc fit; cum vero sontes ferro depugnabant, auribus fortasse multa, oculis quidem nulla poterat esse fortior contra dolorem et mortem disciplina.' Again, at *Tusc.* 4. 48, Cicero argues against anger as a prerequisite for courage, by observing the calm of the gladiator, and, at *Ep.* 30. 8, Seneca uses the gladiator to demonstrate the courage which a man can show when faced with imminent death. Finally, it is essential to note Sen. *Ep.* 70. 19–27, which deliberately chooses three examples of suicide by gladiators at the recent games rather than the exalted behaviour of a Cato, and concludes at 70. 26–27, 'Tanto hoc speciosius spectaculum fuit quanto honestius mori discunt homines quam occidere', then puts the question to Lucilius, 'Quid ergo? Quod animi perditi quoque noxiosi habent non habebunt illi quos adversus hos casus instruxit longa meditatio et magistra rerum omnium ratio?'

gladiator was intended to inspire his watching audience to leap down from their seats and take his side. In the immediate term, at least, the gladiatorial audience was conditioned passively to watch and marvel, and in Roman literature it is the sense of passive spectatorship on the part of the audience that comes across most strongly in accounts of the amphitheatrical experience. A clear example is offered by the possibly Neronian seventh *Eclogue* of Calpurnius Siculus,[18] in which Corydon returns from the city to explain to Lycotas his experiences in what has often been taken to be the new wooden amphitheatre built by Nero in AD 57.[19]

The *Eclogue* opens with Corydon returning late from the city. At lines 4–6 he gives the reason why:

> O piger, o duro iam durior axe, Lycota,
> qui veteres fagos *nova* quam *spectacula* mavis
> *cernere*, quae patula iuvenis deus edit harena.

Lycotas, you dullard, harder of head than the hardest axle, you who would sooner see the ancient beeches than the new spectacles which the young god puts on in the spreading arena.

Similarly, at 13–18, Corydon replies to news that he has lost a singing contest to Stimicon by his absence, commenting that, line 16, 'Yet he will not equal my delight' (*Non tamen aequabit mea gaudia*) and that the gift of every herd in the Lucanian woods would not be 'more pleasing than what I watched at Rome' (*grata magis . . . quam quae spectavimus Urbe*). The great joy of Corydon is in his looking and marvelling, a point which he underlines at 23–7:

[18] The dating of Calpurnius Siculus is a vexed problem. Haupt (1854) separated Calpurnius from Nemesianus and attributed the former to Neronian times. This view was very largely consensual for a long time, but has lately been challenged, most significantly in Champlin (1978) and (1986), Armstrong (1986), and Courtney (1987). It has been defended in Townend (1980), Mayer (1980), and Wiseman (1982). Since Wiseman's article assumes the correctness of Mayer's stylistic arguments, while these, along with those of Townend, are closely scrutinized and rejected in Champlin (1986) and Armstrong (1986), it seems fair to say that the Neronian dating looks ever harder to defend. In particular, I am impressed with the argument of Armstrong that Calp. *Ecl.* 1. 46–52 imitates Luc. 1. 2–6 and 10–12. On the other hand, di Salvo (1990) 21–4 and Amat (1991), while noting the objections to the traditional dating, still prefer to treat Calpurnius as Neronian. Happily, the uses of Calpurnius to be made here depend not on allusion to specifically and exclusively Neronian happenings, but on the description of an institution and experience which straddles all the imperial period and is independently attested and analysed by Seneca.

[19] See Townend (1980) and Amat (1991) 61, citing Tac. *Ann.* 13. 31 and Suet. *Ner.* 12. 1. This seems the strongest argument for a Neronian dating.

Vidimus in caelum trabibus *spectacula* textis
surgere, Tarpeium prope *despectantia* culmen
immensosque gradus et clivos lene iacentes.
Venimus ad sedes, ubi pulla sordida veste
inter femineas *spectabat* turba cathedras.

I saw the theatre that rose to the heavens on interwoven timbers and almost looked down on the top of the Capitoline, and I saw the huge steps and the gentle incline of the slopes. I came to my seat where amongst the women's benches the poor people watched in their dingy clothes.

This theme then reaches its climax at lines 35–46, where the city slicker by his side admits that he is as amazed as the poor country boy:

Quid tibi nunc referam, quae vix suffecimus ipsi
per partes *spectare* suas? Sic undique fulgor
percussit. Stabam *defixus et ore patenti*
cunctaque *mirabar* necdum bona singula noram,
cum mihi tum senior, lateri qui forte sinistro
iunctus erat: 'Quid te *stupefactum*, rustice', dixit,
'ad tantas *miraris* opes, qui nescius auri
sordida tecta, casas et sola mapalia nosti?
En ego iam tremulus et vertice canus et ista
factus in Urbe senex, *stupeo* tamen omnia: certe
vilia sunt nobis quaecumque prioribus annis
vidimus, et sordet quidquid *spectavimus olim*.'

Why should I tell you now of all the things I myself was scarce able to look at in all their details? So did the gleam strike me from every side. I stood dumbfounded and with gaping mouth and marvelled at everything and was still short of understanding every treat when then an older man who happened to be seated next to me on my left said, 'Country boy, why wonder that you are amazed at such great wealth, you who, ignorant of gold, know only the cottages and huts which are your humble homes. Look, I, now trembling with age and white of hair and grown old in Rome itself, am still amazed at it all: truly, all those things we saw in previous years we hold at little value, whatever we once watched we now hold mean.'

These observations could easily stretch into the second half of the poem and the descriptions of the *venatio* and of the sighting of Nero,[20] but by now the centrality to the amphitheatrical experience of *spectare* and *mirari* should be clear.[21]

[20] e.g. Calp. *Ecl.* 7. 49 'spectacula', 7. 50 'ebur admirabile', 7. 66 'spectavi'.

[21] At root, of course, these are terms conventionally used to describe θαῦματα (see R. F. Thomas (1988) at Verg. *G.* 2. 82, 4. 3–5, 4. 309, 4. 554), but the amphitheatre is the home of the θαῦμα in imperial Rome, and any scene of the *Pharsalia* containing both thaumastics and gladiators or *naumachiae* has to denote the amphitheatre. The element of the θαῦμα in the *naumachia* is stressed by Coleman (1993).

The point is that the metaliterary reference to the amphitheatrical has a consistently disruptive role. On the one hand, it subverts the conventions of epic pathos by reminding the reader of the emotions felt when attending the games. On the other, it undermines the category of the exemplary, of the Senecan Stoic sense of that 'theatre of the world' (*theatrum mundi*), by permitting or encouraging the reader to treat the episode just as a show. The close of this chapter returns to the disruption wrought by reference to the amphitheatrical and develops the theoretical conceptions outlined here. First, however, it is necessary to examine more closely the individual passages which have prompted these considerations, and to suggest how they are affected by the spectacularity which the narrator invites us to see in them. In some cases, more emphasis is put on the emotional, in others on the exemplary, but, as a rule, both disruptions can be identified, and all contain elements to disturb the reader.

SCAEVA: LUCAN'S GLADIATOR

That there is an element of the gladiatorial arena in the Scaeva episode was first proposed by Housman, in order to explain the oddity of the comparison of the centurion to a Pannonian bear being hunted by a Libyan.[22] This theme was then taken up by Aymard, who observed that Lucan on three occasions compares Scaeva to animals normally alien to epic, but common to the amphitheatre.[23] Conte, who cites Housman but not Aymard, is uncertain as to the *pardus* at 6. 180–4, but he has no need to be.[24] At Livy, 44. 18. 8 *Africanas* is normally translated as lions, leopards, or panthers, while Martial, *De Spectaculis* 15. 7 and Claudian, 17. 303 (Hall) definitely mention the use of the *pardus* in the amphitheatre.[25] As for the Libyan elephant at 6. 208–13, there exist

[22] Housman (1926) at 6. 220–3: 'Locus ubi Pannonis ursa et venator Libys una consistant amphitheatrum est Romanum, videratque poeta quae describit'.

[23] Aymard (1951) ch. 3, 'Le Thème de l'animal', 61–3. This work is a useful source, though its explanation of Lucan's amphitheatrical imagery in terms of 'nouvauté' and 'originalité' is rather inadequate.

[24] Conte (1974) ad loc.

[25] Cf. Prudent. *Perist.* 1. 57 and Marcellus, *Chron.* II p. 102, *ad annum* 521. Toynbee (1973) 82 notes that 'The earliest use of the Latin word "pardus" for leopard dates from the time of Nero', citing this passage of Lucan. Plin. *HN* 8. 64–5 records an old *Senatus Consultum* banning the importation of *Africanae* to Rome, but adds that Gnaeus Aufidius, tribune of the plebs, in 114 BC carried a resolution in the assembly of the people, permitting their introduction 'Circensium gratia'. Plin. *HN* 8. 63 also states that the *varia* is the female of the *pardus*, and records the showing of the former by Scaurus in 58 BC, by Pompey, and by Augustus. If the female, why not the male?

numerous parallels.[26] Aymard, while he notes that an elephant simile is not unparalleled in epic, citing Rabirius fr. 3 p. 121 Morel (= fr. 3 Courtney), still concedes that Lucan is innovating and wishes to conjure up the atmosphere of the amphitheatre. Finally, the comparison at 6. 220–3 to a Pannonian bear is paralleled, *inter alia*, in Horace and Pliny,[27] while the particular fact of representing Scaeva as a she-bear may be explained with reference to Apuleius, *Metamorphoses* 4. 13 where it seems that *ursae* are particularly fierce.[28]

The animal similes are crucial, but there are many other suggestions of the gladiatorial about the Scaeva scene. The inclusion of two such at the opening of Book 6 has a programmatic function. Thus, with the very first sentence of the book, Lucan describes Caesar and Pompey as a gladiatorial pair.[29] Further, since the intimate connection between Caesar's walling operations at Dyrrachium and the imagery of Scaeva as a man-wall has already been established, it will be conceded that the conclusion to Lucan's reflections on the walling at 6. 60–3 has a strong symbolic value:

> Coit *area* belli:
> hic alitur sanguis terras fluxurus in omnis,
> hic et Thessalicae clades Libycaeque tenentur;
> aestuat angusta rabies civilis *harena*.

The field of war grows smaller: here feeds the blood which will flow to every land and here is contained the slaughter of Thessaly and of Libya; the madness of civil war seethes in a narrow arena.[30]

The walls create a ring in which the gladiators of civil war can compete. In particular, Scaeva will perform that role. From now on, there follows a succession of allusions to the life of the ring. Here again, lines

26 *TLL* v. 2. 357. 78 ff. gives, *inter alia*, Cic. *Fam.* 7. 1. 3; Livy, 44. 18. 6; Vell. Pat. 2. 56. 1; Val. Max. 2. 7. 14; Sen. *Brev.* 13. 6; Plin. *HN* 8. 17–20; Mart. *Spect.* 19. 4; Suet. *Jul.* 39. 3. Cicero and Pliny both record the *admiratio* coloured with *misericordia* felt by the people of Rome in sympathy with the elephants slaughtered by Pompey in 55 BC. For this famous episode cf. Sen. *Brev.* 13. 6 and Dio Cass. 39. 38. 2–4.

27 Hor. *Epist.* 2. 1. 182–6; Plin. *HN* 8. 130–1 cf. Livy, 44. 18. 8; *CIL* 4. 1989.

28 The fact that the range of animals cited here is almost exactly paralleled at Livy, 44. 18 may not be coincidental. For the range and number (up to 9,000) animals slaughtered in any given show, see Hopkins (1983) 9–12.

29 Luc. 6. 1–5: 'Postquam castra duces pugnae iam mente propinquis | inposuere iugis admotaque comminus arma | *parque suum videre dei*, capere omnia Caesar | moenia Graiorum spernit Martemque secundum | iam nisi de genero fatis debere recusat'.

30 For 'area' as the open space used for the games, see *TLL* ii. 497. 75 ff., which offers, *inter alia*, Ov. *Ars Am.* 1. 39, Livy 33. 32. 4, Luc. 3. 513. Despite the scepticism of Hunink (1992) ad loc., I am sure that 3. 513 is a paradoxical reference to the arena.

already discussed in another context invite rereading. At 6. 158–60, it is hard to exclude the sense that Scaeva pursues an imperial audience:

'Peterem felicior umbras
Caesaris in voltu: testem hunc fortuna negavit:
Pompeio laudante cadam.'

I would sooner die under the gaze of Caesar: fortune has denied me this witness—let Pompey praise me as I fall.'[31]

This interpretation of Scaeva's ambitions is suggested by the narrator, who also invokes the concept of the pair, 6. 191–2:

Parque novum Fortuna videt concurrere, bellum
atque virum.

And Fortune sees a new pair come to blows: war and a man.[32]

The reading audience may share the pleasures of the internal audience, 6. 225–7:

Laetus fragor aethera pulsat
victorum: maiora viris e sanguine parvo
gaudia non faceret conspectum in Caesare volnus.

The victors' happy cry strikes the heavens: the sight of Caesar wounded would not cause greater joy to the men than that of this plebeian blood.

All these elements cohere with the appeal for clemency at 6. 230; the abandonment of the shield at 6. 202–6 as an echo of the old Latin practice of gladiators fighting without body armour or of the modern lunchtime treat of naked combat;[33] and the sureness of each blow, 6. 189–90:

Illum tota premit moles, illum omnia tela,
nulla fuit non certa manus, non lancea felix.

[31] For his ambition as originally typical of the Caesarian legionary, see Ch. 6, pp. 199–203. However, with all the surrounding amphitheatricality, it is impossible to exclude the idea that Scaeva represents a bizarre form of 'gladiatorial voluntarism'. Scaeva's gladiatorial ambition is stressed by Barton (1992) ch. 1, 'Despair', 21, which develops the thesis of voluntarism, though on the basis of a theory of discourse which appears to demand only the most minimal contextualization of evidence. Infuriating though this work may be, it is also extremely suggestive, and it will be clear that my analysis of Murrus, Mucius, and Seneca (see below, pp. 279–82) bears the general stamp of Barton's concerns.

[32] For Masters (1992) and Ahl (1976) on *par* in Lucan, see above p. 235 and nn. 3–4.

[33] Cf. Sen. *Ep.* 7. 3–5, 'Nihil habent quo tegantur . . . non galea, non scuto repellitur ferrum. Quo munimenta? Quo artes? Omnia ista mortis morae sunt . . . "Plagis agatur in vulnera, mutuos ictus nudis et obviis pectoribus excipiant."' See also Mart. *Ep.* 8. 80.

All the army, every weapon attacked him, nor was any hand awry, nor did any lance miss the mark.[34]

Finally, the general resemblance to Cocles established in Chapter 5 might be taken as a parallel to the tendency to re-create exemplary deeds of heroism in the amphitheatre. Martial, *Spect.* 21 and *Ep.* 8. 30 and 10. 25 all celebrate re-creations at the games of Mucius Scaevola's attempt on the life of Lars Porsenna.[35]

The manner in which the spectatorship of the *iuvenes* confounds the Valerian association of the exemplary with the spectacular, the eccentric position of Scaeva in the context of the Roman culture of public display of wounds, these have already been discussed in detail. In this instance, therefore, two observations must suffice. First, the function of the constant reference to the amphitheatre is to make the young men's attitude of disengaged spectatorship accessible to the readers. When the heroic *exemplum virtutis* repeatedly becomes an animal whose destruction is paraded before the public for their entertainment, it is easier to sympathize with the audience within the text, who choose just to sit down and watch. Second, the similarities between Scaeva and Horatius Cocles should be related to those discussed later in this chapter between Murrus at 9. 828–33 and Mucius Scaevola. In both instances, we have early Roman heroes represented by Seneca as paradigms of Stoic resistance to denigration,[36] yet described through the gladiatorial analogy available only to one who has been present at (and has participated in) that same process of denigration. This point is taken up below.

MASSILIA AND THE FAMILY AUDIENCE: VERGIL AND LUCAN OPPOSED

The notion that Lucan makes accessible to his reader a mode of response to suffering akin to the sadistic disengagement of the amphitheatre is disturbing. In particular, it suggests a radical contrast to what is traditionally taken as the pathetic sensibility of Vergilian epic. This problem may be considered in greater depth.

Most's discussion of dismemberment in Neronian literature observes that Lucan takes three to four times as long as other epicists to describe individual wounds while showing markedly little interest in

[34] Cf. Sen. *Ep.* 7. 3, 'ad ictum totis corporibus expositi numquam frustra manum mittunt'.

[35] This and similar episodes are excellently discussed in Coleman (1990).

[36] For Horatius Cocles, see Sen. *Ep.* 120. 7. For Mucius Scaevola see below, pp. 279–82.

the mental suffering of the victim.[37] This distinction should be compared to that made by Williams, who traces 'the exploitation of cruelty and physical suffering as a sort of fantasy theme' back to Ovid, but insists on treating Vergil as different. Quoting the splitting of the head at *Aen.* 9. 749–55 and the terror it causes among the Trojans, he defines Vergil's perspective as follows: 'The physical details are objective, unemotional, and restricted to a minimum. The poet is the recorder of terrible facts that must be told. When emotion is an ingredient of such scenes in Virgil, it is projected on the victim in pity and remembrance.'[38]

What is implicit in Most and explicit in Williams is the dissociation of the *Aeneid* from the guilty voyeurism of Neronian verse. There are dangers in this procedure. It is particularly important to be careful not to describe Vergil in Williams' terms either for the sake of a comfortable opposition with which to structure our thought, or because we too badly want Vergil to be like what we take to be 'our aesthetic'. This point should be made not just because one can, with Heuzé, trace a consistent use of gladiatorial imagery and language in the *Aeneid*, and with it the suggestion of the pleasures of his readers,[39] but also because it is in these, or similar terms, that Vergil anticipates his own poem in the preface to the third *Georgic*. Most striking here is the double role of the poet at 3. 16–22 as both ringmaster and competitor in his new Italian games:

> In medio mihi Caesar erit templumque tenebit:
> illi victor ego et Tyrio conspectus in ostro
> centum quadriiugos agitabo ad flumina currus.
> Cuncta mihi Alpheum linquens lucosque Molorchi
> cursibus et crudo decernet Graecia caestu.
> Ipse caput tonsae foliis ornatus olivae
> dona feram.

I will have Caesar at the centre and he will possess a temple: victorious and splendid in Tyrian purple, I will drive a hundred four-horse chariots by the river

[37] Most (1992) 400, 'Like Seneca, Lucan lingers on mutilation; yet it is striking that, in both authors, the mental sufferings of the physically wounded are scarcely ever mentioned. The fictional bodies are gashed; but the persons whose sufferings seem to concern these authors are not the victims, but ourselves.'

[38] G. Williams (1978) 188–9.

[39] Heuzé (1985) 178–94, 'Les Combats de l'épopée et la gladiature'. Harrison (1991) pp. xxii and xxiv sees the presence of 'Iliadic battle-description' as 'the principal barrier to modern appreciation' of the closing books of the *Aeneid*, but sees such writing, like the gladiatorial shows, as 'an appropriate form of entertainment for a military-minded people'.

for him. All of Greece will quit the Alpheus and the groves of Molorchus for me and will compete in running races and boxing with the rough [Roman] glove. I myself will bring gifts, my head decorated with leaves of shorn olive.[40]

The proem concludes in similar terms at 3. 46–8 with the promise that:

> Mox tamen ardentis accingar dicere pugnas
> Caesaris et nomen fama tot ferre per annos,
> Tithoni prima quot abest ab origine Caesar.

Yet soon I shall gird myself to tell of burning battles and in fame to carry the name of Caesar through as many years as separate Caesar from the birth of Tithonus.

It is therefore evident that an analogy is being drawn between the Italian games and epic. Vergil will both compete, challenging the poets of Greece—that is, square off in the ring with Callimachus *et al.*—and be the ringmaster for the bouts of Turnus and Aeneas.

In short, Vergil the ringmaster recalls the euergetist emperor and suggests that he is advertising a very imperial poetics. And every emperor knows that his games appeal not just for their pathos, but also for their 'spectacles' (θεάματα) and 'wonders' (θαύματα). It is not possible to exclude sadistic or voyeuristic elements in the reading of the *Aeneid*.

Vergil's advertisement for an epic in the proem to *Georgic* 3 should encourage a certain critical self-consciousness. Yet it may still be observed that what makes the *Aeneid* so distinctively different from the *Augustiad* there anticipated is the nature of the pathos which characterizes the work as a whole and particularly the battle narratives. Two of the passages from the close of the *Aeneid* in which the amphitheatre is suggested will both illustrate the poet's concerns and reveal the distance at which he stands from Lucan. The first is at *Aen.* 10. 441–3, where it is Turnus who first conditions his fight with Pallas as single combat, and then openly describes it in gladiatorial terms:

> 'Tempus desistere pugnae;
> solus ego in Pallanta feror, soli mihi Pallas
> debetur; cuperem ipse parens *spectator* adesset.'

'It is time to quit the fight; I alone am borne against Pallas, Pallas is owed to me alone; I might only wish his father himself were here to watch.'

[40] Note that Vergil's dress in these lines anticipates that of Aeneas at *Aen.* 5. 774. For a discussion of the proem to *Georgic* 3 as a programme for the *Aeneid*, see R. F. Thomas (1986).

The most recent commentator on this scene notes the desire of Turnus to treat Evander as a spectator at the amphitheatre and appends some useful remarks on the death of sons before fathers as a thing of horror in ancient literature.[41] In Vergil, it is the character who suggests the image, one which is all the more moving first because the dying gladiator is not a worthless person or feared criminal but the beloved lieutenant of Aeneas and tragic débutant;[42] and second because the narration of his duel with Turnus will be given from his perspective.[43] In other words, Turnus can regard the death of Pallas with the satisfaction of the gladiatorial audience, but the effect of his words is to measure the distance between his emotional reaction and that of the reader. Thus, when the sense of the gladiatorial duel returns in the hunting of Turnus by Aeneas in Book 12,[44] the action is seen largely from the point of view of the Italians[45] or of Turnus himself.[46]

In Vergil, the gladiatorial theme is introduced subject to different mediating character-perspectives and speeches. In Lucan, the reader is faced with a different technique. When, in the middle of the naval battle, the narrator comments that, 3. 633–4:

> Multaque ponto
> praebuit ille dies *varii miracula fati*.

And that day gave the sea many wondrous and varied deaths.

he suggests to the reader one way to approach the subsequent narrative: that is, with an eye to the freakish rather than the pathetic, and this in the same terms as Corydon used to describe his reaction to the amphitheatre. Hunink remarks on the degree to which *varii miracula fati* summarizes the concerns of the poet in this episode and offers as parallels, 3. 652–3, 'Then was seen a unique form of dire death' (*Tunc unica diri* | *conspecta est leti facies*), as well as 9. 736, 'unusual deaths'

41 Harrison (1991) ad loc. One might add two striking parallels: Livy, 2. 5. 5 for Brutus ('et qui spectator erat amovendus, eum ipsum fortuna exactorem supplicii dedit') and Sen., *Ira* 3. 14. 3 for the father who praised the accuracy of Gaius in shooting his son ('eius rei laudator fuit, cuius nimis erat spectatorem fuisse') exploit the presumption of horror in such a spectacle in order to overbid it.

42 See the discussion of the Belt of Pallas in the last chapter of Conte (1986), and the useful comments in Putnam (1987) 792. See also Fowler (1987).

43 For the point of view in Vergilian duels always being that of the victim, see ch. 1 of Bonfanti (1985).

44 See the excellent discussion of this passage at Hardie (1986) 151–4.

45 See the discussion of the simile of the farmers facing a storm in G. Williams (1983) 166–8 and in Lyne (1987) 5–8.

46 See the discussion of the reworking of the Hom. *Il.* 22 dream-simile to emphasize the plight of the pursued at G. Williams (1983) 172–3.

(*insolitas . . . mortes*) and 9. 805, 'spectacles' (*spectacula*).[47] The parallels to the snakes episode are investigated further later in this chapter; that in Book 3 might be put alongside the paradoxical 3. 680–1:

> Nulla tamen plures hoc edidit aequore clades
> quam pelago diversa lues.

Yet on this sea no mode of destruction slaughtered more men than that element which is enemy to the deep.

and the emphasis on multiplicity at 3. 689–90:

> Mille modos inter leti mors una timori est
> qua coepere mori.

Among the thousand ways to die the only one they fear is that by which they begin to die.

Lucan seems to be parading a certain strategy in describing this battle and to be inviting his audience to read or to watch with the same amazed and amused perspective. The reader sees 'dire death' (*dirum . . . letum*), but she sees only the 'surface' (*facies*), is not emotionally involved with the pathos of the victims' experiences.

Models for watching are often of the essence in ancient descriptions of the departure of a naval expedition or of a naval battle. The narrative habitually records the reaction of the crowds gathered to watch the ships leave the harbour or following the battle from the shore.[48] These descriptions offer the hopes and fears of those who love the combatants, thus giving a view of the world left behind, the world typically evoked in a Homeric or Vergilian battle obituary.[49] Further, this is exactly the technique employed in Caesar's account of the

[47] Hunink (1992) ad loc., who says of 'varii miracula fati' that it is 'a remarkable phrase revealing the main interest of the poet in these horrific scenes of violence and death'.

[48] The most famous examples are the description of the departure of the Sicilian expedition at Thuc. 6. 30–2 and of the naval battle off Syracuse at Thuc. 7. 70–1. Thuc. is described at Dion. Hal. *De Imit.* 2. 3. 425 as supreme ἐν τοῖς παθητικοῖς. Note also that Isoc. *Paneg.* 97 declines to use all the pathetic devices conventional to the description of a sea battle. This might be compared to Livy and the description of the departure of Scipio from Sicily at Livy, 29. 26. 1 ('Multae classes Romanae e Sicilia atque ipso illo portu profectae erant; ceterum non eo bello solum—nec id mirum; praedatum enim tantummodo pleraeque classes ierant—sed ne priore quidem ulla profectio tanti *spectaculi* fuit') and at Livy, 29. 26. 7–8 ('Concurrebat ad *spectaculum* in portum omnis turba non habitantium modo Lilybaei sed legationum omnium ex Sicilia quae et ad prosequendum Scipionem officii causa convenerant et praetorem provinciae M. Pomponium secutae fuerant; ad hoc legiones quae in Sicilia relinquebantur ad prosequendos commilitones processerant; nec classis modo prospectantibus e terra, sed terra etiam omnis circa referta turba *spectaculo* navigantibus erat').

[49] See J. Griffin (1980) 103–43 and (1985) 163–82.

Massilia sea battle, first before the battle,[50] then during the action,[51] finally at its close, as the news of the disaster is received.[52] It is the equivalent of the tragic historical topos of the women, children, and old as audience on the walls of a city as it is sacked or a battle is fought at the gates for its survival.[53] In Lucan, however, the perspective of the watchers on the shore is decidedly marginalized and makes a pointedly late appearance, one which is unmistakably different from the tone of the preceding narrative, 3. 756–62:

> Quis in urbe parentum
> fletus erat, quanti matrum per litora planctus!
> Coniunx saepe sui confusis voltibus unda
> credidit ora viri Romanum amplexa cadaver,
> accensisque rogis miseri de corpore trunco
> certavere patres. At Brutus in aequore victor
> primus Caesareis pelagi decus addidit armis.

How the fathers in the city wept! How the mothers lamented along the shore! Features were so disfigured by the water that often a wife embraced the corpse of a Roman and thought it the face of her husband. And when the pyres were lit, wretched fathers wrestled over a headless body. Yet out at sea the victorious Brutus was the first to add the glory of a naval battle to the military achievements of Caesar.

[50] Caes. *B. Civ.* 2. 4. 3: 'Tali modo instructa classe omnium seniorum, matrum familiae, virginum precibus et fletu excitati, extremo tempore civitati subvenirent, non minore animo ac fiducia quam ante dimicaverant navis conscendunt.'

[51] Ibid. 2. 5. 3: 'Facile erat ex castris C. Treboni atque omnibus superioribus locis prospicere in urbem, ut omnis iuventus, quae in oppido remanserat, omnesque superioris aetatis cum liberis atque uxoribus ex publicis locis custodiisque aut e muro ad caelum manus tenderent, aut templa deorum immortalium adirent et ante simulacra proiecti victoriam ab diis exposcerent. Neque erat quisquam omnium, quin in eius diei casu suarum omnium fortunarum eventum consistere existimaret. Nam et honesti ex iuventute et cuiusque aetatis amplissimi nominatim evocati atque obsecrati naves conscenderant, ut, si quid adversi accidisset, ne ad conandum quidem sibi quicquam reliqui fore viderent; si superavissent, vel domesticis opibus vel externis auxiliis de salute urbis confiderent.' Cf. 2. 6. 1 for the desperate *virtus* of Massilians who fight 'memores eorum praeceptorum, quae paulo ante ab suis acceperant', and 2. 7. 1 for the ships of Nasidius: 'Sed Nasidianae naves nullo usui fuerunt celeriterque pugna excesserunt; *non enim has aut conspectus patriae aut propinquorum praecepta* ad extremum vitae periculum adire cogebant'.

[52] Ibid. 2. 7. 3: 'At ex reliquis una praemissa Massiliam huius nunti perferendi gratia cum iam appropinquaret urbi, omnis sese multitudo *ad cognoscendum* effudit, et re cognita tantus luctus excepit, ut urbs ab hostibus capta eodem vestigio videretur.'

[53] For this topos in tragic history, see pp. 36–9. This sort of audience is apparent at Livy, 1. 25. 1–2, 5. 42. 4–6, 7. 11. 6, 7. 30. 21–3. It is perhaps typical of Lucan that it features only at 1. 481–4, where it is anticipated in rumour and at 7. 369–76, where Pompey employs it as a rhetorical figure for his men to imagine. For more on this theme, see Borzsák (1973).

The lamentation of the parents here might be compared to two instances of the actual battle narrative in which Lucan reworks traditional themes relating to fathers and sons in battle. Both scenes are marked by a chilling of the reader's emotional relationship to the victims, though these effects are achieved in different ways.

The first scene to be considered, the episode of the twins at 3. 603–34, has been excellently analysed by Metger,[54] who identifies a series of significant changes from the scene's model at *Aen.* 10. 390–2. Metger's first observation is that Vergil, unlike Lucan, names and apostrophizes his twins, creating an emotional engagement only heightened by their triple description as 'children most like each other . . . indistinguishable to their family . . . a happy source of error for their parents' (*simillima proles, indiscreta suis gratusque parentibus error*). The last offers a sentimentally charged oxymoron,[55] which contrasts strongly with the evocation of the violation wrought by Pallas, soon himself to be a victim, in the phrase 'harsh distinctions' (*dura discrimina*).[56] By contrast, Lucan's 'glory of a fertile mother' (*fecundae gloria matris*) does not express the tender joy of indistinguishability, and 'savage death distinguished the men' (*discrevit mors saeva viros*) has a decidedly brutal ring.[57] Further, Lucan's 'when the error was removed' (*sublato errore*), while finally introducing the theme of indistinguishability, does so in a very new way. Instead of both brothers bearing injuries, both being victims, the one, by surviving, becomes the 'cause of endless tears' (*aeternis causam lacrimis*) in that he offers the picture of his 'better' and now dead twin, 3. 607–8:

Tenet ille dolorem
semper et amissum fratrem lugentibus offert.

He keeps their grief ever alive and shows the mourners the image of his lost brother.

Finally, Metger observes that the killing of the victim twins by victim Pallas, the mourning of two sets of parents, sets up an emotional continuum in the reader's response to Vergilian battle. In the Lucanian re-formation, the fight to the death of the one twin is temporally and locally quite isolated from the reflections on the division of the twins.[58]

[54] Metger (1957) 48–63 = Rutz (1970*b*) 423–38.

[55] Metger describes it as 'mit einem leicht sentimentalen Anflug, das aber wohl gerade darum so eindrucksvoll wird' (Rutz, p. 424).

[56] Metger notes that this 'den Leser die Zerstörung dieses kleinen Familienidylls nachfühlen lasst' (Rutz, p. 425).

[57] Ibid. 425, 'brutal klingen'.

[58] Ibid.

It is also thirty-five lines in length, as opposed to the six lines of obituary. Where Vergil expresses the whole and single sense of his twin episode in two lines, Lucan sets up two separate passages, which close examination reveals to operate on each other rather darkly. For instance, the hero-twin is less a flower cut down at the edge of the meadow, than an example of suicidal *aristeia* in the manner of Scaeva. He assaults the enemy ship and has a hand cut off, but still independently grips the ship. Nor does the rest of the body desist from combat, but, 3. 614–16:

> Crevit in adversis *virtus*: plus nobilis *irae*
> *truncus* habet fortique instaurat proelia laeva
> rapturusque suam procumbit in aequora dextram.

Valour grew in adversity, once mutilated he had more noble anger and renewed the battle with his brave left hand and leaned down into the sea to reach for his right.

This is the typically disastrous *virtus* which one expects in Lucan, and the suicidal attitude reaches its gladiatorial acme at 3. 618–22:

> Iam clipeo telisque carens, non conditus ima
> puppe sed expositus *fraternaque pectore nudo*
> *arma tegens*, crebra confixus cuspide perstat
> telaque multorum leto casura suorum
> emerita iam morte tenet.

Bereft now of shield and weapons, he is not buried in the depths of the ship but stands his ground, exposed to the enemy, protecting his brother's arms with his naked breast and pierced by a succession of darts; and, his death already earned, he catches spears that would have fallen fatally on many of his comrades.[59]

Strange. On the one hand, the very idea of exposing oneself to all the darts of the enemy, even if heroic self-sacrifice, is a *miraculum fati* at which to marvel. It bespeaks a lunatic vigour which, however admirable, is so superhuman as to alienate the tender response felt in Vergil. Further, it is also an action that raises questions as to the other half of the pair. Roman heroes bear scars on their chests with great pride, but do not actively seek them, and wear body armour in order to avoid them. Lucan's hero-twin pursues a hypallagous relationship with his brother, his *pectus* protecting the other's armour, and the impression is of an excessive, an insane *virtus*. Further, we only now see properly

[59] For lack of armour, see above, p. 245 and n. 33.

why the other brother is a cause of tears to his parents. It is not just that his *incolumitas* is bought at the expense of his brother's life, but also that, in a family where the dead man's insane heroism is so valued, it is hard not to question exactly what the survivor was up to. If the one is crazily heroic, the other, who is willing to use his brother's body to protect his own armour, is just a little short of the desired standard.

The action of the Massilia sea battle is more bizarre than heroic, and it is natural to react to the bizarre with amazement and not sympathy. In the second example, that of the fatal wounding of the unfortunate Argus and the double suicide of his father, 3. 723–51, it is apparent from the beginning that the poet can see a comic dimension to his story. The chance success of the blinded Tyrrhenus in striking a character called Argus is amusing enough in itself. That Lucan should move so wonderfully from the figurative to the concrete in his description of the shot confirms the point. In ancient literature, Fortune often operates 'with a blind hand' (*caeca manu*); the phrase is also used for soldiers sending unseen weapons or themselves attacking randomly, but only Lucan uses it to describe the shot of a man who actually is blind and who contrives to hit someone with the same name as the hundred-eyed Argus *panoptes*.[60]

As the narrative progresses, a further degree of strangeness emerges paradoxically from the characters' heightened awareness of the constituent parts of pathos in ancient literature. Perhaps Lucan gives warning of what is to come when, at 3. 729–30, the father of Argus is described as:

Fessusque senecta
exemplum, non miles erat.

And weary with age he served as an example, not a soldier.

Scaeva is too aware of his capacity for exemplarity in his situation, and the father of Argus shares the same literary consciousness of his position. At 3. 737–40, the dying son lifts his head and urges his father to offer him the last rites:

Ille *caput labens et iam languentia colla*
viso patre levat; vox faucis nulla solutas

[60] For Argus *panoptes*, see Wernicke at *RE* ii. 1. 791–5; Fortune is blind at Pac. tr. 366 (Ribbeck), Cic. *Phil.* 13. 10, Ov. *Pont.* 4. 8. 16, Sen. *Phoen.* 632, and acts *caeca manu* at Sen. *Phaed.* 980 and Stat. *Silv.* 2. 6. 8–9; arms are sent *caeca manu* from an unseen hand at Sil. *Pun.* 10. 235–6, and seized at random *caeca manu* at Val. Flacc. *Arg.* 3. 79; attacks are made thus at Claud. *Carm. Min.* 53. 110 (Hall).

> prosequitur, tacito tantum petit oscula voltu
> invitatque patris claudenda ad lumina dextram.

At the sight of his father he lifts his lolling head and his now languishing neck; no words follow when he opens his mouth, he just asks for a kiss with silent facial expression and requests his father's right hand to close his eyes.

A Roman wishes for a family member to be by his side as he dies, to be there with the dying.[61] One thinks of Anna's lament at being apart from the death of her sister, of the bedside retinue enjoyed by the philosophical Cato, Atticus, and Thrasea. It is important to consider this general context when noting that 3. 737 recalls in particular Vergil's description of the death of Euryalus at *Aen.* 9. 434–6:

> Purpureus veluti cum flos succisus aratro
> *languescit* moriens, lassove papavera *collo*
> demisere *caput* pluvia cum forte gravantur.

Just as when a purple flower cut by the plough languishes in death, or poppies with weary neck bend down their heads when the rain weighs heavy on them.

At *Aen.* 9. 444–5, Nisus joins Euryalus and they are not separated in death. On the other hand, the horror of a father outliving his children expressed in the *Aeneid* by Evander and Mezentius is a familiar commonplace in ancient literature.[62] In short, Lucan presents the conflict of two obligations, each supported by *exempla*. The son is already fatally wounded, yearns not to die alone, but the father is still convinced that he must act to avoid being the exemplary unhappy father, the one who outlives his son. Lucan has overloaded his scene with pathetic commonplaces but the effect is not to heighten the emotional impact on the reader. The account of the father's speech and of his suicide is absurd, but it typifies the satirical genius which Lucan brings to Roman epic, 3. 742–51:

[61] At Luc. 5. 280–2, among the requests the mutinous soldiers will make is not to 'atque oculos morti clausuram quaerere dextram', and to 'coniugis inlabi lacrimis, unique paratum | scire rogum'. For other instances of this theme, cf. Stat. *Theb.* 2. 629–43; Sil. *Pun.* 9. 141–3, 149–51; Val. Flacc. *Arg.* 1. 333–4, 3. 278–9.

[62] At Verg. *Aen.* 8. 572–83, Evander prays either to see Pallas alive again or to die before he does, and at 11. 158–61 asserts that he has lived too long: '"Tuque, o sanctissima coniunx, | felix morte tua neque in hunc servata dolorem! | Contra ego vivendo vici mea fata, superstes | restarem ut genitor."' Similarly, at 10. 846–56, Mezentius speaks of the horror of outliving his son; note esp. 855–6: '"Nunc vivo neque adhuc homines lucemque relinquo. | Sed linquam"'. Cf. 10. 861–2 to his horse: '"Rhaebe, diu, res si qua diu mortalibus ulla est, | viximus"'. Harrison (1991) at *Aen.* 10. 441–3 cites the comments of Solon to Croesus in Herodotus and makes some useful points. For parallels in later Latin epic, see Stat. *Theb.* 8. 113; Val. Flacc. *Arg.* 1. 323–7, 1. 344., 1. 457–60. See also Eur. *Alc.* 939–40, and Lattimore (1962) 187–91. Lattimore sees this theme as typical of the Roman sensibility.

'Non perdam tempora' dixit
'a saevis permissa deis, iugulumque senilem
confodiam. Veniam misero concede parenti,
Arge, quod amplexus, extrema quod oscula fugi.
Nondum destituit calidus tua volnera sanguis,
semianimisque iaces et *adhuc potes esse superstes*.'
Sic fatus, quamvis capulum per viscera missi
polluerit gladii, tamen alta sub aequora tendit
praecipiti saltu: *letum praecedere nati*
festinantem animam morti non credidit uni.

'I shall not waste the time,' said he, 'granted by the savage gods and shall cut my aged throat. Pardon your poor father, Argus, if I flee your embrace, if I flee the final kiss. The hot blood has not yet quit your wounds, you lie half-conscious and can still outlive me.' So he spoke and, though he polluted the hilt of the sword he thrust through his guts, he still jumped into the deep sea with a headlong leap: he did not entrust to just one death a soul hastening to precede the extinction of his son.

It is now clear how far we are from the pathos characteristic of Homeric and Vergilian epic. Past literature provides a series of related scenes which both reflect and structure the pathetic sensibility of the reader. A literary father outliving his son is not just the lamenting father familiar from Roman epitaphs, but also an Evander, a Mezentius. And yet, in Lucan, it is that heightened consciousness of literary precedent which now creates a rigid system of obligation for the father. In every sense it is too late for the 'unhappy father of Argus' (*infelix Argi genitor*) to be happy, but it is not too late for him to avoid becoming the unhappy father of literature. Where Evander laments at *Aen.* 11. 160–1 that:

'Ego vivendo vici mea fata, *superstes*
restarem ut genitor.'

'I have lived beyond my destiny, that I might remain a father who survived his son.'

the father of Argus leaps to his death, because thus 'you can still survive me' (*adhuc potes esse superstes*). The reader, in turn, faced with the task of unravelling the basis of the obligations, of reconstructing the model, is denied the simple sympathy felt with a Priam or an Evander.

Lucan engages with the pathetic devices of epic but only in a manner which subverts his inheritance. The attitudes of the twins, of their parents, of Argus and his father, defy the engagement of the reader trained to the traditional emotional reactions of epic, of tragic history. The signal marginalization of the conventional watchers on the shore at 3. 756–62 helps measure the distance at which Lucan's poetry stands from the old presumption that the sorrow of relatives is emotionally accessible to the reader. While this presumption underpins the pathetic impact of almost every Homeric and Vergilian battle obituary, here it finds itself in competition with a second perspective, one which emphasizes the viewing of *varii miracula fati*.

The importance of *miracula fati* is recognized in German criticism of this episode. Metger observes the transformation of the Acilius story which underlies the account of the twins, the movement from an *exemplum virtutis* requiring emulation to a narrative of freakish death, while Opelt emphasizes the abandonment of narrative progression in favour of an extended description of the bizarre and the unusual.[63] As with much post-war German criticism, Opelt is too quick to resort to the simplistic concept of *Steigerung des Pathos*, but her study contains a number of other observations of great significance.[64] Of these the most significant is the suggestion later in the discussion that the scene described is in some way inspired by the experience of attending an imperial *naumachia*.[65] This idea has lately been endorsed by Newman

[63] Metger (1957) 63 = Rutz (1970*b*) 438, 'Diese Episode galt in den Prosaberichten [*viz.* in the Acilius model] als ein *exemplum fortitudinis*, ein Beispiel einzigartiger Tapferkeit, das verdient, der Nachwelt erhalten zu bleiben, und gleichzeitig ein Ansporn zu ähnlichen Leistungen sein soll.' Cf. ibid.: 'Statt eines solchen *exemplum fortitudinis* sieht Lucan sie als ein *miraculum fati* (634). *Nichts mehr von nachahmenswerter Tapferkeit, nur noch ein seltsames Todesschicksal*'. For Acilius, cf. Val. Max. 3. 2. 22 and Suet. *Jul.* 68. 4. Cf. Opelt (1957) 437, 'Seine Darstellung ist eine Beschreibung, keine Erzählung im Sinne der HEINZEschen Unterscheidung (VET p. 396), d.h. die Vorgänge stehen nebeneinander, der Akzent der Gestaltung liegt nicht auf dem zeitlichen Ablauf, sondern auf der Modalität des Geschehens.'

[64] See ibid. 443–4: 'Das Hauptanliegen ist das der Steigerung des Pathos. Dies wird durch die Auswahl der Einzelszenen erreicht. Das Aussergewöhnliche wechselt mit dem Einmaligen, und auch die Grausigkeit des allgemeinen Schlachtgeschehens, in das die Einzelszenen eingebettet sind, *strebt in einer ansteigenden Kurve immer neuen Höhepunkten zu*.' The passages to which Opelt is referring are 634 ('varii miracula fati'), 641–2 ('nullius vita perempti | est tanta dimissa via'), 652–3 ('unica diri | conspecta est leti facies'), 696–7. ('Pugna fuit unus in illa | eximius Phoceus'). Perhaps the best statement of the Massilia sensibility is at 444: 'Der Kampf ist für Lucan das Erleiden aussergewöhnlichen Todes . . . Dies ist ganz unvergilisch; denn Vergil "vermeidet" nach Heinze "komplizierte Verwundungen und beschränkt sich auf das Einfache, Nächstliegende". Ovid hat jedoch Vergleichbares.'

[65] Ibid. 443, 'Der Geschmack dafür und das Interesse des Publikums mag durch die Naumachiae des Zirkus geweckt gewesen sein. Lucan selbst dürfte die beiden Seegefechte, die Nero 57 oder 58 und 64 veranstalten liess, gesehen haben.'

and by Hunink,[66] and, any general impression apart, is strongly supported by the description at 3. 513 of the joining of the Roman ships as 'a stable field for naval warfare' (*stabilis navalibus area bellis*).

There is agreement as to the effect which the *naumachia* might have had on Lucan's imagination, an effect which it is not hard to conceive when one considers the enormity of the spectacles attested in the sources.[67] On the other hand, none of Lucan's critics has as yet brought together the notion of the *naumachia* firing Lucan's imagination with the agreedly metaliterary markers such as *varii miracula fati*. A rather crude consensus therefore arises in which all imagine Lucan going to Lake Fucino as a boy of 13, or as an adult to a Neronian *naumachia*, getting excited by what he sees, and reproducing it, with a fleeting statement of his interests, on the printed page. What none of Lucan's critics offers is any discussion of the function of the metaliterary markers to distinguish the body of the narrative from the model of sympathetic watching which he largely pushes aside until the very close. While something is said of the mentality of the poet, nothing is said as to the mode of reaction he offers to his readers.

The final appearance of sympathetic watching has the effect of parading the ethical conflict as to the rights and wrongs of two different responses to human suffering. The juxtaposition of two modes of watching disrupts any sympathetic emotional continuum in the description of battle. Any complacent Vergilianism takes a jolt. In short, do we always react to death in battle with sorrow, or do we, as Harrison would have it, regard martial epic as 'an appropriate form of entertainment for a military-minded people'?[68] The answer, one suspects, lies in an uncomfortable combination of the two.

[66] Newman (1986) 211–12 cf. Hunink (1992) 201, 'In the individual scenes, Lucan often seems to have invented new themes, though often echoes of literary models may be detected here as well. It is tempting to speculate about the literary source of Lucan's ideas. It does not seem unnatural to suppose that theatrical performances influenced his fantasy. Since 46 BC several "naumachiae" had been performed in or near Rome, one or possibly two of them during the reign of Nero.'

[67] The following catalogue of *naumachiae* is based on Coleman (1990): (i) Julius Caesar, 46 BC, 4,000 oarsmen and 2,000 soldiers play 'Tyrians' vs. 'Egyptians,' Suet. *Jul.* 39. 4 and App. *B. Civ.* 2. 102; (ii) Augustus, 2 BC, 3,000 soldiers in battle of 'Athenians' vs. 'Persians', *Res Gestae* 23 and Dio Cass. 55. 10. 7; (iii) Claudius, AD 52, 19,000 soldiers play 'Sicilians' vs. 'Rhodians' on Fucine Lake, Suet. *Claud.* 21, Tac. *Ann.* 12. 56 and Dio 60. 33. 3; (iv) Nero, 'Athenians' vs. 'Persians,' Dio Cass. 61. 9. 5 and 62. 15 cf. Suet. *Ner.* 12. 1; (v) Titus, 'Corcyreans' vs. 'Corinthians,' Dio Cass. 66. 25. 3, and 3,000 combatants for 'Athenians' vs. 'Syracusans', Dio Cass. 66. 25. 4; (vi) Domitian has almost everyone die in an exhibition recorded at Dio Cass. 67. 8. 2. Sextus Pompeius is also reported at Dio Cass. 48. 19. 1 to have held a *naumachia* off Rhegium in 40 BC.

[68] Harrison (1991) p. xxiv.

VULTEIUS: THE THEATRE OF SUICIDE

The combination of the exemplary and the spectacular in the mass suicide of the crew of Vulteius in Book 4 of the *Pharsalia* has already been noted in Chapter 5.[69] At the same time, it is important to assert that Vulteius' determination that the suicide should be carried out in the light of day—a determination expressed with all the key words in place[70]—carries with it the desire for the theatrical. While no one has yet suggested that there is a *naumachia* element in this,[71] the sense of the theatre has some place in a recently published study of Vulteius, Saylor's *Lux Extrema.*[72] This study observes that 'the suicide is bright, conspicuous, visible to all',[73] places great emphasis on the ostentation of the Opitergini, and notes 'the use of topography as a theatre and of rafts as a stage'.[74]

Trapped on the sea, the Opitergini are in a form of natural theatre,[75] and, though they could die fighting, they seem determined to condition their assailants as a passive audience. In his initial exhortation to his men, for instance, Vulteius bemoans the want of theatre in a conventional battle situation, 4. 488–91:

> 'Non tamen in caeca bellorum nube cadendum est
> aut cum permixtas acies sua tela tenebris
> involvent. Conferta iacent cum corpora campo,
> in medium mors omnis abit, perit obruta virtus.'

'Yet it is not necessary to die in the blind cloud of war or when their own arms shroud the commingled armies in darkness. When the bodies lie thick upon the field, each death becomes part of the mass, valour is buried and goes to waste.'

These are the crucial lines. They illustrate perfectly the impossibility of separating the exemplary from the amphitheatrical, and they operate a succession of complex combinatorial allusions. The episode works on at least the following two levels.

[69] See Ch. 5, pp. 182–3.

[70] e.g. Luc. 4. 495 'spectabunt' cf. 4. 569 'spectare' cf. 4. 572 'ducibus mirantibus'.

[71] Except perhaps Hardie (1992) 53–4, who observes that 'The "virtuous" self-sacrifice of Vulteius and his men before the wondering eyes of the Pompeian spectators forms a "gladiatorial" pair with the final episode of the book, the "sacrifice" to the African ghosts of Curio and his men.'

[72] Saylor (1990). Heyke (1970) 149 quotes 4. 493–5 and talks of the transformation of the landscape to 'ein hervorragender Zuschauerraum'.

[73] Saylor (1990) 297.

[74] Ibid. 298.

[75] Luc. 4. 492–5, '"Nos in conspicua sociis hostique carina | constituere dei; praebebunt aequora testes, | praebebunt terrae, summis dabit insula saxis, | spectabunt geminae diverso litore partes."'

(i) This episode contains all the elements of a *naumachia* except one. Massilia at least has two sides fighting; this is stylized shipboard slaughter under the gaze of an audience, but it is also a suicide. When one considers the situation of the condemned men fighting in the *naumachia*, the distinction between suicide and battle is, however, rather less clear-cut. Further, we are surely compelled to bring this event into comparison with an episode from a contemporary *naumachia* made famous by Lucan's uncle Seneca, *Ep.* 70. 25–6, in which the spectacularity of the noble suicide of a prisoner participating in a mock sea battle allows all to see the superiority of death to killing:

> Ex eodem tibi *munere* plura *exempla* promisi. Secundo naumachiae *spectaculo* unus e barbaris lanceam quam in adversarios acceperat totam iugulo suo mersit. 'Quare, quare' inquit 'non omne tormentum, omne ludibrium iamdudum effugio? Quare ego mortem armatus expecto?' *Tanto hoc speciosius spectaculum fuit quanto honestius mori discunt homines quam occidere.*
>
> I have promised you more examples from the same games. In the second spectacle [show] of the sea battle, one of the barbarians buried in his own throat the full length of the lance which he had been given to use against his adversaries. 'Why, why,' said he, 'have I for so long not fled every torture, every insult? Why when I am armed do I wait for death?' This show was all the more glorious for the fact that men learn from it that it is better to die than to kill.

Once again, the situation is one where the categories of exemplarity and amphitheatricality are not discrete. This passage is an important resource for anyone wishing to rebut the conventional wisdom that gladiators were simple non-persons, the only lamentable aspect of whose suffering lay in the possibility of their innocence and in the harmful effect on the audience of watching. Instead, the barbarian prisoner's response to his Roman masters is an *exemplum* to a Roman audience of the superiority of dying over killing, Seneca's anecdote in part functioning as a Stoic cosmopolitan critique of his country's racism and of its affected unconcern for the fate or worth of the gladiator.[76] Lucan, however, reforms this story and its interpretation in two significant ways. On the one hand, Vulteius, though he might not have chosen to be trapped where and how he is, can be shown to maximize the amphitheatricality of his own death. He is thus complicit

[76] For a *barbarus* to give lessons on how to live as a *homo* recalls the horror felt at Sen. *Ep.* 95. 33 that 'Homo, sacra res homini, iam per lusum ac iocum occiditur'. It is a characteristic of Seneca's dialogues that, the greater his disillusionment with the Roman State, the more he should appeal to the second *res publica* of which we are all members—see Sen. *Ot.* 4. 1–2, 6. 4, *Vit. Beat.* 20. 3, 24. 3, *Tranq.* 1. 10, 4. 3–4.

with the pleasures of his audience in a way that Seneca's *barbarus* is not. Further, Lucan's narrative is surely an unmasking of the latent dissidence in Seneca's story. Vulteius, like Scaeva, is conscious of his own potential for exemplarity, and sees the suicide as a model of loyalty to one's general, 4. 496–9:

> 'Nescio quod nostris magnum et memorabile fatis
> *exemplum*, Fortuna, paras. Quaecumque per aevum
> exhibuit *monimenta* fides servataque ferro
> militiae pietas, transisset nostra iuventus.'

'Fortune, you are preparing some great and memorable example by our death. Whatever records loyalty and military duty preserved by the sword have left through time, our youthful band would have surpassed them.'

Vulteius serves under Caesar, is devoted to Caesar. By contrast, Seneca's barbarian obviously finds himself in the centre of Caesar's games, and refuses to endure the torture and insult of such an experience. In other words, it is his attitude and not that of Vulteius, which is most obviously endorsed as Lucan offers his own alternative interpretation of the exemplarity of Vulteius at 4. 573–81:

> Nullam maiore locuta est
> ore ratem totum discurrens Fama per orbem.
> Non tamen ignavae post haec *exempla* virorum
> percipient gentes quam sit non ardua virtus
> servitium fugisse manu, sed regna timentur
> ob ferrum et saevis libertas uritur armis,
> ignorantque datos, ne quisquam serviat, enses.
> Mors, utinam pavidos vitae subducere nolles,
> sed virtus te sola daret.

Fame running through all the world has spoken of no ship with louder voice. Yet even after the example set by these men, craven races will not perceive how little valour is required to escape slavery by suicide, but the sword of the monarch is feared and liberty is oppressed by savage arms, and they do not realise that they have been given swords that no man may be a slave. Death, would that you refused to kill the cowardly and that you were the gift of valour alone.

(ii) The Vulteius scene does more than extract an *exemplum* true to its model in *Ep.* 70 but alien to the loyalties which the Opitergini think they are expressing. The episode contains a supplementary irrationality which invites the reader to view it as the very amphitheatrical spectacle which Seneca's slave sought to escape. This can be illustrated with regard to the very paradoxical lines 4. 488–91 with which we began.

At 4. 488–91, Vulteius praises death in his sea-borne natural amphitheatre in terms which are normally employed for death on land by those facing extinction in a storm at sea. The paradoxicality of his claim starts to become clear if it is compared to the words of the messenger at Sen. *Ag.* 514–19 as he describes the great storm and evokes the emotions of the Greeks:

> Quisquis ad Troiam iacet
> felix vocatur, cadere qui meruit gradu,
> quem fama servat, victa quem tellus tegit.
> 'Nil nobile ausos pontus atque undae ferent?
> Ignava fortes fata consument viros?
> *Perdenda mors est*?'

All those who died at Troy are called fortunate, those who earned the right to fall where they stood, whom fame preserves, whom the conquered earth covers. 'Will the sea and the waves carry us off who have dared no noble deed? Will spiritless deaths destroy courageous men? Must our death go to waste?'

Here, on one level, Lucan's *perire* and Seneca's *perdere* express the same idea. Yet the latter's sense of the waste of a death met at sea is the conventional wisdom of antiquity, and the *μακαρισμός* of the dead of Troy alludes to the famous words of despair of the storm-tossed heroes at Hom. *Od.* 5. 306–7 and Verg. *Aen.* 1. 94–101.[77]

However, the element of the *spectaculum* in the Vulteius episode should remind us of another passage of Seneca, which, on one crucial level, is closer to the spirit of the actions of the Opitergini. For the fear expressed in *Ag.* 519 'Must our death go to waste?' (*Perdenda mors est?*) is that of a death wasted because not endured while slaying the enemy on the field of battle. As such, it is very similar to *Pharsalia* 3. 706–7, and the mentality of the dying sailors at Massilia, all determined to fight to the last:

> Non perdere letum
> maxima cura fuit.

Their greatest concern was not to waste their deaths.[78]

[77] Cf. also Ov. *Fast.* 3. 597–8: 'Tum primum Dido felix est dicta sorori | et quaecumque aliquam corpore pressit humum'.

[78] This is also the sense of Sen. *Her. O.* 1175–6, 'Pro cuncta tellus, Herculis vestri placet | mortem perire?' The text 'mortem perire' is defended at Housman (1923) 163. For a similar problem, cf. Ker (1953) 177 defending 'perdere mortes' at Stat. *Theb.* 9. 58.

On the other hand, the point of *Pharsalia* 4. 491, 'each death becomes part of the mass, valour is buried and goes to waste' (*in medium mors omnis abit, perit obruta virtus*), is that one's death, one's heroism, is wasted if unseen. This is an expression of the Senecan idea of *theatrum mundi*, of the morality play performed for the gods by Cato at *Prov.* 2. 7–9, discussed in Chapter 3,[79] of the 'Stoic athleticism' and 'self-dramatisation' discussed by Rosenmeyer.[80] Senecan tragic heroes revel in their metatheatrical pursuit of an audience for their deeds from within the characters of the drama. Crucial here is the resolution of Medea at Sen. *Med.* 976–7:

Non in occulto tibi est
perdenda virtus; approba populo manum.

You must not waste your valour in some hidden corner: commend your hand to the audience.[81]

and her reaction to the arrival of Jason at 991–4:

Voluptas magna me invitam subit,
et ecce crescit. Derat hoc unum mihi,
spectator iste. Nil adhuc facti reor:
quidquid sine isto fecimus sceleris perit.

Great pleasure enters me however reluctant and, look, it rises. I lacked only one thing: him as a spectator. Nothing, I deem, has been achieved hitherto: whatever crime I committed without him went to waste.

Medea's function as an intertext for Vulteius is to highlight the uncomfortable element in his action: the obsession with an audience. When Medea tells herself, 'commend your hand to the audience' (*approba populo manum*), she sees herself as the gladiator showing off his *virtus* to please the audience. Yet, since her *virtus* expresses itself in the vicious killing of her children, she can only be speaking in irony. With Vulteius, the case is less clear-cut. His crew's actions are not criminal, they can even serve as an *exemplum* of Stoic suicide as resistance to tyranny, but they carry with them some uncomfortable extra baggage. The heroes of the *Agamemnon*, like the sailors off Massilia, feared that they would lose their deaths by not dying in battle. Vulteius and his men do not face this problem. They have every opportunity to

[79] See above, pp. 94–6.
[80] Rosenmeyer (1989) ch. 3, 'Truth, Speech, Posture', 37–62.
[81] The athletic ring of 'approba populo manum' is striking. *Approbare* is used very similarly at Stat. *Silv.* 2. 6. 46–7, 'teneri sic integer aevi | Elin adit primosque Iovi puer adprobat annos'.

die fighting the enemy, but instead choose suddenly to turn away fro their opponents and on themselves. Thus, at 4. 533–40, the *devo iuventus* first resist the enemy, but then turn away from battle an *perdere letum* by their refusal to compensate with the death of as man of the enemy as possible:

> Stabat devota iuventus
> damnata iam luce ferox securaque pugnae
> promisso sibi fine manu, nullique tumultus
> excussere viris mentes ad summa paratas;
> innumerasque simul pauci terraque marique
> sustinuere manus: tanta est fiducia mortis.
> Utque satis bello visum est fluxisse cruoris
> versus ab hoste furor.

The doomed band of young men stood, ferocious now that they had rejecte life and unconcerned at the battle because sure of the death they had promise themselves by their own hands, nor could any uproar distract the minds of me set on finality; and few in number they resisted innumerable opponents fror sea and land at once: so great is the certainty of death. And when it seemed tha enough blood had been spilt in the fight, they turned their madness from th foe.

This suicide is carried out 'to the wonderment of the commander (*ducibus mirantibus*). And well they may wonder. The suicide is bemus ing because it is less a necessary resistance to oppression than th expression of a theatrical aesthetic, the fear of wasting a truly dramati magnificently staged ending. Their opponents may now only *mirar* for they are denied any role save that of audience. Bemusement ma turn into the spectator's appreciation of θαῦμα. And the reade should she choose not to look for an edifying *exemplum*, but to rea their deaths as if watching in the amphitheatre, has only been invite to do as much, directly by the characters, indirectly by the narrator.[82]

[82] Note how Sil. *Pun.* 4. 603–11, describing the fighting in the Trebia, fussily unravel the contradictions which give Lucan's episode its bite—Fibrenus both kills an enemy an finds an audience: 'Explorant adversa viros, perque aspera duro | nititur ad laudem virtu interrita clivo. | Namque inhonoratam Fibrenus *perdere mortem* | et famae nudan impatiens "*Spectabimur*," inquit, | "*nec, Fortuna, meum condes sub gurgite letum.* | Experiar sitne in terris, domitare quod ensis | non queat Ausonius, Tyrrhenave permeet hasta" (with which he assaults an elephant).

CATO IN THE *HARENA*: THE *VENATIO* REVERSED

Introduction

At *Epistle* 104. 33, Seneca comes to one of the most remarkable of the achievements of the younger Cato:

> Vides posse homines laborem pati: per medias Africae solitudines pedes duxit exercitum. Vides posse tolerari sitim: in collibus arentibus sine ullis impedimentis victi exercitus reliquias trahens inopiam umoris loricatus tulit et, quotiens aquae fuerat occasio, novissimus bibit.
>
> You see that men can bear hardship: Cato led an army on foot through the midst of the deserts of Africa. You see that thirst can be endured: on parched hills, dragging the remains of a beaten army and with no train of supplies, he went without water though wearing a heavy cuirass, and, whenever there was some supply of water, he was the last to drink.

The long journey across the Libyan desert completed by the troops of Cato is recounted by Lucan at *Pharsalia* 9. 294–949. On top of the toil and thirst mentioned by Seneca, the poet introduces a third and more serious horror in the succession of grotesque snakes encountered along the way. Cato's ensuing encounter with these beasts has long been perceived as a form of Stoic march towards the truth, the wise man unshaken by the horrors that the world can throw at him.[83] It is the aim of this section to put a rather more unedifying construction on events.

The temptation to interpret this passage as a Stoic metaphor or allegory is encouraged a priori by the construction put on the episode by Seneca and further heightened by a number of factors in the narrative, not least Lucan's consistent tendency to elevate anything said by Cato to the point of sanctity. At 9. 255, for instance, Cato's magnificent response to his disheartened troops is introduced with: 'Speech burst forth from the holy breast of the general' (*Erupere ducis sacro de pectore voces*); at 9. 564–5, the refusal to consult the oracle of Jupiter at

[83] This view is stated most completely in Viarre (1982). It has recently been modified and restated in Fantham (1992*b*). See also Aumont (1968*a*), esp. 318, and (1968*b*). Ahl (1976) 268–74 compares Cato to the other great Stoic hero, Hercules. Other treatments of a Stoicizing tendency are somewhat more subtle and make some excellent points. I think in particular of Morford (1967), Shoaf (1978) and R. F. Thomas (1982) ch. 5, 'The Stoic Landscape of Lucan 9'. Billerbeck (1986) 3122 sees Cato as 'orthodox stoisch ... geradezu sektierisch', but says little about the desert. George (1991) makes a very good case for the coherence of Cato's politically engaged Stoicism in Book 2 and at the start of Book 9, but again avoids commenting on his fortunes in Libya.

Hammon is described in terms which appropriate the language use by Lucretius of Epicurus in order to apply it to the celebration of th Stoic:

Ille deo plenus tacita quem mente gerebat
effudit dignas adytis e pectore voces.

He, full of the god whom he bore in his silent mind, poured forth from h breast speech worthy of a shrine.[84]

Finally, at 9. 593–604, Lucan breaks off to lavish the highest praise o the leader, marking him as a figure of true greatness where previou heroes have enjoyed only *fortuna*, preferring to follow Cato across th desert rather than to mount the Capitol in triumph with Pompey, an marking him not just as an oracle but as the one mortal Rome migh rightly deify, 9. 601–4:

Ecce parens verus patriae, dignissimus aris,
Roma, tuis, per quem numquam iurare pudebit
et quem, si steteris umquam cervice soluta,
nunc, olim, factura deum es.

Lo, the true father of the country, most worthy of your altars, Rome, by whom you will never be ashamed to swear and whom, if ever you stand with your nec free from the yoke, now, one day, you will make a god.[85]

This repeated recourse to undiluted eulogy appears to dictate to th reader the appropriate response to Cato and his achievement. Ye Lucan is a past master of the art of autosubversion. It is this poin which is taken up by Johnson when he argues that Lucan enlivens hi relentlessly, aridly virtuous Cato with some comic shots at th austerity of the position which he has occupied, but Johnson's analysi functions best in its account of the ridiculously frigid virtues of Cato i the second book of the *Pharsalia*,[86] and rather runs out of steam whe it comes to interpreting the ninth book. It is not enough simply t

[84] For these lines, cf. Lucr. 5. 110–13 on Epicurus. The topos of the poet or philo sopher as oracle can also be seen at Sen. *Brev.* 2. 2 and *Vit. Beat.* 26. 7.

[85] For Seneca on the divinity of Cato, see *Epp.* 64. 10, 67. 12–13, *Marc.* 25. 2, *Tran* 16. 4.

[86] Johnson (1987) ch. 2, 'Cato: The Delusions of Virtue'. For a sense of Johnson's pos tion, see p. 37 and Cato's 'puritanical extravagance, his unfailing inhumanity', or p. 4 'This Cato is, in short, something of a pain in the neck, something of a bore. Or rather, h would be tiresome, were he not also fascinating and vital and funny . . . If I dislike him . . I nevertheless find myself enjoying him. Is this how Lucan intended his audiences to fe about his Cato?'

enumerate the descriptions of the different snakes and thus to confront one's audience with Lucan's wonderful, scandalous character.[87]

Two dangerous temptations are apparent. On one side it is possible to determinedly to seek virtuous action with a virtuous message as to strip Lucan of the unsavoury iconoclasm which makes him worth reading; on the other it is too easy to translate frustration with Cato into boredom with the entire question of the Stoic virtues he parades. The analysis offered here steers a different course, putting the Stoic mode of interpretation at the centre of its concerns but using it to argue for a radically subversive manipulation of the nostra of that sect.

Panaetius associated Stoicism with the concept of the *theatrum mundi*, of the wise man as an actor performing for the admiration of the gods.[88] A characteristic of Senecan Stoicism is to put equal emphasis on the notion of the *sapiens* as an athlete or gladiator flexing his moral muscles in the *amphitheatrum mundi*.[89] Lucan's Cato is located firmly in this second tradition, but he is confronted with two levels of subversion. First, he is made to look ridiculous, his struggles inviting interpretation as ethical allegories but sadly only as allegories of virtue defeated. Next, this comic failure opens up the space within which the narrator can exploit the instability of the Stoic amphitheatre as a concept. When the focus shifts away from the triumph of heroic virtue, when the narrator persistently brings into view all the pomp, all the miraculous spectacle of the games, less elevated responses are at hand and the temptation just to sit back and enjoy the show can become too strong. This second problem will be dealt with later on. First, however, it is essential to consider closely the potential for flawed Stoic allegory by examining Lucan's first serpent, the *dipsas*.

The Dipsas, Sitis, *and the Failure of Stoic Wisdom*

The first death among Cato's centurions provides an excellent example of the dysfunctionality of his Stoic march to wisdom. In it the poet goes out of his way to invite an allegorical interpretation, but only one which shows the hopeless failure of Cato's moral instruction. The cup of philosophy is dashed from our lips.

[87] This tactic was first employed in Thierfelder (1934–5), which gives a précis of the various deaths off Massilia. The author's confidence that such grotesque horrors could mean nothing to the Germany of 1933 may now be read with a certain scepticism.

[88] For the Panaetian concept of the πρόσωπον of the Stoic actor and its influence on Roman thought, see the appendix to Brunt (1975).

[89] For the Stoic actor in Seneca, see *Vit. Beat.* 20. 4–5; for the Stoic gladiator *Prov.* 3. 3–4 and 4. 4, *Constant.* 16. 2, *Tranq.* 11. 4–5; for the Stoic athlete, *Prov.* 2. 3–4, 4. 1–2, *Constant.* 9. 5.

One of the great torments of the desert is thirst. This is a recurrent leitmotiv in the ninth book, and one which has always been taken as enforcing Cato's claims to Stoic wisdom and the virtue of the good general. At the start of the march, Cato lists the hazards to be faced, 9. 402, as 'snakes, thirst, heat, sand' (*serpens, sitis, ardor, harenae*), and promises that he will share completely in any hardships, 9. 398–401:

> '*Sitiat*, quicumque [sc. me] bibentem
> viderit, aut umbras nemorum quicumque petentem
> aestuet, aut equitem peditum praecedere turmas
> deficiat: si quo fuerit discrimine notum
> dux an miles eam.'

'Whosoever sees me drinking, let him be thirsty, whosoever sees me seeking the shade of the woods, let him be hot, whosoever sees me pass by on horseback the regiments of the footsoldiers, let him fail: if by any distinction it is known whether I march as leader or soldier.'

This promise is first put to the test at 9. 500–10, an episode which has been demonstrated by Rutz to develop a story famous from the Alexander tradition and recorded at Curtius Rufus, 7. 5. 9–12, Plut. *Alex.* 42, and Arr. *Anab.* 6. 26.[90] When the parched army comes on a stream so meagre as to fill only the helmet of one centurion, Cato is offered the invidious chance alone to drink, but responds angrily and, 9. 509–10:

> Sic concitus ira
> excussit galeam, *suffecitque omnibus unda.*

Thus, stirred by anger, he dashed away the helmet and there was water enough for all.

Later, at 9. 591–3, when water is finally found, Cato drinks last of all, waiting even for the camp-followers. More paradoxical is the episode at 9. 607–18, when the soldiers come across the only copious fount in the middle of the desert, but are deterred by the presence of a large crowd of snakes, 9. 607–10:

> Inventus mediis fons unus harenis
> largus aquae, sed quem serpentum turba tenebat
> vix capiente loco; stabant in margine siccae
> aspides, in mediis sitiebant dipsades undis.

In the midst of the desert a single spring was discovered, and its waters were copious, but a host of serpents beset it, almost more than the ground could contain: parched asps had their station on the brink and the dipsades were thirsty in the midst of the waters.

[90] Rutz (1970*a*) 233–49.

Cato, however, dismisses this, 9. 612, as 'an empty semblance of death' (*vana specie . . . leti*), and, with a clever twist on the motif of the good general as *primus*, for this one time is first to drink the waters of Libya, 9. 617–18:

> Et in tota Libyae fons unus harena
> ille fuit de quo primus sibi posceret aquam.

And in all the desert of Libya that was the one fount from which he demanded water for himself first.[91]

Apart from a passing reference in the catalogue at 9. 718 to *torrida dipsas*, Lucan then leaves the theme of thirst until 9. 734–61, the introduction to the attack of the snakes, and the fate of Aulus. At this point, it is perhaps useful to quote a conventional Stoicizing judgement of the action which ensues. Morford's version of the scene is as follows: 'Aulus, the standard-bearer, is the first to die, victim of a *dipsas* (737–50): his sufferings are treated with much hyperbole, but he dies in the end with the courage of a Stoic, opening his veins in order to drink his own blood. He would have failed in his agony had Cato not been present: thanks to him Aulus died master of his fate.'[92] This interpretation is therefore consonant with Morford's conclusion that: 'the linking *motif* of the ninth book is death and its central theme is the superiority of Stoic virtue, as exemplified by Cato, to pain and death.'[93] Yet it is far from self-evident that this is true to what Lucan actually describes. Various observations might here be made.

First, Morford is surely correct to see Aulus' opening of his own veins as an imitation of the classic Stoic mode of suicide. It is less clear that it is true to orthodox Stoicism to open one's own veins in order to satisfy a raging thirst. Rather, Aulus wages civil war with himself, recalling the Bellona of Calpurnius Siculus and the Erysichthon of Ovid.[94]

Second, it is unclear how Morford can portray Cato as helping Aulus to conquer his own sufferings unless this is an extrapolation from the statement at 9. 884 that 'though just one man he was present at every death' (*omnibus unus adest fatis*); for Lucan suggests something quite different at 9. 747–50:

[91] For *primus*, see p. 106 n. 60. Apart from the inversion at 9. 591, when Cato is 'ultimus', note his promise at 9. 394–5, '"Dum primus harenas | ingrediar primusque gradus in pulvere ponam"'.

[92] Morford (1967) 128.

[93] Ibid. 129.

[94] Calp. *Ecl.* 1. 47–50, Ov. *Met.* 8. 875–8.

> Non decus imperii, non maesti iura Catonis
> ardentem tenuere virum, ne spargere signa
> auderet totisque furens exquireret arvis
> quas poscebat aquas sitiens in corde venenum.

Not the glory of his post, not the commands of the austere Cato could stop th burning man from daring to throw down his standard and madly seeking a over the desert the water demanded by the thirsty poison in his heart.

If anything, Aulus is overwhelmed by his appetite, and not even Cat can hold him back. I shall return to this point.

It is instructive to measure the distance between what Morfor presumes the episode to tell, and the actual details of Lucan's account Further, Morford's concentration on the conquest of death leads hin to ignore the allegory which Lucan undoubtedly presents. For this, one must return to the first appearance of the *dipsas*, infesting the foun from which Cato dares to drink. There, programmatically, we are tol that:

> Stabant in margine siccae
> aspides, in mediis sitiebant dipsades undis.

Parched asps had their station on the brink and the dipsades were thirsty in the midst of the waters.

The distribution of the snakes is significant. For, the *dipsas* thirsty in the middle of the water is now quite clearly equated with Tantalus, the greedy, avaricious man of myth *par excellence*. Lucan directly conflates Ovid *Am.* 3. 7. 51, 'so thirsts the man who divulged the secret in the middle of water' (*sic aret mediis taciti vulgator in undis*) and *Met.* 9. 761, 'we shall be thirsty in the midst of water' (*mediis sitiemus in undis*), but the theme is a commonplace in Latin literature and thought.[95]

The first appearance of the *dipsas* almost instructs the reader to look out for an allegory when it returns. And such there is. The effect of the bite is to induce an unbearable, uncontrollable thirsting disease closely akin to the hydropsy described at Horace, *Carm.* 2. 2. 13–16. Nisbet and Hubbard demonstrate that hydropsy is regularly used by Cynics and Stoics as an allegory for the insatiability of desire, the constant provocation of one desire by the sating of another. More generally, too,

[95] See Sen. *Thy.* 4–6: 'Peius inventum est siti | arente in undis aliquid et peius fame | hiante semper?'; cf. Lucr. 4. 1100, Prop. 1. 9. 15–16, Ov. *Tr.* 5. 4. 10, Petron. fr. 35. 5 Bucheler and Otto (1890) 138–9. A huge of body of material associating the avaricious Tantalus with this topos is collected in di Simone (1993).

a succession of Latin writers all use *sitis* as a synonym for *cupiditas*, and there is a considerable hinterland of ancient ethical writing which represents avarice as a disease.[96]

In the light of this extensive tradition in ethical writing, it is not surprising to find that the language which Lucan uses to describe the physical effects of the *dipsas* on the centurion echoes previous poetic applications of the metaphor of burning to express mental disturbance. This emerges most clearly at 9. 741–2, which combines two passages of *Aeneid* 4:

> Ecce, subit virus *tacitum*, *carpitque medullas*
> *ignis* edax calidaque incendit viscera tabe.

But lo! the silent venom rises; the devouring fire consumes the marrow and ignites the guts with hot wasting.

These lines draw on both *Aeneid* 4. 2, *caeco carpitur igni*, and 4. 66–7:

> Est mollis flamma *medullas*
> interea et *tacitum* vivit sub pectore vulnus.

Meanwhile the flame eats the soft marrow bone and the silent wound lives beneath her breast.[97]

Similarly, the description of Aulus at 9. 748 as *ardentem* might remind one *inter alia* both of Vergil's description of Dido at *Aeneid* 4. 101 (*ardet amans Dido*) and of Ovid's précis of *Aeneid* 4 at *Fasti* 3. 545–6:

> Arserat Aeneae Dido miserabilis igne,
> arserat exstructis in sua fata rogis.

Wretched Dido had burned with fire for Aeneas, had burned on the pyre built for her death.[98]

Vergil uses the imagery of burning to express the passion of Dido. Lucan invites the reader to allegorize the burning thirst of Aulus as the *sitis* of appetite and cupidity, the 'thirsty poison in his heart' (*sitiens in*

[96] For *sitis* as *cupiditas*, see Sen. *Phaed.* 542, Sil. *Pun.* 5. 265, Hor. *Epist.* 1. 18. 23, Cic. *Par.* 6, and Lucr. 3. 1084 . For avarice as a disease, see the detailed discussion of Nisbet and Hubbard (1978) at Hor. *Carm.* 2. 2. 13–6 and cf. Commager (1957) and Bramble (1974) 35–6.

[97] Similar locutions are aparent at Ov. *Met.* 3. 490, 10. 369–70, *Am.* 2. 19. 43, and *Rem. Am.* 105–6. The phrasing of the last, 'interea tacitae *serpunt* in viscera flammae | et mala radices altius arbor agit' is significant. *Serpere* is used regularly in Latin for the spread of plague amongst a people (see Sil. *Pun.* 14. 596–7 and 613) and for the diffusion of physical illness inside the body (see Lucil. fr. 53 (Marx), Ov. *Met.* 2. 825–6, Celsus, *Med.* 5. 26. 34d) and it must be this latter linguistic resonance which underpins Allecto's injection of passion into Amata by means of a snake at Verg. *Aen.* 7. 346–53.

[98] For the metaphorical use of *ardere*, see the wealth of material at *TLL* ii. 485. 20 ff.

corde venenum).[99] Aulus becomes an *exemplum* of the sermon given by Seneca at *Epistle* 21 on the Epicurean text:

Si vis . . . Pythoclea divitem facere, non pecuniae adiciendum sed cupiditati detrahendum est.

If you want to make Pythocles rich, you must not add to his wealth but subtract from his desires.[100]

His big problem is that he does not know exactly what is wrong with him, and thinks that his thirst, now understood as both real and metaphorical, can be satisfied simply by drinking more, 9. 756–60:

> Nunc redit ad Syrtes et fluctus accipit ore,
> aequoreusque placet, *sed non et sufficit*, umor.
> Nec sentit fatique genus mortemque veneni,
> *sed putat esse sitim*; ferroque aperire tumentis
> sustinuit venas atque os inplere cruore.

Now he returned to the Syrtes and drank the waves and he liked the sea-water, *but still it was not enough*. Nor did he sense the way he was dying and the poison that was killing him, but *he thought that it was thirst*, and he bore to open his swollen veins with the steel and to fill his mouth with blood.

Aulus thus serves to demonstrate the failure of Cato's moral lessons. At 9. 510, Cato refuses to drink, casts the cup to the ground 'and there was water enough for all' (*suffecitque omnibus unda*). In the short term, we see the conquest of *sitis*. Now, however, the *dipsas* of appetite strikes: Aulus is driven to drink the brine of the Syrtes, 'but still it was not enough' (*sed non et sufficit*).[101] Cato does not conquer *sitis*. Far from it, he merely hurries on, lest anyone should see its full power, 9. 761–2:

> Iussit signa rapi propere Cato: discere nulli
> permissum est hoc posse sitim.

[99] Luc. 9. 750. For the metaphorical use of *venenum*, see *OLD* 'venenum' 3b. For representation of the illness of the *cor* as moral or psychological, see Commager (1957) 105–6 and n. 4.

[100] Epicurus, fr. 135 (Usener). Note how the *sitis* metaphor later appears in the concretized satisfaction of the Gardens of Epicurus, where, Sen. *Ep*. 21. 10, 'Non irritant . . . hi hortuli famem sed extinguunt, nec maiorem ipsis potionibus sitim faciunt'. Cf. Commager (1957) 111–12 and n. 24 on *sitis* at Lucr. 3. 995–7, 4. 1100, and 6. 1176–7, and its victims deluded as to its cure: 'The notion of a false or seeming nourishment which is actually destructive underlies all three cases'. Martindale (1976) 45 and n. 3 notes the connection between the description of the austere Cato at Luc. 2. 384–7 and Seneca's use of Epicurus fr. 477 (Usener) at *Ep*. 4. 10. *Ep*. 4 like *Ep*. 21 develops the idea of the Gardens of Epicurus.

[101] Cf. Ov. *Met.* 8. 832–3 *re* Erysichthon: 'quodque urbibus esse, | quodque satis poterat populo, *non sufficit uni*'.

Cato ordered them to hurry the standards along: nobody was allowed to learn that thirst was as powerful as this.

The once-triumphant philosopher is now forced to cover up the truth; the vice which he thought he had conquered is now seen in all its power and, literally, has the last word. Cato's Stoic march is an allegory, but it is an allegory for the impotence of philosophy.[102]

Spectatorship and Lucan's Venatio

Lucan's Cato is left high and dry. There is a considerable distance to be measured between what an orthodox Stoicizing critic would like the episode to tell and what is actually told. Cato, it will be argued, becomes an increasingly isolated figure, at once unable to make his sermons relevant to the sufferings of his men and strikingly ill-equipped to engage with them. This isolation, moreover, is repeatedly evoked by Lucan by emphasizing one factor which coheres with the potential emotional detachment of the reader.

[102] The episode of the *dipsas* is of special importance because it is the first of the snakes and because it so subverts the principal vehicle for moral admiration of Cato in the first half of the desert narrative. At the same time, others of the snakes have a similar function. Philip Hardie points out to me that the simile of the melting of snow and wax for the impact of the *seps* at Luc. 9. 780–2 looks back to Callim. *Cer.* 91–2 and the classic figure of appetite, Erysichthon, and to Narcissus at Ov. *Met.* 3. 487–90. That the torments of Narcissus are Tantalean is most evident at Ov. *Met.* 3. 427–9, 'Inrita fallaci quotiens dedit oscula fonti! | in mediis quotiens visum captantia collum | bracchia mersit aquis nec se deprendit in illis'. For more on this, see Hardie (1988) but note also two further elements of Ovid's narrative pertinent to this context. First, at *Met.* 3. 415, Narcissus leans down to drink from the pool and 'dumque sitim sedare cupit, sitis altera crevit'; second, at *Met.* 3. 426, 430, 464, and 487–90, esp. 490 'tecto paulatim carpitur igni', the passion of Narcissus is equated with burning. No less striking is the impact of the 'prester' at 789–804. Ael. *NA* 6. 51 says that *prester* is another name for the *dipsas* but Lucan uses its bite to concretize the impact of another passion, anger. While the idea of the 'sanies' passing 'humanum . . . egressa modum' at 794–5 is the opposite of Cato at 2. 381, who lives determined to 'servare modum', and while it recalls the tumidity of arrogance at Sen. *Ben.* 6. 3. 2 and 6. 31. 1 and *Polyb.* 17. 5, the swollen and distended body of the soldier, the redness of his face, is most strikingly reminiscent of the description of the body afflicted by anger at Sen. *Ira* 1. 1. 4, 2. 20. 2, 2. 35. 3, 2. 36. 2, 3. 4. 1. Striking therefore that Pollux, 2. 134 uses the word πρηστῆρες for the veins of the neck when swollen by anger (τὸ ἔξωθεν ὑπὸ τὰς ὀργὰς ὑπὸ τοῦ φυσᾶσθαι πιμπράμενον καὶ ἀνοιδούμενον, πρηστὴρ ὀνομάζεται). For the distance at which Lucan's narrative stands from that of Vergil, compare the reference at Luc. 9. 790 to Nasidius as 'Marsi cultorem . . . agri' to Verg. *Aen.* 7. 750–60 and the anticipation of the death of Umbro. In Vergil, the skill of the Marsian in curing snake-bite is contrasted plangently with the irremediable impact of a Trojan spear; Lucan's recollection of this traditional art amongst the Marsi while describing the impact on Nasidius of the *prester* is one of his very best jokes. For the role of the *marsus* or 'snake-charmer' in ancient medicine, see the fascinating Nutton (1988).

The factor here apparent is the metaphor of the amphitheatre. Consider, for instance, 9. 881–3, which first decribes Cato as the defeated gladiator, then uses the language of single combat to show how he fights on:

> Cogit tantos tolerare labores
> summa ducis virtus, qui *nuda fusus harena*
> excubat atque omni fortunam *provocat* hora.

The exceptional valour of the general makes them endure such great toils—laid out on the bare sand he keeps watch and challenges fortune at every hour.

Two points emerge from this passage. First, the image of the hero 'laid out on the bare sand' permits the sand of the desert to transcend its status and recalls instead the sand of the arena.[103] This is particularly true when Lucan employs the word *provocat* for his response to fortune, a term drawn directly from the repertoire of the Stoic athlete or gladiator.[104] The strong impression that this is an instance of the ethical celebration of the Stoic gladiator then receives an unusual form of confirmation from the lines which follow, 9. 884–9:

> Omnibus unus adest fatis; quocumque vocatus
> advolat atque ingens meritum maiusque salute
> contulit, in letum vires; puduitque *gementem*
> *illo teste* mori. Quod ius habuisset in ipsum
> ulla lues? Casus *alieno in pectore* vincit
> *spectatorque* docet magnos nil posse dolores.

Though just one man he was present at every death. He rushed to wherever he was called and brought a huge boon, greater than salvation, strength against death, and they were ashamed to die groaning with him looking on. What

[103] In this case, the paradox is that Cato is 'fusus' because just lying down but *fusus* is regularly used for a fighter, an army laid low in combat (see *TLL* vi. 1. 569. 70 ff.). 'Nuda . . . harena' suggests the location of that combat.

[104] For *provocare* as a challenge to a fight in general, see *OLD provoco* 3a. A *provocator* was a specific type of gladiator, for which see Cic. *Sest.* 134 and *CIL* v. 4502. *CIL* v. 2884 also offers 'provocare' in the sense of following the profession of *provocator*. It must also be noted that *provocare* is a key term in Seneca's 'Stoic athleticism'. Thus, at Sen. *Q. Nat.* 6. 32. 3, he claims that 'Ingenti . . . animo mors provocanda est', and at *Ep.* 64. 4 comments that the effect of reading Sextius is that 'Libet omnis casus provocare, libet exclamare, "Quid cessas, fortuna? Congredere: paratum vides"'. Cf. also Sen. *Ep.* 67. 6 and *Prov.* 2. 9, the latter passage already discussed *re* Luc. 7. 385–459. For 'provocare', cf. ἐπηγγείλατο at Schol. Nic. *Ther.* 15a. *Provocare* is also used at Luc. 4. 725 for the challenge of the ichneumon to the snakes of Egypt. At Plut. *Mor.* 980 E, the ichneumon is compared to an athlete, at Plut. *Mor.* 966 D, Plin., *HN* 8. 88, Strab. *Geog.* 17. 1. 39, and Gell. *NA* 3. 22 to a soldier.

power could any plague have had against him? He conquered fortune in the breasts of others and taught them as he watched that pain was without power.

This passage is not without its own surface ironies. While it is asserted that Cato's lessons bring 'a huge boon, greater than salvation' (*ingens meritum maiusque salute*), it is hard to forget that the one service this huge boon of 'strength against death' (*in letum vires*) cannot perform is actually to stop the men from dying. Yet the lesson which Cato does give is one straight from the Stoic textbook, convincing his followers of the indifference of their pain. The deeper level of irony emerges from the position which the teacher adopts. While at 9. 881–3 he was described as directly challenging fortune, the Stoic gladiator has now become a witness and a spectator. What then of his men? True, the shame they feel at emitting a groan provokes the comportment proper to a Stoic, but the motivation attested, the simple wish not to disappoint Cato, puts the whole affair in a more equivocal light. To put the point more harshly, Cato the *spectator*, the man involved with the surfaces of things, may believe himself to have taught them philosophy, to have challenged and beaten fortune, but it is a fair bet that, as soon as he has left the ward, the patients redouble their lamentation, first from the agonies which they endure, second from the realization of what a prig they have for a general.[105]

In the transformation of Cato the gladiator into Cato the spectator there emerges the possibility that Lucan's Stoic amphitheatre is verging on the dysfunctional. More dramatically subversive is the manner in which the pious viewing of Cato contrasts with the narrator's suggestion of a far more ambiguous perspective. This second perspective is invited at the very opening of the attack of the snakes, at 9. 734–6, where what Cato sees is described as both sad and 'most unusual':

[105] This is perhaps a little harsh but 'illo teste' does not suggest much philosophical αὐτάρκεια in their comportment. The Stoic objection to groaning is owed to the doctrines of ἀναλγησία and ἀπάθεια, the classic exposition of which is that given at Gell. *NA* 12. 5, the visit of Taurus the philosopher and his retinue to the sick Stoic who would not groan. Note especially 12. 5. 8, 'pugnat autem cum his semper' and 12. 5. 9, 'philosophum . . . conluctantem, nihil cedentem, nihil confidentem', where the Stoic appears as soldier or wrestler; and compare 12. 5. 13, where he is likened to a gladiator. For more on this scene and on Panaetius' scepticism concerning these doctrines, see Holford-Strevens (1988) 68–9. The notion of the Stoic Pompey is heightened by his dignified refusal to groan at Luc. 7. 680–2, 8. 618–21, and 633–4, though Johnson (1987) would refer his behaviour at his execution to the need to generate awe in his audience.

Has inter pestes duro Cato milite siccum
emetitur iter, tot *tristia* fata suorum
insolitasque videns parvo cum volnere mortes.

Cato made his thirsty way with his doughty soldiers amidst these plagues seeing so many sorry deaths of his men, so many unusual ways of dying with a tiny wound.

The two adjectives sum up two different responses to visual experience which have been contrasted throughout this chapter: the pathetic and the thaumastic. It would not be too much to allege that lines 734–6 have a strongly metaliterary quality. Certainly, they anticipate the treatment of the *seps* episode at 9. 761–3:

Iussit signa rapi propere Cato; discere nulli
permissum est hoc posse sitim. Sed *tristior* illo
mors erat *ante oculos*.

Cato ordered them to hurry the standards along: nobody was allowed to learn that thirst was as powerful as this. Yet a sorrier death than that was before their eyes.

Cato the Victorian covers things up and will not let others see. Immediately, however, they get to see sadder and more fascinating things still. Or, at least, they are fascinating to the narrator, who devotes twenty-five lines of description to them, and finds them not without scientific interest, 9. 777–80:

Quidquid homo est, aperit pestis natura profana:
vincula nervorum et laterum textura cavumque
pectus et abstrusum fibris vitalibus omne
morte patet.

All that makes a man the horrible nature of the plague lays open: the ligature of the muscles and the rib-cage and the cavity of the chest and all that the vital organs hide—all is revealed in death.[106]

Cato, if given the benefit of the doubt, reacts to the killing with horror and sympathy for the victim. The narrator, on the other hand, affects a sympathetic response, but then breaks into the gleeful fascination of the pseudo-scientist. While the attitude of the reader is left open, it is hard not to be drawn into the mentality of the narrator.

[106] For another case of affected scientific fascination, one might cite the Psylli at 9. 922–4: 'At, siquis peste diurna | fata trahit, tunc sunt magicae *miracula* gentis | Psyllorumque ingens et rapti pugna veneni.' For scientific justifications of looking at horrible things, see Ar. *Part. An.* 645^{a}11–15.

The subversive temptation implied by this second mode of viewing recalls the suggestive oxymora of the Massilia narrative. At 9. 789–90, in particular, 'lo! there comes a form of death different from that by melting' (*ecce, subit facies leto diversa fluenti*), is strikingly reminiscent of 3. 652–3 and the 'unique form of dire death' (*unica diri* | . . . *leti facies*). Yet here there is a further factor which works very powerfully to represent the desert narrative not so much as a Stoic amphitheatre as just simply an amphitheatre: the collusion between the narrator and his snakes. This collusion is apparent at 787–8, where the narrator concludes his description of the effect of the *seps* with the following apostrophe:

> Cinyphias inter pestes *tibi palma nocendi est*:
> eripiunt omnes animam, tu sola cadaver.

Amongst the plagues of Cinyphia you take the prize for damage: all take away the soul, you alone the corpse.

The poet's intervention gives the *seps* the status of a human athlete or of a gladiator.[107] Nor is the celebration of this serpent's power to cause ruin an isolated phenomenon. In this context, one might also mention 9. 833–8 and the praise meted out to *scorpion* and *salpuga*:

> Quis fata putarit
> scorpion aut vires maturae mortis habere?
> Ille minax nodis et recto verbere saevus
> *teste tulit caelo victi decus Orionis.*
> Quis calcare tuas metuat, salpuga, latebras?
> Et tibi dant Stygiae ius in sua fila sorores.

Who would think the scorpion could kill or possessed the power to deal out a swift death? Menacing with his knotted tail and savage with his sting erect he had heaven as his witness when he won the glory of beating Orion. Salpuga, who would fear to step on your lair? Yet the Stygian sisters give power to you as well over the threads they spin.[108]

[107] For the *palma* as the prize awarded to a gladiator, see Cic. *Rosc. Am.* 17: 'Plurimarum palmarum vetus ac nobilis gladiator habetur T. Roscius Capito', cf. ibid. 84, 'alias quoque suas palmas cognoscet'. Schol. Cic. Gron. p. 311, 16 adds 'palmas . . . dicimus victorias gladiatorum'. See also *TLL* x. 1. 144. 8 ff. Johnson (1987) 50 describes this as 'a nice epinician touch'.

[108] Cazzaniga (1957) 31–2 notes that 'teste tulit caelo victi decus Orionis' refers to the alternative version of the Orion story offered in the Schol. Nic. *Ther.* 13 ff., in which Orion challenged Artemis and Leto (ἐπηγγείλατο), boasting that no beast could escape him when hunting. Cazzaniga stresses the element here, peculiarly pertinent to our notion of a *venatio* reversed, of the great hunter now hunted: 'Orione è dunque per Lucano il grande cacciatore per antonomasia che avendo sfidato Artemide Cacciatrice, fu

Line 836 clearly implies single combat, while the apostrophe to the *salpuga* at 837–8 takes on the same celebratory, perhaps epinician tone already heard in the address to the *seps*. Not dissimilar are lines 9. 724–6 and the description of the *basiliscus* as 'king of the ring':

> Sibilaque effundens cunctas terrentia pestes,
> ante venena nocens, late sibi summovet omne
> vulgus et *in vacua regnat basiliscus harena.*

And pouring forth hisses that terrify all the plagues, doing damage even before his venom strikes, he drives all the mob away from him and reigns in an empty desert.[109]

King of the desert or king of the ring? Not all instances of *harena* in this passage move beyond the simple sense of 'desert', but the density of reference to the games means that the acquired resonance is always strong.[110] More significantly, it is often the action of the snakes which expresses their determination to transform the *harena* from desert to arena. This is a *venatio* on their terms and they are the hunters. Remarkable creatures, each with his own special way of killing, they can slaughter animals far bigger than themselves.[111] If Cato thinks he is presenting a display of elevated Stoic virtue, they by contrast are sure

punito dalla dea per la sua μεγαλαυχία con la puntura del piccolissimo rettile e da esso fu ingloriosamente ucciso, per pena quasi di contrapasso: lo Scorpione riportò così la palma sul grande campione.'

[109] Here, of course, we must not ignore the etymological play on the name *basiliscus* and the consequent kingly *regnat*. The line deliberately echoes Verg. *G.* 4. 90, advising the killing of the lesser king bee: 'melior vacua sine regnet in aula'.

[110] For instance, I do not see anything evidently amphitheatrical about 9. 715–16 'concolor exustis atque indiscretus harenis | hammodytes' or about 9. 755 'harenae', 9. 913 'harenas' and 9. 941 'harenivagum ... Catonem'. At 9. 704–7 it is hard to see an explicit reference to the display of snakes in the amphitheatre. One must presume that Lucan's exclamation refers to private poisonings or to the keeping of asps as pets. For poisoning, cf. Heges. 1. 43. 8, 'Veneficii genus ... compositum ex sucis serpentum et veneno aspidum'. For the use of asps as pets, performing tricks at dinner parties, see the refs. to Phylarchus at Plin. *HN* 10. 208 and Gell. *NA* 17. 5. It is true that Suet. *Aug.* 43. 4 cites the use of an enormous 'anguis' in a 'venatio' (perhaps to recreate the duel of Regulus?), and that Diod. 3. 36. 3–37. 9 tells of a giant snake taken from the marshes of the Upper Nile and appearing in the collection of Ptolemy II as μέγιστον καὶ παραδοξότατον θέαμα, but an asp is probably too small to be a hit at the box office. Auguet (1972) 86 cites evidence from the monuments of a bear wrestling a python.

[111] See 9. 729–32, where the choice of victims of the 'dracones' may be made in order to emphasize their enormity. However, they are also typical victims of the arena: 'Ducitis altum | aera cum pinnis, armentaque tota secuti | rumpitis ingentes amplexi verbere tauros; | nec tutus spatio est elephans'. Similarly, at 9. 946–7, the paradox of the arrival in Libya depends on the relief at last to see conventional amphitheatrical animals: 'Quanta dedit miseris melioris gaudia terrae | cum primum *saevos contra videre leones*!'

that they are putting on a show. When Lucan introduces his fourth serpent at 9. 805 it is with the remarkable 'but the plagues of Libya are preparing greater spectacles' (*Sed maiora parant Libycae spectacula pestes*) and when the *haemmorhois* makes his kill, he has Tullus squirt forth liquid just like the crocus water sprayed in the arena, 9. 808–10:

> Utque solet pariter totis se fundere signis
> Corycii pressura croci, sic omnia membra
> emisere simul rutilum pro sanguine virus.

And just as water dyed with Corycian saffron often pours from every part of a statue at once, so all the limbs together gave out a ruddy slime in place of blood.[112]

The devastating effect of the collusion between narrator and snakes is to present an amphitheatre unburdened with Stoic elevation, as just a source of spectacle, a theatre of blood. Moreover, what is especially disturbing about this second perspective is its terrifying truthfulness to the mentality of the spectator. The dire pleasure of the amphitheatre is discussed in detail in the conclusion to this chapter but its consistent power to invade and to corrupt may be given some brief exemplification in the last scene from the desert narrative to be discussed.

The confusion of roles in Cato's Stoic hospital visits has a bizarre counterpoint in the story of Murrus. At 9. 829–33, the distinction between Stoic gladiator and Stoic spectator grows even more blurred, as the speedy self-mutilation of Murrus gives him the chance to take a seat and observe what might have happened to the rest of him:[113]

> Velox currit per tela venenum
> invaditque manum; quam protinus ille retecto
> ense ferit totoque semel demittit ab armo,
> *exemplarque sui spectans miserabile leti*
> *stat tutus* pereunte manu.

The swift poison ran through his spear and attacked his hand; he immediately drew his sword and struck it and in one blow chopped his whole arm off from

[112] For the spraying of saffron water at the games, see Lucr. 2. 416; Ov. *Ars. Am.* 1. 104; Prop. 4. 1. 16; Sen. *Q. Nat.* 2. 9. 2, *Ep.* 90. 15; Plin. *HN* 21. 33; Mart. *Spect.* 3. 8, *Ep.* 5. 25. 7–8, 8. 33. 4. Lucan's reference to statues suggests the sort of technological experimentation deplored at Sen. *Ep.* 90. 15. If Calpurnius Siculus is truly Neronian, an important parallel is offered at Calp. *Ecl.* 7. 71–2, 'et in isdem saepe cavernis | aurea cum subito creverunt arbuta nimbo', where artificial golden arbutes rise in the middle of the amphitheatre and spray forth yellow crocus water.

[113] Cazzaniga (1956) notes the separate testimony to the power of the *basiliscus* at Pliny *HN* 8. 78, but argues that the inspiration for Lucan's account may be found in the lost *De Situ et Sacris Aegyptorum* of Seneca.

the shoulder, and he stood safe looking at the wretched model of his own death as his hand perished.[114]

Here, even more than in the case of Cato the Stoic gladiator, the action replicates themes familiar from the exemplary tradition and from a field of behaviour marked in Chapter One as archetypically Stoic.[115] For Morford has observed that the spectatorship of Murrus recalls the Stoics' favourite *exemplum*, Mucius Scaevola, and particularly Seneca, *Epistle* 24. 5, 'He stood and watched his right hand melt away in the enemy fire' (*spectator destillantis in hostili foculo dexterae stetit*).[116] To this one might add that the theme recurs at *Epistle* 66. 51:

> Stetit hostium flammarumque contemptor et manum suam in hostili foculo destillantem *perspectavit*, donec Porsina cuius poenae favebat gloriae invidit et ignem invito eripi iussit.
>
> He stood, scorning the enemy and the flames, and watched to the very end his own hand melting away in the enemy fire, until Porsina, though he wanted to see him punished, envied his glory and told them to deny him the fire even against his will.

and that it relates to a number of other passages in Seneca in which the exemplary Stoic is unmoved by the sight of his own suffering.[117]

The problem, however, is more complicated. Murrus is both like Seneca's Mucius and also unlike him. There is a striking paradox in the fact that the dismembered Murrus is actually safe, and thus can stand by and watch the destruction of his hand with as much detachment as anyone else. This, surely, is a classic case of the disruption wrought by reference to the amphitheatre. At once, the theme of watching one's

[114] For an intriguing parallel to these lines, see col. v, lines 1–2 of the fragmentary *Carmen De Bello Actiaco* re-edited in Benario (1983): '[Dele]ctumqu[e loc]um quo noxia turba co[i]ret | praeberetque suae spectacula tri[s]tia mortis'. Benario believes that the *Carmen* is anterior to Lucan and possibly attributable to Rabirius. For a much more detailed statement of this position, see Cozzolino (1975). Oddly, neither writer offers this parallel.

[115] See pp. 28–30.

[116] Morford (1967) 128 and n. 2.

[117] One might compare the attitude of the noble Epicurean Bassus at Sen. *Ep.* 30. 3: 'Hoc facit Bassus noster et eo animo vultuque finem suum spectat quo alienum spectare nimis securi putares'. Both Mucius and Bassus are like the experienced soldier at *Prov.* 4. 7: '. . . ad suspicionem vulneris tiro pallescit, audacter veteranus cruorem suum spectat, qui scit se saepe vicisse post sanguinem'. See also Ch. 1, pp. 28–30 for discussion of *Ep.* 74. 22. All these passages should be compared with Mart. *Ep.* 8. 30. 5, where an amphitheatrical execution replicates Mucius' burning of his own hand and Mucius is dubbed 'ipse sui spectator'. The imperturbable attitude of one able to look on his own degradation is very appealing to Christian martyrologists, e.g. Prud. *Perist.* 10. 906–10, where the tongue of the martyr is cut out, the blood runs down and he 'cruenti pectoris spectat decus'.

hand burn or die is so eminently Stoic that one cannot help but equate the attitude of Murrus with his model Mucius. At the same time, the density of association between spectatorship and the amphitheatre which the surrounding narrative has provided makes it impossible to exclude an attitude on the part of the reader which treats the dismemberment of Murrus as θαῦμα and an entertainment. The reaction of the *safe* spectator Murrus offers a surrogate for such behaviour in a way that Mucius never could.

Nor does it end here. Lucan's evocation of conflicting responses to suffering operates in turn as an acute commentary on certain contradictions in Seneca's forms of analogy. Hitherto, for instance when discussing Vulteius, it has been possible to describe the reference to the amphitheatre as a disruptive supplement to exemplary narrative. In this instance, the exemplary and the amphitheatrical are even less easy to separate.

It is a familiar contradiction in Seneca's writing that while he provides some of the best evidence for the entertainment offered by the sadistic voyeurism of the amphitheatre,[118] certain passages, most notably *Ep.* 7. 2–5 and *Helv.* 17. 1, betray an attitude of considerably greater complicity. Moreover, the realization that the philosopher cannot completely dissociate himself from the crowd amongst whom he sits casts a new light on the repeated leitmotiv of Senecan argumentation which lies behind Cato's challenge to fortune at *Pharsalia* 9. 881–9: the gladiator who resists unbowed is used as an analogy for the Stoic who will not give way to oppression and pain.

Just as at *Prov.* 2. 7–12, the gods admired the spectacle of Cato's suicide so much that they brought him back on stage for a second time, so, one must allege, Seneca the spectator must participate in the denigration of the gladiator whose resistance he admires. It is hard to escape this implication at *Constant.* 16. 1–2, *Tranq.* 11. 4, *Ep.* 37. 1–2 and 71. 23, and, most significantly for the Murrus passage, at *Prov.* 3. 4–5:

Ignominiam iudicat gladiator cum inferiore componi et scit eum sine gloria vinci qui sine periculo vincitur. Idem facit fortuna: fortissimos sibi pares quaerit, quosdam fastidio transit. Contumacissimum quemque et rectissimum adgreditur, adversus quem vim suam intendat: ignem experitur in Mucio, paupertatem in Fabricio, exilium in Rutilio, tormenta in Regulo, venenum in Socrate, mortem in Catone. Magnum exemplum nisi mala fortuna non invenit. Infelix est

[118] See Sen. *Epp.* 7. 2–5, 90. 45, 95. 33, *Tranq.* 2. 13, *Clem.* 1. 25. 2, *Ira* 1. 2. 4, *Helv.* 17. 1.

Mucius, quod dextra ignes hostium premit et ipse a se exigit erroris sui poenas, quod regem quem armata manu non potuit exusta fugat? Quid ergo? Felicior esset, si in sinu amicae foveret manum?

A gladiator judges it ignominy to be pitted against a lesser man and knows that he is beaten without glory who is beaten without risk. Fortune does the same: she seeks the bravest opponents for herself, disdains others and passes them by. She attacks all the most unyielding and stubborn men against whom she may direct her force: she tries Mucius with fire, Fabricius with poverty, Rutilius with exile, Regulus with torture, Socrates with poison, Cato with death. Only ill fortune produces a great example. Is Mucius unhappy because he grasps the fire of the enemy in his right hand and punishes himself for his mistake, because with a burnt hand he puts a king to flight whom he could not [put to flight] with one that was armed? What then? Would he be happier if his hand were caressing the bosom of his girlfriend?

The conclusion to which I am moving should be clear: just as Seneca admires while he denigrates, so Lucan can denigrate as he admires. The categories cannot be held apart.

CONCLUSIONS AND SPECULATIONS: THE POETICS OF THE AMPHITHEATRE

In summarizing the argument of this chapter, I wish to restrict myself to outlining three general contentions: that Lucan's references to *par* and *harena* must be studied in the context of his metaliterary references to *spectaculum* and *miraculum*; that these terms liken the reading of an epic to the watching of the games and must be studied in the context of what we know of the experience of spectatorship; most important of all, that this experience is intimately connected with the political system which Lucan is accustomed to deplore.

Antiquarian and Imperial Interpretations of the Amphitheatre

The fundamental question is: what was the experience of the amphitheatre? The frame of reference adopted in order to answer this is substantially imperial, but not narrowly Neronian. The presumption of a diachronic continuity which this implies is justified by the institutional continuity between emperors: there is always someone to inhabit the royal box, always a regal *editor*. The concerns which motivate this investigation are rather different from the antiquarian preoccupations of some previous interpretations of Lucan.

Antiquarianism fixes the meaning of Lucan's games by reference to the ritual origins of the *munus*. Explanation by original meaning is the practice of Ahl,[119] who is principally concerned with the amphitheatrical in the African episode of Book 4, thus with the sacrifice of Roman blood to propitiate the shades of Hannibal and his troops. Ahl emphasizes Tertullian, *De Spectaculis* 12 and the other ancient authorities for the origin of the *munus* in antique ritual.[120] When one considers the specific argument which Ahl is developing, this approach is not illegitimate, but its limitations are swift to emerge. On the one hand, Ahl concedes that by the time of the Gracchi the gladiatorial *munus* had little to do with rites for the dead; on the other, he asserts that Seneca and Lucan must have been aware of its original function. [121]

The faith in origins becomes a lodestone. It is hard to believe that this is the whole story as regards the games. Of course it is important to know what Varro said about the antiquarian background to the amphitheatre, but there is no less value in investigating contemporary Roman formulations of the actual experience of being there in the present. Different meanings are attached to the same experience in different times and it is an instance of what one might call the Indo-European fallacy always to privilege the oldest.[122]

The Experience of the Amphitheatre

The 'imperial' or 'modern' meaning of the amphitheatre centres on the interaction of *editor*, gladiators, and crowd. It is expressed most

[119] Ahl (1976) 84–8, esp. 86 and n. 8.

[120] e.g. Tert. *Spect.* 12. 1–2: 'Munus dictum est ab officio, quoniam officium etiam muneris nomen est. Officium autem mortuis hoc spectaculo facere se veteres arbitrabantur, posteaquam illud humaniore atrocitate temperaverunt. Nam olim, quoniam animas defunctorum humano sanguine propitiari creditum erat, captivos vel mali status servos mercati in exequiis immolabant.' Cf. Ahl (1976) 84–8, who also cites Val. Max. 2. 4. 7; Livy, *Per.* 16; Serv. at Verg. *Aen.* 3. 67; Pauly, *RE* Suppl. 3. 760–84, esp. 760–1; Athen. 4. 153–4, while Castorina (1961) ad loc. cites Hom. *Il.* 23. 175–83 and Serv. at Verg. *Aen.* 10. 519: 'Inferiae sunt sacra mortuorum quod inferis solvuntur. Sane mos erat in sepulchris virorum fortium captivos necari: quod posteaquam crudele visum est, placuit gladiatores ante sepulchra dimicare, qui a bustis bustuarii appellati sunt'. Also cited are Livy, 7. 15. 10, 23. 30. 15, 31. 50. 4 and Werber (1896) 30–1.

[121] Ahl (1976) 86.

[122] I find a similar attitude to my own in relation to the significance of another Roman spectacle, the triumph, in Marshall (1984); p. 126 is admirable: 'But if the "meaning" of the triumph is allowed to have evolved, the investigator of the social significance of the developed ceremony within its contemporary setting need not assume that an understanding of its archaic origins was requisite in the participants' minds for it to retain significance. Nor need he assume that such an understanding holds the *only* key with which the modern historian may unlock the constant "meaning" of the triumph . . . The significance of any social institution cannot be restricted entirely to its earliest beginnings and must accordingly be traced through time as an evolving function of the historical life of the parent society.'

consistently in meditation on the experience of spectatorship. This was first instantiated with reference to the seventh *Eclogue* of Calpurnius Siculus and Corydon's emphasis on his own watching (*spectare*), his marvelling (*mirari*), and on the delights this afforded (*gaudium*). The purpose of the following catalogue is to demonstrate that these are the classic emotions of the spectator in literary accounts of the games.

To begin in Neronian times, it will be noted that the first and third of these experiences are also emphasized in Seneca, *Ep.* 7. 2–3, which gives us a chilling description of the sheer thrill of going to a *munus*, of the degrading pleasures of Seneca's peers:

> Nihil vero tam damnosum bonis moribus quam in aliquo *spectaculo* desidere; tunc enim per *voluptatem* facilius vitia subrepunt. Quid me existimas dicere? Avarior redeo, ambitiosior, luxuriosior? Immo vero crudelior et inhumanior, quia inter homines fui.
>
> Truly, nothing is more harmful to good morals than to waste time at some spectacle; for then pleasure allows vices to creep in more easily. What do you think I am saying? That I return greedier, more ambitious, more extravagant? On the contrary: that I am more cruel and more inhuman because I have been amongst men.

The emphasis on the pleasures of spectatorship is a recurrent theme in Seneca's writing on the games. For instance, at *Ep.* 95. 33, he writes that:

> *Voluptas* ex omni quaeritur. Nullum intra se manet vitium: in avaritiam luxuria praeceps est. Honesti oblivio invasit; nihil turpest cuius placet pretium. Homo, sacra res homini, iam *per lusum ac iocum occiditur* et quem erudiri ad inferenda accipiendaque vulnera nefas erat, is iam nudus inermisque producitur *satisque spectaculi ex homine mors est.*
>
> Pleasure is sought from every quarter. No vice stays within itself: extravagance turns straight into avarice. Once you have forgotten what is right, nothing then is foul as long as the price is right. Man, a sacred thing to man, is now killed for play and for a joke and he whom it was sinful to train to deal and to bear wounds is now brought forth naked and unarmed and a man's death provides a sufficient spectacle.

This is paralleled at *Ep.* 90. 45, where Seneca, writing that primitive man was far from modern killing, asserts:

> Illi quidem non aurum nec argentum nec perlucidos ⟨lapides in⟩ ima terrarum faece quaerebant parcebantque adhuc etiam mutis animalibus: *tantum aberat ut homo hominem non iratus, non timens, tantum spectaturus occideret.*

Indeed, they did not seek gold and silver and shining stones in the very deepest strata of the earth and they still spared even dumb animals: so far were things from the state where a man would kill another man not because he was angry, not because he was afraid but just because he wanted something to watch.[123]

Further instances of the same phenomenon are not hard to find. Livy 41. 20. 10–12, quoted at the beginning of this chapter, considers the games of Antiochus both in terms of their *spectaculum* and the *voluptas* provided. Pliny, *Panegyric* 33. 1, also cited, continues, 33. 3:

Iam quam libera *spectantium* studia, quam securus favor! Nemini impietas ut solebat obiecta, quod odisset gladiatorem; nemo e *spectatore spectaculum factus* miseras *voluptates* unco et ignibus expiavit.

How free now are the passions of the spectators, how safe their favour! Nobody is accused of impiety—as used to be the case—because he hated a gladiator; nobody, turned from spectator into spectacle, has paid for his wretched pleasures with hook and fire.[124]

And Martial's *Liber de Spectaculis*, analysed by Coleman[125] and Moretti[126] for its emphasis on the thaumastic element in the games as proof of the divinity of Titus, returns repeatedly to the experience of *spectare* and *mirari*.[127]

Yet it is Tertullian, previously used only for his remarks on the ritual origins of the games, who develops the theme most penetratingly. Consider the immediate continuation of *De Spectaculis* 12 from the statement of origins, 12. 3–4:

[123] Compare Sen. *Brev.* 16. 3, where people who have a dinner-date and know not how to spend the time up to then are not 'otiosi' but suffer a pain like that 'cum *dies muneris gladiatorii* edictus est, aut cum alicuius alterius *vel spectaculi vel voluptatis* expectatur constitutum, transilire medios dies volunt'. For similar statements in Seneca, cf. *Tranq.* 2. 13: people choose to head for town because '. . . nimis diu a plausu et fragore aures vacaverunt, *iuvat iam et humano sanguine frui*: "Iam flectamus cursum ad urbem." Aliud ex alio iter suscipitur et spectacula spectaculis mutantur'; *Clem.* 1. 25. 2: 'Tunc illi dirus animi morbus ad insaniam pervenit ultimam, cum crudelitas versa est in voluptatem et *iam occidere hominem iuvat*'; *Ira* 1. 2. 4: the fundamental disengagement of the spectator is described: 'Quid? Gladiatoribus quare populus irascitur, et tam inique ut iniuriam putet quod non libenter pereunt? Contemni se iudicat et vultu gestu ardore *ex spectatore in adversarium vertitur*'. Essential too is the attitude of the audience at the human sacrifice in the *Troades*. See *Tro.* 1128–9, 'Magna pars vulgi levis | *odit scelus spectatque*', and 1148 '*mirantur ac miserantur*', and cf. *Tro.* 1086–7.

[124] Cf. Tac. *Hist.* 2. 67. 2 and 3. 83. 3 for the *voluptas* of Vitellius and his subjects in the shows; cf. 2. 70. 3 for 'strues corporum intueri mirari'.

[125] Coleman (1990).

[126] Moretti (1992).

[127] For *spectare* and cognates, see Mart. *Spect.* 2. 5, 3. 2, 15. 5, 21. 1, 24. 1, 24. 5, 28. 9; for *mirari* and cognates, see Mart. *Spect.* 1. 1, 2. 7, 5. 3, 21. 3, 25. 2; for the pleasures of the audience, see 2. 12, 20. 4.

Postea placuit impietatem *voluptate* adumbrare . . . Haec muneri origo. Sed paulatim provecti ad tantam gratiam, ad quantam et crudelitatem, quia feriarum *voluptati* satis non fiebat nisi et feris humana corpora dissiparentur.

Later they decided to cover over their impiety in pleasure . . . This is the origin of the games. Yet little by little they advanced as far in refinement as in cruelty, for the pleasure of the festival was not satisfied unless human bodies too were torn apart by wild beasts.[128]

Again, at 14. 1–2, Tertullian tries to persuade Christians not to go to the amphitheatre, and lambasts the evil pleasures which it affords:

Quasi parum etiam de *spectaculis* pronuntietur, cum concupiscentiae saeculi damnantur. Nam sicut pecuniae vel dignitatis vel gulae vel libidinis vel gloriae, ita et *voluptatis* concupiscentia est; species autem *voluptatis* etiam *spectacula.*

As if enough is not said about the games when the desires of the age are condemned. For the desire of pleasure is the same as the desire of wealth or respect or food or sex or glory; the games too are a type of pleasure.[129]

In the same way, at 20. 1, Christians who defend their presence do so 'for fear of losing pleasure' (*tergiversatione amittendae voluptatis*).[130]

Finally, Tertullian, 21. 2–4 emphasizes the distance between the attitude of the spectators to violent death in the amphitheatre and that shown even to peaceful death outside. This should be quoted in full:

Sic ergo evenit, ut qui in publico vix necessitate vesicae tunicam levet, idem in circo aliter non exuat nisi totum pudorem in faciem omnium intentet; et qui filiae virginis ab omni spurco verbo aures tuetur, ipse eam in theatrum ad illas voces gesticulationesque deducat; et qui in plateis litem manu agentem aut compescit aut detestatur, idem in stadio gravioribus pugnis suffragium ferat; *et qui ad cadaver hominis communi lege defuncti exhorret, idem in amphitheatro derosa et dissipata et in suo sanguine squalentia corpora patientissimis oculis desuper incumbat*; immo qui propter homicidae poenam probandam ad spectaculum veniat, idem gladiatorem ad homicidium flagellis et virgis compellat invitum; et qui insigniori cuique homicidae leonem poscit, idem gladiatori atroci petat rudem et pileum

[128] 'feriarum' = Klussmann, Reifferscheid-Wissowa, Boulanger, and Hoppe; cf. 'ferorum' or 'inferiarum' Glover, 'ferarum' Castorina.

[129] Note that Tertullian continues in much the same vein: 'Opinor, generaliter nominatae concupiscentiae continent in se et *voluptates*: aeque generaliter intellectae *voluptates* specialiter et in *spectacula* disseruntur'.

[130] Cf. Prudent. *c. Symm.* 1126–9: 'Nullus in urbe cadat, cuius sit poena *voluptas*, | nec sua virginitas oblectet caedibus ora. | Iam solis contenta feris infamis harena | nulla cruentatis homicidia ludat in armis', and Prudent. *Perist.* 6. 65–6: 'ac vilis gladiator ense duro | percussus cadit et fremit *voluptas*'.

praemium conferat, *illum vero confectum etiam mortis spectaculo repetat, libentius recognoscens de proximo quem voluit occidere de longinquo*, tanto durior si non voluit.

Thus it therefore happens that a man, who would not lift his tunic in public unless driven to urinate, takes it off in the circus in such a way as to show everyone his genitals; it happens too that a man, who guards his daughter's ears from every coarse word, himself takes her down to the theatre to hear all those oaths and see all those gestures; and that the same man, who checks or shuns anyone fighting over some quarrel in the street, shows his approbation in the stadium for more serious blows; and that the same man, who shudders at the corpse of someone who has died a natural death, lingers with the most patient eyes in the amphitheatre on bodies that have been gnawed and torn apart and arestiff with their own blood; indeed that the same man, who comes to the games to show approval of a punishment for murder, drives a reluctant gladiator to commit murder with whips and beatings; and that the man who demands the lions for all the worst murderers grants a terrible gladiator the reward of the wooden staff and the cap of liberty, and indeed demands to see the corpse of the loser, delightedly examining close up the man he wanted to kill at a distance, all the harsher if he did not.[131]

The significance of the passages italicized should be clear. Spectators in the amphitheatre take an attitude to violent death, which they do not take even to peaceful death in real life. They no longer abhor it, but look on at close range and take pleasure in what they are doing. This is not at all the attitude of pathetic lament with which we are familiar from Vergilian epic, and which Chapters 2–4 have shown Lucan to double and redouble. The invitation to view sections of the *Pharsalia* with the emotions with which it is conventional to view a gladiatorial combat might be equated with Tertullian's description of the reversal of conventional attitudes once inside the amphitheatre: the death of the young man you lament so tenderly when reading the *Aeneid*, now you can enjoy as a spectacle and a wonder.

Yet it does not end there. It is not so easy to mark off some episodes as amphitheatrical and deny the possibility of reading others with the same perspective. Ancient writers on poetics knew the pleasure of seeing an

[131] Note that Tert. *Spect.* 29 emphasizes the alternative *voluptates* and *spectacula* offered by the life of Christian virtue. For another good Christian brought low by a group visit to the amphitheatre, see Augustine, *Confessions* 6. 8 and the story of Alypius. Augustine's friend is forced to go to the games by his friends, but refuses to open his eyes. The games will not affect him, he asserts. Yet he is ruined by the simple sound of the amphitheatre, and his downfall is completed as soon as he opens his eyes: 'Ut enim vidit illum sanguinem, immanitatem simul ebibit et non se avertit, sed fixit aspectum et hauriebat furias et nesciebat, et delectabatur scelere certaminis et cruenta *voluptate* inebriabatur. Et non erat iam ille qui venerat sed unus de turba ad quam venerat, et verus eorum socius a quibus adductus erat.'

artistic mimesis of something horrible, but staved off charges of irrationality and corruption: the motivation was the universal human thirst for knowledge or the pleasure one took solely in the execution of the representation. The experience of such representations, it should be noted, was expressed in terms which might almost have been translated to create the triad catalogued above: θέαμα for *spectaculum*, θαῦμα for *miraculum*, ἥδεσθαι or χαίρειν for *voluptas*.[132] Now, the intrusion of the amphitheatre reminds the reader that the sight of horrible things is a pleasure which extends far beyond the admiration felt for the execution of the artist. And once the reader has dispensed with the myth of artistic admiration, she can begin to ask what exactly are the pleasures afforded by epic.

The Politics of the Amphitheatre

The problem to be confronted in this section might be introduced by means of an anecdote from Seneca. At *De Ira* 2. 5. 1–3, Seneca asserts that some forms of sadistic violence owe more to pleasure than to anger, that in these cases:

> Nec . . . verbera lacerationesque in ultionem petuntur sed in voluptatem.
>
> Beatings and rendings are not sought in the name of punishment but of pleasure.

Those who act thus:

> Rident itaque gaudentque et voluptate multa perfruuntur plurimumque ab iratorum vultu absunt, per otium saevi.
>
> Therefore [they] laugh and rejoice and enjoy great pleasure and are quite different in expression from those who are angry, for they are savage in the name of leisure.

Who are these villains? At 2. 5. 4–5 a first example is given, that of Hannibal who, on seeing a ditch full of human blood, proclaimed 'O what a beautiful spectacle!' (*O formosum spectaculum!*) The words used by Hannibal recall the 'beautiful sight' (τοῦ καλοῦ θεάματος) of Leontios quoted at the start of the chapter, but the Senecan story has a more specific application. This is clear from the pairing of the Hannibal story with that at 2. 5. 5 of Volesus, proconsul of Asia, who, on examining the corpses of the 300 men he had executed in one day, cried out in pride 'O what a kingly deed!' (*O rem regiam!*). The spectatorship described is that of the tyrant.

[132] See esp. Ar. *Poet.* 1448b8–19, *Rh.* 1371b4–9, *Part. An.* 645a11–15; Plut. *Mor.* 18 A–B, 674 A–C.

The problem raised by Seneca's anecdote goes to the heart of the ideology of the *Pharsalia.* Two figures in Lucan are particularly close to the scene from the *De Ira.* These two will dominate not just the close of this chapter but also the Epilogue which follows. The first is Sulla, described at 2. 207–8 by the old men of Rome:

> Intrepidus tanti sedit securus ab alto
> spectator sceleris.

Fearless he sat on high and watched the enormous crime without concern.

The second, much more closely observed, is Caesar, relishing his handiwork after the close of Pharsalus, 7. 786–99:

> Tamen omnia passo,
> postquam clara dies Pharsalica damna retexit,
> nulla loci facies revocat feralibus arvis
> haerentis oculos. Cernit propulsa cruore
> flumina et excelsos cumulis aequantia colles
> corpora, sidentis in tabem spectat acervos
> et Magni numerat populos, epulisque paratur
> ille locus, voltus ex quo faciesque iacentum
> agnoscat. Iuvat Emathiam non cernere terram
> et lustrare oculis campos sub clade latentes.
> Fortunam superosque suos in sanguine cernit.
> Ac, ne laeta furens scelerum spectacula perdat,
> invidet igne rogi miseris, caeloque nocenti
> ingerit Emathiam.

Though he endured all this, when the light of day revealed the destruction wrought by Pharsalus, no aspect of the place drew his lingering gaze away from the murderous fields. He saw rivers running with gore and bodies heaped up as high as lofty hills, he looked at the piles as they rotted away and counted the peoples allied to Magnus; and a place was got ready for his breakfast from which he might recognize the faces and features of the dead. Pleasing it was not to see the soil of Emathia and pass over with his eyes the fields lying hidden under the slaughter. In the blood he saw the favour of Fortune and the gods. And, lest he should lose the happy spectacle of his crimes, he would not let the wretches be burnt on the pyre and inflicted [the sight of] Emathia on guilty heaven.[133]

Sulla is, so to speak, the first Republican king at Rome, Caesar the first emperor. Of Sulla, Fantham comments that 'L. follows his uncle in

[133] The connection between Hannibal's appearance in Seneca and that of Caesar in Lucan is perhaps highlighted by the terms of the narrator's appeal at Luc. 7. 809, 'Nil agis hac *ira*'.

condemning sadistic voyeurism',[134] and it is evident that the attitude of both men is meant to be as invidious as that of Hannibal in Seneca. In particular, the seated posture of Sulla is rightly compared by Fantham to *Troades* 1086–7:

Atque aliquis (nefas)
tumulo ferus spectator Hectoreo sedet.

And some savage spectator (the sin!) sits and watches on the tomb of Hector.

As for Caesar, 'and, lest he should lose the happy spectacle of his crimes' (*ac ne laeta furens scelerum spectacula perdat*) surely marks his pleasure as mad and criminal.

For a Neronian writer, the choice of King Sulla and Emperor Caesar is significant. By this period, the amphitheatre is the classic meeting-point of the emperor with his people, the place where he panders to their pleasures and receives their acclaim. For Lucan the Republican, it might seem only consistent to represent the predecessors of Nero presiding over their own theatre of blood. And the very manner in which Lucan depicts these tyrants suggests that he has the wherewithal to mount a critique of the arena of the sort made by his uncle.[135]

The problem is that it is too easy to represent Lucan as taking a very different position. The poet who talks to Caesar of *Pharsalia nostra* (9. 985), the poem 'you made and I wrote', pays ample tribute to his aesthetic affinity with the conqueror. If Caesar sits down to admire the slaughter of Pharsalus, he also admires the slaughter of the *Pharsalia*, the so eloquent account which Lucan affected not to be able to give (7. 551–6). The *laeta... scelerum spectacula* of Caesar, the *laeta... spectacula* of Roman defeat denied to the Moor at 4. 784—all these are provided by Lucan.

All these games must be put together with those examined more closely in this chapter. The civil war is described too often through the metaphor of the entertainment now so closely associated with the power of the winners. The end result, however, is not to make Lucan simply a partisan of Caesar or a loyal Neronian. Rather, it makes him a writer the vigour of whose historical consciousness is sparked primarily by his vivid awareness of the culture of the present, one who

[134] Fantham (1992*a*) ad loc. Fantham cites as parallels Sen. *Ep.* 7. 4, *Tro.* 1086–7, and *Thy.* 903–4.

[135] For the association of the *foedum spectaculum* motif with tyranny, see Keitel (1992), esp. 342–4 and Vitellius at Tac. *Hist.* 2. 70. 1–4, feasting his eyes on the body-strewn battlefield. Cf. 2. 67. 2 for the *voluptas* he takes in gladiatorial combat.

can set up a dialectic between nostalgia for the lost past he evokes and the guilty pleasures of the present he lives.

The dialectic to which I refer is evoked time and again. Let me close with two examples pertaining to Pharsalus itself. The first is already familiar: while Caesar enjoys the *laeta... scelerum spectacula*, the retreating Pompey is asked at 7. 698–9:

> Nonne iuvat pulsum bellis cessisse *nec istud*
> *perspectasse nefas*?

Is it not pleasing to have been defeated and quit the battle and not watched that horror through to the end?[136]

It is hard for the reader unselfconsciously to associate with either position, with the voyeurism of the former or the defeatism of the latter. This should be compared with the address in Book 4 to the dead Curio, forced to miss the show which the readers have still to 'enjoy', 4. 803–4:

> Ante iaces quam *dira* duces *Pharsalia confert*,
> *spectandumque* tibi *bellum civile* negatum est.

You lie dead before dire Pharsalia pits the generals and you are denied the chance to watch a civil war.[137]

In this last instance, moreover, it does not matter whether one entitles the poem *Pharsalia* or *Bellum Civile*—both are present to force the metapoetic interpretation on the reader. Poor Curio, the loyal Caesarian, is not present to see his general's and his author's greatest performance, but the reader will be, and then must be ever more sure to know whether the battle is truly *dira*, and not a source of spectacle and pleasure. Such, I suggest, is the political dynamic of Lucan's amphitheatre.

[136] For 'perspectasse', see Hutchinson (1993) 87 and n. 17.

[137] For 'conferre' cf. Germanicus, *Aratea* 655, 'Scorpion ingenti maiorem contulit hostem'. Lucan's use of 'confert' here is also a barbed echo of Curio's foolish musing at 4. 705–7, 'Eripe consilium pugna: cum *dira voluptas* | ense subit presso, galeae texere pudorem, | quis *conferre duces* meminit?' The return to an amphitheatrical sense of *conferre* at 4. 803–4 and the description of the death of Curio's men as a spectacle denied to the Moors is exquisite revenge against Curio the ringmaster of the famous revolving wooden amphitheatre deplored at Plin. *HN* 36. 116–20. For more on this, see Ahl (1976) 113–15.

Epilogue—Ecstatic Vision and the Tyrant's Spectacle

RIVERS OF BLOOD AND THE CAESARIAN SPECTATOR

The last chapter closed with the kingly visions of Sulla and Caesar, two murderers feasting their eyes on the spectacle of Rome's transformation. It is pertinent to pause longer on these scenes, to examine further the mentality they depict.

This study opened with Lucan's reaction to the ecstatic vision of Cornelius as recorded by Livy. The claim that one can see something so vividly in one's mind's eye as to seem to be present as a witness was seen to be common to the language of prophecy, of narrative and of rhetoric. In Lucan, one topos combines these categories and in the process offers an essential commentary on the significance of being a spectator at a civil war. That topos is apparent in Caesar's *paraceleusis* at 7. 292–4:

'Videor fluvios spectare cruoris
calcatosque simul reges sparsumque senatus
corpus et inmensa populos in caede natantis.'

'I seem to look at once on rivers of blood, on the kings trodden down and the scattered body of the Senate and peoples swimming in immeasurable gore.'[1]

The general offers what has the ring of an ecstatic prophecy. At 7. 786–99, as Caesar takes his breakfast on the morning after the battle and gazes down on the spectacle of his handiwork, his prophecy takes on a different tone:

Tamen omnia passo,
postquam clara dies Pharsalica damna retexit,
nulla loci facies revocat feralibus arvis

[1] In terms of language, Lucan's model might be said to be Ov. *Her.* 19. 59, 'Nam modo te videor prope iam spectare natantem'. The sense here would seem to be quite different, though this may be a cruel joke—Lucan, 8. 43–54 describes the mental state of Cornelia in terms very similar to those of Hero at and around *Her.* 19. 59.

haerentis oculos. Cernit propulsa cruore
flumina et excelsos cumulis aequantia colles
corpora, sidentis in tabem spectat acervos
et Magni numerat populos, epulisque paratur
ille locus, voltus ex quo faciesque iacentum
agnoscat. Iuvat Emathiam non cernere terram
et lustrare oculis campos sub clade latentes.
Fortunam superosque suos in sanguine cernit.
Ac, ne laeta furens scelerum spectacula perdat,
invidet igne rogi miseris, caeloque nocenti
ingerit Emathiam.

Though he endured all this, when the light of day revealed the destruction wrought by Pharsalus, no aspect of the place drew his lingering gaze away from the murderous fields. He saw rivers running with gore and bodies heaped up as high as lofty hills, he looked at the piles as they rotted away and counted the peoples allied to Magnus; and a place was got ready for his breakfast from which he might recognize the faces and features of the dead. Pleasing it was not to see the soil of Emathia and pass over with his eyes the fields lying hidden under the slaughter. In the blood he saw the favour of Fortune and the gods. And, lest he should lose the happy spectacle of his crimes, he would not let the wretches be burnt on the pyre and inflicted [the sight of] Emathia on guilty heaven.

This passage deserves close attention for its relationship first to the *Georgics*, then to the *Aeneid*.

Vergil's Georgics and the Killing Fields of Civil War

One of the great pathetic topoi of Roman writing on the civil wars is that first expressed at Vergil, *Georgics* 1. 489–92, where the poet laments the double enrichment of the plains of Thessaly with the blood of Rome:

Ergo inter sese paribus concurrere telis
Romanas acies iterum videre Philippi;
nec fuit indignum superis bis sanguine nostro
Emathiam et latos Haemi pinguescere campos.

Therefore Philippi again saw Roman battle-lines meet each other in battle with like spears; nor did the gods disdain twice to enrich Emathia and the broad fields of the Haemus with our blood.

Thomas's commentary on the *Georgics* makes some fascinating observations on these lines, emphasizing the repeated use elsewhere in the *Georgics* of *pinguis* for the richness of soil and comparing Vergil's words with the story at Plut. *Mar.* 21 that the corpses used by the Massilians to surround their vineyards after the battle of Marius with the Ambrones produced an exceptional crop the next year.[2] Roman literature is understandably sceptical as to the final value of this sort of fertilizer, the idea recurring in evocations of the waste of civil war, for instance at Horace, *Carm.* 2. 1. 29–31:

> Quis non Latino sanguine pinguior
> campus sepulcris impia proelia
> testatur?

Which field, enriched with Latin blood, does not testify with tombs to impious battles?

and, crucially for present concerns, in Lucan's emotional response to the battle and to Caesar's spectatorship at 7. 847–54:

> Thessalia, infelix, quo tantum crimine, tellus,
> laesisti superos, ut te tot mortibus unam,
> tot scelerum fatis premerent? Quod sufficit aevum
> immemor ut donet belli tibi damna vetustas?
> Quae seges infecta surget non decolor herba?
> Quo non Romanos violabis vomere manes?
> Ante novae venient acies, scelerique secundo
> praestabis nondum siccos hoc sanguine campos.

Wretched land of Thessaly, with what crime did you so hurt the gods that they should oppress you alone with so many deaths, so many criminal dooms? How much time will it take for forgetful posterity to forgive you the losses of war? What crop will not rise discoloured and with tainted blades? With which ploughshare will you not violate Roman ghosts? Before that time, new battle-lines will come and you will give your fields, not yet dry from this blood, for a second crime.[3]

The attitude of Caesar the spectator gazing at the dead of Pharsalus relates intriguingly to the background to these lines. For here it is by

[2] For rich soil as *pinguis*, see Verg. *G.* 2. 92, 139, 184, 203, 248, 274. At *G.* 1. 495, 'exesa inveniet scabra robigine pila', Thomas compares 2. 220 again on types of soil, 'nec scabie et salsa laedit robigine ferrum'. For blood as fertilizer, Plut. *Mar.* 21 states that the claim goes back to Archilochus, but see also Aesch. *Sept.* 587; Ov. *Her.* 1. 54; Petron. 120. 99; Sil. *Pun.* 3. 261, 14. 130; Stat. *Theb.* 7. 545–6.

[3] Cf. Petron. and the speech of Dis, 120. 96–9, which imitates Vergil and Lucan's language in order to invert it: '*Iam pridem* nullo perfundimus ora cruore, | nec mea Tisiphone sitientis perluit artus, | ex quo *Sullanus bibit ensis* et horrida tellus | extulit in lucem *nutritas sanguine fruges*.' A more conventional attitude is that ascribed to Ascanius at Stat. *Silv.* 5. 3. 39–40, who sets Alba Longa on the hills, 'Phrygio dum pingues sanguine campos | odit et infaustae regnum dotale novercae'. The relationship between Verg. *G.* 1. 489–92 and Luc. 7. 847–72 is first discussed in Paratore (1943) 58–60.

imitation of the same basic text, the *Georgics*, that Lucan evokes his perspective. Lucan, 7. 791: 'he looked at the piles' (*spectat acervos*) depicts Caesar as the successful farmer looking at his own crop, thus reversing Verg. *G.* 1. 158:

> Heu magnum alterius frustra spectabis acervum.

Alas, you will look in vain at the great pile of your neighbour.

Another pun on Pompeius Magnus? One might also consider the warning of Cymodocea to Aeneas at *Aen.* 10. 244–5,

> 'Crastina lux, mea si non inrita dicta putaris,
> ingentis Rutulae spectabit caedis acervos.'

'Tomorrow's light, if you do not think my words are empty, will look on huge piles of Rutulian dead.'

Yet the *Georgic* intertext is more pertinent, since the frustration of the disappointed farmer has now become the satisfaction of the successful Caesar. Again, 7. 794, 'Pleasing it was not to see the soil of Emathia' (*Iuvat Emathiam non cernere terram*) surely recalls a further *Georgic* intertext, Verg. *G.* 2. 437–9,

> Et iuvat undantem buxo spectare Cytorum
> Naryciaeque picis lucos, iuvat arva videre
> non rastris, hominum non ulli obnoxia curae.

And it is pleasing to look at Cytorus waving with box-wood and the groves of Narycian pitch, it is pleasing to see fields not subject to rakes or to any human care.[4]

Rivers of Blood and the Aesthetics of Tyranny

The *Georgics* tell only half the story. The *Aeneid* might have something to contribute as well. For an instance of the prophetic ring of the assertion of a vision, one need look no further than the voice of the Sibyl at *Aeneid* 6. 86–7:

> 'Bella, horrida bella,
> et Thybrim multo spumantem sanguine cerno.'

'I see wars, horrible wars, and the Tiber foaming with much blood.'[5]

This example has a terrible resonance for the *Pharsalia*, for the epic tradition. For it is the sight of rivers of blood, of rivers foaming with

[4] I owe this second parallel to Michael Winterbottom.

[5] For *cerno* in prophecies, see p. 10 n. 4. The image of rivers full with bodies or foaming with much blood has already been used at Verg. *Aen.* 1. 100–1 and the Sibyl's prophecy is then realized repeatedly at 8. 537–40, 10. 20–4, and esp. at 12. 34–6.

much blood, that Caesar so eagerly anticipates at 7. 292–4 and then actually enjoys at 7. 789–91. Caesar therefore relishes what Vergil's Sibyl must abhor, that is an experience to which epic poetic memory grants a privileged position amongst the worst, most horrific moments of the *Iliad*: the killing-spree of Achilles and his final conflict with the Scamander in Book 21. The horror of this moment is kept alive in Greek tragedy and historiography[6] and in Roman poetry before Vergil, for instance at Accius frr. 322–3 (Ribbeck) from the *Epinausimache*:

> Scamandriam undam salso sanctam obtexi sanguine,
> atque acervos alta in amni corpore explevi hostico.

I have covered the holy water of the Scamander with salt blood and have piled up heaps of enemy bodies in the deep river.[7]

And at Catullus, 64. 356–60:

> Currite ducentes subtegmina, currite, fusi.
> Testis erit magnis virtutibus unda Scamandri,
> quae passim rapido diffunditur Hellesponto,
> cuius iter caesis angustans corporum acervis
> alta tepefaciet permixta flumina caede.

Run, spindles, run, drawing out the weft. The wave of Scamander shall witness his great deeds of valour, which pours out in every direction in the swift Hellespont, choking whose course with slaughtered heaps of bodies he will warm the deep river with admixture of blood.

Vergil's Sibyl exclaims 'cerno' in order to give voice to a horrific vision only too vividly perceived in her mind's eye. When she sees the

[6] The motif recurs in tragedy with the threats of the avenger Heracles at Eur. *HF* 572–3. In historiography, Plut. *Dem.* 19. 2 and *Thes.* 27. 6 comment on the disappearance of the river Thermodon and presumes that its name was changed to Haemon because, Plut. *Den.* 19. 2, αἵματος ἐμπλησθέντα καὶ νεκρῶν during the battle of Chaeronea. This offers an intriguing parallel to the gloss 'Haemi . . . campos' as 'fields of blood' identified by R. F. Thomas (1988) at Verg. *G.* 1. 492.

[7] Vergil's language in *Aen.* 6, however, bears a closer relationship to Ennius, *Scaen.* frr. 117–18 (Jocelyn): 'alia fluctus differt dissupat | visceratim membra; maria salsa spumant sanguine'. Later Roman tragedy also employs the motif, for instance Sen. *Tro.* 185–7. The Achillean epic conception of the conflict between hero and river is also prominent in Silius and Statius. At Sil. *Pun.* 4. 625–6, the fighting in the Trebia is described in these terms, 'corporibus clipeisque simul galeisque cadentum | contegitur Trebia, et vix cernere linquitur undas'. At 4. 638–40, the conflict of Scipio with the river takes over, with the addition of the Xerxes-style threat to divide the Trebia into many channels and at 660–6 the anguished reply of the river, modelled closely on the lament of Homer's Scamander. This is paralleled by the conflict at Stat. *Theb.* 9. 225–569 of Hippomedon with the Ismenos, which features the lament of the river at 429–39. For other references to the theme in Silius, see *Pun.* 7. 147–50, 11. 550–2, 13. 743.

Tiber foaming with much blood, she sees 'wars, horrible wars' (*bella, horrida bella*). When Caesar cries 'I seem to look' (*videor spectare*), when he offers his own anticipatory vision of rivers of blood, of the trampled body of the Senate, he omits any reference to the horror, the pathos of the scene. This silence is left inert until he returns for his breakfast the morning after—now the Sibyl's ghastly sight has become something very different, has become a source of aesthetic satisfaction.

The depiction of the victor gazing contentedly at the dismembered, heaped-up bodies of his defeated opponents is a powerful image of the transformation of the Roman State wrought by civil war. Much the same effect is obtained in Books 8 and 9 by the emphasis placed by Lucan on the beheading of Pompey and on the very different reactions to this sight first of his wife and son, then of Caesar, before whose eyes the head is brought by the vile Pothinus.[8] In each case, the reaction of the viewers becomes a measure of their acceptance or refusal of the consequences of civil wars.

When Vergil's Sibyl anticipates the Tiber foaming with much blood, it is insufficient to state that she alludes solely to Homer, Achilles, and the Scamander. For, inasmuch as the *Aeneid* is a story of civil war and an attempt through a myth-historical epic narrative to exorcize the terrible memory of recent Roman history, her words must also have some reference to the horrific days of the first century BC and especially of the 80s. Thus, Cic. *Sest.* 77 describes the conflict in the forum on 23 January 57 BC, when an armed force of gladiators and slaves broke up the assembly at which Q. Fabricius was preparing to propose a motion in favour of the recall of Cicero:

> Meministis tum, iudices, corporibus civium Tiberim compleri, cloacas refarciri, e foro spongiis effingi sanguinem, ut omnes tantam illam copiam et tam magnificum apparatum non privatum aut plebeium, sed patricium et praetorium esse arbitrarentur.

> Members of the jury, you remember that then the Tiber was filled with the corpses of citizens, that the sewers were blocked, that blood was wiped off the forum with sponges, so that everyone thought that a force so great as that, an apparatus so magnificent, could not be that of a private citizen or a plebeian but of a patrician and a praetor.

[8] For the development of the theme, see Luc. 7. 674–5, 8. 632–5 with Mayer (1981) ad loc., 8. 637–9, 8. 646–7, 8. 674–84, 8. 687–91, 9. 104–5, 9. 126–8, 9. 133–40. For the horror of displaying or abusing severed heads, see Sulla at Sen. *Prov.* 3. 7, Livy 3. 5. 9, 'legati . . . caput ferociter ostentantes', and Braund (1993). Perhaps the best parallel is Plut. *Ant.* 20. 3–4, where Anthony ἐθεᾶτο γεγηθὼς καὶ ἀνακαγχάζων the head and right hand of Cicero. For further parallels, see Pelling (1988) ad loc.

Note, however, how the continuation then looks back to the horrific days of the 80s:

Nihil neque ante hoc tempus neque hoc ipso turbulentissimo die criminamini Sestium. 'Atqui vis in foro versata est.' Certe; quando enim maior? Lapidationes persaepe vidimus, non ita saepe, sed nimium tamen saepe gladios: caedem vero tantam, *tantos acervos corporum exstructos*, nisi forte illo Cinnano atque Octaviano die, quis umquam in foro vidit?

You make no accusation against Sestius either before this time or on this most turbulent day. 'Yet there was violence in the forum.' Certainly—when greater? We have very often seen stonings, not so often but still too often swords, but so great a slaughter, so many heaps of bodies piled up, who ever saw this in the forum save perhaps on that day when Cinna and Octavian fought?

Cicero refers to 87 BC, when the consul Cn. Octavius attacked his colleague L. Cinna with an armed force and defeated him. Compare the reference to these events at Cic. *Cat*. 3. 24:

Cn. Octavius consul armis expulit ex urbe conlegam: omnis hic locus *acervis corporum* et *civium sanguine* redundavit.

Cn. Octavius when consul expelled his colleague from the forum by force: all this place abounded with heaps of bodies and with the blood of citizens.

And, by extension, to the vision conjured up by Cicero at *Cat.* 4. 11 in order to defend his 'peculiar humanity and compassion':

Videor enim mihi *videre* hanc urbem, lucem orbis terrarum atque arcem omnium gentium, subito uno incendio concidentem. *Cerno* animo sepulta in patria miseros atque insepultos *acervos civium*, versatur mihi *ante oculos* aspectus Cethegi et furor in vestra caede bacchantis.

For I *seem to see* this city, the light of all the earth and the citadel of all the peoples, collapsing suddenly in one inferno. *In my mind I see* in our buried homeland the wretched and unburied heaps of citizens, *before my eyes moves the sight of Cethegus* playing the mad bacchant in your slaughter.

Most important of all for this context, Valerius Maximus, 9. 2. 1 records that the Sullan terror actually featured the jamming with bodies of the flow of the Tiber:

Lacerata ferro corpora Tiberis inpatiens tanti oneris cruentatis aquis vehere est coactus.

The Tiber rebelling at so great a burden was forced to bear in its bloody waters the bodies torn by the sword.

The importance of this to Lucan will soon become apparent.

Books 1 and 2 of Lucan establish from the start that Roman history is not to be understood in terms of a gradual and painful progress from humble origins to imperial glory but rather as a cyclic pattern of experience culminating every generation in a burst of civil bloodshed.[9] At the close of Book 1, this emerges in another ecstatic vision, that of the matron turned bacchante who anticipates all of Roman history from Pharsalus to Philippi and who closes with a telling response to the idea at Verg. *G.* 1. 489–92 that the two battles were fought on the same field.[10] Vergil's lament has already been cited for the fertilization of the fields; now a second element comes to prominence,

> Ergo inter sese paribus concurrere telis
> Romanas acies *iterum videre* Philippi;
> nec fuit indignum superis bis sanguine nostro
> Emathiam et latos Haemi pinguescere campos.

Therefore Philippi again saw Roman battle-lines meet each other in battle with like spears; nor did the gods disdain twice to enrich Emathia and the broad fields of the Haemus with our blood.

For it is the repetitious nature of the cycle, the second *vision* of civil war, which the matron finally rejects, Lucan 1. 690–4:

> 'Patriae sedes remeamus in urbis,
> inpiaque in medio peraguntur bella senatu.
> Consurgunt partes *iterum*, totumque per orbem
> rursus eo. Nova da mihi *cernere* litora ponti
> telluremque novam: *vidi iam, Phoebe, Philippos*.'

I return to the seat of my ancestral city and impious wars are being waged in the midst of the Senate. The sides rise again and again I go through all the world. Let me *see* new shores of the sea and new land—Phoebus, I have already *seen* Philippi.'

The idea of a cycle of repetition is then underlined in Book 2, which opens with a quasi-choric recollection by the old men of Rome of the previous cycle of civil bloodshed in the 80s.[11] The climax to this

[9] This conception of Rome as passing through repeated cycles of internecine slaughter is even more richly pessimistic than that apparent in Sen. ap. Lact. *Inst.* 7. 15. 14, Flor. *Epit.* 1, pref. 4–8, and Amm. Marc. 14. 6. 4, where the growth and decline of Rome is explained through the analogy of the ages of man. For this, see M. T. Griffin (1976) 194–201.

[10] For the idea of Pharsalus and Philippi fought on the same field, see Ov. *Met.* 15. 823–4, Manil. 1. 910–11, Petron. 121. 111–12, Flor. *Epit.* 2. 13. 43.

[11] For the old men as a chorus, see Conte (1968).

description—most significant for the issues raised here—might first be put into better context by a contrast with Seneca. At Sen. *Prov.* 3. 7 Rutilius turns his back on Sulla's tyranny and distinguishes himself from those who stay behind and see what follows:

'*Viderint*' inquit, 'isti quos Romae deprehendit felicitas tua: *videant largum in foro sanguinem* et supra Servilianum lacum (id enim proscriptionis Sullanae spoliarium est) *senatorum capita* et passim vagantis per urbem percussorum greges et multa milia civium Romanorum uno loco post fidem, immo per ipsam fidem trucidata; *videant* ista qui exulare non possunt'. Quid ergo? *Felix* est L. Sulla quod illi descendenti ad forum gladio summovetur, quod capita sibi consularium virorum patitur ostendi et pretium caedis per quaestorem ac tabulas publicas numerat? Et haec omnia facit ille, ille qui legem Corneliam tulit.

'Let those behold,' he says, 'whom your happy era has caught at Rome. Let them *see* the blood flowing in the forum and, over the Servilian Lake (for that is the trophy-room of the Sullan proscriptions), the heads of senators, and the gangs of executioners wandering everywhere through the city, and the many thousands of Roman citizens slaughtered in one place after you had promised them salvation, even because you had promised them salvation; let them *see* those things, who cannot bear to go into exile.' What then? Is L. Sulla fortunate because his path down to the forum is cleared by the sword, because he allows the heads of former consuls to be shown to him and because he has the quaestor and the public accounts pay out the reward for murder? And he does all these things who passed the Cornelian law.

Lucan too closes with a barb against the *felicitas* of Sulla but now this emerges in the context of the latter, like Caesar, seated aloft so as to get a proper perspective on the bodies too tightly packed to fall, on the corpses clogging the bloody flow of the Tiber, 2. 201–24:

Densi vix agmina volgi
inter et exsangues inmissa morte catervas
victores movere manus; vix caede peracta
procumbunt, *dubiaque labant cervice*; sed illos
magna premit strages peraguntque cadavera partem
caedis: viva graves elidunt corpora trunci.
Intrepidus tanti sedit securus ab alto
spectator sceleris: *miseri* tot milia volgi
non timuit iussisse mori. Congesta recepit
omnia Tyrrhenus Sullana cadavera gurges.
In fluvium primi cecidere, in corpora summi.
Praecipites haesere rates, et strage cruenta
interruptus aquae fluxit prior amnis in aequor,
ad molem stetit unda sequens. Iam sanguinis alti

vis sibi fecit iter campumque effusa per omnem
praecipitique ruens Tiberina in flumina rivo
haerentis adiuvit aquas; nec iam alveus amnem
nec retinent ripae, redditque cadavera campo.
Tandem Tyrrhenas vix eluctatus in undas
sanguine caeruleum torrenti dividit aequor.
Hisne salus rerum, felix his Sulla vocari,
his meruit tumulum medio sibi tollere Campo?
Haec rursus patienda manent, hoc ordine belli
ibitur, hic stabit civilibus exitus armis.

The victors could scarcely move their hands amongst the regiments of the thick-set crowd and the companies pale at the coming of death. Even when they had died they could scarce fall down and they tottered with lolling neck; but the great slaughter weighed on them and the corpses carried out part of the massacre: the heavy corpses crushed the bodies of the living. Fearless he [Sulla] sat on high and watched the enormous crime without concern; he felt no qualm that he had ordered so many thousands of the wretched crowd to die. The Etruscan stream received all the bodies of Sulla's victims heaped together. The first fell into the river, the last onto bodies. Ships heading downstream stuck fast; the river of water was blocked by the bloody slaughter, the front part flowed into the sea, the back stopped at the dam. Now the might of the steeped blood forced a way for itself and, flooding over all the fields and rushing with headlong spate into the Tiber, it aided the blocked water. No longer did the bed and the banks hold back the river and it returned the corpses to the field. Finally and with difficulty it forced its way out into the Tyrrhene waters and split the blue sea with a torrent of red. Was it by these deeds that Sulla earned the title of saviour, of happy, and to build a tomb for himself in the middle of the Campus? These things remain to be endured again, this is the course the war will follow, this will be the end appointed for civil war.[12]

Here again, Lucan introduces elements very closely modelled on *Iliad* 21. Fantham notes in particular the similarity between Lucan, 2. 211–13 and *Il.* 21. 218–20: 'My lovely channels are full of dead men's bodies. I am so choked with corpses that I cannot pour my waters into the sacred sea', and between Lucan 2. 217–18 and *Il.* 21. 235–8: 'He flung up on dry land the innumerable bodies of Achilles' victims that had choked him'. Sulla is unmoved. Nor is he any more affected by what is exquisitely Vergilian in the pathos of his scene. At 2. 196–7, Lucan has opened this scene with the lines:

[12] Lucan here is strikingly different from Sen. *Prov.* 3. 7. It is a topos of consolation in Latin literature to assert the fortune of the dead because they did not live to see the horrors which followed—cf. Cic. *De Or.* 3. 9–10, *Brut.* 4–6; Sen. *Tro.* 145–164. The point of Lucan's representation of Sulla the spectator is that it intensifies the degree of his complicity with events he would normally have been deemed lucky not to see.

> Tum *flos Hesperiae*, Latii iam sola iuventus,
> concidit et *miserae maculavit* ovilia *Romae.*

Then the *flower of Italy*, the only young men of Latium now left, fell down and stained with their blood the Sheepfold of wretched Rome.

The representation of the young men of a country as its flower is characteristic of Vergil.[13] As the scene advances, Lucan extends the impact of this metaphor and describes the sufferings of the youthful victims of the terror in terms drawn from the same metaphorical system: Lucan, 2. 204, 'and they tottered with lolling neck' (*dubiaque labant cervice*), like 3. 737, directly echoes the death of Euryalus at *Aen.* 9. 433–7:

> Volvitur Euryalus leto, pulchrosque per artus
> it cruor inque humeros cervix conlapsa recumbit:
> purpureus veluti cum flos succisus aratro
> languescit moriens, lassove papavera collo
> demisere caput pluvia cum forte gravantur.

Euryalus fell dead, and the blood went over his lovely limbs and his neck collapsed and fell on his shoulders, just as when a purple flower cut by a plough languishes in death, or poppies with weary neck bend down their heads when the rain weighs heavy on them.

Lucan thus concretizes his original metaphor and alludes to the pathetic connotation it customarily bears.[14] It is possible also that his use of 'stained' (*maculavit*) at 2. 197 emphasizes the Vergilian association between the death of virgin soldiers and the spilling of blood at defloration.[15] In this way, yet again, Lucan intrudes an image charged

[13] Fantham (1992a) ad loc. notes the reminiscence of Verg. *Aen.* 8. 499–500, 'iuventus | flos veterum virtusque virum', and 7. 162, 'pueri et primaevo flore iuventus'.

[14] One might also describe Lucan's practice here in the terms of West (1969) as 'transfusion of metaphor' or of Lyne (1989) as 'trespass'. Lyne (1989) 41 n. 7 also relates his ideas to those of Silk (1974) and talks of 'metaphor in place of what would be the ground term'. What is perhaps most characteristic of Lucan is that the pathetic metaphor which he permits to transfuse or trespass in his narrative is his only at second-hand, and derives its impact from its original manipulation in the pathetic repetoire of Vergil.

[15] The metaphorical system here at issue is that discussed in Fowler (1987). Lucan's 'maculavit' recalls Catull. 63. 7, 'recente terrae sola sanguine maculans', used for what might be termed the counterproductive avoidance of defloration of Attis. At Catull. 63. 64 Attis says of himself that 'ego gymnasi fui flos'. The picking of a flower is used as a metaphor for defloration in Catull. 62, and Fowler (1987) explores the bloodshed which connects sexual defloration with the description throughout epic of the death of virgin soldiers as the cutting-down of a flower. 'Maculo' surely translates the Greek μιαίνω, quoted by Fowler in the context of defloration at *Il.* 4. 141–7, Stesichorus, *Geryoneis* (*SLG* S15 ii. 12), and Aesch. *Ag.* 206–16. For the *maculo*–μιαίνω equation, see *TLL* viii. 1. 28. 47. All of this, however, must remain secondary to the fundamental

with the highest pathos by Vergil and uses it as a measure by which to gauge the very different perspective implicit in the impassive response of Sulla. The repeated use of *miseri* and *miserae* at 2. 197 and 208 imposes one interpretation, Sulla offers another.[16]

Conclusion: Cornelius, Caesar and Rhetorical Theory

It is time to return to Cornelius in Gellius, who:

Mota mente conspicere se procul dixit pugnam acerrimam pugnari.

His mind suddenly in a turmoil [he] said that far off he had caught sight of a most bitter battle being fought.

and:

Proinde ut si ipse in proelio versaretur, coram videre sese vociferatus est.

[He] proclaimed that he could see before him, just as if he himself were caught up in the battle.

His language, like that of Caesar's 'I seem to look' (*videor spectare*) is very much the language of the prophetic vision. At the same time, it also recalls that of the orator, and the narrator attempting to draw a verbal picture for his audience. Cicero's repeated employment of the assertion 'I seem to see' (*Videor videre*) is not casual but functions as an implicit claim to have attained the special vividness associated with the family of rhetorical terms related to ἐνάργεια.[17]

observation of Fantham (1992*a*) ad loc. that 'maculavit' emphasizes the death of the young men in the 'Ovilia' as being like the slaughter of sheep taken to market.

[16] Lucan emphasizes the viciousness of Sulla's attitude by making him a spectator immediately at the scene of the slaughter. This is considerably more disturbing even than the versions given at Sen. *Clem.* 1. 12. 1–2 and Plut. *Sull.* 30. 3, where Sulla holds a meeting of the Senate by or in the temple of Bellona on the Campus Martius and bids them ignore the cries of the 6,000 men being killed in the Circus Flaminius. Plutarch's account of Sulla in the temple offers a particularly interesting comparison for Lucan's 'securus spectator': κραυγῆς δέ, ὡς εἰκός, ἐν χωρίωι μικρῶι τοσούτων σφαττομένων φερομένης καὶ τῶν συγκλητικῶν ἐκπλαγέντων, ὥσπερ ἐτύγχανε λέγων ἀτρέπτωι καὶ καθεστηκότι τῶι προσώπωι προσέχειν ἐκέλευσεν αὐτοὺς τῶι λόγωι, τὰ δ' ἔξω γινόμενα μὴ πολυπραγμονεῖν· νουθετεῖσθαι γὰρ αὐτοῦ κελεύσαντος ἐνίους τῶν πονηρῶν. Fantham (1992*a*) at Luc. 2. 207–8 compares Sulla watching from aloft to Xerxes at Hdt. 8. 69 and 90 sitting on his throne in order to watch the Battle of Salamis from land. Certainly, Plut. *Sulla* 30. 4 is quick to attest the political implications of Sulla's behaviour here, stating that even the slowest of the Romans now perceived that what had taken place was a change in tyrant, not an end to tyranny (ἀλλαγὴ . . . τυραννίδος, οὐκ ἀπαλλαγή). Cf. Seneca's introduction to the same anecdote, *Clem.* 1. 12. 1–2: 'Et L. Sullam *tyrannum* appellari quid prohibet, cui occidendi finem fecit inopia hostium?'

[17] See, for instance, *De Or.* 2. 33, *Cat.* 4. 11, *Leg. Ag.* 2. 93, *Phil.* 6. 9. Note how 'I seem to see' is the central notion in various theoretical definitions of ἐνάργεια and its

The prophetic and rhetorical resonances of *videor spectare* offer a key to interpretation of the drastic slippage in Caesar's position between his *paraceleusis* before the battle and his gaze after. If the employment of *videor spectare* to describe the image of rivers of blood seems at first to borrow a trope from ecstatic prophecy, and particularly from the prophecy of Vergil's Sibyl, for the worst of epic warfare—the worst also of civil war—it turns out actually to anticipate a profoundly aesthetic satisfaction in the victor's rearrangement of the body of the State. This aestheticization of the spectacle of civil war is shared by Sulla. In both cases, the new perspective of these figures is made clear by the manner in which their spectacles present them with various archetypes of Homeric and Vergilian pathos (the rivers clogged with bodies, the fields fertilized with blood, the virgin soldier as a flower cut down) now incapable of disturbing their pleasure.

This study closes with Lucan's most potent representation of the Caesarian mentality. The vivid spectacle of civil war presented by Cornelius the *augur* and so eagerly performed by Caesar's centurions finds the audience it always sought. Lucan is the supreme poet of imperial spectator-society. As he describes the coming of the age of the emperors he also describes its coming into being, portrays scenes and episodes which stand as the most vivid metaphors for the experience of contemporary life.

The voice of the narrator in Lucan repeatedly pillories those who accept historical change as treating its moments of crisis as a spectacle to be observed. This is as true of the troops who sell the pass to clemency as it is of Jupiter too indolent to intervene in mortal affairs. For those who cannot make their peace with the Caesars, a number of responses are at hand. For the matron who cannot bear to see Philippi a second time, the only response is a disaffected refusal to see the show through to its close. When Pompey flees the battle at 7. 698–701, Lucan can engage with his reaction in similar terms:

cognates. [Cic.] *Rhet. Her.* 4. 65, for instance, notes that 'Demonstratio est, cum ita verbis res exprimitur, ut geri negotium et res ante oculos esse videatur', while Quint. *Inst.* 9. 2. 40 defines as follows, 'Ab aliis ὑποτύπωσις dicitur, proposita quaedam forma rerum ita expressa verbis ut cerni potius videantur quam audiri'. Similarly, Quint. *Inst.* 8. 3. 61–6 also associates 'videor videre' closely with the concept of ἐνάργεια, 8. 3. 62 asserting that 'Magna virtus res de quibus loquimur clare atque ut cerni videantur enuntiare'. Of the boxing match at *Aen.* 5. 426, it is stated that it is such 'ut non clarior futura fuerit spectantibus', while *Inst.* 8. 3. 65 says of Cic. *Verr.* 2. 5. 86 that 'Ego certe mihi cernere videor et vultum et oculos et deformes utriusque blanditias et eorum qui aderant tacitam aversationem ac timidam verecundiam'. Finally, *Inst.* 8. 3. 66 quotes a fragment of the lost Cic. *Pro Gallo* opening, 'Videbar videre'.

> Nonne iuvat pulsum bellis cessisse nec istud
> perspectasse nefas? *Spumantes caede catervas*
> *respice, turbatos incursu sanguinis amnes,*
> et soceri miserere tui.

Is it not pleasing to have been defeated and quit the battle and not watched that horror through to the end? Look back at the regiments foaming with gore, the rivers disturbed with the flow of blood, and feel sorry for your father-in-law.

Pompey's flight reveals the distortions of his perspective: the soldiers of the Republic fight for him, the army is his corpse. As he moves away from the battle, the narrator's address marks a succession of transformations. Pompey abdicates the power he has so long contested, retreats from the egotism of monarchical pretensions into the struggle for individual dignity which characterizes his best moments in Book 8. Yet it is in his final appearance, as the immortal soul of Book 9. 1–18, that he is ultimately reconciled with the cause. For a Pompey full of the true light of reason and sinking into the avenging breasts of Brutus and Cato is now a quite different figure. This Pompey has transcended the solipsism which turns its back on the struggle as much as the spectacle of civil war. He has found a place for himself in the Republican tradition, the firm ideological grounding of which could once only clearly be perceived after he had run away.

The contribution made by Lucan to the continuing struggle has been my theme throughout this study. The notion that the *Pharsalia* is a form of manifesto, that its function is crudely propagandistic, has never appealed. For all his wildness, Lucan is too meditative a thinker for that; for all his radical dedication to one tradition, he is intellectually too courageous not to engage with the mentality of his opponents, and too discourteous, too funny not to take some shots at the pretensions of his leaders. To found a Republican interpretation of the *Pharsalia* on a wilful disregard for the complexities of the poem would be as futile as to premise an Augustan reading of the *Aeneid* on the resolute obfuscation of irresolution and misgiving.

The prominence in the *Pharsalia* of the disengaged and aesthetically satisfied spectator poses problems which are richly political. To suggest that Lucan employs this figure simply as a mirror for the problem of writing, of reading something as woeful as a civil war would be to make him conform to the introspective, or, more rightly, self-regarding standards of our age. When Lucan contrasts the mentality of the spectator with that of those passionately engaged in resistance to

Caesar, to his heirs, the point is that spectacle—most obviously amphi-theatrical spectacle—is the narcotic with which dissent is lulled into forgetfulness: the theatre resounds, the Senate is silent. You can go along and cheer the king, you can relish the pleasures of his grisly show, or you can turn your back on the spectacle and retreat into inaction. These are two choices, but there is a third: you can think through what is wrong with the empire, you can assert that there are other political values on which to found the State. For those who refuse to accept the finality of Pharsalus, for those willing to attach themselves to the enduring Republican tradition, Lucan's story will always be one of 'venientia fata, non transmissa'.

APPENDIX 1
Apostrophe

Essential to the impact of the narrator's intervention in the *Pharsalia* is his repeated use of apostrophic address to his characters. It is therefore important to offer some brief comment on the nature and function of the apostrophe in ancient narrative and rhetoric.

Quintilian, *Inst.* 9. 2. 38 discusses the apostrophe in the following terms:

> Aversus quoque a iudice sermo, qui dicitur apostrophe, mire movet, sive adversarios invadimus ... sive ad invocationem aliquam convertimur ... sive ad invidiosam inplorationem.
>
> That speech which turns away from the judge, which is called apostrophe, is wonderfully moving, whether we attack our adversaries ... or turn to some invocation ... or to some lamentation designed to cause resentment [of our opponent].

The affective character of the apostrophe is also emphasized in the definitions offered by Cousin and Lausberg.[1] In each case, it is assumed that the apostrophe involves not just a simple shift of addressee, but also a shift deliberately intended to heighten the pathos of the speech or narrative. However, the consensus suggested by these definitions is far from universal. Alternative views of the apostrophe are propounded by the following interpretative traditions.

The first tradition is that represented by the other ancient rhetoricians. Apart from Alexander,[2] none of Phoebammon, Herodian, Aquila Romanus, Julius Rufinianus, Fortunatianus, C. Julius Victor, or Martianus Capella goes beyond the concept of *aversio*, that is of a simple shift of addressee. These writers may have assumed that the apostrophe was pathetic in its effect, but they did not leave any record of such an assumption.

The second tradition is that which treats some or all instances of the poetic apostrophe as a simple metrical convenience. This interpretation of the apostrophe is common in Homeric studies. Nitzsch, for instance, argued early on that the use of the vocative *Μενέλαε* was a resource to overcome the metrical

[1] Cousin (1935) 463–4 cf. Cousin (1936) 53–4; Lausberg (1960) 377–9, §§ 762–5. The affective interpretation is also stressed in Zyroff (1971) and Block (1982).

[2] Alexander at Spengel (1885–6) iii. 23 .28, *Ἀποστροφὴ δ᾿ ἐστίν, ὅταν πρόσωπον ἕτερον ἀνθ᾿ ἑτέρου αἰτιώμεθα, ἤτοι πραΰνειν, ἢ ἐποτρύνειν ἐθέλοντες.*

complexity of the other cases of the name,[3] and the identification of the apostrophe as a simple metrical resource became an orthodoxy among the followers of Milman Parry.[4] The poet as composing machine overcomes a minor difficulty in the construction of his hexameter without affecting the nature of his narrative. This view is, of course, both out of tune with the understanding of the Homeric scholia,[5] and one of the principal targets of the recent reaction to Parry,[6] but it does have a certain fundamental rigour.

The oralists' view of the apostrophe does have an underlying, if limited validity. This might be illustrated with reference to one of the series of apostrophes to Menelaus in the *Iliad*. For instance, at *Il.* 4. 127–8, the narrator reacts to the arrow-shot of Pandarus, addressing Menelaus directly and reassuring him of the protection of the gods:

> οὐδὲ σέθεν, Μενέλαε, θεοὶ μάκαρες λελάθοντο
> ἀθάνατοι.

Nor did the blessed, immortal gods forget you, Menelaus.

Here, one might invoke the distinction between the *propositional content* of the sentence and the *mode of locution*.[7] If the *propositional content* alone were considered, one might say that the sentence printed above and one reading 'Nor did the blessed, immortal gods forget Menelaus', passed on effectively the same message. Only the *mode of locution* was at all different.

The limitation to this view is that ancient criticism can identify at least one type of apostrophe where the distinction between propositional content and mode of locution is denied. What emerges as critical is the degree of seriousness attributed to the notion that the narrator is actually addressing his characters. This is an essentially subjective judgement. One passage of Quintilian can thus be used both to illustrate the continuing suspicion of the overuse of apostrophe and to reveal a significant converse view for when the apostrophe is treated seriously. At *Inst.* 9. 3. 23–4, Quintilian discusses different ways to disrupt the flow of narrative by interjecting the person of the speaker:

[3] Nitzsch (1860). Very similar is C. Bonner (1905). For a cogent reply to Nitzsch, see Endt (1905) 124–5.

[4] For a sceptical account and rebuttal of this view, see A. Parry (1972). Another early piece of scepticism is Hoekstra (1965) 139. Recently, the metrical position has been revived in Matthews (1980). This article, however, does not cite or take account of Parry and is no more able to dismiss every example of apostrophe than Bonner.

[5] De Jong (1987) 13 cites the T-scholion at *Il.* 16. 787: 'The apostrophe shows that [the poet] condoles with you, O Patroclus, who were loved so much by Achilles, who had exerted yourself to save your fellow Greeks, who had patiently endured Nestor's garrulity, who had lovingly tended Eurypulus, who had shed tears because of [the disaster of] the Greeks, who had persuaded unyielding Achilles, who had secured a way out [for the Greeks] at the cost of your own life. By relating all this to the apostrophe one can detect its highly pathetic meaning'. Matthews (1980) 93 parallels this with a number of other citations from Eustathius and the scholia.

[6] Apart from Parry (1972) and Hoekstra (1965), see especially Kahane (1994).

[7] I use 'mode of locution' to translate Quintilian's 'forma eloquendi' (9. 3. 23–4), and do not wish to be taken as using the language of speech-act theory.

Illa quoque ex eodem genere possunt videri: unum quod *interpositionem* vel *interclusionem* dicimus, Graeci παρένθεσιν ⟨sive⟩ παρέμπτωσιν vocant, cum continuationi sermonis medius aliqui sensus intervenit: 'Ego cum te (mecum enim saepissime loquitur) patriae reddidissem': cui adiciunt *hyperbaton* qui id inter tropos esse noluerunt; *alterum quod est ei figurae sententiarum quae ἀποστροφή dicitur simile, sed non sensum mutat, verum formam eloquendi:* 'Decios Marios magnosque Camillos, | Scipiadas duros bello et te, maxime Caesar'.

The following too may be considered to belong to the same class: first, that which we entitle *interpositio* or *interclusio* and which the Greeks call *parenthesis* or *paremptosis*, that is when some remark interrupts the continuous flow of speech, for example 'When I had restored you (for he speaks to me very often) to the fatherland'; to this those who refuse to class it amongst the tropes add *hyperbaton*; then there is that one which is similar to the figure of thought which is entitled *apostrophe* but which does not change the sense, only the mode of locution: 'the Decii, the Marii, and the great Camilli, | the Scipios tough in war and you, greatest Caesar'.

What is clear here is that Quintilian does not regard the use of a vocative simply to break up and enliven a catalogue as an apostrophe proper. This is significant, for it is just this sort of figure which becomes particularly commonplace in imperial Latin epic,[8] and which leads to judgements condemnatory of the use of apostrophe in general. These are traditionally harshest towards Lucan, who uses the apostrophe with greater statistical frequency than any other Latin epicist. Thus, Duff's Loeb translation simply suppresses most instances of the apostrophe, restricting the use of the figure to the few occasions which the author considers justify it.[9] The sense of a figure diluted by undue repetition is also evident in the standard German studies of the apostrophe, those of Endt and Hampel.[10] In the case of the latter, evangelical theology seems to take over as he laments the fall of the apostrophe from its proper condition.[11]

According to Quintilian, casual use of the vocative is not the same as apostrophe. In this, he propounds a view shared by many modern critics. On the

[8] e.g. Sil. *Pun.* 3. 287–9, 4. 235, 4. 635, 5. 544, 8. 392, 12. 526, 14. 223, 14. 226, 14. 229, cf. Val. Flacc. *Arg.* 1. 391, 1. 398, 5. 106.

[9] Duff (1928) p. viii observes that 'In Latin apostrophe is often a metrical device, and often a meaningless convention. There are indeed in Lucan many passages where it adds to the rhetorical effect. Yet even here I believe that more is gained than lost, if it is generally ignored in the translation. The combination of apostrophe and plain statement, common in Lucan, is hardly endurable in English.' Cf. Marti (1975) 83–4, 'Such syntactical changes of focus are not warranted by logic or grammar and can hardly be translated into English. The translators regularly eliminate them and proceed as if Lucan had used the straight authorial narrative, with nominative subjects and verbs in the third person.'

[10] Endt (1905) and Hampel (1908).

[11] Ibid. 37 and 42–3. In the latter case, Hampel dates the fall as far back as Φοῖβε at Hom. *Il.* 15. 365.

other hand, the particular address which he quotes, to 'maxime Caesar', i hardly the most obvious instance of a casual and meaningless vocative. Moreover, the manner in which he distinguishes the casual from the serious apostrophe suggests a susceptibility to the full implications of the form which Du and his peers might find disturbing. Quite simply, if the figure like the apostrophe but distinct from it is characterized by its 'mechanical' change in th *forma eloquendi*—that is the *mode of locution*—one must ask in what way the apostrophe proper changes the *sensus*—that is the *propositional content*. The answe coheres with the conclusions drawn from the analysis of Homer's address t Menelaus: the poet changes the *propositional content* of his statement in that h would not have the reader dismiss the apostrophe as just a particular choice o phrasing, which communicates a message capable of full translation into third person narration. Rather, he truly is talking to his characters, does have a special relationship with the world of his verse, and, like it or not, this is part o the message communicated.

Apostrophe is a famously embarrassing form.[12] In Lucan, however, apostrophe is also deadly serious. Quintilian's distinction should not be used to support a generalizing prejudice against the figure, rather as a statement of its true potential. If the second implication of his judgement is accepted, that the poet involves himself actively with his characters, then it is possible fully to engage with Lucan's narrative technique.

[12] Culler (1981) 135–44 demonstrates this in his analysis of attitudes to apostrophe among critics of the Romantics.

APPENDIX 2

Theories of Tensing in Narrative, the Latin Present Historic, and Lucan's Vivid Present

TRANSGRESSIVE TENSES

The use of the apostrophe in Lucan is only one of the elements in the poet's creation of a vivid presence at the time and place of the narrative. In particular, he combines his use of the apostrophe with a sophisticated manipulation of tense and temporality of narrative. The purpose of this appendix is to set out the terms in which it is possible to analyse the poet's use of the present-tense form and, in particular, to state what distinguishes the highly abnormal use in narrative of a 'vivid present' from the quite conventional use of the Latin present historic. I therefore begin with two linguistic models for analysing tenses in speech and in narrative.

JAKOBSON AND MARKEDNESS RELATIONS

The concept of markedness[1] posits that in many morphological, grammatical, and semiotic systems there exists an asymmetrical binary relationship between a property which will be denoted as unmarked because 'normal' and another which is considered marked because 'abnormal'. For instance, in spoken language, the convention is the present tense, which is therefore considered unmarked. The introduction of a past tense is less usual and is thus marked. The factor which renders it marked, that of time before now, is given the title of *x*, and sentences may be analysed as follows:

(*a*) Zero-interpretation: 'Politicians cheat the electorate'. Here, the sentence applies the fundamental atemporal function of the present-tense system, one which makes statements of relevance across the temporal spectrum. This is entitled the zero-interpretation because the presence or absence of the factor *x* is deemed non-pertinent.

(*b*) Minus-interpretation: 'I am going to Exeter today'. Here, the absence of *x*

[1] My remarks here are based on Jakobson (1990) Ch. 8, 'The Concept of Mark', and on the discussion offered in Fleischman (1990) 52–61.

is specifically noted in that the time-frame of the action described is clearly located in the present.

(*c*) Plus-interpretation: 'I went to Pisa yesterday'. Here, the presence of *x* is specifically noted in that the time-frame of the action is clearly located in the past.

The above is an outline of the apparent dynamics of markedness in spoken English. It will be noted that the relationship is essentially asymmetrical in that the present-tense system, the unmarked category, by its generic or atemporal uses, has the capacity to speak both for non-*x* and for *x* in a way in which the past cannot. This point is given a wide range of examples by Waugh.[2]

However, it would be wrong to assume that the dynamics of markedness are the same for written narrative as they are for spoken English. In fact, there is a clear reversal in that the conventional tense of narrative, the unmarked category, is actually the past. Further, in modern English there is no presupposition of a specific time-location either for narrator or for subject-matter. Thus, as narrator, I can begin a novel: 'Only 30 years ago, just after the end of the Korean war', when my time-location for both categories will be clear; or I can begin 'Jim got up, packed his trunk and left . . .', where the time-location of the characters will be left unstated and perhaps only vaguely ascertainable from the context of the action, and that of the narrator simply left out of consideration. However, it will be marked, or unusual, for a narrator either to relate the experience of the narrative to the now of narration, or to pretend, as Lucan occasionally does, that the now of the narrator is contemporaneous with that of the action. For whatever reason, there is an underlying metaphysical preconception which leads us to tell almost any story in the past. This is an instance of what Fleischman describes as the reversal of markedness relations in oppositions dominated by marked contexts, of the contrast between 'global' markedness relations and 'local' divergences.[3]

It will be seen from the formalization of English written narrative as a description of something placed clearly or arbitrarily in the past that the marked element in such a process is the present-tense system. Here, two distinct effects can be attributed to the use of the present tense. The first is the creation of the air of vivid immediacy which we associate wth story-telling in the present historic. This is most commonly connected with the notion of perception without reflection, of events recorded as they pass the eye.[4] This is a

[2] Waugh (1980).

[3] Fleischman (1990) 54–5: 'The idea that markedness values often reverse in oppositions dominated by marked contexts provides a strong linguistic foundation for the view that the unmarked tense of narrative is the (PFV) P [perfective preterite].'

[4] This is the conclusion of Casparis (1975). Cf. Barthes (1967) 32: 'When, within the narration, the preterite is replaced by less ornamental forms, fresher, more full-bodied, and nearer to speech (the present tense or present perfect), literature becomes the receptacle of existence in all its destiny and no longer just its meaning alone. The acts it recounts are still separated from History, but no longer from people.'

contentious issue—and one where linguistic surveys are constantly wrong-footed by the latest experiments of the twentieth-century novelists they take as a sample—but it would not be too crude to say that one possible effect is to suggest that the temporal position of the narrator is contemporary with that of the narrative.

The second use of the present-tense system is that which gives clear signalization to the perspective, comment, reaction of the narrator to her story. This can either have the effect of expressing a high level of immediate emotional involvement of the speaker with the event or it can actually emphasize the distance between speaker and event. In the latter case, the narrator's comment or assessment can give the story a different communicative purpose, turning a simple story for its own sake into one used as an example, with the aim of convincing the reader of a given point of view in her own world. My point of reference here is the distinction between *histoire* and *discours* drawn by Benveniste, and it is to this theory that I now turn.

BENVENISTE ON NARRATIVE AND DISCOURSE

Consideration of the concept of mark leads inevitably from an abstract sense of the markedness of the past in oral speech, or of the present in narrative, to consideration of the practical impact of employing a marked tense. It is at this point, therefore, that it is necessary to consider Benveniste's model[5] for explaining and assessing that impact.

Benveniste identifies two separate systems of communication, *histoire* and *discours*, terms normally translated in English as 'narrative' and 'discourse'. He then allocates certain tenses and persons to one system or the other, implying that the presence of tenses and persons belonging to the one system in a communication dependent on the other would be seen as marked. *Histoire* is therefore defined as that form of historical statement which characterizes a narrative of past events and which recounts those events without any intervention by the narrator;[6] *discours*, by contrast, as presupposing a speaker and a listener and the intention of the former somehow to influence the latter.[7]

Benveniste's purpose in identifying these two systems is to offer an explanation for the distribution of the *passé simple* and *passé composé* in French. Yet his

[5] The work under discussion is Benveniste (1966). A similar model is offered by Weinrich (1964) 36–8 and the concept of the 'Tempusgruppen'. If the following discussion concentrates on the system of Benveniste, and rather ignores Weinrich, it is first, because his exclusion of the past tense from the world of comment seems far too rigid; second, because it is Benveniste who has attracted the most creative response.

[6] Benveniste (1966) 238–9 defines *histoire* as 'L'énonciation historique, aujourd'hui réservée à la langue écrite, caractérise le récit des événements passés. Les terms "récit", "événement", "passé" sont également à souligner. Il s'agit de la présentation des faits survenus à un certain moment du temps, sans aucune intervention du locuteur dans le récit.'

[7] Ibid. 242.

system moves beyond the simple observation that the former is now restricted to written narrative, the latter generally to spoken French. Rather, this division is only part of the broader phenomenon, in which the category of *histoire* dispenses entirely with the *passé composé*, the present, the future, and the first and second persons, while that of *discours* can adopt all persons and all tenses save the *passé simple*. The exclusion of the *passé composé* from *histoire*, and preference for the *passé simple*, therefore, is only one aspect of the objective, distanced attitude of this mode.[8] While *discours* relates everything to the present of the speaker, and is permeated with the relation of one person to another, *histoire* adopts forms (the third person, the *passé simple*) which maintain the maximum separation of the writer from his material. This principle extends logically to the exclusion of *hic* and *nunc* deictics.[9]

Benveniste's argument is impressive, but not absolutely watertight. Comparison of his conception of narrative (founded on examples from Grote and Balzac) with that of the story-teller in Benjamin is revealing and it is hard not to feel that Benveniste extrapolates universal rules from what Benjamin regards as the specific historical experience of the 'bourgeois novel'.[10] No less troubling is the direct reply of Genette, who demonstrates that even an apparently absent Balzac (or his invented narrator) actually permeates his text.[11] However, such criticism does not entirely undermine the thesis. Indeed, it reveals the fundamental strength of Benveniste's model. For Genette operates by demonstrating the implicit presence of the narrator and his values, and not the explicit markers of perfect, present, and future tenses, first or second person, and consequently his response should be taken essentially as an instantiation of what the narrator in *histoire* ends up doing in spite of himself, and not as a complete debunking of the concept.

What emerges as of paramount importance is the testing of Benveniste's schema against empirical data. The viability of his system as a working model

[8] Ibid. 248: 'À mesure que l'aoriste se spécifie comme le temps de l'événement historique, il se distance du passé subjectif qui, par tendance inverse, s'associe à la marque de la personne dans le discours. Pour un locuteur parlant de lui-même, le temps fondamental est le présent; tout ce qu'il prend à son compte accompli en l'énonçant à la première personne du parfait se trouve rejeté immanquablement dans le passé.'

[9] Ibid. 239: 'Nous définirons le récit historique comme le mode d'énonciation qui exclut toute forme linguistique "autobiographique". L'historien ne dira jamais "je" ni "tu", ni "ici" ni "maintenant", parce qu'il n'empruntera jamais l'appareil formel du discours, qui consiste d'abord dans la relation de personne je:tu. On ne constatera jamais dans le récit historique strictement poursuivi que des formes de troisième personne'. Cf. ibid. 245: 'Le présent serait nécéssairement alors le présent de l'historien, mais l'historien ne peut s'historiser sans dementir son dessein. Un événement pour être posé comme tel dans l'expression temporelle, doit avoir cessé d'être présent, il doit ne pouvoir plus être énoncé comme présent.'

[10] Benjamin (1969).

[11] Genette (1969). Genette (1984) 66–9 goes on to describe 'le récit sans narrateur, l'énoncé sans énonciation' as a chimera, a mythical beast he would, in any case, not care to meet.

on which to base a pattern of markedness relations in narrative is not global, but dependent substantially on the literary history of the texts to which it is applied and on the specific language in which those texts are composed.

The first point, therefore, is that the concept of *histoire* is of undeniable pertinence to Lucan's literary history. For the wider genre of ancient epic is particularly careful to establish the relationship of the narrator to the world of his narrative, and essentially to keep that relationship distanced and objective. Where Vergil differs from the Homeric 'ideal form' of epic, his innovations occur within a system and a sensibility very conscious of its fundamental identity.

The specific qualities of the Latin language, however, demand a considerable modification of Benveniste's original model. In the ensuing sections of this Appendix and of Appendix 3, therefore, close attention is given to the role of the present and of the future tenses in Latin epic narrative. Of these, the use of the future causes far fewer problems. In its historic form, it is seen to be a surprising usage; it is as marked and as rare in Latin narrative as Benveniste would wish it to be in French, because it depends on a conception of the temporal present. In order to understand its role in epic narrative, however, it is necessary to classify its different functions. By contrast, the use of the present tense in past-tense narration will be seen to defy the crude application of English or French linguistic experience, and to function according to a very different set of rules. This does not preclude discussion of a vivid present in Lucan, but only where the use of temporal and local deixis gives the grammatical present the specific rhetorical sense of describing the temporal present of the speaker.[12]

PRESENT HISTORIC AND VIVID PRESENT IN LATIN LITERATURE

Which modifications is it necessary to make in order to apply Benveniste's model of narrative and discourse to Latin narrative? Two facets of the Latin verb, above all, must be emphasized.

The first facet is the absence in Latin of the twin forms of *passé composé* and *passé simple*, there being only what is known as the perfect tense. Meillet and his disciples initially identified this tense as the *praesens-praeteritum*, but the latest assessment concludes that the Latin perfect is essentially aoristic in aspect.[13] This latter point is, however, less significant. What is fundamental is that, whatever the real aspect of the perfect, it stands alone and one cannot look for the dynamics of markedness relations between two tenses of the past-tense system.[14]

[12] It is in this sense that I will talk henceforth of the 'rhetorical present' of the narrator.

[13] Serbat (1975) and (1976). For a discussion of Meillet, see Serbat (1976) 330–4, esp. 330 n. 4.

[14] For this, see also Bergsland (1942) 29.

Or, at least, the perfect stands alone except in relation to the second facet which must be underlined: the prominence of the present historic. To Benveniste, the French present historic is just an artifice of style. By this, he must mean that the present historic is an artificial mode designed to inject a degree of urgency, vividness, and immediacy into the narration of past events of the sort discussed above with regard to markedness.[15] In Latin the situation is rather different.

The Latin present historic has often been explained in the same terms of vividness and urgency. Szantyr, for instance, asserts that the present historic is used for the crises in a narrative and that these events are thus felt to be closer because rendered vividly present.[16] Kühner, Heinze, and Otis adopt very similar positions.[17] Yet this mode of interpretation is far from satisfactory. The presumption of vividness seems to be drawn instinctively from an association of the grammatical present tense with the rhetorical expression of the speaker's present. There exists, however, an alternative approach far truer both to linguistic theory and to the empirical reality of Latin literature.

The fundamental contention of linguistic theory with regard to the present is that it is atemporal. The interpretation of the present historic as vivid, on the other hand, depends essentially on an equation of the present tense with an implicit 'now' which cannot be justified. To state the point simply, the past tense in all languages essentially describes only those events occurring before the 'now' of the speaker, the future only those events occurring after. Of course, some languages possess a gnomic perfect or future, but neither tense so naturally or frequently serves the universalizing function as the present. A statement such as 'All poets are lunatics' inevitably transcends the 'now' of the speaker and makes a claim with regard to poets both of the past and the future. This is equally true of French and Latin.[18]

The atemporality of the Latin present is the basis of the alternative interpretation of the Latin present historic. Following this premise, Serbat,[19] von Albrecht,[20] and Quinn[21] all develop the same two fundamental observations. The first is that the present historic preponderates to such an extent over the perfect and imperfect in, for instance, Caesar and Vergil, that it can hardly be regarded as a specially selected stylistic device.[22] The second is that the

[15] For Long. *Subl.* 25 and the similar effect of the Greek present historic see p. 13 n. 9.

[16] Leumann, Hofmann, and Szantyr (1965) ii. 305–7.

[17] Kühner (1912) ii. i. 114; Heinze (1915) 374; Otis (1963) 46. I engage below with the example offered by Otis, that of Vergil's boat race.

[18] The atemporality of the present is the basis of the analysis of the present historic offered at Serbat (1975) 383 ff. For this, see also Bergsland (1942) 27–8 and Pinkster (1983) 275 and 310–14.

[19] Serbat (1975) 383–90.

[20] Von Albrecht (1970). See also von Albrecht (1968).

[21] Quinn (1963) ch. 8, 'The Tempo of Virgilian Epic'.

[22] Serbat (1975) 387 quotes the figure of 520 historics to 121 perfects in Caes. *B. Civ.* 1. Quinn (1963) 222 and n. 1 notes that historics outnumber perfects in Vergil in a ratio of 3 : 1.

present historic never appears unless preceded by an introductory past tense.[23]

The second observation leads Quinn and von Albrecht to the paradoxical conclusion that it is actually the Latin perfect which has a properly stylistic function, serving to mark the crucial points in the narrative. Both authors offer plentiful examples for this point, but it will not hurt to offer two further instances, both from the boat-race in *Aeneid* 5. Thus, at *Aeneid* 5. 202–6, a succession of perfects mark the crucial crash of Sergestus:

> Namque furens animi dum proram ad saxa suburget
> interior spatioque subit Sergestus iniquo,
> infelix saxis in procurrentibus *haesit*.
> Concussae cautes et acuto in murice remi
> obnixi *crepuere* inlisaque prora *pependit*.

For while Sergestus mad of mind drove his boat in towards the rocks and came up on the inside where there was not enough room, the wretch stuck firm on the rocks that jutted out. The cliffs were shaken and the oars made a din as they crashed against the sharp stone and the crushed prow hung useless.

This should be compared with *Aeneid* 5. 239–43, which marks another turning-point in the action, that is the successful prayer of Cloanthus, this time with four perfects:

> *Dixit*, eumque imis sub fluctibus *audiit* omnis
> Nereidum Phorcique chorus Panopeaque virgo,
> et pater ipse manu magna Portunus euntem
> *impulit*: illa Noto citius volucrique sagitta
> ad terram *fugit* et portu se *condidit* alto.

He spoke and all the chorus of the Nereids and of Phorcus and the maid Panopea heard him in the very depths of the sea, and father Portunus himself drove him on his way with his own great hand: the boat sped to land faster than the South wind or a winged arrow and buried itself in the deep harbour.

However, it is Serbat who offers a linguistic explanation for the patterns of appearance of the historic present: the preceding past tense acts as a 'paragraph-marker', qualifying the present historics as past in the manner that *hodie* combined with the first person would mark as present a sentence reading *hodie eius gladios pertimesco*.[24]

23 This point was first established in Emery (1897) with regard to Plautus. See also Pinkster (1983) 310–14.

24 Serbat (1975) 390 concludes that 'Il est plus correct de dire qu'une forme dénommée à tort "présent" s'oppose comme non temporelle à toutes les autres formes, qui sont temporelles.'

This is an important idea. It will again be helpful if it is given practical exemplification. An obvious case is the opening of Vergil's boat race, *Aeneid* 5. 104–23:

> Exspectata dies *aderat* nonamque serena
> Auroram Phaethontis equi iam luce *vehebant*,
> famaque finitimos et clari nomen Acestae
> *excierat*; laeto *complerant* litora coetu
> *visuri* Aeneadas, pars et certare *parati*.
> Munera principio ante oculos circoque *locantur*
> in medio, sacri tripodes viridesque coronae
> et palmae pretium victoribus, armaque et ostro
> perfusae vestes, argenti aurique talenta;
> et tuba commissos medio *canit* aggere ludos.
> Prima pares *ineunt* gravibus certamina remis
> quattuor ex omni delectae classe carinae.
> Velocem Mnestheus *agit* acri remige Pristim,
> mox Italus Mnestheus, genus a quo nomine Memmi,
> ingentemque Gyas ingenti mole Chimaeram,
> urbis opus, triplici pubes quam Dardana versu
> *impellunt*, terno *consurgunt* ordine remi;
> Sergestusque, domus *tenet* a quo Sergia nomen,
> Centauro *invehitur* magna, Scyllaque Cloanthus
> caerulea, genus unde tibi, Romane Cluenti.

The awaited day had come and the horses of Phaethon were bringing in the ninth dawn with serene light and the news and the name of famous Acestes had stirred the neighbouring peoples; they had filled the shores in a happy throng, meaning to see the men of Aeneas, and some of them ready to compete. First of all, the prizes are set out before their eyes in the middle of the arena: sacred tripods and green garlands and palms, the reward for the victors, and weapons and garments dyed with purple and talents of silver and gold. And a blast of the trumpet from the central mound proclaims the start of the games. Matched with heavy oars, four ships chosen from all the fleet enter the first contest. Mnestheus and his eager oarsmen drive the swift *Pristis*, soon to be Mnestheus the Italian, from whose name comes the family of the Memmii, and Gyas the *Chimaera* huge with a huge mass, the size of a city, which three rows of Trojan youth drive on, the oars rising in three ranks; and Sergestus, from whom the house of the Sergii takes its name, rides the great *Centaur* and Cloanthus, from whom stems your family, Roman Cluentius, the blue *Scylla*.

The function of the present historic observed by von Albrecht and related by Serbat to the concept of the paragraph-marker is apparent in this passage. A cluster of present historics is noticeable, from 5. 109 (*locantur*) to 5. 122

(*invehitur*).[25] This cluster is introduced by past-tense paragraph-markers in the form of the mixture of two pluperfects and two imperfects at 5. 104–7. It is interrupted by the atemporal present of the ecphrastic *est* locution at 5. 124–8, and closed completely by *constituit* and *scirent* at 5. 130–1. This, in turn, however, introduces a further cluster of historic presents from *legunt* at 5. 132 to *haurit* at 5. 137.[26]

It is clear that Serbat's concept of the paragraph-marker does go a long way towards explaining the significance of the present historic in Latin narrative.[27] No less important is his explanation of the effect of the present historic: that is, as a lightening agent for a narrative weighed down by the consciousness of its own pastness.[28]

This is a crucial observation. It might, however, be pushed further. For the present tense in Latin is not marked just by its atemporality, but also by another lightening quality, that is its lack of any clear *aspect*. The situation is made explicit only by the context or by the *performance type* of the verb itself, and not by the explicit evidence of the verbal form.

By *aspect*, I refer to 'the manner in which the verb action is regarded or experienced'.[29] In English, the distinction can be made between verbal forms which describe single, completed actions, and which therefore are deemed *perfective*, and those which describe habitual or repeated actions and states, which are deemed *imperfective*. One can also mark an action in progress but expected at some time to end by the *progressive* form, 'he was doing his best', 'is still walking'.[30] In Latin narrative, the perfect and pluperfect tenses can represent only the perfective, the imperfect tense can represent only the imperfective or

[25] This does not, however, include *tenet* at 5. 121, which refers to the rhetorical present of the narrator.

[26] Other segments conforming to the rule are 5. 139–43 and 5. 148–58; 5. 159–61; 5. 164–5; 5. 166–71; 5. 172–7; 5. 178–82; 5. 183–9 and 197–200; 5. 201–12 and 218–24; 5. 244–9; 5. 268–72 and 280–5. Of those segments conforming to the rule, 5. 104–23, 159–61, 166–71 and 268–72 begin with a backgrounding imperfect or pluperfect; the other segments begin with a perfect, except for 244–9, which begins with an ablative absolute and *tum*.

[27] Norden (1957) at *Aen.* 6. 3–5 offers an unintended illustration of the principle of the paragraph-marker. Citing 6. 212–25 as an instance of the 'regellos' exchange of imperfects, perfects, and historics, he ignores the sequence of two backgrounding imperfects, one perfect, and nine continuous historics. He is wrong to see metre as the only criterion.

[28] Serbat (1975) 389 argues that 'La fonction principale du "présent historique" est donc de rendre un énoncé moins lourd, plus économique; riche de la même information qu'un récit au passé, bien qu'il évite de répéter constamment l'appartenance des faits à la "Zeitstufe" du passé, le récit au présent sera moins chargé, plus agile.'

[29] Quirk *et al.* (1972) 90–9. Much of what follows is dependent on their definitions.

[30] The progressive form is obviously imperfective in the broadest sense of the word. However, there is also the important distinction between dynamic and stative verbs, the latter very rarely appearing in the progressive form, generally in the imperfective. The Latin historic present is used for the progressive form of dynamic verbs. For the basic distinction, see Quirk *et al.* (1972) 93–7.

progressive aspects. On the other hand, the *background* events of a narrative are liable to be represented by the pluperfect or imperfect, the *foreground* by the imperfect or perfect. As for the present historic, it is used for *foreground* events, and after a backgrounding paragraph-marker, but is still able to operate either perfectively or progressively. There thus evolves a narrative which is no longer weighed down by constant indication of aspect: *currit* can stand for 'he was running' (*currebat*) or for 'he ran [to the end of the road]' (*cucurrit*). Free from the burden of constant change of suffix or prefix, or both, a narrative may advance smoothly, while the reader is drawn in and experiences the involvement which others have taken to be the effect of a vivid rhetorical present.[31]

The ability of the present historic to depict all categories of aspect can be discerned from the passage cited above. Here, while 5. 114 *ineunt* seems to describe the advance of all the competitors, and can legitimately be described as a perfective present historic describing a single completed action, it is unclear how far the following verbs describe further individual actions in sequence, or whether they are actually progressive or imperfective in aspect and form an ecphrasis of the scene before the off. For example, *agit* is much more difficult to read as one single action 'drove' than as progressive 'was driving'. This is true of other phrases as well. Lines 118–20, for instance, clearly describe an incomplete situation. Thus, the repeated adjectival description of the boat as huge, with a huge mass, and the size of a city, is given verbal elucidation by the description of the triple banks of men in the lines that follow. Similarly, *invehitur* at 122 is surrounded by the adjectives *magna* and *caerulea*, the two of which together put the emphasis of the sentence less on the action of riding than on the description of the scene as the competitors ride out. The verb must be read as progressive, and the section as a whole as the narrative pause typical of ecphrasis.

The ability of the present historic to assume different aspects is also prominent in a further passage from the boat race. Here, however, the action is reaching its climax, and it is important to note the use made of the historic form's various facilities in constructing an involving narrative, *Aeneid* 5. 225–43:

> Solus iamque ipso *superest* in fine Cloanthus,
> quem *petit* et summis adnixus viribus *urget*.
> Tum vero *ingeminat* clamor cunctique sequentem
> *instigant* studiis, *resonatque* fragoribus aether.
> Hi proprium decus et partum *indignantur* honorem

[31] For this, see Pinkster (1983) 313–14. The present-tense system, free from aspectual mark, not only provides a continuous narrative, but also one which is genuinely morphologically lightened because free from the suffixes (*parat* cf. *para-vit* or *para-bat*) which constantly identify the aspect of perfects and imperfects. Cf. Koller (1951), who argues for an *inceptive* aspect to the present historic in the Greek historians and in Latin, but whose reasoning becomes overcomplicated and loses the thread. Serbat (1975) 389 n. 1 is harsh in his censure.

ni teneant, vitamque *volunt* pro laude pacisci;
hos successus *alit*: *possunt*, quia posse *videntur*.
Et fors aequatis *cepissent* praemia rostris,
ni palmas ponto tendens utrasque Cloanthus
fudissetque preces divosque in vota *vocasset*:
'Di, quibus imperium *est* pelagi, quorum aequora *curro*,
vobis laetus ego hoc candentem in litore taurum
constituam ante aras voti reus, extaque salsos
proiciam in fluctus et vina liquentia *fundam*.'
Dixit, eumque imis sub fluctibus *audiit* omnis
Nereidum Phorcique chorus Panopeaque virgo,
et pater ipse manu magna Portunus euntem
impulit: illa Noto citius volucrique sagitta
ad terram *fugit* et portu se *condidit* alto.

And now there remains Cloanthus virtually at the finishing line; he chases him and presses him, straining with all his might. Then truly the shouting redoubles and all eagerly urge on the pursuer and the heavens resound with the din. The one crew think it shameful should they not hold the glory that is theirs and the honour they have won and are willing to trade life for praise; success feeds the others—they are able because they are seen to be able. And perhaps they would have shared the prizes with their beaks locked in a dead heat had not Cloanthus, stretching out both hands to the sea, offered prayers and called the gods to listen to his vows, 'Gods who rule the sea, whose waters I run, if my prayer is fulfilled, on this shore I will happily set before your altars a shining white bull and will cast the entrails into the salt waves and will pour flowing wine.' He spoke and all the chorus of the Nereids and of Phorcus and the maid Panopea heard him in the very depths of the sea, and father Portunus himself drove him on his way with his own great hand: the boat sped to land faster than the South wind or a winged arrow and buried itself in the deep harbour.

These lines form the second half of a continuous movement from the crash of Sergestus at 5. 202–6. The movement describes the rise of Mnestheus and pursuit of Cloanthus. At line 225, however, a new phase in the narrative is marked with *iamque*. This line uses the imperfective present historic, *superest*, to describe the background scene on which the actions of Mnestheus will occur. One is struck by how 'ipse in fine' freezes Cloanthus in a tantalizingly incomplete situation. The action is introduced at 226 with *petit* and *urget*. Neither of these verbs can be regarded as describing a single completed action because they reflect an effort which is begun but not yet completed. This conative force renders them progressive in aspect. This sense is enhanced by the phrase 'summis adnixus viribus'.

Lines 5. 227–8 leave the action of the race in suspense and return to the shore and to the cries of support presumed continuous since 148. Here again, there is an action, namely the redoubling of the cries of the crowd ('tum vero ingeminat clamor'), but there is also the start of a situation which will be regarded as continuous ('instigant . . . resonat . . .') until the close of the race. The progressive sense of *instigant* is enhanced by its reference, namely the obviously conative, and clearly progressive, *sequentem*, and by the emphasis on the vivid *studiis* of the watchers.

The effect of 225–6 and 227–8 is to depict two ongoing and simultaneous situations in two different places. The picture of Cloanthus on the very finishing-line, of the zealous enthusiasm of the audience—all this co-operates with the imperfective use of the present historic to evoke the scene. The following lines are crucial to the understanding of the present historic and of the nature of vivid narration in Vergil, for they take the reader straight into the immediate emotional states of the competitors. The sense of a still-open situation, where the result is undecided, is unmistakable. One cannot help but note how Vergil uses all his effects to build in the suspense of the incomplete and immediate. For instance, the men of Cloanthus regard the *decus* as *proprium* and *partum*, much as Vergil has called the Pristis *victam* at 156 and Gyas *victor* at 160. The victory seems already won, but the sudden rise of Mnestheus means that what seemed complete no longer is. Equally, 'vitamque volunt pro laude pacisci' evokes the feelings of anguish experienced by the men of Cloanthus, while the eager optimism of the men of Mnestheus is expressed in terms of advances already made ('hos successus alit') and the sense of others still there to come ('possunt quia posse videntur').

Perhaps the most important element in these three lines is the protasis to an unreal vivid condition in *ni teneant*.[32] This should be compared to 5. 323–6, lines from Vergil's foot-race which Otis highlights as examples of the vivid effect of the present tense in narrative:

> Euryalumque Helymus sequitur; quo deinde sub ipso
> ecce volat calcemque terit iam calce Diores
> incumbens umero, *spatia et si plura supersint*
> *transeat* elapsus prior ambiguumque *relinquat*.

And Helymus pursues Euryalus; and right behind him lo! flies Diores and rubs his heel with his heel, pressing on his shoulder, and, should there be more room, he might slip out past him and take the lead or leave the contest in doubt.[33]

[32] For the unreal vivid condition, see Austin (1971) and Conington (1883) at Verg. *Aen.* 1. 56–9, Austin (1964) at *Aen.* 2. 598–600, R. Williams (1960) at *Aen.* 5. 325–6, Norden (1957) at *Aen.* 6. 290 ff. Norden and Austin make the simple but important observation that the imperfect and pluperfect subjunctives often just will not fit the metre. However, this makes all the more interesting the way in which the pluperfect subjunctive is made to fit the metre at 5. 232–4.

[33] Otis (1963) 46 and 50.

It is important to state more accurately the nature of the unreal vivid condition. What Vergil does is to employ a form which, while communicating the incompleteness of the situation *then*, does not suggest that the *then* of the narration is also the rhetorical *now* of the speaker.[34] Vergil never writes *supersint (superfuerint)* . . . *transibit* . . . *relinquet*. Instead, at 1. 56–9, 2. 598–600, 6. 290–4 and 11. 912–13 he repeatedly uses a form which, as a substitute for the imperfect subjunctive, does not suddenly change its own temporality or that of the historic presents around it.[35] In this way, the condition functions in the spirit of those historics, lightening the narrative by omitting unnecessary reminders of a pastness which has already been marked.

At 5. 232–4, however, Vergil reverses the situation in the most abrupt fashion. If the constant use of the present historic and of the unreal vivid condition allows the reader to slip into a state of empathetic involvement with the crisis of the characters, the employment here of the past *irrealis* condition, the most distancing, analytical form of the conditional, has the opposite effect of reminding the reader that this is a narrative of a long past event, and that Vergil is in charge. The use of this form of the conditional to break the suspense coheres with another reminder of the activity of the narrator, that is the first major break in iconic sequence in the entire account of the race.[36] Instead of stating that Cloanthus prayed and that the prayer was successful, Vergil speculates on the possibility of a tie, and makes it clear that the outcome of the prayer was that it was heard and successful, before he ever gives the words of Cloanthus. The effect of this sentence is thus to break the chain of engagement with the characters. The prayer of Cloanthus at 5. 235–9 may still embed his immediate experience and anguish, but the succession of perfects at 5. 239–43 closes the account with decision.

It must therefore be concluded from the various passages assessed that the present historic can be put to 'vivid' effect, but that its usefulness in this context depends essentially on its lack of temporal or aspectual identification. Its counterpart, the unreal vivid condition, gives the sensation of a situation frozen and as yet incomplete, but not of the genuine contingency which would be suggested if the future indicative were used in the apodosis. Therefore, it cannot be argued that the present historic creates a vivid situation by merging

[34] Cf. Woodcock (1959) 154–5, 'The use of the present (and perfect) subjunctive in conditions referring to the present . . . has not died out in classical Latin, but both become rarer as time goes on. The present subjunctive is still used with reference to the present, if the speaker or writer does not wish to rule out the idea of ultimate fulfilment . . . As the present and the perfect subjunctive represent a hypothetical condition more vividly, they are found more frequently in poetry than prose, in contexts where we should expect the imperfect and pluperfect.'

[35] For this, see Ronconi (1959) 176–8.

[36] By 'iconic sequence', I mean the recounting of the events of the race in the order in which they may be presumed actually to have happened. The violation of this sequence breaks the flow of 'perception without reflection' often considered typical of present-historic narratives.

the time of the narrative with the rhetorical present of the narrator. This is only achieved when the present tense coheres with the triple axis of deictic terms *hic* ... *ego* ... *nunc*, or with future forms dependent on the sense of a rhetorical present. This is exactly what lines such as Lucan, 4. 191–2, 'magnum nunc saecula nostra | venturi discrimen habent', provide and which gives them their unique sense of describing fates that are coming and not yet past.

APPENDIX 3
The Future Tense in Latin Epic Narrative

THE FUTURE IN EPIC

The employment of the future tense by the narrator in Latin epic is extremely rare and occurs in specific stylized contexts. However, its use in Lucan is central to his conception of epic time and features prominently in the passages examined in Chapters 2–4. It is therefore pertinent briefly to codify the various uses to which the future is put in epic from Vergil to Valerius, and to identify those forms which are unique to Lucan.

CODIFICATION OF FUTURES IN EPIC NARRATIVE

The Future Historic

The classic example of the Latin future historic is to be found in Vergil. At *Aeneid* 10. 503–5, immediately after the killing and stripping of Pallas by Turnus, the narrator offers the following prophecy:

> Turno tempus erit magno cum optaverit emptum
> intactum Pallanta, et cum spolia ista diemque
> oderit.

There will come a time to Turnus when he will wish to pay even at a great price not to have touched Pallas and when he will hate those spoils and the day.

The future historic functions as a prolepsis, anticipating the final scene of the poem and underlining the fatal error of stripping Pallas of his armour. Flavian epic offers examples of both homodiegetic (or internal) and heterodiegetic (or external) prolepses using the future indicative[1] and the future participle.[2]

The Future of Common Memory

The future of common memory is different from the future historic in the sense that the future it anticipates does not concern the experiences the character

[1] See Sil. *Pun.* 2. 699–707, 8. 401–11, 9. 426–7, 11. 122–8, 16. 272–4; Stat. *Theb.* 3. 106–7; Val. Flacc. *Arg.* 1. 378–9, 1. 441–3, 1. 450–2.

[2] See Sil. *Pun.* 4. 228–9, 8. 544–5; Stat. *Theb.* 2. 295–6, 2. 523–4; Val. Flacc. *Arg.* 1. 370–2, 1. 391–3, 1. 441, 8. 235–6.

will undergo in life, but rather the popular fame which he will win in life and hold long after his death. An obvious example is Livy, 7. 1. 1, which anticipates the most significant aspect of the coming year:

> Annus hic erit insignis novi hominis consulatu.
>
> This year will be remarkable for the consulate of a new man.

Similarly, Livy, 21. 46. 8 predicts future glory for Scipio:

> Hic erit iuvenis, penes quem perfecti huiusce belli laus est, Africanus ob egregiam victoriam de Hannibale Poenisque appellatus.
>
> This youth will be the one to win the glory for finishing this war, called Africanus on account of his great victory over Hannibal and the Carthaginians.[3]

Finally, the same phenomenon is observable in the aition offered for the Pyrenees in the erotic sufferings of Pyrene at Silius, *Punica* 3. 440–1:

> Nec honos intercidet aevo,
> defletumque tenent montes per saecula nomen.
>
> Nor will her honour die in time, and the mountains maintain her lamented name through the centuries.[4]

The Future of Literary Immortality

Closely related to the future of common memory is that in which the narrator guarantees a figure immortal fame specifically as a character in a literary work. This is the case in the address to Lausus at Vergil, *Aeneid* 10. 791–3:

> Hic mortis durae casum tuaque optima facta,
> si qua fidem tanto est operi latura vetustas,
> non equidem nec te, iuvenis memorande, silebo.
>
> Here I shall not pass over in silence the cruel fortune of your harsh death, your excellent deeds (if antiquity be trusted as it tells of so great a feat), nor indeed shall I pass over you, O memorable youth.

[3] Both Samuelsson (1905) and Wackernagel (1956) quote these lines. Samuelsson (1905) 36 also offers the imitation of Livy at Flor. *Epit.* 1. 22. 11: 'Hic erit Scipio, qui in exitium Africae crescit, nomen ex malis eius habiturus' and at Paul. Diac. *Hist. Misc.* 4. 9. 1 (Eyssenhardt): 'Anno ab urbe condita sexcentesimo . . . Publius Scipio, qui post Africanus erit, ultro se militaturum in Hispania obtulit, cum tamen in Macedoniam sorte iam deputatus esset.'

[4] For this theme, compare Sil. *Pun.* 2. 696–8, 5. 186–90, 9. 351–3, 12. 312–13, 14. 679–83, 17. 651–4; and Stat. *Theb.* 10. 503–8. One should here add a further related category, that of the apostrophe and imperative addressed to a character at the moment of death, for instance at Sil. *Pun.* 2. 696–8, 7. 16–19; Stat. *Theb.* 3. 109–13, 11. 574–9, 12. 810–19 (to his book). These apostrophes are modelled on Vergil's addresses for instance to Pallas, Lausus, and Nisus and Euryalus. It is striking that Lucan's successors only felt comfortable giving instructions to their characters at the liminal point between life and death, where the range of actions to which the character can be invited is severely circumscribed.

Here, the poet talks to Lausus at the moment of his death, and the future he offers him is the ersatz immortality of becoming and remaining a part of the poem. This sort of future reappears at Vergil, *Aeneid* 7. 133–4, 9. 446–7, 10. 185–6, Lucan 4. 811–14, 7. 207–13, and 9. 980–6. It is also very common in Flavian epic, for instance at Statius, *Thebaid* 10. 445–8:

> Vos quoque sacrati, quamvis mea carmina surgant
> inferiore lyra, memores superabitis annos.
> Forsitan et comites non aspernabitur umbras
> Euryalus Phrygiique admittet gloria Nisi.

You too are consecrated and, though my songs rise on a lesser lyre, will survive through the remembering years. And perhaps Euryalus will not spurn the companionship of your shades and the glory of Phrygian Nisus will accept you.[5]

In no sense beyond the presumption of the narrator's ability to talk to the character does it set up a vivid situation. Hence, it will be known as the future of literary immortality.

The Future for the Creation of a Text

The poet uses the future to discuss his own act of composition. Valerius Flaccus, *Argonautica* 6. 134–6 also uses *silebo* but now in a slightly different sense:

> Non ego sanguineis gestantem tympana bellis
> Thyrsaget⟨en⟩ cinctumque vagis post terga *silebo*
> pellibus et nexis viridantem floribus hastas.

I shall not pass over in silence the Thyrsagetae who carry drums in bloody war and tie fluttering skins behind their backs and are green with the flowers with which they bind their spears.[6]

The Hypothetical Future

This is a device designed to give vigorous expression to an unreal condition, one which can have no real bearing on the action of the poem. *Pharsalia* 10. 151–4 employs this form to evoke the wealth of Cleopatra's banquet:

5 For other examples, see Sil. *Pun.* 4. 396–400, 6. 63–4; Stat. *Theb.* 12. 810–19; Val. Flacc. *Arg.* 2. 242–6, 6. 103–5. Some of the Vergilian and Lucanian examples are discussed at Endt (1905) 120–2 as instances of a lyric topos.

6 For other examples, see Sil. *Pun.* 1. 20, 11. 1–3, 11. 304–6; Stat. *Theb.* 1. 4, 1. 9, 1. 15–16, 1. 32–3, 1. 41, 2. 267–8, 3. 103–4, 5. 207, 5. 218–19; Val. Flacc. *Arg.* 2. 216–17. Some of these instances may be claimed for the first-person singular of the present subjunctive. For examples of ambiguity of mood or evident use of the subjunctive, see Sil. *Pun.* 11. 1–3; Stat. *Theb.* 2. 240, 2. 268, 3. 103–4, 4. 145, 5. 206–7, 5. 218–19, 7. 343–4, 7. 452, 10. 273–4, 12. 797–9; Val. Flacc. *Arg.* 2. 216–19, 2. 439–40, 4. 718–21.

Pone duces priscos et nomina pauperis aevi
Fabricios Curiosque graves, hic ille recumbat
sordidus Etruscis abductus consul aratris:
optabit patriae talem duxisse triumphum.

Set down the leaders of old and the famous names of a frugal age, the Fabricii and the grave Curii, let that consul summoned unwashed from his Etruscan plough recline here: he will wish that he had celebrated such a triumph for the homeland.

The hypothetical future is purely stylistic and has no real importance for the broader conception of epic time.[7]

The Contingent Future

By contrast with the hypothetical future, the contingent future takes as its point of reference potential future conditions easily realizable if only the characters make one basic decision instead of another. This is seen only in the *Pharsalia*. This interpretation is inescapable, for instance, for the following assertion at 4. 187–8:

Iam iam civilis Erinys
concidet et Caesar generum privatus amabit.

Now, now the Fury of civil strife will fall and Caesar, a private citizen, will love his son-in-law.

What is essential is that Lucan intervenes as a character in order to put to the soldiers future propositions which are represented dramatically as still open, although, of course, most of them are foreclosed by the final, inevitable reality of history. Real conditions and choices exist: not 'If you were to do *x*, *y* would happen', but 'If you do *x*, *y* will happen.'[8]

EXTRAPOLATION FROM CODIFICATION

It is essential to codify the future in Latin epic narrative by function. The categories proposed are a development of those suggested in the earlier study of Samuelsson but are designed to avoid the fundamental flaw in that work: the treatment of each future as a subcategory of the future historic.[9] Rather, I would argue that the contingent future, though adopting the same verbal form as the

[7] For other instances, see Ov. *Met.* 12. 399–402 and Luc. 7. 755–7.

[8] Samuelsson (1905) has one category of the 'hypothetical future', which merges both the hypothetical future proper and the contingent future. He cites Ov. *Fast.* 2. 801, *Met.* 12. 399–400; Luc. 4.187–8, 7. 755–7, 10. 151–4, 10. 420–1; Claud. *Carm.* 3. 196–9 (Hall), 4. 425–6 (Hall), *Carm. Spur.* 2. 39–42 (Hall). These examples do not all belong to one category. Ov. *Met.* 12. 399–400, Luc. 7. 755–7 and 10. 151–4 have very little in common with the dramatic appeal at Luc. 4. 187–8.

[9] Samuelsson (1905).

future historic, actually serves to express a quite different perspective on the narrative.

The future historic involves a temporary change of narrative perspective from retrospection to an affected prophetic prospectivity, the verbal form being dependent on the adoption of a position of simultaneity with the action narrated.[10] In terms of propositional content, the future historic is only one of a number of forms of narrative prolepsis in Latin. In terms of its mode of locution, however, its very rarity makes it notable. It is therefore not surprising that the Livian and Vergilian examples all involve prediction of events of the highest import: the coming of Scipio, the death of Turnus, are not minor events in their respective stories.

The appearance of a future historic in Latin epic narrative is therefore a moment of some significance. So too is the appearance of a *contingent future*, but for reasons which are quite different. A sentence in which the intervening narrator uses a contingent future to back up his pleas to a character is no longer narrative as such, but rather a form of dramatic speech. As such, it has no 'historic' role. While the prophecies of the future historic actually enclose reader and characters in an inevitably unfolding process, the contingent future suggests that the final outcome is still open and that significant choices remain to be made. Much of the point of Lucan's futures is gained from the juxtaposition of contingent and historic futures, often over large narrative movements, creating an effect of architectonic unity. It is only possible to appreciate these effects if one maintains a strict distinction between the different functions of the future.

[10] See the definitions of Leumann, Hofmann, and Szantyr (1965) ii. 310 and Wackernagel (1928) i. 207–8. Perhaps the best definition is that contained in Wackernagel (1956) 443, 'Dass das Futurum von etwas Vergangenem gebraucht wird, ist gar nicht unerhört. Für uns am verständlichsten ist es, wenn im lauf einer Erzählung eine futurische Zwischenbemerkung auf etwas hinweist, was aus dem Rahmen der Erzählung ganz herausfällt und viel später eintritt als das, was in der Erzählung unmittelbar folgt. Das Futurum erklärt sich hier sehr natürlich daraus, dass sich Erzähler und Hörer in die Zeit der Haupterzählung zurückversetzen; von diesem Standpunkt aus ist das Spätere zukünftig.' Samuelsson (1905) 29–30 is unduly loaded.

Bibliography

Adam, T. (1970), *Clementia Principis: Der Einfluss hellenistischer Fürstenspiegel auf den Versuch einer rechtlichen Fundierung des Prinzipats durch Seneca* (Stuttgart).

Ahl, F. (1974), 'The Pivot of the Pharsalia', *Hermes*, 102: 305–20.

— (1976), *Lucan. An Introduction* (Ithaca).

Alfonsi, L. (1947), 'Pompeo in Manilio', *Latomus*, 6: 345–51.

Amat, J. (1991), *Calpurnius Siculus Bucoliques: Texte établi et traduit* (Paris).

Anderson, W. S. (1963), 'Multiple Change in the Metamorphoses', *TAPhA* 94: 1–27.

Armstrong, D. (1986), 'Stylistics and the Date of Calpurnius Siculus', *Philologus*, 130: 113–36.

Auguet, R. (1972), *Cruelty and Civilization: The Roman Games* (London).

Aumont, J. (1968*a*), 'Caton en Libye (Lucain, Pharsale, 9.294–949)', *REA* 70: 304–20.

— (1968*b*), 'Sur l'épisode des reptiles dans la Pharsale de Lucain (9.587–937)', *BAGB* 103–19.

Austin, R. G. (1948) (ed.), *Quintiliani Institutionis Oratoriae Liber XII* (Oxford).

— (1964), *P. Vergili Maronis Aeneidos Liber Secundus, with a Commentary* (Oxford).

— (1971), *P. Vergili Maronis Aeneidos Liber Primus, with a Commentary* (Oxford).

— (1977), *P. Vergili Maronis Aeneidos Liber Sextus, with a Commentary* (Oxford).

Aymard, J. (1951), *Quelques séries de comparaisons chez Lucain* (Montpellier).

Baehrens, A. (1882–3) (ed.), *Poetae Latini Minores*, 5 vols. (Leipzig).

Bal, M. (1988), *Narratology* (Buffalo, Toronto, London).

Barchiesi, M. (1986), *Il testo e il tempo* (Urbino).

Barratt, P. (1979), *M. Annaei Lucani Belli Civilis Liber V: A Commentary* (Amsterdam).

Barthes, R. (1967), *Writing Degree Zero*, trans. A. Lavers and C. Smith (New York).

Barton, C. (1992), *The Sorrows of the Ancient Romans* (Princeton).

Benario, H. W. (1983), 'The Carmen de Bello Actiaco and Early Imperial Epic', *ANRW* II.30.3: 1656–62.

Benjamin, W. (1969), 'The Storyteller', in *Illuminations*, trans. Harry Zohn (New York).

Benveniste, E. (1966), 'Les Relations des temps dans le verbe français', in id., *Problèmes de linguistique générale* (Paris), i. 69–82.

Béranger, J. (1953), *Recherches sur l'aspect idéologique du principat* (Basle).
Bergsland, K. (1942), 'Remarques sur la valeur des temps latins', *SO* Suppl. 11: 25–32.
Bettini, M. (1991), *Anthropology and Roman Culture: Kinship, Time, Images of the Soul*, trans. J. van Sickle (Baltimore and London).
Bickel, E. (1951), 'Vates bei Varro und Vergil', *RhM* 94: 257–314.
Billerbeck, M. (1986), 'Stoizismus in der römischen Epik neronischer und flavischer Zeit', *ANRW* II.32.5: 3116–51.
Block, E. (1982), 'The Narrator Speaks. Apostrophe in Homer and Vergil', *TAPhA* 112: 7–22.
Bömer, F. (1969–86), *P. Ovidius Naso, Metamorphosen, Kommentar*, 7 vols. (Heidelberg).
Bonfanti, M. (1985), *Punto di vista e modi della narrazione nell'Eneide* (Pisa).
Bonner, C. (1905), 'The Use of Apostrophe in Homer', *CR* 19: 383–6.
Bonner, S. F. (1966), 'Lucan and the Declamation Schools', *AJPh* 87: 257–89.
Booth, W. C. (1961), *The Rhetoric of Fiction* (Chicago).
Borghini, A. (1979), 'Codice antropologico e narrazione letteraria. Il comportamento del soldato valoroso (Nevio, Bellum Poenicum fr. 42M)', *Lingua e stile*, 14: 165–76.
Borzsák, I. (1973), 'Spectaculum. Ein Motiv der 'Tragischen Geschichtsschreibung' bei Livius und Tacitus', *ACD* 9: 57–67.
Bourazelis, K. (1988), 'Floret Imperium. The Age of Septimius Severus and the Work of Q. Curtius Rufus', *Ariadne*, 4: 244–64.
Bowie, A. M. (1990), 'The Death of Priam: Allegory and History in the Aeneid', *CQ* NS 40.2: 470–81.
Bramble, J. C. (1974), *Persius and the Programmatic Satire* (Cambridge).
— (1982), 'Lucan', in E. J. Kenney and W. V. Clausen (eds.), *Cambridge History of Classical Literature* (Cambridge), ii. 533–57.
Braund, D. (1993), 'Dionysiac Tragedy in Plutarch *Crassus*', *CQ* NS 43.2: 468–74.
Braund, S. (1988), *Beyond Anger* (Cambridge).
Brena, F. (1988), 'L'elogio di Nerone nella Pharsalia: Moduli ufficiali e riflessione politica', *MD* 20–1: 133–45.
Brink, C. O. (1960), 'Tragic History and Aristotle's School', *PCPhS* NS 6: 14–19.
Brisset, J. (1964), *Les Idées politiques de Lucain* (Paris).
Broch, H. (1983), *The Death of Vergil*, trans. J. S. Untermeyer (Oxford).
Brown, P. G. McC. (1992), 'Menander, Fragments 745 and 746 K–T, Menander's Kolax and Parasites and Flatterers in Greek Comedy', *ZPE* 92: 91–107.
Brunt, P. (1966), 'The "Fiscus" and its Development', *JRS* 56: 75–91.
— (1975), 'Stoicism and the Principate', *PBSR* 43: 7–35.
Buchheit, V. (1971), 'Epikurs Triumph des Geistes', *Hermes*, 99: 303–23.
Burke Jr., P. F. (1978), 'Drances Infensus. A Study in Vergilian Character Portrayal', *TAPhA* 108: 15–20.
Burton, R. W. B. (1980), *The Chorus in Sophocles' Tragedies* (Oxford).

Butler, H. E., and Barber, E. A. (1933), *The Elegies of Propertius, Edited with an Introduction and Commentary* (Oxford).

Butrica, J. L. (1993), 'Propertius 3.11.33–38 and the Death of Pompey', *CQ* NS 43.1: 342–6.

Cairns, F. (1972), *Generic Composition in Greek and Roman Poetry* (Edinburgh).

—— (1983), 'Horace Epode 9. Some New Interpretations', *ICS* 8.1: 80–93.

—— (1989), *Virgil's Augustan Epic* (Cambridge).

Campbell, J. B. (1984), *The Emperor and the Roman Army, 31 B.C.–A.D. 235* (Oxford).

Camps, W. A. (1966), *Propertius Elegies Book 3* (Cambridge).

Carcopino, J. (1947), *Les Secrets de la correspondance de Cicéron* (Paris).

Carter, J. M. (1993), *Caesar Civil War Book 3* (Warminster).

Casparis, C. P. (1975), 'Tense Without Time: The Present Tense in Narration', *Schweizer Anglistische Arbeiten*, 84 (Berne).

Castorina, E. (1961) (ed.), *Tertullian De Spectaculis* (Florence).

Caviglia, F. (1966), 'Note su alcuni frammenti delle Historiae di Sallustio (Bellum Sertorianum)', *Maia*, NS 18: 156–61.

Cazzaniga, I. (1956), 'Osservazioni a Lucano no. 1, 9.828–33: L'avventura di Murro col basilisco', *Acme*, 9: 7–9.

—— (1957), 'L'episodio dei serpi libici in Lucano e la tradizione dei Theriaka nicandrei', *Acme*, 10: 27–41.

Champlin, E. (1978), 'The Life and Times of Calpurnius Siculus', *JRS* 68: 95–110.

—— (1986), 'History and the Date of Calpurnius Siculus', *Philologus*, 130: 104–12.

Cizek, E. (1972), *L'Époque de Néron et ses controverses idéologiques* (Leiden).

Codrignani, G. (1958), 'L'aition nella poesia greca prima di Callimaco', *Convivium*, NS 26: 527–45.

Coleman, K. M. (1990), 'Fatal Charades: Roman Executions Staged as Mythical Enactments', *JRS* 80: 44–73.

—— (1993), 'Launching into History: Aquatic Displays in the Early Empire', *JRS* 83: 48–74.

Commager, H. S. Jr. (1957), 'Lucretius' Interpretation of the Plague', *HSPh* 62: 105–18.

Conington, J. (1883), *The Works of Virgil, with a Commentary*, 3rd edn. (London).

Conte, G. B. (1966), 'Il proemio della Pharsalia', *Maia*, NS 18: 42–53.

—— (1968), 'La guerra civile nella rievocazione del popolo: Lucano 2.67–233', *Maia*, 20: 224–53.

—— (1974), *Saggio di commento a Lucano. Pharsalia 6. 118–260. L'Aristia di Sceva* (Pisa).

—— (1986), *The Rhetoric of Imitation*, trans. C. P. Segal (Ithaca, NY).

—— (1988), *La 'Guerra Civile' di Lucano* (Urbino).

Cook, A. B. (1914–40), *Zeus*, 3 vols. (Cambridge).

Courtney, E. (1980), *A Commentary on the Satires of Juvenal* (London).

—— (1987), 'Imitation, chronologie littéraire et Calpurnius Siculus', *REL* 65: 148–57.

Cousin, J. (1935), *Études sur Quintilien*, i (Paris).

—— (1936), *Études sur Quintilien*, ii (Paris).

Cozzolino, A. (1975), 'Il Bellum Actiacum e Lucano', *BCPE* 5: 81–6.

Crook, J. A. (1967), *Law and Life of Rome* (Ithaca, NY).

Culler, J. (1981), *The Pursuit of Signs: Semiotics, Literature, Deconstruction* (London).

Dahlmann, H. (1948), 'Vates', *Philologus*, 97: 337–53.

De Jong, I. (1987), *Narrators and Focalizers: The Presentation of the Story in the Iliad* (Amsterdam).

Deratani, N. F. (1970), 'Der Kampf für Freiheit, Patriotismus und Heldentum im Gedicht Lucans "Über den Bürgerkrieg"', in W. Rutz (ed.), *Lucan* (Darmstadt).

Dewar, M. (1991), *Statius Thebaid IX, Edited with an English Translation and Commentary* (Oxford).

Di Salvo, L. (1990) (ed.), *T. Calpurnio Siculo, Ecloga VII, introduzione, edizione critica, traduzione e commento* (Bologna).

Di Simone, M. (1993), 'I fallimenti di Encolpio, tra esemplarità mitica e modelli letterari: Una ricostruzione (Sat. 82,5; 132,1)', *MD* 30: 87–118.

Dick, B. F. (1963), 'The Technique of Prophecy in Lucan', *TAPhA* 94: 37–49.

—— (1967), 'Fatum and Fortuna in Lucan's Bellum Civile', *CPh* 62: 235–42.

Dilke, O. A. W. (1960), *M. Annaei Lucani De Bello Civili Liber VII*, revision of J. P. Postgate ed. (Cambridge).

Dobson, B. (1974), 'The Significance of the Centurion and Primipilaris in the Roman Army and Administration', *ANRW* 2.1: 392–434.

Dougan, T. W., and Henry, R. M. (1934), *M. Tulli Ciceronis Tusculanarum Disputationum Libri Quinque: A Revised Text with Introduction and Commentary and a Collation of Numerous MSS* (Cambridge).

Due, O. S. (1962), 'An Essay on Lucan', *C&M* 23: 68–132.

—— (1970), 'Lucain et la philosophie', in *Entretiens de la Fondation Hardt*, 15, *Lucain*, 203–32 (Geneva).

Duff, J. D. (1928), *Lucan with an English Translation* (Cambridge, Mass.).

—— (1970), *D. Iunii Iuvenalis Saturae XIV* (2nd edn., Cambridge).

Dupont, F. (1985), *L'Acteur-roi* (Paris).

Dyson, S. (1970), 'Caepio, Tacitus and Lucan's Sacred Grove', *CPh* 65: 36–8.

Earl, D. (1967), *The Moral and Political Tradition of Rome* (London).

Else, G. F. (1957), *Aristotle's Poetics: The Argument* (Cambridge, Mass.).

Emery, A. C. (1897), *The Historical Present in Early Latin* (Ellsworth, Me.).

Endt, J. (1905), 'Der Gebrauch der Apostrophe bei den lateinischen Epiker', *WS* 27: 106–29.

—— (1909) (ed.), *Adnotationes super Lucanum* (Leipzig).

Erbig, F. E. (1931), *Topoi in den Schlachtenberichten römischer Dichter*, Diss. (Würzburg).

Fairweather, J. (1981), *Seneca the Elder* (Cambridge).

—— (1987), 'Ovid's Autobiographical Poem, Tristia 4.10', *CQ* NS 37.1: 181–96.

Fantham, E. (1982), *Seneca's Troades: A Literary Introduction with Text, Translation and Commentary* (Princeton).

—— (1985), 'Caesar and the Mutiny: Lucan's Reshaping of the Historical Tradition in De Bello Civili 5.237–373', *CPh* 80: 119–31.

—— (1992*a*), *Lucan, De Bello Civili, Book 2* (Cambridge).

—— (1992*b*), 'Lucan's Medusa Excursus: Its Design and Purpose', *MD* 29: 95–119.

Fears, J. R. (1975), 'Nero as the Viceregent of the Gods in Seneca's De Clementia', *Hermes*, 103: 486–96.

—— (1976), 'Silius Italicus, Cataphracti, and the Date of Q. Curtius Rufus', *CPh* 71: 214–23.

—— (1981), 'The Cult of Jupiter and Roman Imperial Ideology', *ANRW* II.17.1: 3–141.

Fedeli, P. (1980), *Sesto Properzio, Il Primo Libro delle Elegie, introduzione, testo e commento* (Florence).

—— (1985), *Sesto Properzio, Il Libro Terzo delle Elegie, introduzione, testo e commento* (Bari).

Feeney, D. C. (1986*a*), '"Stat Magni Nominis Umbra". Lucan on the Greatness of Pompeius Magnus', *CQ* NS 36: 239–43.

—— (1986*b*), 'History and Revelation in Vergil's Underworld', *PCPhS* NS 32: 1–24.

—— (1991), *The Gods in Epic* (Oxford).

Fitch, J. G. (1987), *Seneca's Hercules Furens: A Critical Text with Introduction and Commentary* (Ithaca, NY, and London).

Fleischman, S. (1990), *Tense and Narrativity* (Austin, Tex.).

Fowler, D. P. (1987), 'Vergil on Killing Virgins', in M. Whitby, P. Hardie and M. Whitby (eds.), *Homo Viator, Classical Essays for John Bramble* (Bristol), 185–98.

—— (1990), 'Deviant Focalization in Virgil's Aeneid', *PCPhS* NS 36: 42–63.

Fraenkel, E. (1964), 'Lucan als Mittler des Antiken Pathos', in *Kleine Beiträge*, ii. 233–66 (Rome).

Fucecchi, M. (1990), 'Il declino di Annibale nei Punica', *Maia*, 42: 151–66.

Fusillo, M. (1985), *Il tempo delle Argonautiche, un'analisi del racconto di Apollonio Rodio* (Rome).

Gagliardi, D. (1970), *Lucano: Poeta della libertà* (2nd edn., Naples).

—— (1985), 'La letteratura dell'irrazionale in età neroniana', *ANRW* II.32.3: 2047–65.

—— (1975) (ed.), *M. Annaei Lucani Belli Civilis Liber VII* (Florence).

Galinsky, K. (1969), 'The Triumph Theme in the Roman Elegy', *WS* 82: 75–107.

Garzetti, A. (1954) (ed.), *Plutarchi Vita Caesaris* (Florence).

Geiger, J. (1979), 'Munatius Rufus and Thrasea on Cato the Younger', *Athenaeum*, 67: 48–72.

Genette, G. (1969), 'Frontières du récit', in id., *Figures II* (Paris), 49–71.
— (1980), *Narrative Discourse*, trans. Jane E. Lewin (Ithaca, NY).
— (1984), *Nouveau discours du récit* (Paris).
George, D. B. (1991), 'Lucan's Cato and Stoic Attitudes to the Republic', *ClAnt* 10.2: 237–58.
Glenn, J. (1971), 'Mezentius and Polyphemus', *AJPh* 92: 129–55.
Goff, B. E. (1991), 'The Sign of the Fall: The Scars of Orestes and Odysseus', *ClAnt* 10.2: 259–67.
Gray, V. (1987), 'Mimesis in Greek Historical Theory', *AJPh* 108.3: 467–86.
Greenhalgh, P. (1981), *Pompey: The Republican Prince* (London).
Grenade, P. (1950), 'Le Mythe de Pompée et les Pompéiens sous les Césars', *REA* 52: 28–63.
Griffin, J. (1980), *Homer on Life and Death* (Oxford).
— (1985), *Latin Poets and Roman Life* (London).
Griffin, M. T. (1968), 'Seneca on Cato's Politics. Epistle 14.12–13', *CQ* NS 18: 373–5.
— (1976), *Seneca: A Philosopher in Politics* (Oxford).
— (1984), *Nero: The End of a Dynasty* (New Haven).
Grimal, P. (1960), 'L'Éloge de Néron au début de la Pharsale est-il ironique?', *REL* 38: 296–305.
— (1970), 'Le Poète et l'histoire', in *Entretiens de la Fondation Hardt*, 15, *Lucain* (Geneva), 51–117.
— (1971), Le De Clementia et la royauté solaire de Néron', *REL*, 49: 205–17.
Guerrini, R. (1980), 'Tipologia di fatti e detti memorabili', *MD* 4: 77–96.
Guillemin, A. (1951), 'L'inspiration virgilienne dans la Pharsale', *REL* 29: 214–27.
Gundel, W. (1936) (ed.), *Neue Astrologische Texte des Hermes Trismegistos* (Munich).
Habinek, T. N. (1987), 'Greeks and Romans in Book 12 of Quintilian', in A. J. Boyle (ed.), *The Imperial Muse: Ramus Essays on Roman Literature of the Empire* (Victoria), 192–202.
Haffter, H. (1957), 'Dem Schwanken Zünglein Lauschend Wachte Cäsar Dort', *MH* 14: 118–26.
Halliwell, S. (1986), *Aristotle's Poetics* (London).
Hamilton, J. R. (1988), 'The Date of Quintus Curtius Rufus', *Historia* 37: 445–56.
Hamburger, K. (1957), *Die Logik der Dichtung* (Stuttgart).
Hampel, E. (1908), 'De Apostrophae apud Romanorum Poetas Usu', Diss. (Jena).
Hardie, P. (1986), *Virgil's Aeneid: Cosmos and Imperium* (Oxford).
— (1988), 'Lucretius and the Delusions of Narcissus', *MD* 20–1: 71–89.
— (1993), *The Epic Successors of Virgil* (Cambridge).
Harmand, J. (1967), *L'Armée et le soldat à Rome de 107 à 50 avant notre ère* (Paris).
Harnack, A. von (1981), *Militia Christi*, trans. David McI. Gracie (Philadelphia).

Harrison, S. J. (1991), *Vergil Aeneid 10, with Introduction, Translation and Commentary* (Oxford).

Haskins, C. E. (1887), *M. Annaei Lucani Pharsalia, Edited with English Notes* (London).

Haupt, M. (1854), *De Carminibus Bucolicis Calpurnii et Nemesiani* (Berlin).

Headlam, W. (1922), *Herodas: The Mimes and Fragments* (Cambridge).

Heinze, R. (1915), *Virgils epische Technik* (3rd edn., Leipzig and Berlin).

— (1960), 'Ovids elegische Erzählung', in E. Burck (ed.), *Vom Geist des Römertums* (3rd edn., Stuttgart), 308–403.

— and Kiessling, A. (1957), *Q. Horatius Flaccus Satiren* (2nd edn., Berlin).

Hellegouarc'h, J. (1963), *Le Vocabulaire latin des relations et des partis politiques sous la république* (Paris).

Heuzé, P. (1985), *L'Image du corps dans l'œuvre de Virgile*, Collection de l'École Française de Rome, 86.

Heyke, W. (1970), *Zur Rolle der Pietas bei Lucan*, Diss. (Heidelberg).

Hickson, F. V. (1993), *Roman Prayer Language: Livy and the Aeneid of Vergil* (Stuttgart).

Hinds, S. J. (1987), *The Metamorphosis of Persephone* (Cambridge).

— (1992), 'Arma in Ovid's Fasti, Parts 1 and 2', *Arethusa*, 25.1: 81–153.

Hine, H. (1987), 'Aeneas and the Arts (Vergil, *Aeneid* 6.847–50)', in M. Whitby, P. Hardie and M. Whitby (eds.), *Homo Viator: Classical Essays for John Bramble* (Bristol), 173–84.

Hoekstra, A. (1965), *Homeric Modifications of Formulaic Prototypes* (Amsterdam).

Holford-Strevens, L. (1971), *Select Commentary on Aulus Gellius Noctes Atticae Book 2*, D.Phil. thesis (Oxford).

— (1988), *Aulus Gellius* (London).

Hopkins, K. (1983), *Death and Renewal* (Cambridge).

Hosius, C. (1893), 'Lucan und seine Quellen', *RhM* NF 48: 380–97.

Housman, A. E. (1923), 'Notes on Seneca's Tragedies', *CQ* 17: 163–72.

— (1926), *M. Annaei Lucani Belli Civilis Libri Decem* (Oxford).

Hübner, U. (1972), 'Hypallage in Lucans Pharsalia', *Hermes*, 100: 577–600.

Hudson-Williams, A. (1952), 'Lucan 1.76–7', *CR* NS 2.2: 68–9.

Hunink, V. (1992), *M. Annaeus Lucanus: Bellum Civile, Book 3, a Commentary* (Amsterdam).

Hunter, R. (1993), *The Argonautica of Apollonius: Literary Studies* (Cambridge).

Hutchinson, G. O. (1993), *Latin Literature from Seneca to Juvenal* (Oxford).

Jakobson, R. (1960), 'Closing Statement: Linguistics and Poetics', in T. A. Seboek (ed.), *Style in Language* (Cambridge, Mass.).

— (1990), 'The Concept of Mark', in L. R. Waugh and M. Monville-Burston (eds.), *On Language* (Cambridge, Mass.).

Jal, P. (1961), 'Pax Civilis, Concordia', *REL* 39: 210–31.

— (1962), 'Bellum Civile . . . Bellum Externum dans la Rome de la fin de la République', *LEC* 30: 257–67 and 384–90.

— (1963), *La guerre civile à Rome: Étude littéraire et morale* (Paris).
— (1982), 'La Place de Lucain dans la littérature antique des guerres civiles', in J.-M. Croisille and P.-M. Fauchère (eds.), *Neronia 1977* (Clermont-Ferrand).
Janko, R. (1989), 'Review of S. Halliwell, *Aristotle's Poetics*', *CPh* 84: 151–9.
Johnson, W. R. (1987), *Momentary Monsters* (Ithaca, NY).
Kahane, A. (1994), *The Interpretation of Order* (Oxford). .
Kebric, R. B. (1977), *In the Shadow of Macedon. Duris of Samos*, Historia Einzelschriften, 29 (Wiesbaden).
Keitel, E. (1992), '"Foedum Spectaculum" and Related Motifs in Tacitus Histories II–III', *RhM* 135. 3–4: 342–51.
Ker, A. (1953), 'Notes on Statius', *CQ* NS 3.4: 175–82.
Kitto, H. D. F. (1966), *Poiesis: Structure and Thought*, Sather Classical Lectures, 36 (Berkeley and Los Angeles).
Klotz, A. (1940), 'L. Siccius Dentatus', *Klio*, 15: 173–9.
Koller, H. (1951), 'Praesens Historicum und Erzählendes Imperfekt. Beitrag zur Aktionsart der Praesensstammzeiten im Lateinischen und Griechischen', *MH* 8: 63–99.
Kroll, W. (1924), *Studien zum Verständnis der römischen Literatur* (Stuttgart).
Kühner, R. (1912), *Ausführliche Grammatik der lateinische Sprache*, 3 vols. (Hanover).
Labate, M. (1991), 'Città morte, città future: Un tema della poesia augustea', *Maia*, 43.3: 167–84.
L'Orange, H. P. (1947), *Apotheosis in Ancient Portraiture* (Oslo).
La Penna, A. (1952), 'Tendenze e arte del Bellum Civile di Cesare', *Maia*, 5: 191–233.
— (1963), 'Le Historiae di Sallustio e l'interpretazione della crisi repubblicana', *Athenaeum*, NS 41: 201–74.
— (1967), 'Sul cosidetto stile soggettivo e sul cosidetto simbolismo di Virgilio', *Dialoghi di archeologia*, 1: 220–44.
— (1978), 'Il ritratto "paradossale" da Silla a Petronio', in id., *Aspetti del pensiero storico latino* (Turin), 193–221.
— (1979), 'Spunti sociologici per l'interpretazione dell'Eneide', in id., *Fra teatro, poesia e politica romana* (Florence), 153–65.
— (1980), 'Mezenzio: Una tragedia della tirannia e del titanismo antico', *Maia*, 32: 3–30.
Lapidge, M. (1979), 'Lucan's Imagery of Cosmic Dissolution', *Hermes*, 107: 344–70.
Lattimore, R. (1962), *Themes in Greek and Latin Epitaphs* (Urbana, Ill.).
Lausberg, H. (1960), *Handbuch der literarischen Rhetorik* (Munich).
Leach, E. W. (1973), 'Corydon Revisted: An Interpretation of the Political Eclogues of Calpurnius Siculus', *Ramus*, 2: 53–97.
Lebek, W. D. (1976), *Lucans Pharsalia: Dichtungsstruktur und Zeitbezug*, Hypomnemata, 44 (Göttingen).

Le Bonniec, H. (1970), 'Lucain et la religion', in *Entretiens de la Fondation Hardt* 15, *Lucain* (Geneva), 159–200.

Leigh, M. G. L. (1993), 'Hopelessly Devoted to You: Traces of the Decii in Vergil's Aeneid', *PVS* 21: 89–110.

— (1995), 'Wounding and Popular Rhetoric at Rome', *BICS*: 195–212.

— (forthcoming) 'Livy and Lucan on the Augury of Gaius Cornelius'.

Leumann, M., Hofmann, J. B., and Szantyr, A. (1965), *Lateinische Grammatik*, 3 vols. (Munich).

Litchfield, H. W. (1914), 'National Exempla Virtutis in Roman Literature', *HSPh* 25: 1–71.

Loraux, N. (1977), 'La Belle Mort spartiate', *Ktema*, 2: 105–20.

Lounsbury, R. (1975), 'The Death of Domitius in the Pharsalia', *TAPhA* 105: 209–12.

— (1976), 'History and Motive in Book Seven of Lucan's Pharsalia', *Hermes*, 104: 210–39.

— (1986), 'Lucan, the Octavia and Domitius Nero', in C. Deroux (ed.), *Latomus Studies in Latin Literature*, 4 (Brussels), 499–520.

Lubbock, P. (1921), *The Craft of Fiction* (London).

Lyne, R. O. A. M. (1987), *Further Voices in Vergil's Aeneid* (Oxford).

— (1989), *Words and the Poet: Characteristic Techniques of Style in Vergil's Aeneid* (Oxford).

McGushin, P. (1977), *C. Sallustius Crispus, Bellum Catilinae: A Commentary* (Leiden).

Mackail, J. W. (1930) (ed.), *The Aeneid of Vergil* (Oxford).

Mackay, L. A. (1953), 'Lucan 1.76–7', *CR* NS 3.2: 145.

Mckeown, J. C. (1989), *Ovid: Amores, Text, Prolegomena and Commentary in Four Volumes*, ii. *A Commentary on Book One* (Leeds).

Malcovati, E. (1940), *M. Anneo Lucano* (Milan).

— (1955), *Oratorum Romanorum Fragmenta*, 2nd edn., i (Turin).

Marshall, A. J. (1984), 'Symbols and Showmanship in Roman Public Life: The Fasces', *Phoenix*, 38: 120–41.

Marti, B. (1945), 'The Meaning of the Pharsalia', *AJPh* 66: 352–76.

— (1964), 'Tragic History and Lucan's Pharsalia', in C. Henderson Jr. (ed.), *Classical, Mediaeval and Renaissance Studies in Honor of Berthold Louis Ullman* (Rome), i. 165–204.

— (1966), 'Cassius Scaeva and Lucan's Inventio', in L. Wallach (ed.), *The Classical Tradition: Literary and Historical Studies in Honor of H. Caplan* (Ithaca, NY), 239–57.

— (1975), 'Lucan's Narrative Techniques', *Parola del passato*, 30: 74–90.

Martin, T. R. (1983), 'Quintus Curtius' Presentation of Philip Arrhidaeus and Josephus' Accounts of the Accession of Claudius', *AJAH* 8: 161–90.

Martindale, C. A. (1976), 'Paradox, Hyperbole and Literary Novelty in Lucan's De Bello Civili', *BICS* 23: 45–54.

Maslakov, G. (1984), 'Valerius Maximus and Roman Historiography: A Study of the Exempla Tradition', *ANRW* II.32.1: 437–96.
Masters, J. (1992), *Poetry and Civil War in Lucan's Bellum Civile* (Cambridge).
— (1994), 'Deceiving the Reader: The Political Mission of Lucan Book 7', in J. Elsner and J. Masters (eds.) *Reflections of Nero* (London), 151–77.
Matthews, V. J. (1980), 'Metrical Reasons for Apostrophe in Homer', *LCM* 5.5: 93–9.
Maxfield, V. (1981), *The Military Decorations of the Roman Army* (London).
Mayer, R. (1978), 'On Lucan and Nero', *BICS* 25: 85–8.
— (1980), 'Calpurnius Siculus: Technique and Date', *JRS* 70: 175–6.
— (1981), *Lucan Civil War VIII, Edited with a Commentary* (Warminster).
— (1991), 'Roman Historical Exempla in Seneca', in *Entretiens de la Fondation Hardt*, 36, *Sénèque et la prose latine* (Geneva), 141–76.
Mayor, J. E. B. (1889), *Thirteen Satires of Juvenal* (4th edn., London and New York).
Meister, K. (1975), *Historische Kritik bei Polybios*, Palingenesia, 9 (Wiesbaden).
Menz, W. (1952), *Caesar und Pompeius im Epos Lucans. Zur Stoffbehandlung und Charakterschilderung in Lucans Pharsalia*, Diss. (Berlin: Humboldt-Universitat).
Metger, W. (1957), *Kampf und Tod in Lucans Pharsalia*, Diss. (Kiel).
Millar, F. (1963), 'The "Fiscus" in the First Two Centuries', *JRS* 53: 29–42.
Minissale, F. (1977), *L. Annaei Senecae De Constantia Sapientis: Introduzione, testo. commento* (Messina).
Moore, C. H. (1921), 'Prophecy in the Ancient Epic', *HSPh* 32: 99–175.
Moretti, G. (1984), 'Formularità e techniche del paradossale in Lucano', *Maia*, 36: 37–49.
— (1992), 'L'arena, Cesare e il mito. Appunti sul De Spectaculis di Marziale', *Maia*, 44.1: 55–63.
Morford, M. P. O. (1966), 'Lucan and the Marian Tradition', *Latomus*, 25: 107–14.
— (1967), 'The Purpose of Lucan's 9th Book', *Latomus*, 26: 123–9.
Most, G. W. (1992), 'The Rhetoric of Dismemberment in Neronian Poetry', in R. Hexter and D. Selden (eds.), *Innovations of Antiquity* (New Haven).
Müller, C. W. (1989), 'Der Schöne Tod des Polisbürgers oder "Ehrenvoll ist es für das Vaterland zu Sterben"', *Gymnasium*, 96: 317–40.
Narducci, E. (1973), 'Il tronco di Pompeo (Troia e Roma nella Pharsalia)', *Maia*, 25: 317–25.
— (1979), *La provvidenza crudele. Lucano e la distruzione dei miti augustei* (Pisa).
Newman, J. K. (1967), *Augustus and the New Poetry* (Brussels).
— (1986), *The Classical Epic Tradition* (Madison, Wis.).
Nicolai, R. (1992), *La storiografia nell'educazione antica* (Pisa).
Nisbet, R. (1978), 'Notes on the Text of Catullus', *PCPhS* NS 24: 92–115.
— and Hubbard, M. (1970), *A Commentary on Horace: Odes Book 1* (Oxford).
— (1978), *A Commentary on Horace: Odes Book 2* (Oxford).

Nitzsch, G. W. (1860), 'Die Apostrophe in Ilias und Odyssee', *Philologus*, 16: 151–4.

Nock, A. D. (1926), 'The Proem of Lucan', *CR* 40: 17–18.

Norden, E. (1957), *P. Vergilius Maro, Aeneis Buch VI* (4th edn., Stuttgart).

Nutton, V. (1988), 'The Drug Trade in Antiquity', in id., *From Democedes to Harvey: Studies in the History of Medicine* (London), 138–45.

Oakley, S. P. (1985), 'Single Combat in the Roman Republic', *CQ* NS 35.2: 392–410.

Ogilvie, R. (1965), *A Commentary on Livy, Books 1–5* (Oxford).

O'Hara, J. J. (1990), *Death and the Optimistic Prophecy in Vergil's Aeneid* (Princeton).

O'Higgins, D. (1988), 'Lucan as Vates', *ClAnt* 7.2: 208–26.

Oltramare, A. (1926), 'Les Origines de la diatribe romaine', Diss. (Geneva).

Opelt, I. (1957), 'Die Seeschlacht vor Massilia bei Lucan', *Hermes*, 85: 435–45.

Otis, B. (1963), *Virgil: A Study in Civilized Poetry* (Oxford).

— (1970), *Ovid as an Epic Poet* (2nd edn., Cambridge).

Otto, A. (1890), *Die Sprichwörter und sprichwörtlichen Redensarten der Römer* (Leipzig).

Paratore, E. (1936), *L'Elegia 3.11 e gli atteggiamenti politici di Properzio* (Palermo).

— (1943), 'Virgilio Georgico e Lucano', *ASNP* 12: 40–69.

Parry, A. (1972), 'Language and Characterization in Homer', *HSPh* 76: 1–22.

Pascal, C. B. (1982), 'Do ut Des', *Epigraphica*, 44: 7–16.

— (1990), 'The Dubious Devotion of Turnus', *TAPhA* 120: 251–68.

Passerini, A. (1934), 'Caio Mario come uomo politico', *Athenaeum*, NS 12: 10–44, 109–43, 257–97, 348–80.

Paul, G. M. (1982), 'Urbs Capta: A Sketch of an Ancient Literary Motif', *Phoenix*, 36: 144–55.

— (1984), *A Historical Commentary on Sallust's Bellum Jugurthinum* (Liverpool).

Pease, A. S. (1935), *P. Vergili Maronis Aeneidos Liber Quartus* (Cambridge, Mass.).

— (1973), *M. Tulli Ciceronis De Divinatione Libri Duo* (Darmstadt).

Pelling, C. B. R. (1988) (ed.), *Plutarch, Life of Antony* (Oxford).

Phillips, O. C. (1968), 'Lucan's Grove', *CPh* 63: 296–300.

Pichon, R. (1912), *Les Sources de Lucain* (Paris).

Pinkster, H. (1983), 'Tempus, Aspect and Aktionsart in Latin', *ANRW* II.29.1: 270–319.

Pöschl, V. (1950), *Die Dichtkunst Virgils: Bild und Symbol in der Aeneis* (Innsbruck and Vienna).

Postgate, J. P. (1913), *M. Annaei Lucani De Bello Civili Liber VII* (Cambridge).

Prato, C. (1969) (ed.), *Tyrtaeus, Fragmenta* (Rome).

Putnam, M. J. (1987), 'Review of G.B. Conte, *Rhetoric of Imitation*', *AJPh* 108: 787–93.

Quinn, K. (1963), *Latin Explorations: Critical Studies in Latin Literature* (New York).

— (1968), *Vergil's Aeneid: A Critical Description* (London).

— (1979), *Texts and Contexts: The Roman Writers and their Audience* (London).

Quint, D. (1993), *Epic and Empire* (Princeton).

Quirk, R., Greenbaum, S., Leech, G., and Svartvik, S. (1972), *A Grammar of Contemporary English* (London).

Rambaud, M. (1953), *L'Art de la déformation historique dans les Commentaires de César*, Annales de l'Université de Lyon, 3e série (XXIII) (Paris).

— (1955), 'L'Apologie de Pompée par Lucain au Livre VII de la Pharsale', *REL* 33: 258–96.

Rawson, E. (1969), *The Spartan Tradition in European Thought* (Oxford).

Ribbeck, O. (1895), *P. Vergili Maronis Opera, Apparatu Critico in Artius Contracto*, 3 vols. (Leipzig).

Richardson, L. (1977), *Propertius Elegies I–IV, Edited, with Introduction and Commentary* (Oklahoma City).

Richardson, N. J. (1980), 'Literary Criticism in the Exegetical Scholia to the Iliad. A Sketch', *CQ* NS 30.2: 265–87.

Ridgeway, W. (1912), 'Three Notes on the Poetics of Aristotle', *CQ* 6: 235–45.

Roloff, H. (1936), *Maiores bei Cicero*, Diss. (Leipzig).

Ronconi, A. (1959), *Il verbo latino. Problemi di sintassi storica* (Florence).

Rosenmeyer, T. (1989), *Senecan Drama and Stoic Cosmology* (Berkeley, Los Angeles, and London).

Rosenstein, N. (1990), *Imperatores Victi: Military Defeat and Aristocratic Competition in the Middle and the Late Republic* (Berkeley).

Rosner-Siegel, J. (1983), 'The Oak and the Lightning: Lucan, Bellum Civile 1. 135–57', *Athenaeum*, NS 61: 165–77.

Rostagni, A. (1964) (ed.), *Suetonio De Poetis e Biografi Minori* (Turin).

Rothstein, M. (1924) (ed.), *Die Elegien des Sextus Propertius*, ii (2nd edn., Berlin).

Rudich, V. (1993), *Political Dissidence under Nero* (London and New York).

Russell, D. (1964), *'Longinus', On the Sublime, Edited with Introduction and Commentary* (Oxford).

— (1983), *Greek Declamation* (Cambridge).

Rutz, W. (1960), 'Amor Mortis bei Lucan', *Hermes*, 88: 462–75.

— (1970*a*), 'Lucan und die Rhetorik', in *Entretiens de la Fondation Hardt*, 15. *Lucain* (Geneva), 233–65.

— (1970*b*) (ed.), *Wege der Forschung*, 235. *Lucan* (Darmstadt).

Sacks, K. (1981), *Polybius on the Writing of History*, University of California Publications in Classical Studies, 24 (Berkeley and Los Angeles).

Samuelsson, J. (1905), 'Futurum Historicum im Latein', *Eranos*, 6: 29–44.

Saylor, C. (1978), 'Belli Spes Inproba: The Theme of Walls in Lucan, Pharsalia 6', *TAPhA* 108: 243–57.

— (1986), 'Wine, Blood and Water. The Imagery of Lucan Pharsalia 4.148–401', *Eranos*, 84: 149–56.

— (1990), 'Lux Extrema: Lucan Pharsalia 4.402–581', *TAPhA* 120: 291–300.

Scheller, P. (1911), *De Hellenistica Historiae Conscribendae Arte*, Diss. (Leipzig).

Schiesaro, A. (1985), 'Il "locus horridus" nelle Metamorfosi di Apuleio', *Maia*, 37: 211–23.

Schnepf, H. (1953), *Untersuchungen zur Darstellungskunst Lucans im 8. Buch der Pharsalia*, Diss. (Heidelberg).

Schrijvers, P. (1990), *Crise poétique et poésie de la crise: La Réception de Lucain aux XIX et XX siècles, suivi d'une interprétation de la scène 'César à Troie' (la Pharsale 9.950–999)*, (Amsterdam).

Schumann, G. (1930), *Hellenistische und griechische Elemente in der Regierung Neros*, Diss. (Leipzig).

Schwartz, E. (1897), 'Die Berichte über die Catilinarische Verschwörung', *Hermes*, 32: 554–608.

— (1903), 'Duris (3)' in Pauly, *RE* v. 2. 1853–6.

Seitz, K. (1965), 'Der Pathetische Erzählstil Lucans', *Hermes*, 93: 204–32.

Serbat, G. (1975), 'Les Temps du verbe en Latin: I', *REL* 53: 367–405.

— (1976), 'Les Temps du verbe en Latin: II', *REL* 54: 308–52.

Seyffert, M., and Müller, C. F. W. (1876) (eds.), *M.T. Ciceronis Laelius* (Leipzig).

Shackleton Bailey, D. R. (1956), *Propertiana* (Cambridge).

Shoaf, R. A. (1978), 'Certius Exemplar Sapientis Viri: Rhetorical Subversion and Subversive Rhetoric in Pharsalia 9', *PhQ* 57: 143–54.

Silk, M. S. (1974), *Interaction in Poetic Imagery with Special Reference to Early Greek Poetry* (Cambridge).

Skard, E. (1941), 'Marius' Speech in Sallust, Jug. Chap. 85', *SO* 21: 98–102.

— (1956), *Sallust und seine Vorgänger. Eine sprachliche Untersuchung*, *SO* Suppl. 15 (Oslo).

Skutsch, O. S. (1985) (ed.), *The Annals of Ennius* (Oxford).

Smith, W. (1870), *Dictionary of Greek and Roman Geography*, 2 vols. (London).

Solodow, J. (1988), *The World of Ovid's Metamorphoses* (Chapel Hill).

Spaltenstein, F. (1986–90), *Commentaire des Punica de Silius Italicus*, 2 vols. (Geneva).

Spengel, L. (1885–6) (ed.), *Rhetores Graeci*, 3 vols. (Leipzig).

Stevens, C. E. (1952), 'The Bellum Gallicum as a Work of Propaganda', *Latomus*, 11: 3–18, 165–79.

Strasburger, H. (1966), *Die Wesensbestimmung der Geschichte durch die antike Geschichtsschreibung*, Sitzungsberichte der Wissenschaftlichen Gesellschaft an der Johann Wolfgang Goethe-Universität, Frankfurt/Main, 5.3 (Wiesbaden).

Syme, R. (1937), 'Who Was Decidius Saxa?', *JRS* 27: 127–37.

— (1938), 'Caesar, the Senate and Italy', *PBSR* 14: 1–31.

— (1939), *The Roman Revolution* (Oxford).

Syndikus, H. P. (1958), *Lucans Gedicht vom Bürgerkrieg Untersuchungen zur epischen Technik und zu den Grundlagen des Werkes*, Diss. (Munich).

Tandoi, V. (1963), 'Intorno ad Anth. Lat. 437–438 R. e al mito di Alessandro fra i Pompeiani', *SIFC* 35: 69–106.

Tarkow, T. A. (1981), 'The Scar of Orestes: Observations on a Euripidean Innovation', *RhM* 124: 143–53.

Tarrant, R. J. (1976), *Seneca, Agamemnon, Edited with a Commentary* (Cambridge).

— (1985), *Seneca's Thyestes Edited with Introduction and Commentary* (Atlanta).

Thierfelder, A. (1934–5), 'Der Dichter Lucan', *AKG* 25: 1–20.

Thomas, J. A. C. (1975), *The Institutes of Justinian* (Amsterdam).

Thomas, R. F. (1982), *Lands and Peoples in Roman Poetry: The Ethnographical Tradition*, *PCPhS*, Suppl. vol. 7.

— (1986), 'From Recusatio to Commitment. The Evolution of the Vergilian Programme', *PLLS* 5: 61–73.

— (1988) (ed.), *Vergil Georgics, Commentary in 2 Vols.* (Cambridge).

Thome, G. (1979), *Gestalt und Funktion des Mezentius bei Vergil, mit einem Ausblick auf die Schlusszene der Aeneis* (Frankfurt).

Thompson, L., and Bruère, R. T. (1968), 'Lucan's Use of Virgilian Reminiscence', *CPh* 63.1: 1–21.

Townend, G. B. (1980), 'Calpurnius Siculus and the Munus Neronis', *JRS* 70: 166–74.

Toynbee, J. M. C. (1973), *Animals in Roman Life and Art* (London).

Ullman, B. L. (1942), 'History and Tragedy', *TAPhA* 73: 25–53.

Vahlen, J. (1867), 'Beiträge zu Aristoteles' Poetik III', *Sitzungsberichte der Kaiserlichen Akademie der Wissenschaften* (Vienna), 56: 213–343, 351–439.

Venini, P. (1965), 'Echi lucanei nel l.xi della Tebaide', *RIL* 99: 149–67.

— (1970) (ed.), *P. Papini Stati Thebaidos Liber XI, Introduzione, testo critico, commento e traduzione* (Florence).

Vernant, J.-P. (1982), 'La Belle Mort et le cadavre outragé', in G. Gnoli and J.-P. Vernant (eds.), *La Mort, les morts dans les sociétés anciennes* (Paris and Cambridge), 45–76.

Versnel, H. S. (1976), 'Two Types of Roman Devotio', *Mnemosyne*, 29: 365–400.

— (1981), 'Self-Sacrifice, Compensation, and the Anonymous Gods', in *Entretiens de la Fondation Hardt, 2. Le Sacrifice dans l'antiquité* (Geneva), 135–94.

Vessey, D. W. T. C. (1971), 'Menoeceus in the Thebaid of Statius', *CPh* 66: 236–43.

Veyne, P. (1990), *Bread and Circuses: Historical Sociology and Political Pluralism*, trans. B. Pearce (London).

Viansino, G. (1974), *Studi sul Bellum Civile di Lucano* (Salerno).

Viarre, S. (1982), 'Caton en Libye; l'histoire et la métaphore (Lucain, Pharsale, 9.294–949)', in J.-M. Croisille and P.-M. Fauchère (eds.), *Neronia 1977* (Clermont-Ferrand), 103–10.

Ville, G. (1981), *La Gladiature en occident, des origines à la mort de Domitien* (BEFAR 245; Rome).

Von Albrecht, M. (1968), 'Zur Funktion der Tempora in Ovids Elegische Erzählung (Fasti 5.379–414)', in *Ovid*, ed. M. von Albrecht and E. Zinn (Darmstadt), 451–67.

— (1970), 'Zu Vergils Erzähltechnik: Beobachtungen zum Tempusgebrauch in der Aeneis', *Glotta*, 48: 219–29.

Von Arnim, H. (1903–24), *Stoicorum Veterum Fragmenta*, 4 vols. (Leipzig).

Vretska, K. (1976) (ed.), *C. Sallustius Crispus, De Catilinae Coniuratione*, 2 vols. (Heidelberg).

Wackernagel, J. (1928), *Vorlesungen über Syntax*, 2nd edn., 2 vols. (Basle).

— (1956), 'Futurum Historicum im Altpersischen', *Kleine Schriften* (Göttingen), i. 444–7.

Walbank, F. W. (1955), 'Tragic History. A Reconsideration', *BICS* 2: 4–14.

— (1957–79), *A Historical Commentary on Polybius*, 3 vols. (Oxford).

— (1960), 'History and Tragedy', *Historia*, 9: 216–34.

— (1972), *Polybius* (Berkeley, Los Angeles, and London).

Walker, A. (1993), 'Enargeia and the Spectator in Greek Historiography', *TAPhA* 123: 353–77.

Waugh, L. R. (1980), 'Marked and Unmarked: A Choice Between Unequals in Semiotic Structure', *Semiotica*, 38.3–4: 299–318.

Weinrich, H. (1964), *Tempus* (Stuttgart).

Weinstock, S. (1971), *Divus Julius* (Oxford).

Weissenborn, W., and Müller, H. J. (1965), *Titi Livi Ab Urbe Condita Libri*, iii (8th edn., Zurich and Berlin).

Werber, K. (1896), *Tertullians Schrift De Spectaculis in ihrem Verhältnis zu Varros Rerum Divinarum Libri* (Teschen).

West, D. A. (1969), 'Multiple Correspondence Similes in the Aeneid', *JRS* 59: 40–9.

Wheeler, E. L. (1991), 'The General as Hoplite', in V. D. Hanson (ed.), *Hoplites: The Classical Greek Battle Experience* (Berkeley), 121–70.

Wilkins, J. (1993) (ed.), *Euripides Heraclidae with Introduction and Commentary* (Oxford).

Williams, G. (1978), *Change and Decline: Roman Literature in the Early Empire* (Berkeley, Los Angeles, and London).

— (1983), *Technique and Ideas in the Aeneid* (New Haven).

Williams, R. D. (1960) (ed.), *P. Vergili Maronis Aeneidos Liber Quintus with a Commentary* (Oxford).

Wirszubski, C. (1950), *Libertas as a Political Idea at Rome during the Late Republic and Early Principate* (Cambridge).

Wiseman, T. P. (1971), *New Men in the Roman Senate 139 B.C.–A.D. 14* (Oxford).

— (1982), 'Calpurnius Siculus and the Claudian Civil War', *JRS* 72: 57–67.

— (1992), 'Lucretius, Catiline, and the Survival of Prophecy', *Ostraka*, 1.2: 275–86.

— (1994), *Historiography and Imagination* (Exeter).

Woodcock, E. C. (1959), *A New Latin Syntax* (London).

Woodman, A. J. (1977), *Velleius Paterculus: The Tiberian Narrative (2.94–131)* (Cambridge).

— (1983), *Velleius Paterculus: The Caesarian and Augustan Narrative (2.41–93)* (Cambridge).

— and Martin, R. H. (1989) (eds.), *Tacitus Annals Book IV with a Commentary* (Cambridge).

Woodruff, P. (1992), 'Aristotle on Mimesis', in A. Oksenberg Rorty (ed.), *Essays on Aristotle's Poetics* (Princeton), 73–95.

Yavetz, Z. (1983), *Julius Caesar and his Public Image* (London).

Zanker, G. (1981), 'Enargeia in the Ancient Criticism of Poetry', *RhM* NF 124: 297–311.

Zetzel, J. E. G. (1980), 'Two Imitations in Lucan', *CQ* NS 30: 257.

Zwierlein, O. (1982), 'Der Ruhm der Dichtung bei Ennius und seinen Nachfolgern, *Hermes*, 110: 85–102.

— (1986), 'Lucans Caesar in Troia', *Hermes*, 114: 460–78.

— (1988), 'Statius, Lucan, Curtius Rufus und das hellenistische Epos', *RhM* NF 131: 67–84.

Zyroff, E. (1971), 'The Author's Apostrophe in Epic from Homer through Lucan', Diss. (Johns Hopkins University).

Index Locorum

Index Rerum et Nominum